MW01267775

Meeting the Challenge of
Cultural Diversity in
Higher Education
in the New Millennium

WYNDHAM HALL PRESS
Lima, Oh. 45806
Copyright © 2002
The Rhodes-Fulbright International Library

ISBN 1-55605-342-8
Library of Congress Control Number 2002107885

Edited by
Vernon L. Farmer

Contents

iii

iv

Dedication

This book is dedicated to my son, Vernyatta L. Farmer, and all the other students of color with the hope that it will help to make their lives in the new millennium better than ours.

Preface

The work of the authors in *Meeting the Challenge of Cultural Diversity in Higher Education in the New Millennium* is an important and significant contribution to cultural diversity in the field of higher education. The insightfulness of the authors takes us into the new millennium. The challenge of higher education in the new millennium to meeting the needs of culturally diverse students may be difficult for some to understand and even more difficult for others to accept. The work of these authors provide us with a means to analyze, discuss, reflect, and generate a new vision for the 21st century.

Meeting the Challenge of Cultural Diversity in Higher Education in the New Millennium consists of twelve chapters. In Chapter One, Vernon L. Farmer develops a conceptual framework for understanding the needs of culturally diverse college students in America. This chapter provides a perspective for developing programs and services to meet the needs of a culturally diverse student body. The author suggests that having a conceptual framework and perspective to respond to challenges related to diversity is an important blueprint needed to guide the attitudinal development of such an effort in higher education. Martin O. Edu, in Chapter Two, examines classroom diversity in higher education and discusses the challenges for developmental education in the 21st century. The author makes a case for college-level developmental education programs as an integral component of college education, and discusses some unresolved challenges in the field.

In Chapter Three, Margaret A. McLaughlin and Eleanor Agnew report on a comparative analysis of writing skills of high risk African American and European American students with matched verbal SAT score.

The major research question this chapter addresses is "What happens to high-risk students after remedial English, particularly, African Americans?" Evelyn Shepherd-Wynn, in Chapter Four, advocates the use of collaborative writing as an instructional approach to address the writing skills of a changing college clientele. The author reports on a study she conducted to investigate the impact of collaborative learning on African American English composition students' writing apprehension, anxiety, attitude, and overall writing quality.

In Chapter Five, Neari F. Warner provides insights into the processes, pressures, and people that shaped the lives of four African American first generation college students. She examines the contradictions, paradoxes, and ambivalence in the lives of marginalized groups that prompted these students to leave the educational system, particularly the urban school setting.

In Chapter Six, Gwen Spencer discusses attitudes and attribution that influence the academic performance of college students of color. This chapter examines causal attribution and self-efficacy among African American, Native American, and Hispanic students. Implications for educational support and intervention are discussed in relations to ethnic minority students' attribution belief patterns.

Frances Swayzer Conley, in Chapter Seven, examines the relationship of achievement and academic and support services at tribally controlled colleges. The specific purposes were to identify the components of developmental education programs at tribally controlled colleges and to determine the relationship between each component and underrepresented achievement. In Chapter Eight, Laura D. Brown and Gordon Kitto help educators understand why so few American Indian students attend and graduate from American higher education institutions and how tribal colleges are changing the face of American Indian higher education. The authors discuss how self-determination has changed the American Indian higher education system and how tribal colleges are responding to the needs of their students by aligning developmental education programs.

Betty J. Farmer, in Chapter Nine, discusses the relationship between critical thinking ability and success of African American nursing students on the National Counsel Licensure Examination for nurses at five historically black colleges and universities (HBCUs). The author also discusses the impact of HBCUs on African American nursing students' success. In Chapter Ten, Heather A. Katz examines the interrelated and combined effects of African American and Latina American women's goal orientation on their cognitive tool use and achievement in an interactive hypermedia environment. The author suggests that her findings can assist in understanding how college students learn in an interactive hypermedia environment as well as facilitate research-based integration of interactive hypermedia programs into the college curriculum .

Lee Jones, in Chapter 11, discusses how higher education institutions can create an affirming culture to retain African American college students. The author presents characteristics of an effective retention model that focuses on the needs of the student in both the affective and cognitive domains.

In Chapter 12, Wilton A. Barham, proposes a literacy skills model for helping culturally diverse college students understand and conduct educational research. The author points out that the literacy skills model can also be used to simply emphasize the integration of literacy skills for their general understanding.

Finally, this book should set the "context" for a discourse of the educational challenges confronting higher education institutions in America, for all college students, specifically for culturally diverse students. America's educational future will be very different from its educational past. Higher education institutions will need to respond to a variety of structural, global, and value transformations. Moreover, this will be done with a highly diverse set of college students who will provide a particularly challenging set of agendas. Historically, higher education institutions' efforts have been flawed conceptually and have not produced academic success for all college students. However, new conceptual insights, new research, and new educational practices suggest that higher education institutions can successfully meet this challenge.

Acknowledgments

Meeting the Challenge of Cultural Diversity in Higher Education in the New Millennium would not have been possible without the help of many people, and I extend my gratitude and appreciation to all who have helped me along the way to make it a reality. In particular, I thank the contributing authors for their insightful and inspiring chapters and for their commitment to the theme of this book which is evident in their diligent work and adherence to demanding research agendas.

Of course, the book would not have been possible without the outstanding efforts of the editorial and production staff at Wyndham Hall Press, most notably Mark S. McCullough and John Morgan, managing editors. I especially thank Mark S. McCullough and Wyndham Hall Press for selecting this book to be published in *The Rhodes-Fulbright International Library* series. My deep appreciation and gratitude are extended to Evelyn Shepherd-Wynn, who not only contributed a chapter, but also for her organizational and technical assistance. Special thanks to Ernesta P. Pendleton and Robby Lindsay for critiquing portions of the manuscript; their editorial advice was invaluable in helping to bring this book to realization.

I would like to thank student assistants, Octavia Daniels and Tremika Montgomery, and graduate students, Xanthe Seals, Paul Ifeanyi and Lihua Wang, for helping with the word processing and indexing of the final manuscript. Finally, I would like to thank Jordan Wynn for patiently and quietly doing her homework each afternoon as we completed this book.

CHAPTER 1

Introduction: Developing a Framework for Meeting the Challenge of Cultural Diversity

Vernon L. Farmer

> It is through a holistic and well developed framework that universities can be fully inclusive in attaining equal learning outcomes for all students. The framework . . . [must be] built upon a foundation of administrative leadership, faculty involvement and community support. It is comprised of curriculum reform, varied instructional methods, a supportive campus environment, program development and assessment. These components are interdependent, and each is critical to the endeavor. (Rodriguez 1991, p. 9)

Educating a culturally diverse student population is a major challenge for American higher education in the new millennium. Institutions of higher learning have experienced major demographic changes in the composition of the student population during the past three and a half decades, with increasing numbers of students from culturally diverse groups in the United States and throughout the globe. It is predicted that this change in demography will continue and even accelerate in the new millennium. The presence of students from culturally diverse groups in higher education began to show a substantial increase between 1965 and 1975. Since 1975, the number and proportion of total enrollment of Hispanic and Asian American students has continued to increase at all levels of the educational ladder while the number of African American students has tended to level off. African American and Hispanic American students as a proportion of the college population has continued to fall short of their presence in the general population. Although there was a substantial increase in their presence on college campuses between 1965-1975, their participation in higher education, nevertheless, has tended to decline at each successive level of the educational ladder (Commission on National Challenges in Higher Education, 1988, p. 32). In the 1990s, the number of African American students again began to show a substantial increase in the college population.

As we entered the new millennium, the Census 2000 data show that America's demography has changed significantly, and with this change comes the responsibility of America to reform higher education to educate a culturally diverse student population. In 1992, Locke predicted African Americans, Hispanic Americans, Native Americans, Asian Americans, and Alaskan Natives will make up the majority of the general population of America by 2075. Morganthau predicted in 1997 that by the year 2050, the general population will increase by more than 500 million, doubling the general population reported in the 1990 census.

Therefore, it seems to follow that the number of culturally diverse students on college campuses will have increased substantially by the 2010 Census. Anthony P. Carnevale, vice president for public leadership, and Richard Fry, senior economist, at the Educational Testing Service, reported that 80 percent of the 2.6 million new students in higher education by 2015 will consist of African Americans, Hispanic Americans, and Asian/Pacific Islanders (*Educational Testing Service Series*, 2000). This new population of students is expected to rise, according to Carnevale and Fry, both in absolute number of students (up to 2 million) and in percentage terms, up from 29.4 percent of the undergraduate population to 37.2 percent. Roach (2001) reports that the Census 2000 data demonstrate that the population of America is undergoing a radical change. The large increases in the Latino and Asian American populations are said to be changing the complexion of America. He argues that the color of American institutions of higher learning will experience significant change in the student population during this decade. This substantial increase in the number of culturally diverse students will undoubtably result in a major challenge for higher education in the new millennium.

A change in philosophy regarding the purpose of a college education has, in turn, caused a change in the numbers of culturally diverse students who pursue their basic right to a higher education. Consequently, many of these students bring with them different cognitive styles, learning styles, and lifestyles causing them to be at a learning disadvantage in the traditional college classroom. These population changes have generated a new consciousness of diversity and the many challenges that America is confronted with in the effort to meet the educational needs of students from culturally diverse groups. Despite the many positive attributes of higher education, there is growing evidence that most colleges and universities are responding to neither the uniqueness nor the cultural diversity of minority students on their campuses. Dr. Yolanda Moses, president of the American Association for Higher Education (AAHE) in Washington, reported that in the 1980s and 1990s, predominantly White colleges and universities experienced a period where they focused heavily on recruiting minority students but paid virtually no attention to their retention (qtd. in Roach, 2001, p. 29). This problem is evident by the excessively high attrition rates of students from culturally diverse groups. Dr. Yolanda Moses explains by saying that while elite higher education institutions, such as Ivy League schools, and Historically Black Colleges and Universities have experienced success in recruiting and retaining minority students from culturally diverse groups, "it's not clear that other campuses are cognizant that they have populations they have to pay attention to" (qtd. in Roach, 2001, p. 29).

Creating a positive campus environment for a culturally diverse student population must be a priority for American higher education. Many educators conceptualize this issue purely in terms of the numbers of students or faculty from culturally diverse groups on their campuses. Meanwhile, there are other educators who tend to focus on the curriculum, infusing a wider representation of perspectives. However, creating a culturally diverse campus environment consists of a number of key components, including recruitment, retention, climate, issues, pedagogy and the curriculum, organizational values, culture and structure, faculty and staff development, and so on. Therefore, colleges and universities that consider themselves committed to cultural diversity are those that foster environments that promote mutual respect, value individual differences, and facilitate collaboration among their administrators, faculty, staff, students, programs, and society at large. These higher education institutions must not only recognize cultural differences, but more importantly, make those differences the basis of educating a culturally diverse student population.

The time is ripe for higher education to assume the leadership role in meeting the challenge of America's diversity in the new millennium. The changing nature of the student population, renewed interest in interdisciplinary and collaborative research and teaching, re-examination of the college curriculum, and issues of cultural pluralism in a rapidly changing society within a global economy all provide fertile soil for the seeds of reform in American higher education. What must America do, then, to meet the challenge of cultural diversity in higher education in the new millennium? America must first be genuine and admit that it has not achieved educational quality for students from culturally diverse groups in higher education. If this goal is to be achieved, then higher education must develop a conceptual framework for responding to the challenge of America's diversity. Colleges and universities will then be able to develop a supportive environment that will enhance the success of culturally diverse students and to help prepare them to make significant contributions to society while retaining their sense of identity within their own culture in a pluralistic society.

Increasing the retention and graduation rates of culturally diverse students will depend on how effective higher education institutions are in creating academic climates that are comfortable for students from culturally diverse groups. Educating faculty to be culturally knowledgeable and sensitive is a daunting task for American higher education but a necessary one for creating a supportive environment that has a positive academic climate for a culturally diverse student population.   Historically, higher education institutions have prepared faculty to work primarily with traditional college students who were young, White, full-time, and native English speakers. So it is no surprise that the typical faculty on today's college campuses find themselves unprepared to work with a nontraditional student population. Recognizing the problem and the magnitude of this challenge, what must higher education do? It appears obvious that higher education must broaden its knowledge base regarding America's diversity. Often times faculty are unprepared to acknowledge the cultural differences and educational inequalities that exist the higher education environment. Some faculty find it difficult to understand that while culturally diverse students have the potential to be successful, they often are not given the opportunity to develop their academic and social skills in a traditional classroom. Research has indicated that faculty who are not knowledgeable about and sensitive to the needs of culturally diverse students in the classroom tend to be unaware of the cultural conflicts that cause barriers in the learning processes which may result in students' underachievement (Gilbert & Gay, 1985; Sleeter & Grant, 1986; Webster, 1974). Faculty must be trained not to dwell upon these differences but rather to use them to create a learning environment that is effective for all students, regardless of cultural background (Pine & Hilliard, 1990).

Professional development programs must be an integral part of college and university infrastructures designed to train faculty to be more effective in a culturally diverse student environment (LaBare, 1993; Wadsworth, 1992). It is obvious that if faculty are to become effective teachers in a pluralistic classroom, they must examine recent research that has redefined the nature of culturally diverse students' educational vulnerability. Much of this research has destroyed both stereotypes and myths and has laid the groundwork upon which to reconceptualize present educational theories and practices and establish new initiatives. This groundwork recognizes the homogeneity and heterogeneity within and between such populations.

Though cultural diversity is essential in American higher education, recruiting and retaining faculty from culturally diverse groups remains an arduous challenge. One of the most persistent issues has been the absence of tenured faculty from culturally diverse groups on American college and university campuses (Aguirre, 2000; Granger, 1993; Hocker, 1991). In a nation that is scampering to meet the challenges of a changing demography, a growing population of minority students from culturally diverse groups is putting pressure on higher education institutions to recruit and retain faculty from culturally diverse groups. The problem, according to Turner and Sotello (2002), is that good (i.e. qualified, tenurable) faculty is difficult to locate. This perhaps is true to a great extent; therefore, colleges and universities must recruit, retain, and graduate larger numbers of students from culturally diverse groups with the terminal degrees needed to qualify for and to help increase the nation's pool of faculty candidates. These institutions must also increase their efforts to recruit, hire and approve tenure to more of the qualified individuals from culturally diverse groups who are already in the faculty pipeline.

Despite modest gains in recent years, faculty from culturally diverse groups continue to be gravely underrepresented in American higher education institutions, according to a report from the National Center for Education Statistics (NCES). In 1997, a vast majority of full-time faculty positions were held by whites, 84 percent. However, this proportion is slightly less than the 1995 level of 87.1 percent. Individuals from culturally diverse groups have experienced only modest gains in the make up of college faculty in recent years. Asians or Pacific Islanders made up 5.5 percent of all faculty in 1997, up from 5.1 percent in 1995; African Americans, 4.9 percent, basically the same as the 1995 level of 5 percent; Hispanics, 2.6 percent, up from 2.4 percent; and American Indians or Alaskan Natives, 0.4 percent, the same as in 1995. In 1997, there were nearly 28,000 African Americans employed as full-time faculty; 14,769 Hispanic Americans; 31, 259 Asian Americans or Pacific Islanders; and 2,291 American Indians or Alaskan Natives. In comparison, there were more than 477,100 full-time White faculty.

Finding the financial resources necessary to meet the needs of this new student population is a major challenge for higher education in the new millennium. Culturally diverse students often find it difficult to meet the expenses of a college education. Working is not necessarily the answer, for this often exacerbates the pressure they are already experiencing. These students will need adequate financial support if they are to obtain a college education; however, their expectations for financial support is often not fulfilled. While higher education officials believe that there is enough space to handle the new student population, it's not clear to some whether colleges and universities are financially prepared to accommodate them. Dr. Jamie Merisotis, president of the Institute for Higher Education Policy, argues that current state and federal policies reveal too minimum investment in need-based financial aid programs. He suggests that the demographic profile of this new student population will require a larger investment in financial aid programs in the new millennium than in the past (qtd. in Roach, 2001, pp. 29-30).

There are many of us in the academia who believe that higher education already knows most of what it needs to know to meet the challenge of cultural diversity in the new millennium. However, what it lacks is the will to do so. Therefore, higher education must commit itself to implementing dynamic educational reform if it is to be effective in educating students from culturally diverse groups. This lack of will to educate this new student population is a major shortcoming of American higher education today. If higher education fails to meet the challenge of America's diversity, it could become America's Achille's heel. For it is in the best interest of America to utilize the relevant research in the field to develop initiatives to educate culturally diverse students and to help them be successful, for they will become the majority in the student population very soon and will lead America to either a bright or a beleaguered future.

The increasing presence of students from culturally diverse groups has forced many higher education institutions to call into question existing policies and practices regarding programs and services, in turn calling for revision in the ways in which they conduct their business with and for students. In higher education's effort to respond to the challenge of cultural diversity, many colleges and universities have sought to design and implement programs and services before they have developed a conceptual framework to guide the attitudinal development of their effort (Anderson, 1991). Prior to designing and implementing such activities, higher education institutions must express their commitment to cultural diversity in their mission statements and demonstrate this commitment by fostering a campus environment that encourages cultural pluralism and values cultural differences among their students.

The task at hand, then, is to utilize the relevant research literature on cultural diversity to develop and implement support programs and services designed to enhance the learning outcomes of this new student population. Tomlinson (1989) argues that from a global perspective, successful programs tend to have two major characteristics in common: comprehensiveness in their support services and integration within the academic mainstream of the institution. Farmer and Barham (2001) suggest that educating a culturally diverse student population is more than simply a matter of providing a few isolated support services, but rather priority must be given to the development of a comprehensive and intensive program of integrated services. Farmer and Barham's "Comprehensive Developmental Education Model" consists of an array of support activities, including basic skills courses, tutorial instruction, supplemental instruction, academic advising, counseling and psychological services, communication skills laboratories and quantitative skills labs to enhance retention of culturally diverse students through graduation. In general, support programs and services designed to help students with their cognitive and affective needs tend to be highly successful when they are well planned, intensive, and comprehensive, and when they employ skilled professionals. When students from culturally diverse groups have the opportunity to participate in such programs, their learning outcomes are greatly enhanced.

Several examples of successful learning strategies employed in a comprehensive program of integrated services designed to enhance the learning outcomes of culturally diverse include, collaborative learning, learning style based instruction, self-regulated learning and supplemental learning (instruction). Instruction in small groups utilizing collaborative learning has proven effective as an instructional approach for teaching culturally diverse students. In using collaborative learning in the classroom, students work with each other and teachers to discover, explore, analyze, synthesize, debate and to think critically and enhance questioning and reasoning abilities to solve problems (Shepherd-Wynn, Cadet, & Pendleton, 2001). Learning style based instruction challenges traditional instructional methods by keying in on the individual learning preferences of students and presenting research evident that, responding to these individual preferences, results in improved academic performance and improved attitudes toward learning. Specifically, learning style-based instruction has promise for responding to the needs of underachieving students and culturally diverse students, resulting in positive learning outcomes (Dunn, Dunn, & Perrin, 1994). Self-regulated learning is an approach that can be used to help culturally diverse students learn to plan, organize, self-instruct, self-monitor, and self-evaluate during various stages of the learning process. The degree to which a student employs self-regulated learning and motivational strategies necessary to convert information into coherent accessible knowledge is the degree to which the student will experience academic success (DuBois, 2001)). The supplemental instruction approach suggests that providing assistance to students has meant relating process-oriented information such as study skills, speed reading, mnemonic devices, time management, and test-taking strategies to facilitate academic success. Supplemental learning is most effective when it is integrated into a comprehensive developmental education program (Barham, 2001).

Finally, America must realize that its future in the new millennium will depend upon how effective it is in educating all of the culturally diverse students who seek a higher education. Higher education should not assume that only a few culturally diverse students are capable of succeeding in college, while many others are ignored. Some colleges and universities tend to recruit only the best from culturally diverse students into their programs, rather than include students whose potential may be less obvious. Admissions criteria should be made more flexible, so that consideration is given to various experiences and other information that may tell more about culturally diverse students' academic potential than do the usual admissions criteria.

The higher education institution that succeeds in admitting, retaining, and graduating students from culturally diverse groups will have garnered faculty commitment and action; will have demonstrated genuine interest in, and commitment to, creating a supportive environment and academic climate; will have developed and made operational positive a plan of action; and will not fail to remember that once the culturally diverse students are on campus, they must be assisted in their educational and career development.

Finally, meeting the challenge of cultural diversity in higher education will be a valuable resource for colleges and universities concerned with developing a framework through which equal learning outcomes can be achieved for all students. If America makes inseparable the goals of inclusion and excellence and draws on the many resources that already exist and will exist, higher education will move from being at the crossroad to being what it can and should be, the foundation for America's diversity.

CHAPTER 2

Classroom Diversity in the New Millennium: The Case for Developmental Education

Martin O. Edu

Introduction

America's cultural language has trouble catching up with the accelerating pace of change faced by the nation. Also, the mainstream media tend to be either exclusionary or dismissive of the realities, thought, history, and representations of "others." To harness cultural diversity as a resource, we must work together with the mainstream media to convey the cultural realities of the new millennium that eliminate some accepted vestiges and patterns of the past (Wilson, 1997). If the successful multicutural classroom is America's goal for the new millennium as the country becomes increasingly culturally diverse, a morphogenetic change that draws its strength from the different cultural voices in the classroom must take place in our school system. This chapter makes a case for college-level developmental education as an integral part of college education, and discusses some unresolved challenges in the field.

Whether called multiculturalism, cultural pluralism, diversity, cross-culturalism or interculturalism, the central idea conveyed by the terms is *difference*. Using the *Webster's New Collegiate Dictionary* as a guide, the terms *multiculturalism* and *cultural pluralism* can be described as multiple but distinct cultures, while *cultural diversity* or diversity, as some people prefer to call it, describes a variety of cultures. Using definitions from Dodd (1995) and Samovar and Porter (1997) the terms *cross-culturalism* and *interculturalism*, can be described as the relationships among and between cultures. These brief definitions demonstrate that whether the terms are used singly or in combination, their meanings revolve around *difference*. Difference is a phenomenon that adds complexity and beauty to nature. We see it everywhere, in trees, animals, weather, people, automobiles, homes and what have you, but the difference at the core of this work is that between and among humans, actual or perceived.

The American Experience

For centuries, American society treated women of all races and minorities and especially men of color as peripheral until black men gained their citizenship and the right to vote after the Civil War in the 1860s. That change eventually paved the way for white and black women to gain a similar status in 1920. But the suzerainty of the white male remained unruffled until the mid 1960s when a social revolution turned American society upside down and downside up as men of color, women of all races, and other minorities began to gain equal access to employment, credit and education (Wilson, 1997).

The social revolution continues unabated by conservative under-currents. It has permeated every facet of American society and business. In the corporate world, most American managers of conglomerates have recognized that cultural difference, if managed well, is a resource. Harris and Moran (1996) suggest that in the past, many of the same managers viewed cultural differences as barriers and handicaps to communication and inter-action. They categorized American multi-national corporations into four types according to how they manage cultural diversity: *ethnocentric, polycentric, regiocentric* and geo*centric.* The ethnocentric corporation is home-oriented, and the managers believe that their home-country nationals are more intelligent, reliable and trustworthy than foreign nationals. The polycentric corporation is host-country oriented that allows the host-country managers to "do it their way" (p. 12). The regiocentric corporation believes that only regional insiders can effectively coordinate functions within the region, and the geocentric corporation is world-oriented. Its central theme is "All for one and one for all. We will work together to solve problems anywhere in the world" (p. 13).

The American corporate world is making every effort to face up to the challenge posed by multiculturalism as projections document a trend toward a culturally more diverse workplace. The profound implication of the trend is that, for business to succeed in the competitive and diverse environment, companies must not only look up to the diverse workers, men and women, drawn from ethnic co-cultures, immigrants and mainstream America, but must also find new ways to combine their efforts. It will not work any other way as noted by Chen and Starosta (1998):

> Diversity looms as one of the biggest learning challenges of the near future. By failing to recognize the importance of demographic trends and of the trends toward multinational commerce, and failing to adjust our beliefs about the contributions that those of diverse backgrounds can make, we will lose their valuable and creative inputs. (p. 215)

An excerpt from a 1987 U.S. Department of Labor report about the state of the American workforce in 2000 further reinforces Chen and Starosta's observation. It indicated that

> more women will enter the workforce...and rapidly enter high-paying professional and technical fields...Co-cultural groups will constitute a larger share of new entrants into the labor force. It is estimated that nonwhites will double their current share of the new entrants...(and) immigrants will represent the largest share of the increase in population and the workforce. (p. 216)

Educational Sector

Since tomorrow's workforce is often prepared today, the educational sector faces many of the same diversity challenges encountered by businesses. The necessity to be more culturally sensitive to diversity in the classroom is more apparent than it ever was. Education not only helps immigrants to make sense of the indigenous culture, but it also offers them survival insights and skills for the changing world. Multicultural and global education helps people to learn about the problems and issues that cut across ethnic, racial, gender, and national boundaries, and to understand how other groups process experience in ways that may be different from traditional perceptions.

The social revolution of the 1960s created an awareness of education as the cornerstone of a better future. The message struck a chord, especially among society's underrepresented and the down-trodden, who have made significant strides since then. Immigrants faced a much tougher situation because most of them have limited English proficiency, which is the official business language in America. As the numbers of these individuals continues to surge in schools, the problem of underpreparedness will exacerbate at K-12 through college, yet some would argue against developmental education at the college level. As was indicated in the abstract, this paper makes a case for college-level developmental education and discusses some unresolved challenges facing the field.

College-level Developmental Education
Opposition to and Support for the Field

Despite developmental education's role in enabling underprepared students to cope with college-level work, its presence in higher education seems to arouse public debate. Some public officials and educators have expressed the view that it should not be the responsibility of post secondary institutions. For example, as Deputy Under-Secretary for Management in the U. S. Department of Education, Linda M. Combs said during an interview that the federal government hoped developmental education would not be needed in post secondary institutions (Combs & Boylan, 1985). Combs and Boylan also cited two reports by the National Endowment for the Humanities and the U. S. Department of Education recommending that colleges and universities phase out remedial instruction. Also, Louisiana State Senator Randy Ewing (Sullivan, 1992), suggested the elimination of developmental courses in the universities to improve Louisiana's higher education. Mickler and Chapel (1989) presented the viewpoints of public officials who support developmental programs in the higher education setting because of their need-based nature. The Miami-Dade Community College Comparative Guidance and Placement is an example of a success-oriented program which assists students with limited educational skills to succeed in college.

As mentioned earlier, the G. I. Bill of 1944 and the Higher Education Act of 1965 encouraged many adults who had been out of school for many years to return. The continuation of developmental education at the college level enabled the new students to acquire the basic skills needed for successful achievement in college courses. Should college-level developmental efforts be eliminated, such adults would have a hard time coping with college work. Some of them might not even try. It should be borne in mind that meeting the needs of adult students whose educational experiences were limited for one reason or another was one of the major reasons community colleges were established (Platt, 1986). Mickler and Chapel (1989) contends that a school that accepts a student for admission "is morally obligated to develop institutional methods that will offer the student those skills" that would enable him or her to succeed academically (p. 3). Landward and Hepworth (1984) suggest that colleges with open-door admission policies should be required to provide support systems necessary to offer their students a reasonable opportunity for success.

The foregoing arguments and counter-arguments make one wonder what students might have to say about the issue. It is rather anachronistic that such a debate could continue to rage without seeking the opinions of students who are directly affected by developmental programs. As consumers, their opinions should help to resolve the issue.

The views expressed by public officials seem to suggest that developmental education still has a long way to go in terms of swaying public opinion to its favor. Public relations experts have learned that the most effective way to influence or shape public opinion is to first build and maintain favorable internal opinions. In the same way, college developmental education professionals must first work to gain the favorable opinions of its internal public which is made up of students, faculty, and staff, before they can positively influence the opinions of their external public. To do so would require the adoption of some of the strategies used by public relations professionals and communication specialists for packaging and promoting goods and services. Such efforts could involve name changes as is common with banks, restaurants, and hospitals seeking new images (DiDomenico, 1992; Morvis, 1991; Wartick, 1992). Credit must be given to these professionals who have made image and brand names to seem to mean everything to the modern-day consumer (Hedden, 1992).

The State of Developmental Education

The spread of developmental education and increased enrollment in the field was reflected in a study by the National Center for Education Statistics (1985), which indicated that about four-fifths of all institutions and nine-tenths of all public colleges and universities offer developmental education courses. Several studies also reported increased enrollment in developmental courses (Abraham, 1987; Beckett, 1985; Hardin, 1988; Lederman, Ribaudo & Ryzewic, 1985; Mickler & Chapel, 1989; Plisko & Stern, 1985). Abraham (1991) contended that about one-third of entering freshmen in the SREB states need remediation. He also noted that entering Black or Hispanic students were more likely to be enrolled in developmental courses than students of any other race or ethnic group. He reported that 57% of Hispanic and 52% of Black students were enrolled in developmental courses in the 606 responding two-year campuses. About 55% of the institutions in the study experienced an increase in remedial enrollment, and 16% experienced a decline. An increase in overall institutional enrollment was the overriding reason for the increase in remedial enrollment. Astin (1984) also reported that inadequately prepared students were one of the fastest growing subgroups in higher education.

The persistent enrollment increase in developmental courses seems to support Pilland's (1983) observation that the problem of underprepared students neither is, nor ever has been, a temporary problem which will someday disappear. He pointed out that the complexity of the problem of underpreparedness calls for long-range rather than short-range solutions. It should be obvious from Pilland's remark that the problem did not begin when minorities first gained access to college educations as some scholars would have their readers believe. Its history dates back much further. For example, when William Rainey Harper, first president of The University of Chicago, encouraged the development of junior colleges, (more commonly referred to as community or two-year colleges), what he had in mind was for the institutions to take over the first two years of courses from senior colleges. He envisaged that such an arrangement would provide a long-term solution to the problem of underpreparedness and allow senior colleges to devote more time to research (Vaughan, 1982). Thus, one of the original missions of junior colleges was to prepare students for the first two years of college so they could transfer to senior or four-year colleges to complete their undergraduate degree requirements (Cohen & Brawer, 1989).

Government Involvement

Increased government involvement in higher education began with the passage of the G. I. Bill in 1944, that provided loans and other forms of financial aid for thousands of military men and women who returned to school in large numbers. It also enabled two-year colleges to begin gradually to assume the developmental function. With the rapid growth of developmental education in the 1960s, the developmental function became an integral part of the missions of two-year colleges. Abraham (1987) reported that Florida, California, Arkansas, Tennessee, and Georgia were among the first states to make developmental education the mission of their two-year colleges (Davis, 1979).

Direct state involvement in college developmental education seems to have increased the most in the 1990s, probably because of the realization of the socio-cultural and long-term nature of the problem. Not only has the direct involvement helped to generate more funds for the field, but it has also led to the recognition of college underpreparedness as a national problem. Pilland (1983) who studied the status of the field nationally found that only 38% of the institutions had official or working definitions of developmental education, while 62% did not have any, and "slightly fewer than one-half of the states have remedial education mission statement or state policy" (p. 11). Though almost 83% of the institutions reported that they had written policies for the placement of students, perhaps a statewide policy would be a preferred option for purposes of uniformity and periodic evaluation of performance.

Diverse Population

The classification of college students into *traditional* and *nontraditional* began with the mass return of veterans to college at the end of the second world war through the provisions of the G. I. Bill of Rights in1944 (Rudolph, 1990). As the number of adult students increased through open admission policies and part-time enrollment in the 1960s, the dichotomy became more obvious.

The terms *traditional* and *nontraditional* have been defined differently by different authors. While a National Center for Educational Statistics report (1985) defines traditional students as those who are 24 years or younger, Holmstrom (1973), defines them as 19 or younger, Solmon, Gordon, and Ochsner (1979) classified them as students 20 years old or younger, while Roelfs (1975) defines them as those 22 years old or younger. These studies seem to suggest that *nontraditional* or *older* students, as they are sometimes called, range in age from the early-to-mid twenties upward. As students differ in their ages and life experiences, so do they also differ in their motives and values about college education. Because of their varied life experiences, nontraditional students tend to have concrete reasons for returning to school and the goals they want to achieve, while the younger and less experienced traditional students do not (Chickering & Associates, 1981).

Weathersby (1977) studied students' reasons for undergraduate enrollment at Goddard College using a participant-observation method. The goals most frequently cited by students for seeking a college degree included work and career development. The study also found that the reasons differed according to the students' ego levels. For example, students at the Conscientious Ego Stage and below (noted for its focus on achievement) cited reorientation and redirection as the most salient reason for college enrollment. "No one at the Self Aware Stage or below gave in-depth study or wanting to pursue one's pressing interests as reasons for enrollment in college" (Chickering & Associates, 1989, p. 64). Compared to younger (traditional) students, older students seem more likely to know what they want out of college (Roelfs, 1985). Another study of students' reasons for returning to school involved 6,000 adult students enrolled in continuing education in Massachusetts (Nolfi & Nelson, 1973). The primary reasons they gave for enrollment was job advancement and motivation. The study also found their finances to be the major reason most of the students dropped out of school initially.

These studies demonstrate that nontraditional and traditional students, some of whom need academic remediation, come from diverse cultural backgrounds and have as different socio-cultural orientations as the traditional students. Also, nontraditional students have motives and values that are distinctly different from those of traditional students. They seem to be more focused toward achievement of their goals than traditional students, some of whom do not know why they are in college; therefore, the perceptions and attitudes of these students toward developmental education are different from those of traditional students (Brown, 1991). For example, a nontradi-tional student would be glad to enroll in developmental courses that would help him or her do well in degree courses; but the traditional student would probably be more concerned with the opinions of his or her peers than the benefit to be derived from the courses.

Cultural Perceptions Viewed From
a Public Relations Perspective

Every culture has its unique ways of doing things and of viewing and interpreting the world around it. People grow up in their unique cultures and societies which train them in the ways of that culture. The training forms the core of their beliefs and values, which, in turn, become rules for governing themselves as they interact with other people and deal with life situations in the world around them. Generally, such cultural training tends to lurk beneath their surface thoughts and actions; and, to a large extent, it serves as our social relations orientation, which describes how people in a culture organize themselves and relate to one another (Lustig & Koester, 1998). The training also allows us to develop our individual social perception, "a process by which we construct our unique social realities by attributing meaning to the social objects and events we encounter in our environments" (Samovar & Porter, 1997, p. 15). Samovar and Porter also identified "three major sociocultural elements that have a direct and major influence on the meanings we develop for our perceptions." They include "our belief/value/attitude systems, world view, and social organization" (p. 15). According to them, these elements influence the individual subjective perceptions and meanings that we derive from social entities. Human perception is defined as "the active process by which we use our sensory organs to sense the world (Chen & Starosta, 1998, p. 33). Because the prevailing social values and beliefs are not held by everybody in society, Americans of different cultural orientations would perceive the developmental education either pejoratively or positively.

Students' perceptions of the field are impacted by their cultural training and orientations. The cultural training we receive growing up forms the bedrock of individual and public perceptions and opinions around which the professional practice of public relations revolves. It is suggested that developmental educators should consider adopting some public relations strategies to reposition the field. Positioning is a promotional strategy used to influence the consumer to view one product more positively than the competition (Wells, Burnett & Moriarty, 1995). Some aspects of the field identified in the literature as having the potential to influence students' perceptions are discussed briefly in the pages that follow. They include the program's name, the relationship of teachers to students, the assessment/ placement method, the level of student involvement or participation in class and campus activities, and peer pressure.

As a two-way management function, public relations utilizes non-selling, non-advertising and persuasive communication activities to influence perceptions and public opinions. Botan and Hazleton (1989) view public relations as a "definitional label for the process of attempting to exert symbolic control over evaluative predispositions" [*attitude, images,* etc. and subsequent behaviors of relevant publics or clienteles (p. 47)]. Shimp (1993) described it as "that aspect of promotion management uniquely suited to fostering goodwill between a company and its various publics" (p. 587).

Sietel (1993) suggests that the impact of public relations efforts depends on human perception that determines how messages are decoded and comprehended. He notes that "everyone is biased and no two people perceive a message identically" (p. 176), and personal biases are nurtured by such factors as "stereotypes, symbols, semantics, peer group pressures, and the media" (p. 177). As communicators, public relations professionals "make their living largely by knowing how to use words effectively to communicate desired meanings" (p. 178). They are expert users of symbols and the media to provide the public agenda through which people form opinions. Understanding public opinion and how it works is fundamental to public relations, as practitioners monitor shifts in public opinion, identify opinion leaders, and determine the kinds of information or communication that matches audience opinions (Sietel, 1993; Wilcox, Ault, & Agee, 1998). Cutlip, Center and Broom (2000) suggest that the power of public opinion must be faced, understood, and dealt with because it provides the psychological environment in which organizations prosper or perish.

Perhaps some examples that demonstrate their power, fragility, and elusiveness of public opinion and perceptions would help. In a *Nightline* interview with Ted Koppel, Mr. Campanis, a veteran baseball player, coach, and an executive of the Los Angeles Dodgers, saw his career capsize with 40 seconds of ill-chosen words as he explained why black people do not get leadership positions in baseball (Desmond, 1989). His public opinion rating plummeted to near zero following the interview. Also, Stuart (1990) reported an incident in which Victor Kiam, successful owner of a shaving products company and the New England Patriots football team, ignited a national anger when he reportedly called a woman news reporter "a classic bitch," after she claimed sexual harassment in the team's locker room. His Lady Remington shaver and Mr. Kiam himself were excoriated by women everywhere. Similar examples also exist in developmental education as shown in the next section.

A Program's Name

The many labels used to refer to developmental education programs may tempt one to ask what is in a name. Names like Campbell soup, Ivory soap, Kelloggs, Betty Crocker, Listerine, Ford, Buick, etc. are well known in American life, but to millions of consumers they mean more than the mere identification of products. Each name, according to Sandage, Fryburger, and Rotzoll (1989) "signifies a unique set of properties that combine over time, to form a picture of the product in the mind's eye. The mental picture is what is often called brand name" (p. 153). Sumrall, (1993) describes each name as a "golden key, ready to unlock a treasure of truth to the inquiring mind" (p. 22).

A person who bears many names, for example, is likely to convey different images to people who know him or her by only one of the names. Such a situation could cause confusion among people who know him or her (Kalat, 1990). College developmental education, unfortunately, has been put in a similar situation because of the different names used to refer to it. The name given to a program is as important as the program's content. It determines the program's definition and image. The lack of uniformity in names given to developmental education programs across the country generates some confusion that could breed negative public opinion. It also conveys a poor image for programs despite their significant role in addressing what is considered a national problem.   Even among educators, some confusion seems to exist, for example, concerning the distinction between the terms *developmental* and *remedial* reading programs offered in colleges and universities (Nist, 1985).

According to Maxwell (1979), the name of an academic learning center is important for its image. For example, Academic Support Services (ASS) may sound like a good name but students may surprise the program's director by dubbing it *ASS* and the staff *ASSES*. Similar occurrences took place at Stanford University where a program called Learning Assistance Center (LAC) was soon dubbed *lack* and staff members were dubbed *lackeys* (Maxwell, 1979, p. 126). The University of Texas quickly changed its Reading Improvement Program (RIP), which was dubbed *rest in peace*, to Reading and Study Skills Laboratory (*RASSL*, pronounced *wrassle*). Lamons (1992) pointed out that companies with positive images tend to have higher market shares, lower selling costs, and higher profits. If the adoption of names that promote positive images works well for businesses, it is reasonable to assume that it will also work well for developmental education programs.

A name, be it individual, family, or corporate, is very important for image and identification purposes. For instance, when the 1914 labor dispute at the Rockefeller-owned Colorado coal mines escalated into violence that resulted in the massacre of about 50 men, women, and children, the family's name just about hit the bottom in public opinion rating. Rockefeller's son quickly regained the positive image and family's good name with the help of public relations genius named Ivy Ledbetter Lee (Dunn, 1986). More recently, when Procter and Gamble was accused of supporting the church of Satan, the company used its public relations department, an outside agency, and millions of dollars to defuse the rumor (Dunn, 1986). The company was probably not as concerned about the rumor as it was about the possible damage to its image and name. These examples from the business world are a strong indication that uniformity in name and redefinition of the goals of developmental education are as much a necessity as the promotion of a new image. It is essential that developmental students be consulted about any changes either being contemplated or planned. Educators may be surprised at how the students' diverse backgrounds and experiences could be used as a powerful resource for creative input.

Student/Teacher Relations

In his book, *Mastering the Techniques of Teaching,* Lowman (1984) described the classroom as both *dramatic* and *human* arenas. The dramatic arena is a setting for intellectual discourse, and the human arena is the setting where the interpersonal dealing of instructors and students takes place. He believes that good teaching arises from teachers' sensitivity toward students. Sensitivity to people entails recognition of and respect for difference. Lowman pointed out that the teachers should always bear in mind that classrooms are made up of different kinds of students. He warns that a teacher who feels that or behaves as if one group of students matters more than the other would be indulging in what he calls "the narrowest form of bigotry" (p. 19). Lowman stressed the need for teachers to recognize that students are "people who like to be challenged, who have strong affective potential to react and to get excited" (p. 19). He stated that the more teachers strive toward raising students' standards, raising their hopes, and getting them excited, the more appreciative the students are likely to become. The more students appreciate their teacher, the greater the effort they would make to maintain good relations with the teacher.

Students want teachers to recognize who they are, to listen to what they have to say, and to respect their efforts. They do not like a classroom where they are put down or made to feel stupid, either by the teacher or by their peers (Phelan, Davidson, & Cao, 1992). Students place a tremendous value on having teachers who care. Their perceptions of teachers either as caring or not caring could have a far-reaching effect on them, especially on low achieving students (p. 698). A teacher who realizes that students from all achievement levels and socio-cultural backgrounds want to succeed and who makes a conscious effort to promote good relations is likely to influence student perceptions of the school environment.

Yager and Penick (1989) reported that teachers tend to perceive high performing students more positively than low performing students, and the attitudes of higher performing students toward their teachers tend to be more positive than those of low performing students. The way students think their teachers perceive them could contribute greatly to the relationship between teacher and student. As Lowman (1984), points out, "everyone has a bias" that is deeply rooted in the cultural training he or she hads. While it is pertinent that developmental education instructors work to maintain positive relationship with students, it is equally important that they monitor students' perceptions or opinions of assessment and placement practices. As consumers, their feedback could help in decisions relating to future changes or improvement.

Assessment/Placement

Educators have expressed several opinions about the assessment and placement of students into developmental education courses. In the Southern Regional Education Board region, there are about 125 combinations of about 75 different tests used to place students in writing, reading, and mathematics (Abraham, 1987). The wide variation in placement standards means that each institution defines college-level work according to its mission.

Reynolds (1985) examined the relationship between remedial programs and diagnostic testing and concluded that diagnostic tests have some serious limitations. She outlined the weaknesses in the Basic Skills Placement Test (BSPT) used by New Jersey public colleges to determine the placement of freshmen in remedial writing, reading, and mathematics. She expressed the viewpoint that the development of tests to measure the reading ability of college students and adults has not kept pace with the instructional programs. She also discussed the shortcomings of the Nelson-Denny Reading Test

(NDRT). Some of the identified shortcomings included the limitation on testing time, the absence of a gradual increase in difficulty of items, questionable results as a pre-post test measure, and the use of passage-dependent items. She claimed that the test is popular not because it is a perfect testing instrument but because of low cost and the short administration time involved. She also listed and discussed ten features that, in her opinion, should be included in diagnostic tests for remedial students, concluding that if a diagnostic test was well matched with, for example, a reading program, the information would assist instructional planning.

Reynolds' findings and views challenge developmental professionals not only to reexamine current assessment and placement practices, but to also find new methods that could eliminate some of the shortcomings. The report is worth being taken seriously, because some developmental educators seem to assume that "all culturally diverse, socio-economically disadvantaged, or first generation college students" are likely to be underprepared (Higbee, Dwinell, McAdams, Goldberg-Belle, & Tardola, 1991, p. 74). Higbee and his associates also stated that it is not easy to categorize or stereotype all underprepared students. They cited the example of the University of California at Los Angeles that admits only the top 12% of graduating high school seniors, yet about one half of those entering freshman require remedial work in mathematics and English.

Studies that focus heavily on the racial representations at developmental education centers rather than the socio-cultural factors that make them underprepared tend to miss the point. By merely comparing racial representations instead of finding solutions, they tend to create the erroneous impression that underpreparedness is associated with only minority groups. That is exactly what mainstream media does best, portraying minorities in ways that suggest they are the society's primary problem. It goes without argument that remediation cuts across racial and class boundaries, and it is not new. It was in existence a long time before minorities gained appreciable access to college education.

The Commission for Educational Quality, set up by the Southern

Regional Education Board (1985) to examine access to higher education and recommend ways to achieve quality education, also had a problem with placement standards. The commission observed that placement standards have dropped "to a point at which students are admitted who cannot learn on the college level...leading to high dropout rates, or forcing faculty, in an attempt to meet the needs of the underprepared, to aim their courses at a level that cheats the prepared students" (p. 7). There is neither a consensus nor common understanding of "what college level work is or how to identify students that require additional preparation before beginning college" (p. 7). The commission pointed to the slowness of higher education to acknowledge that much of what is often called college-level work is not. It called for the re-establishment of college study "as a form of higher learning, with courses that demand learning and thinking skills above the high school level for all students" (p. 7).

In his study of academic placement standards in the member states of the Southern Regional Education Board (SREB), Abraham (1987) found that entry-level placement standards for developmental students vary widely. He expressed concern about the lack of consensus in the tests used and the skills and knowledge necessary for what is often referred to as college-level work. He argued that any attempt to convert or compare the range of low and high cut-off scores is likely to be full of drawbacks. He compared the percentile equivalents of the low cut-off scores in Nelson-Denny, ACT-combined, and MAPS-DTLS, the three nationally norm-referenced tests that were most frequently used by the institutions, and found a variety of drawbacks. In reading and writing, the low cut-off scores ranged from the first to the ninth percentile, and in mathematics they ranged from the ninth to the sixteenth, very few students scored lower.

Wambach and Brothen (1990) provided an alternative to the prediction-placement model. They recommended skills assessment based on current classroom performance since some students who fail to achieve in high school actually have the ability to succeed in college. They pointed out that the high probability of error in placement based on high school records and standardized test scores delays the academic development of many students placed unnecessarily in mandatory skill development programs. They suggested that the tendency of developmental educators to assume that all developmental students are underprepared is misleading. For example, Landward and Hepworth (1984) identified three distinct categories of developmental students. The "false negatives" describes students who are unqualified but can succeed. The "underprepared" are unqualified students who can be enabled to succeed through interventions, and the "true negatives" refers to the unqualified students who cannot be made more qualified by any known intervention.

The three categories of developmental education students described by Landworth and Hepworth and the placement alternative suggested by Wombach and Brothen are important in the discussion of student perceptions of college developmental education programs. Admission to college tends to generate a sense of self worth and achievement. Upon getting to the college, new students expect to be enrolled in degree courses rather than developmental courses. The students whose standardized test scores fall below a certain cut-off point determined by the college, often are required to take a placement test or a series of tests to determine their placement.

A student placed in developmental courses is likely to be disappointed because of the sense of academic deficiency it connotes. The disappointment can lead to disillusionment, poor perception of the school, and an eventual drop out unless appropriate action is taken to help the student understand the reason for the placement. Counseling can help these students develop a positive self perception to encourage active involvement with classroom and selected campuswide activities.

Student Involvement

Classical social psychologists such as George Herbert Mead (1934), Charles Horton Cooley (1971), and psychiatrist Harry Stack Sullivan (1947, 1953) postulated that the way individuals conceive of themselves is based on social interaction with others. Their self-perceptions, in turn, influence and guide their behavior. If developmental students are accepted and respected for who they are, and encouraged to get actively involved in both class and selected campuswide activities, they could develop positive attitudes and perceptions about themselves and developmental education programs. The reverse could result in an environment where students are ridiculed or patronized.

Turnbull (1986) suggests that anything that increases student involvement or commitment irrespective of that student's cultural background would also increase retention and vice versa. Just as a high degree of involvement with home activities and family members promotes harmony and success in a family, so would student involvement with class and campus activities promote self confidence and success in college. He contended that student involvement can be determined by the amount of time a student devotes to studying, whether a student takes an on-campus or off-campus job, participates in campus organizations, and interacts with faculty and other students.

These studies suggest that student perceptions are essential for creating an environment that promotes student involvement in the school community. Sensitivity to students' perceptions and encouragement of their input seems to challenge the traditional norms associated with the school environment, but it is a requirement for maintaining some balance in a multicultural classroom.

Peer Pressure

Ausubel's (1968) classic study described peer groups as distinct groups that tend to develop aggressive attitudes and set distinct standards and training functions of their own. Because members tend to reach out toward one another for support, he said that peer groups not only furnish their members with a sense of belonging and security, but are also a powerful source of loyalty to group norms.

College students form and belong to a variety of organizations both formal and informal, which allows members to provide support, security, and acceptance for one another. Peers also influence one another in different ways. Zanden (1981) notes that one of the most prevalent channels of peer influence is through the pressure that groups put on their members to conform to their various standards of conduct. The requirement makes peer pressure one of the determining factors of the way students perceive certain institutional and academic functions such as developmental education programs.

Jones and Hattie (1991) found that the extra effort students make to conform to peer demands often contributes to academic stress. The study investigated factors that contribute to academic stress among adolescent students. They administered a 35-item questionnaire called the Academic Pressure Scale for Adolescents to 550 high school students. They found peer pressure, the importance of school, and the fear of failure to be significant factors contributing to academic stress.

Egginton, Wells, Gaus, and Esselman (1990) studied the factors that influence the attitudes of underprepared students toward academic work and their propensity to drop out of school. They obtained data from two studies by the Kentucky Department of Education. One study investigated the school dropout rate among young adults who were in programs designed for single parents and/or displaced homemakers. The second study sought to identify the underlying factors associated with being at-risk as reported by 68 white female high school "at-risk" students classified as educationally disadvantaged. The subjects in both groups consistently reported that the freedom they had in their home environments was incompatible to that which they found in school environments. Other factors cited for incompatibility included peer pressure in school, lack of discipline at home, little parental interest in school and/or education, many home responsibilities, financial problems, and abuse.

These studies suggest that peer pressure has a great deal of influence on students. Because of their zeal to imitate one another and to conform to group norms, the perceptions of students in a peer group about the school environment are likely to be similar. Developmental students, whose friends are enrolled in regular degree courses are likely to feel academically inferior and to perceive remediation pejoratively even though they might need it to succeed in college.

Conclusion

Demographic trends make it clear that classroom diversity will rise in the new millennium. Martin and Nakayama (2000) note that "the U.S. population has changed radically in the past two decades and will continue to do so in the future" (p. 5). Hacker (1997) cited projections by the Census Bureau to show that "by the year 2030, the United States will be a global society in which nearly half of all Americans will be from today's racial and ethnic minorities," made up primarily of African Americans, Asians, Hispanics, and Native Americans (p. 121). They believe that the heterogeneity presents opportunities and challenges as efforts are made to bring together the different ways of thinking.

As the country moves toward an increasing wave of diversity, the need for the educational system to explore more inclusionary rather than exclusionary measures becomes obvious. Now is perhaps the opportune time to appreciate the different lifestyles, ways of thinking and learning in the classroom. That underpreparedness is so common among high school graduates illuminates the necessity of such measures at developmental education centers across the country, since they serve as the only bridge through which underprepared students can become college educated. Multiculturalism in American society makes a strong case for college-level developmental education and calls for greater government and public effort in the field to help the professionals meet the challenges that lie ahead.

CHAPTER 3
A Comparison of Writing Skills and Academic Success Rates of High Risk African American and European American Students With Matched Verbal SAT Score

Margaret A. McLaughlin and Eleanor Agnew
Introduction

A 1997 national study, the most comprehensive assessment of the African American postsecondary educational experience yet produced, recently reported that African American students are placed in college remedial classes at a much higher rate than white students (30% to 7%), yet they receive only 6% of all bachelors degrees granted each year (Gray, 1997, p. A-1). Fidler and Godwin have synthesized the topics of several studies into their statement, "Colleges and universities have historically structured their curricula, student services, and campus environment based on a white middle class norm" (p. 35). Additionally, "only five percent of all college faculty are African American" (Gray, 1997, p. A-5), which means that African American students are being taught primarily by white instructors who may be "ill-prepared to teach students who are unlike themselves" (as cited in Harrold, 1995, p. 17). A longitudinal study conducted at our university corroborates these findings and suggests that the inflexible assessment styles of some English instructors impede the progress of students whose home language is African American English (AAE).

At most colleges and universities, the underlying presumption behind the existence of remedial English programs is that underprepared students will not be able to succeed in subsequent college courses without first becoming proficient in college writing skills. Our research, however, reveals that success in a remedial writing course has little effect on students' academic careers. A more troubling finding, however, is the degree to which the academic paths of black and white participants in the study differed. White students who had difficulty passing the remedial course still had more academic success over a five year period than did African American students who passed the course on their first attempt.

In 1993, the year we began the study, 45.3% of the entering freshmen were placed in remedial courses at our school, a regional university in southeast Georgia with about 14,000 students. At the time, the media was giving a great deal of coverage to the large numbers of students in college remedial classes, the low college graduation rate of these students, and the high cost of remediation for tax payers -- reportedly, $25.6 million dollars annually in the state of Georgia. As instructors of remedial students, we wanted to discover whether our efforts on students behalf at the beginning of their college careers [would] make a difference in enabling them to cope afterward (Wolcott, 1994, p. 14).

With the permission of our students and our administrators, we began a longitudinal study. For the past five years, we have followed the academic progress of the 61 students who were randomly placed in two remedial English classes that we were teaching in the 1993 fall quarter. As experienced teachers, we realized that the students in these two classes were quite representative of remedial English students at our university. Virtually all were recent high school graduates; two thirds were African American; and SAT verbal scores ranged from a low of 220 to a high of 410. Most were first generation college students who perceived a college degree as a ticket to a better economic life, and so they entered our classes highly motivated to succeed.

We began our study with one major research question: What Happens to High-Risk Students <u>after</u> Remedial English? Among our related questions were the following:

1. How many of these students will graduate and in how long a time period?
2. Are there correlations between the attrition rate and the students first quarterwork in remedial English?

3.   Will African American dialect interfere with success
in subsequent college courses?

To address these questions, we tracked the academic progress of the students through personal interviews, interviews with the students instructors in subsequent English classes, analyses of the students writings, and analyses of their academic transcripts. Answers are now beginning to emerge. For the question, "How many of these students will graduate and in how long a time period?" we have these facts. Within five years of matriculation, 19 of the 61 students have graduated, a 31% graduation rate, and 4 more of these high risk students are making steady progress toward a 1999 graduation date.

When we looked below the surface of these figures, however, we found disturbing discrepancies: 52% of the white students have graduated but only 17.5 % of the black students have. Appendix 1 profiles the academic progress of all 61 students. The time line moving from left to right shows each students academic progress from the fall of 1993 through the summer of 1998. A column on the right indicates how many attempts the student needed to pass the remedial course, and the column on the far right lists verbal SAT scores. It is readily evident that students' overall academic progress does not correlate with their verbal SAT scores nor with their ability to pass the remedial English class.

When students' progress is assessed according to race, as in Appendices 2 and 3, a distinct difference in academic histories can be seen. These two tables vividly illustrate the disparity between the academic success of the black and white students. Appendix 2 reveals the five-year progress of the African American students. Although a few had smooth sailing--as shown by the uninterrupted straight lines--the majority of their records display "P's," "S's," "E's," and "D's," which stand for Probation, Suspension, Exclusion and Dismissal.   Appendix 3 illustrates the academic histories of the white students. Although certainly not free of "P's," "S's," "E's," and "D's," their academic paths have been smoother. A few had an occasional probation or suspension or exclusion, but none were dismissed from the university for academic reasons.

In an effort to discover whether there was any correlation between academic success and the students first quarter writing abilities, we compared their academic success rates over the five year period with their ability to pass the remedial English class. Appendix 4 shows that 68% of the white students passed the class on their first attempt, and 53% have gone on to successful college careers, but of the 56% Black students who were also successful their first quarter, only 18% have had academic success. In fact, the white students who did NOT exit the remedial class on their first attempt have been more than twice as successful as the black students who DID pass.

In a further attempt to discover what was happening to our African American students, we probed the academic writings and experiences of black/white pairs of students with similar SAT verbal scores . Using the writing portfolios the students completed during their remedial English course, we studied their autobiographical essays, which were a midterm writing assignment, and their final exam essays as samples of their writing abilities early in their remedial class. A summary of the academic histories of one of these pairs illustrates what we found in virtually every case. The writings of a white female whom we will call Laura and a black female whom we will call ChaCha follow:

Introduction to Laura's Autobiography:
English 099 October 1993

One thing that I learned the most in tenth grade is what I call racism. During the year I learned that not all races get along. This was a change in my life because in junior high all races bonded together. Since I went through this awful experience I learned that racism is not only in schools but it is all around you. Every day you hear on the news about racism. I learned that the color of someone's skin does not mean anything.

Introduction to ChaCha's Autobiography: English 099 October 1993

As a young child, around the age of fourteen, my life all commence to fall apart. I faced a number of problems that I could have prevented because I never thought about the consequences. I blamed myself for my parents? separation, which I had no control of. By making my mistakes, I also learned from them. I was such a naive person growing up, but there were some incidents that change my life. With me getting caught for shoplifting, attending an all white private school, and my parents separation, I faced some major experiences that changed my life.

Brief as these excerpts are, they reveal that both students are inexperienced writers. What is meant by Laura's last sentence is certainly unclear, particularly because it follows her assertion that she has had an awful experience with racism. It is as though racism is just a word she has heard, not anything that she has experienced. Laura's writing here is very incoherent, a problem which signals problems with reading comprehension; she does, however, use the conventional expository format for an introduction; the syntax of her sentences is smooth, and, with the exception of the missing apostrophe, her writing is correct. ChaCha also begins with a generalization before narrowing her topic to focus on three life-changing significant personal experiences. Her introduction is more coherent, unified, and focused than Laura's, but it has missing verb endings and AAE vernacular syntax.

We continued by looking at the exit essays the students wrote at the end of the academic quarter. Exit essays are final exams: in-class impromptu writings which are evaluated by English faculty other than the students own instructors. Students choose from several prompts and are required to produce an essay which would merit a "C" grade in a regular freshman English class.

Introduction to Laura's Exit Essay:
English 099 December 1993

TOPIC: Write an essay about an experience that has happened to you since you have been at GSU that has changed you. Describe both the experience and its effect. Now that I am in college, I will face many different experiences. Such as, playing on a varsity sport, dorm life, and meeting new friends. I have enjoyed playing soccer since I was six years old, so I decided to continue playing in college. When I first arrived at GSU on August 19, 1993, I did not know what to suspect because I had never been in a dorm before, and I did not know anyone on the soccer team.

Introduction to ChaCha's Exit Essay:
English 099 December 1993

TOPIC: Yo! Rap music seems to be here to stay. Is it an important new form of musical expression or just noise? Write an essay explaining your answer with specific examples and concrete details. Some rap is very loud and very obscure to understand. I often misinterpret the message that the rappers are trying to stress or what they are trying to get the young kids to perceive. Most of the rap is degrading to woman and some rap provide a good message for the teenagers.

In these excerpts, Laura's introduction is again unfocused; whether it is the new experience of living in the dorm or playing a varsity sport that will be discussed is impossible to discern, and the use of the word *suspect* for *expect* jolts the reader. ChaCha's introduction is more tightly focused, but the AAE noun and verb ending markers are noticeable. What is more interesting, however, is their choice of topics. Laura is playing it safe by writing about her experiences as a new college student. ChaCha, on the other hand, chooses to discuss the significance of rap music. Despite the use of *and* rather than *but* for the coordinate conjunction and the AAE noun and verb endings,

ChaCha's sentence, Most of the rap is degrading to woman and some rap provide a good message for teenagers, offers thoughtful insights in a unified introductory paragraph.

Neither of the two essays was passed by the graders. Both the white student, Laura, and the black student, ChaCha, had to take a second quarter of remedial English, and it was after this second quarter that the academic paths of these two young women began to diverge. Laura passed the remedial English course at the end of the second quarter, received a "B" in Freshman English I, a "D" in Freshman English II, re-enrolled the following quarter, and received the necessary "C." Although Laura got a number of D's and F's in core curriculum classes, she was on academic probation only once during her four college years, and she graduated in December, 1997, exactly four years after completing her first quarter in remedial classes.

ChaCha's story, however is quite different. Unlike Laura, she did not exit her second remedial English class, and she became increasingly frustrated. Near the end of her second college quarter she blew up after receiving yet another failing paper and even threatened to hit her instructor. In an interview with the instructor the following quarter, we asked what she remembered about ChaCha:

Answer:

She was <u>very</u> determined--single most prominent characteristic--she was determined to get out of remedial English. . . She was a hard worker; she did everything; she only missed one class, did workbook exercises, everything.

Question:

What would you say is her biggest strength as a writer?

Answer:

Her ability to phrase an idea in an original way--using some sort of metaphor or image, you know, about what something was like. . .it was as though she really was trying to get the words to make meaning, to match her meaning, and it would be very original and have a lot of strength to it, so every now and then there would be those kinds of sentences that were really very lovely and very expressive.

Question:

Would you predict that ChaCha will graduate from college?

Answer:

If determination will do it, she will. But something I found most disturbing about her, though more on a personal level, was that I never did know when she would explode.

It is little wonder that ChaCha was on the verge of exploding during her second quarter. She was repeating all three remedial classes--Reading, English, Math--and in spite of her hard work and determination, she did not pass any of the three. When we interviewed her third remedial English instructor and asked what she remembered about ChaCha, she said,

> I remember that she kept her head down on her desk a lot.
> At first I thought that she was tuning me out. And then I
> realized that she was paralyzed by stress. I don't know that
> I've seen many students as stressed out as ChaCha.

Question:

How did you recognize that?

Answer:

Because she would sit up and look at me and I could tell that she had been listening to everything that was going on in class, but it helped her to keep her head down. She could hear better with her head down because she was in such a state.

Question:

What would you say is her biggest strength as a writer?

Answer:

She had a voice. She knew who she was, and she could write, and the voice would come through as she wrote.

Question:

And what would you say was her biggest weakness as a writer?

Answer:

Conventions, dealing with conventions. Standard written English.

Question:

Do you predict that she will be able to graduate from college?

Answer:

I don't know. I just don't know. Her determination will serve her well. She has that wonderful determination.

Both of ChaCha's instructors note her strong writing voice and her determination to succeed, and her determination did serve her well--for a while. After one full academic year, she was finally able to pass all three of the non-credit remedial courses, and she did well the first quarter she took regular classes, earning a "B" in Freshman English, a "C" in College Algebra, and a "C" in Spanish. Her determination began to wane, however, and the next quarter her GPA was a 1.5; then the next quarter, a 1.3; and finally, a .50. At the end of her seventh quarter, she did not return to the university. She had completed only 39 credit hours--fewer than six hours per quarter. A study by Otheguy finds that accumulating college credits plays a major role in the retention of minority students (as cited in Soliday, 1996, p. 96). We might think ChaCha's academic story inevitable given her very low SAT verbal score of 230 and inadequate writing skills when she entered college if it were not that Laura's potential for academic success--SAT verbal score 240 and inadequate writing skills --seems so very similar.

Discussion

Since the mid-1960's many studies of African American English (AAE) have been published which document the fact that it is a rule-governed, legitimate language. In acceptance of this new knowledge, the 1974 Conference on College Composition and Communication (CCCC) published a position statement entitled the Students Right To Their Own Language which affirmed the right of students to use their own language without penalty in the classroom; then, in 1988 the CCCC membership unanimously adopted The National Language Policy which validated the legitimacy of native languages and dialects, and called for resources to enable native and non-native speakers to achieve oral and literate competence in English, the language of wider communication (Smitherman, 1990, p. 116). We might thus expect that pedagogical and assessment methods for incorporating AAE language into the classroom would quickly have followed, but, unfortunately, in spite of linguistic research and CCCC resolutions and policies, in many college classrooms writing instruction has not changed much since the course was created a century ago. Because many composition teachers have been trained to be literary critics and teach writing by default, they have little knowledge of or interest in composition theory and research, so they fall back on pedagogies that were in place when they themselves were students and all too often equate the teaching of writing with the eradication of deviant language patterns (Lipscomb, 1985, p. 149).

It is well documented that many teachers have little knowledge about the legitimacy of AAE as a language and thus have negative attitudes about it and those who use it (Balester, 1993; Harrold, 1995; Smitherman, 1977; 1990). These teachers associate AAE with Uncle Remus, the shuffling speech of slavery black urban illiterates, and slovenly, careless speech (Smitherman, 1977, pp. 171-72). That negative attitudes can penalize students is well illustrated by the Ann Arbor Black English Case which focused on the language barriers created by teachers unconscious negative attitudes toward students uses of African American English and the negative effect these attitudes had on student learning (Ball & Lardner, 1997, p 470).

The verdict of the Black English case is significant for English instructors today because it holds the school system responsible for the educational underachievement of African American students. The verdict, however, raises two other questions, questions that remain to be answered today:

1.   How can teachers (and the general public) be taught to accept AAE as a language which differs from English but is just as legitimate?

2.   How can the acceptance of AAE as a legitimate language be demonstrated in the classroom?

These questions become particularly relevant in light of the findings of our research because negative attitudes toward AAE, attitudes similar to those identified in Ann Arbor, appear to have had adverse effects on the academic progress of the many students who are represented by ChaCha.

The generally accepted assumption is that if instructors understand more about language varieties and social dialects, their negative behavior toward AAE will disappear (Shuy, 1971; Ramsey, 1985; Pate, 1996; Ziegler, 1996). The Ann Arbor teachers, however, attended a court ordered series of workshops which introduced them to sociolinguistic information, but they were not able to apply their new knowledge to classroom practice (Ball & Lardner, 1997, p. 475). Teachers need specific pedagogical strategies which they can use to apply the knowledge they gain from the study of sociolinguistics into more accepting classroom attitudes and behaviors.

Taylor (1989) conducted a study which was successful in improving the writing of African American students. In the 11-week study, Project Bidialectialism, she applied TOESL methods to writing instruction. To teach rule-governed patterns in both dialects, she used contrastive analysis techniques with both oral and written pattern-practice drills to help students discriminate between AAE and standard English features. She also assigned literary selections by both black and white writers to heighten ethnosensitivity in her students.. Additionally, she presented herself as not just a teacher but also as a learner by asking African American students to help her understand? their language and by attempting occasionally to speak AAE (p. 131). After the Project Bidialectialism was completed, Taylor continued to use these methods because she found that they helped students master the edited American English skills required by the academy and the professions.

Taylor's methods are directly focused on helping African American students improve their writing skills and becoming proficient in code-switching, but Terry Dean's classes are filled with minority students from more than 30 different cultures. The pedagogical techniques he uses are beneficial to all students regardless of their cultural backgrounds. He assigns culture and language are topics for writing and discussion in his classes, and peer response and peer editing groups ensure that students have an opportunity to share their cultures and to become more familiar with the cultures of their classmates. Because speech patterns are a part of the person's identity and culture, Dean has found that making students home languages the subject of study along with the different kinds of academic discourse they will be required to learn is an effective pedagogical strategy (1989, p. 31).

Although the strategies described above point the way to more inclusive writing instruction, many English instructors do not have the freedom nor the desire to design such innovative classes. No matter what a department prescribes as the curriculum that instructors must follow, it is still the *individual* teachers in their *individual* settings that are the single most important factor in the educational process (Smitherman, 1977, p. 216). Within any writing curriculum, the instructor can use a process-based approach to writing instruction which permits inexperienced writers to engage in prewriting, multiple drafting, revising, and editing sessions. Additionally, instructors can provide different types of writing assignments to help students understand the necessity for identifying an audience and a purpose for their writings which will help them see that different writing styles are appropriate for different rhetorical situations. A most essential element of writing process instruction is to hold editing for Standard American English until the very last step in the composing process. Kamusikiri concluded from her research that many instructors comment on AAE features in early drafts of students writing, and this premature assessment has aborted the composing process for some AAE speakers (1996, p.196). Using portfolios instead of averaging essay grades for final grade assessment gives teachers the opportunity to use students early drafts to teach through such methods as contrastive analysis and gives students the opportunity to demonstrate their writing capabilities at the end of an academic term.

The ChaCha's in our classrooms need our linguistic knowledge as well as our most effective teaching methods. Our acceptance of their culture, their language, and their individuality, however, is the first, and most important, step toward helping them achieve their goals of becoming college graduates who can then improve their economic and social status as well as that of their families and their communities.

CHAPTER 4
Utilizing Collaborative Writing in the College Classroom to Meet the Needs of a Changing Clientele

Evelyn Shepherd-Wynn

Introduction

Writing is one of the most important tools for learning in all academic disciplines. It is an intellectual exercise that empowers students so they will be in a better position to communicate with others in all facets of life. Nevertheless, students continue to enroll in colleges and universities unable to attend regular composition courses. Research reveals that many are from culturally diverse backgrounds. Nine years ago, Locke (1992) reported that by the year 2075, African Americans, Alaskan Natives, Native Americans, Hispanic Americans, Asian Americans, as well as other minorities, will constitute the majority of the United States population. In 1997, Morganthau predicted that by the year 2050, the population of the United States could increase to more than 500 million, more than double the 1990 census.

As America becomes more culturally diverse, the student composition in higher education institutions will also become more culturally diverse. With the emerging demographic changes in society, this changing clientele has caused higher education institutions to revisit instructional and assessment methods for teaching writing because they play a critical role in improving the writing skills of college students. The theory and emergent research on writing suggest that we, as educators, can no longer ignore innovative methods for teaching writing. Therefore, in this chapter, the author draws attention to the status of college students' writing skills and some of the causes contributed to the continuous decline in their writing skills, particularly for culturally diverse college students. The author then discusses the theoretical framework for collaborative learning and its extension, collaborative writing. In a literature review of selected research, the author examines nine studies that investigated the effects of collaborative learning on diverse English composition students' writing skills. Also in the literature review, the author compares nine selected studies spanning from 1977 to 1996 as well as discusses her 1999 investigation. Finally, the author concludes with a discussion of recommendations and implications for the use of collaborative learning in English college classrooms.

Decline in College Students' Writing Skills

No academic area has engendered greater concern among faculty members than the decline in college students' writing skills during the last two and a half decades (Applebee, Langer, & Mullis, 1986; Applebee, et al., 1989; Boyer, 1987; Dieterich, 1977; Dudley, 1976; Jacobs, 1981; Madden & Laurence, 1994; Newkirk & Cameron, 1977; Sailor, 1996; Shrewsbury, 1995; Walker, 1976). These researchers reported that a large percentage of high school students are attaining only minimum writing skills. Consequently, a substantial number of freshmen are unable to communicate in writing from a "reasoned point of view" (Applebee, et al., 1989; Boyer, 1987; Lupack, 1983).

One of the strongest indications of the decline in students' writing ability is the continuous drop in the average scores on college entrance examinations, including the American College Test (ACT), the College Entrance Examination Boards (CEEB), and the Scholastic Aptitude Test (SAT) (Agee, 1977; Butler, 1981; Cameron & Guralnick, 1977; Gossage, 1976; Pomplun, et al., 1991; Shea, 1993). For example, Ornstein (1992) reported in the *National Association of Secondary School Principals (NASSP) Bulletin* that from 1963 to 1990 the average SAT verbal scores dropped from 478 to 424, more than 50 points. Furthermore, the average verbal SAT scores for college-bound students dropped 25 points from 1972 to 1995. The average verbal SAT score for college-bound males in 1995 was 429, down from 454 in 1972.

Meanwhile, the average verbal SAT score for females in 1995 was 426, down from 452 in 1972. Between 1976 and 1995, the average scores of African Americans rose 24 points on the verbal section while the average scores of Anglos fell three points on the verbal section (*The Condition of Education*, 1996). Moreover, the average writing proficiency for eleventh grade scores were slightly lower in 1996 than in 1984. Although scores dropped slightly for Anglo eleventh graders between 1984 and 1996, the average scores for Anglo students were higher than those for African American and Hispanic students (U. S. Department of Education,1997). The verbal performance on both the ACT and SAT remain stable, indicating that the writing skills of college freshmen are not improving (*Fair Test Examiner: SAT/ACT Score*, 1996).

In 1975, the National Assessment of Educational Progress (NAEP) issued a report entitled "Writing Mechanics, 1969-1974: A Capsule Description of Changes in Writing Mechanics." The report revealed that the writing skills of college students had deteriorated in the areas of awkwardness, run-on sentences and incoherent paragraphs. In 1983, The President's Commission on Education published *A Nation at Risk* which reported that 13 percent of 17 year olds living in the United States were illiterate. Moreover, Richardson et al. (1983) conducted a three-year study of an open admission's community college to identify the causes and possible solutions for the decline of literacy in open admission's colleges. These researchers contend that "The predominance of students less concerned with acquiring and developing the reading and writing skills associated with traditional degree programs . . . " (p. 7) contribute to the increase in the literacy rate in community colleges.

Causes of Decline

Many causes have been cited in an attempt to explain the decline in college students' writing skills; however, a consensus has not yet been reached. Some researchers argue that this decline is due to overpopulated classrooms which tend to decrease the amount of time a composition teacher can devote to individualized writing instruction. Other researchers argue that some college students who possess high levels of apprehension and anxiety or who.

possess bad attitudes about writing also contribute to the decline in their writing ability (Bloom, 1980; Daly & Miller, 1975; Faigley, Daly & Witte, 1981; Milligan, 1980; Pfeifer, 1981; Shrewsbury, 1995). Daly and Shamo (1976) reported that college students who experience writing apprehension tend to be frightened by a demand for writing competency, to be afraid of having their writing evaluated, to expect to receive negative comments, and to avoid writing as much as possible.

Of the numerous reasons cited in the research for the decline in college students' writing skills, many researchers tend to agree that the problem lies within the traditional approach to teaching writing. In 1971, Janet Emig conducted a case study that is considered to be one of the groundbreaking investigations concerning students' composing process. In her study on the composing process of twelfth-grade writers, Emig found that there was a need to change the teaching pedagogues in high school composition classes. She reported that the teaching of rigid rules differed from students' own experiences with writing and that students' fear of the instructor's critical comments tended to prevent them from sharing their real feelings.

Shaughnessy (1977) directed a cross-sectional survey of college freshmen enrolled in a basic writing course to understand the reasons behind their writing behaviors. She reported similar findings to Emig in that writers' block stems from students' fear of making errors which could contribute to the decline in college students' writing skills. Shaughnessy concluded that instructors need to change their teaching techniques from a product-oriented approach to a process-oriented approach.

Clifford's (1977) study revealed that developmental freshman writers made substantial gains when guided by the collaborative learning approach. More specifically, their writing quality improved more significantly during the collaborative learning approach than the traditional teacher-lecture approach. Koch and Brazil (1978) argued that it is evident that most students have been taught by the traditional approach, but the research suggests that many of these students have not learned from the traditional approach, or have not learned enough to be proficient writers. These researchers further argue that the traditional practices for teaching composition should be modified or supplemented with other approaches to make composition courses effective and interesting. Hairston (1982) argued that the area of teaching writing and composition has not been given enough attention. She stated that "The overwhelming majority of college writing teachers in the United States are not professional writing teachers . . . they teach by the traditional paradigm, just as they did when they were untrained teaching assistants ten, twenty or forty years ago" (Hairston, 1982, p. 79). However, when drawing general conclusions about college students' writing ability, one has to consider the findings of more than a few selected evaluation studies (Farmer, 1998). Therefore, in a comprehensive review of the literature concerning the teaching of writing from 1963 to 1982, Hillocks (1984) conducted a meta-analysis of 72 studies on teaching approaches and focused on composition instruction at the elementary, secondary, and college levels. Hillocks analyzed the studies concerning mode of instruction, duration of instruction, and focus of instruction, as they relate to the effectiveness of writing instruction. In regards to instructional modes, his findings revealed that the traditional teacher-lecture approach is the least effective instructional mode because the students take on the passive role and in turn become the recipient of examples of essays as opposed to being active participants. Since the traditional approach promotes writing in isolation which discourages social interaction, it tends to focus more on the product rather than the process, and therefore, encourages the student to become a passive than an active writer. It can be derived from Hillocks' findings that the collaborative learning approach is perhaps a more effective approach to teaching writing since it promotes social interaction.

Hillocks' meta-analysis further revealed that when examining the studies in regards to duration of treatment, the studies conducted for less than 13 weeks (61.14), more than 12 (54.72), less than 17 (84.70), or more than 16 (29.13) did not make a significant difference in students' writing ability among groups of treatments; however, the larger studies did show some impact on students' writing quality. The correlation between duration of treatment and raw effect size was -.02 indicating no relationship between duration of treatment and change in the quality of writing performance.

Hillocks further concluded that the focus of instruction employed when teaching composition influenced students' writing performance. Of the areas examined by Hillocks, the studies that examined traditional school grammar revealed no significant improvement in writing quality. In fact, some studies in the meta-analysis revealed that grammar and mechanics instruction may have a catastrophic effect on students' writing performance. Hillocks' findings also revealed that those studies utilizing scales, criteria, and specific questions that students used to evaluate their own and others' writing during the treatments were twice as effective as free writing techniques. He further argued that inquiry as a focus of instruction was almost four times more effective than free writing and more than two and-a-half times more significant than the studies using the traditional model.

Shrewsbury (1995) conducted a study to determine the effect of collaborative learning on the writing apprehension, writing attitude, and writing quality of students enrolled in a basic writing course (native speakers and nonnative speakers). She reported that by the end of the treatment, both groups' writing quality improved. Similarly, Sailor (1996) investigated the effect of peer response groups on freshman composition students' writing apprehension, writing achievement, and revision decisions. She reported that as students' writing apprehension decreased, their writing performance improved. Both studies indicate writing apprehension and writing attitude may contribute to the decline in the writing skills of college students and that collaborative learning may be a possible solution. The studies by Emig (1971), Shaughnessy (1977), Clifford (1977), Shrewsbury, and (1995) Sailor (1996) and the meta-analysis by Hillocks (1984) support the view that there is a need for nontraditional approaches to teaching writing on the college level.

This background information provides evidence that the decline in college students' writing skills is a major problem for the academy. The research further revealed that in many instances the traditional approach to teaching writing is not providing students with the skills necessary to be successful in English composition courses (Clifford, 1977; Daly & Miller, 1975; Emig, 1971; Ford 1973; Hillocks, 1984; Sailor, 1996; Shaughnessy, 1977; Shrewsbury, 1995; Thompson, 1981). Consequently, researchers have begun to investigate collaborative learning, a nontraditional approach, to determine its effects on the writing skills of English composition students.

The Constructivist Theory

Collaborative learning is premised in a learning theory called constructivism. Since the early forties, constructivism has been one of the primary theories applied to teaching and learning in the K-12 system. However, college faculty have recently begun to employ collaborative learning approaches more in higher education institutions. Constructivism is based on the premise that knowledge is generated by the student, making it a more personal experience. Because there are no two students alike, they cannot create the same knowledge. Each has his or her own prior experiences, knowledge structure, learning style, and motivation to learn.

The theoretical underpinnings of constructivism are grounded in two perspectives: social constructivism and cognitive constructivism. Both social constructivism and cognitive constructivism share common principles. Jonassen (1994) posits eight principles common to constructivist learning environments:

Constructivist learning environments provide multiple representations of reality

1. Multiple representations avoid oversimplification and represent the complexity of the real world.
2. Constructivist learning environments emphasize knowledge construction inserted of knowledge reproduction.
3. Constructivist learning environments emphasize authentic tasks in a meaningful context rather than abstract instruction out of context.
4. Constructivist learning environments provide learning environments such as real-world settings or case-based learning instead of predetermined sequences of instruction.

5. Constructivist learning environments encourage thoughtful reflection on experience.
6. Constructivist learning environments "enable context-and content- dependent knowledge construction."
7. Constructivist learning environments "support collaborative construction of knowledge through social negotiation, not competition among learners for recognition."

Although the two perspectives share common characteristics, Jonassen contends they are different in focus. Social constructivists, for example, tend to stress "student discourse as a means of learning, and writing as a manifestation of internalized social interactions" (Dale, 1994, p. 335). Social constructionism is based on the philosophies of psychologists and educators including Bruffee (1984), Rogoff (1986), and Vygotsky (1986). Bruffee's view of social constructionism supports the use of writing in collaboration, particularly peer tutoring. Bruffee (1999) explains that "To write is to use the writer's socially constructed authority to socially construct the authority of the text being written" (p. 57). The central idea of collaborative learning from Bruffee's viewpoint then is that students acquire knowledge involving judgment best by communicating with their peers. Vygotsky emphasizes the influences of cultural and social contexts in learning and supports a discovery model of learning. Cognitive constructivism, on the other hand, is based on the philosophies of Piaget (1968). Piaget argues that students construct understanding in an active and social learning environment where they experience their environment through reading, listening, and exploring. Student are viewed in collaborative groups with peer interaction in an authentic setting.

Because constructivist learning is based on the students' active participation in learning activities, the instructor is viewed as a facilitator guiding and stimulating the students' critical thinking, analysis and synthesis throughout the learning process. Constructivist learning then is a way of providing students with a support group as they become acquainted to the idea of a new community.

In English composition classrooms, faculty who adopt a

constructivist approach to teaching writing view themselves as facilitators and therefore create learning environments for college students to work together during all stages of the writing process including brainstorming, gathering ideas, organizing ideas, writing drafts, proofreading and editing, and completing the final draft. Collaborative learning is perhaps more readily accepted in the English composition classroom perhaps than in other academic disciplines because it is a process approach that can be used to teach writing and to encourage student interaction simultaneously.

The theoretical framework for the collaborative learning model employed in this study was based on the constructionists theory. Collaborative learning is grounded in the theories of constructivism and social constructionism (Dale, 1994). According to Bereiter (1985) and Erickson (1983), constructionists contend that knowledge is derived from the personal experiences of the individual. Meanwhile, social constructionists tend to stress "student discourse as a means of learning, and writing as a manifestation of internalized social interactions" (Dale, 1994, p. 335). Social constructionism is based on the philosophies of a number of major advocates, including Bruffee (1984), Rogoff (1986), and Vygotsky (1986). For the past four decades, many writing instructors have adopted Bruffee's view of social constructionism. Bruffee (1980) argued that the central idea of collaborative learning is that students acquire knowledge involving judgment best by communicating with their peers. Researchers have therefore concluded that college students using the constructivists approach rather than the traditional lecture approach work together more effectively (Deutsch, 1949; Grossack, 1954; Haines & McKeachie, 1967; Nielson, 1994). Social constructionists argue that social interaction is undergirded in collaborative learning used to teach writing. An effective collaborative learning exercise, then, is likely to be socially oriented and consensus driven (Wynn & Cadet, 1997).

Collaborative Learning and Collaborative Writing

The term collaborative learning and cooperative learning are referred to interchangeably in the literature. Slavin (1987) defined cooperative learning as a "set of instructional methods in which students are encouraged or required to work together on academic tasks" (p. 31). Similarly, Johnson, Johnson and Holubec (1990) contend that cooperative or collaborative learning employs the use of small groups so that students may work jointly to maximize their learning. MacGregor (1992) argued that collaborative learning is "a positive interdependence between students, an outcome to which everyone contributes, and a sense of commitment and responsibility to the group's preparation, process, and product" (p. 38). Meanwhile, Shrewsbury (1995) postulated that in collaborative learning " . . . students work with each other and/or a teacher to discover, explore, analyze, synthesize, debate, question, etc., to solve a problem, participate in a writing process, arrive at a mutual understanding of a concept, or develop social and intellectual skills for the purpose of learning" (p. 13).

Although these definitions have been used to describe collaborative learning, this author chose the most commonly referenced definition of collaborative learning identified in the literature to guide this chapter (Bruffee, 1972). Bruffee described collaborative learning as the "least time-consuming, the most self-disciplining, and the most self-corrective" (p. 6) method of learning. Bruffee maintained that it provides an opportunity for students to trust in their own authority rather than being dependent on the instructor's authority. It tends to create a cohesiveness rather than an individualistic or competitive spirit in traditional classrooms. He also affirmed that:

> Collaborative learning provides support groups, or transitional communities, that students can rely on as they go through the risky process of taking on authority as writers and as critical readers. It provides a measure of security as students substitute confidence in their own authority for dependence on the teacher's authority. Students can learn first to vest authority and trust tentatively and for short periods in the members of small, transitional working groups; then, more confidently, in the larger community that constitutes the class; and, finally, in themselves as individuals as they internalize the process and the values of the newly formed community of writers. (Bruffee, 1985, p. 13)

Under the umbrella of collaborative learning, collaborative writing represents a philosophy about the teaching and learning of writing in small groups. Within collaborative writing, there exists definitions and practices that vary, yet share similarities. Dale (1994) defined collaborative writing as dialogic because it "stresses the context of the writing situation and the relationship of the students as they interact" (p. 334). Morgan, Allen, Moore, Atkinson, and Snow (1987) contend that collaborative writing brings purposeful interaction and shared decision making and responsibility among group members in the writing of a shared paper. The author defines collaborative writing as an extension of collaborative learning that promotes interaction among students in small groups during the writing process. Though the definitions may vary, collaborative writing has synergistic benefits for both faculty and students across academic disciplines (Bruffee, 1984). Because of its synergistic benefits, advocates argue that collaborative writing accrue to both faculty and students across disciplines (Bruffee, 1984; Connors & Lunsford, 1993). This tends to be true since collaborative writing is a multifaceted enterprise with many approaches. Collaborative writing makes the writing process less alienating (Gebhardt, 1979).

As higher education institutions seek nontraditional instructional approaches to improve English composition students' writing skills, collaborative writing seems to hold the most promise for writing instruction; thus, research has proliferated (Fleming, 1988; Higgins, Flower, & Petraglia, 1992; Hillocks, 1984; Wynn & Cadet, 1997; Shepherd-Wynn 1999; Wynn, 2000). In a landmark comprehensive review of the literature concerning the teaching of writing from 1963 to 1982, Hillocks (1984) conducted a meta-analysis of seventy-two studies on teaching approaches focusing on composition instruction at the elementary, secondary, and college levels. Hillocks analyzed the studies concerning mode of instruction, duration of instruction, and focus of instruction, as they relate to the effectiveness of writing instruction. In regards to instructional modes, his findings revealed that the traditional teacher-lecture approach is the least effective instructional mode because the students take on the passive role and in turn become the recipient of examples of essays as opposed to being active participants. Since the traditional approach promotes writing in isolation which discourages social interaction, it tends to focus more on the product rather than the process, and therefore, encourages the student to become a passive rather than an active writer. It can be derived from Hillocks' findings that collaborative learning as a nontraditional instructional method is perhaps a more effective approach to teaching writing since it promotes social interaction. This 1984 landmark meta-analysis along with a demand for educational assessment and accountability as a result of the increasing number of culturally diverse students in higher education institutions call much attention to the use of collaborative writing in the college composition classroom (Locke, 1992; Morganthau, 1997).

There are a number of collaborative writing methods; however, the most commonly used in the literature are peer tutoring, peer editing, peer authoring, workshopping, and knowledge making. Peer tutoring is the most frequent collaborative method used by college teachers (Groccia & Miller, 1996). It is the process in which students interface with each other for the purpose of reinforcing and expanding their writing. Myrick (1993) believes that carefully designed and directed peer tutoring programs benefit the tutor and the tutee in the writing process (Franklin, Griffin, & Perry, 1994; Scott, 1995. Peer tutoring was initially used on writing; however, it is being used in other disciplines as well. Bruffee (1999) explains that

> Collaborative peer tutors may sometimes suggest an approach to the course's subject matter and method, but in contrast to monitors, their main purpose is to guide and support. When they instruct, it is to clarify that guidance and enhance that support. They engage in conversation with their tutees, helping them translate at boundaries between the knowledge communities they already belong to and the knowledge communities they aspire to join. The goal of this conversation between peer tutors and tutees is to help tutees internalize the conversation of the community they hope to join so that they can carry it on internally on

their own. (p. 98)

Peer editing is an instructional technique that has been given considerable attention. The writing skills of diverse students can also be enhanced by co-authoring. The author prefers to use the term peer authoring although it is synonymous with co-authoring. Peer authoring is a process in which students jointly compose writing assignments by working together on separate components or working together on the entire writing assignment (Wynn & Cadet, 1997). Peer authoring/co-authoring engenders the social-cognitive dissonance that can lead to effective learning about writing (Daiute & Dalton, 1988). Workshopping is based on the theory of group dynamics. It is a writing feature that is the process of sharing, analyzing, and critiquing in groups. Therefore, students engaged in workshopping are given many opportunities for generating ideas, providing feedback, responding to audience, composing papers, and thinking and writing critically (Strang, 1984).

Finally, writing can be taught as a form of collaboration in learning environments that provide a social context in which college students can practice in the types of writing that society values most in small groups. Collaborative writing ensures that college students have an opportunity to engage in conversation and to experience actual problem-solving throughout the writing process.

A Review of Selected Research

Educators have begun to employ collaborative writing as an innovative instructional method to teach culturally diverse college writers. The matrix below is an illustration of selected research studies that have investigated the effects of collaborative learning on the writing skills of culturally diverse college composition students. The matrix includes the title and purpose of the studies, the sample and population, the instrumentation and treatment employed, the duration of the investigation, the research designs, the statistical techniques used to analyze the date, and the findings of the studies. The author selected these dissertation studies to provide the academic community with an understanding of collaborative writing methods have been employed in college classrooms from 1977 to 1999 (Clifford, 1977; Danis, 1980; Ford, 1973; Hart, 1991; McBride, 1986; Pfeifer, 1981; Sailor, 1996; Shepherd-Wynn, 1999; Shrewsbury, 1995; Swift, 1986). It was during this time period when the culturally diverse college population increased significantly in American higher education institutions. Because the author's study is different in a number of ways, primarily due to the number of variables used in the study, these studies were also selected to show the gradual advancement in classroom research.

Selected Studies from 1977 to 1996

In 1973, Ford conducted a study to determine if a significant difference existed between the freshman composition students' grammar improvement as a result of peer edited and instructor edited paper. Using the Language Knowledge Test as both a pretest and posttest for Grammar-Usage, Ford measured students' theme composition ability by the change in numerical ranking of seven themes written by each student. Ford's finding's revealed there was a significant difference between the amount of grade-point gain experienced by the experimental group and the control group. These results led to the rejection of the null hypotheses and concluded that a significant difference had occurred between the grade-point scores of the two groups as a result of their using different methods of scoring/editing the English essays. Overall, the experimental group achieved significantly higher gains than the control group in both of the tested areas. Ford further reported that students'

A Matrix of Selected Research Studies

Researcher/Title	Purpose	Population Sample	Instrumentation	Duration	Treatment	Research Design	Statistical Technique	Findings
Ford (1973) The Effects of Peer Editing/Grading on the Grammar Usage and Theme-Composition Ability of College Freshman	To investigate the effects of peer edited and instructor edited essays on freshman composition students' grammar and composition ability.	50 freshman composition students (25 Experimental Group and 25 Control Group)	Language Knowledge Test (LKT) Forms A and B	One Semester	Students wrote seven essays; the first and last essays were used as pre-posttest. The experimental group students' essays were peer edited and the control group students' essays were edited by the instructor. Instructor used holistic scoring. The students used checklists.	Pretest-Posttest Design (Control Group Design)	1. Descriptive Statistics 2. ANCOVA	There was a significant difference between the amount of grade-point gain experienced by the experimental and control groups. These results lead to the rejection of the null hypo-theses and concluded that a significant difference had occurred between the grade-point scores of the two groups as a result of their using different methods of scoring/ editing the English compositions.
Clifford (1977) An Experimental Inquiry Into the Effectiveness of Collaborative Learning as a Method for Improving the Experimental Writing Performance of College Freshmen in a Remedial Writing Class	To test the effectiveness of the collaborative writing and traditional approach on freshmen in remedial composition.	92 students in six sections of freshman composition; both Experimental Group and Control Group were divided into three sections each (33 Experi. Group and 49 Cont. Group)	Cooperative English Test (CET) Forms 1A and 1B	One semester	The experimental group students wrote an essay in seven stages with feedback for each stage from peers. The control group students received instruction on punctuation, usage, etc. while the teacher taught the rules, patterns, drills, and used examples of students' papers; instructor focused mainly on various errors common to student essays. Instructor used holistic scoring. Students used checklists.	Pretest-Posttest Design (Control Group Design)	1. Descriptive Statistics 2. 2 x 3 Factorial 3. ANCOVA 4. F-Distribution	There was a slightly higher adjusted posttest gain for the experimental group. There was a total mean gain of .85 for the experimental group while the control group showed a smaller gain of .63. There was no significant interaction between instructor and treatment. Both the experimental (20.90, 22.19) and control (19.16, 20.02) groups pre-posttest mean scores on mechanical knowledge increased respectively, with the experimental group showing a slightly greater increase.

Researcher/Title	Purpose	Population Sample	Instrumentation	Duration	Treatment	Research Design	Statistical Technique	Findings
Danis (1980) Peer-Response in a College Writing Workshop: Students Suggestions for Revising Composition	To identify the discussions which occur in workshop groups to gain insight into writing instruction as it is experienced by students.	24 sophomores in an English 213 Writing Workshop	1. Student Perception Questionnaire (Pretest) 2. Student Goal Setting Questionnaire 3. Student Peer Evaluation Questionnaire 4. Student Attitude Questionnaire 5. Student Perception Questionnaire (Post-test) 6. Tape Recorder	One semester	Students wrote thirteen essays, ten short writings the first six weeks and three long papers using peer response and workshopping. Each small group discussion was tape recorded and transcribed.	Ethnographic Design	Descriptive Statistics	The findings suggest that the use of peer-response groups helped students to internalize the instructor's assumption that the way students learn about their writing is to have an audience. The findings further suggested that peer critics were likely to identify and make recommendations on passages which needed development of ideas, improvement of cohesion, and revision of awkward or ambiguous passages. Finally, the findings revealed that the students were aware of the unique demands for elaboration and explicitness called for by academic writing
Pfeffer (1981) The Effect of Peer Evaluation and Personality on Writing Anxiety and Writing Performance in College Freshmen	To analyze the effectiveness of peer evaluation and individual personality type on freshman composition students' writing anxiety and writing performance.	92 Freshman Composition and Rhetoric students (Two Experimental Groups and Two Control Groups)	1. Writing Apprehension Test 2. Myers' Briggs Type Indicator	One semester	Both experimental and control groups were administered pre-post-test for writing anxiety and writing performance. Students compositions in the experimental group used peer evaluation while the control group's essays were evaluated by the teacher using traditional marginal notes. Instructor used holistic scoring.	Pretest-Posttest Design	1. Descriptive Statistics 2. ANCOVA 3. Pearson Product-Moment Correlation	Peer evaluation did not significantly reduce the level of writing anxiety in the experimental group nor did it significantly improve the writing performance in the experimental group. However, there was a significant relationship between writing performance and personality trait characteristics and between writing anxiety and personality traits.

61

Researcher/Title	Purpose	Population Sample	Instrumentation	Duration	Treatment	Research Design	Special Technique	Findings
McBride (1986) Peer and Traditional Instruction: A Comparison of the Effectiveness of Peer Tutoring/Editing and Traditional Instruction on the Writing Abilities of Freshman Students	To investigate the effectiveness of peer tutoring/editing and traditional instruction on the writing abilities of freshman students.	70 freshmen composition students (36 Experimental Group and 34 Control Group)	Demographic Information Sheet	One semester	Both experiment and control group students wrote ten essays each. The first and last essays were used pre-posttest. The experimental group used peer editing and peer tutoring while the control group was taught by traditional approach. Instructor used Diedrich Analytic Scale while students used checklist.	Nonrandomized Control Group Pre-Posttest Design	1. Descriptive Statistics 2. ANOVA (One-way And Two-By-Two)	No significant differences in pre-posttest gain scores; both groups showed a gain or remained the same pre-test score on the posttest. A significant difference in pre-posttest gain scores between the two groups on the Diedrich Analytic Scale. There was no significant difference between the two groups as a result of the treatment curriculum, but male's gain scores on the posttest were significantly higher than female gain scores.
Swift (1986) The Effect of Peer Review with Self-Evaluation on Freshman Writing Performance, Retention, and Attitude at Broward Community College	To examine the effects of the combined techniques of peer review with self-evaluation on Eng. Composition 1101 students' writing performance, retention, and attitude	176 freshmen in eight sections of English Composition 1101 (Four Experimental Groups and Four Control Groups)	1. Writing Attitude Scale 2. Informal Survey	Two consecutive semesters	Using peer review, both the experimental and control group students wrote pre and posttest essays; the four experimental groups wrote and revised an essay the first half of the term using peer revision, checklists and self-evaluation; control group students wrote essays using the traditional approach.	A Solomon four-group Design	1. Descriptive Statistics 2. ANOVA (2-way) 3. Chi-square Statistics	ANOVA showed a significant F for the experimental group. Pretest nor inter-action was significantly different. ANOVA showed a significant gain from pre to posttest essay using difference in proportions in the experimental group. Informal survey showed students' desire to revise essays before evaluation. Combined peer review and self-evaluation had marginal effects on writing performance. The treatment had a significant effect on writing performance from pre- to posttest.

Researcher/Title	Purpose	Population Sample	Instrumentation	Duration	Treatment	Research Design	Statistical Technique	Findings
Hart (1991) An Investigation of the Effects of Collaborative Learning on the Writing Skills of Composition II Students at Gloucester County College	To explore the effects of collaborative learning techniques on the writing skills of college freshmen.	26 students in two English Composition II (14 Experimental Group and 12 Control Group)	N/A	One semester	Both experiment and control group students were administered pretest-posttest essays. Experimental group used collaborative learning techniques while control group received traditional instruction. Instructor used holistic scoring.	Non randomized control-group pretest/ posttest design.	1. Descriptive Statistics 2. One-tailed t- test with An alpha level of .01.	There was no significant difference in pretest mean scores; however, there was a significant difference between the mean scores of the posttest of both groups.
Shrewsbury (1995) The Effects of Collaborative Learning on Writing Quality, Writing Apprehension, and Writing Attitude of College Students in a Developmental English Program	To investigate the effectiveness of collaborative learning on the writing quality and the writing process of native and non- native college students in a developmental writing program by focusing on their prewriting and revising strategies.	16 Developmental Freshmen (11 native speakers and 5 non-native speakers)	1. Daly-Miller Writing Apprehension Test 2. Emig-King Writing Attitude Scale for Students 3. Faigley and Witte's Taxonomy	One semester	The developmental students were divided into two groups (native and non-native); they wrote seven essays each using revision comments from their group members. Instructor used holistic scoring.	Qualitative and Quantitative Design	1. Descriptive Statistics 2. ANOVA 3. Paired Sample T-test 4. Hycner's Protocols 5. Z-test	The findings revealed no significant difference in the native speakers and the non-native speakers in their writing quality as a result of the treatment (collaborative writing) both groups did produce significantly higher writing quality by the posttreatment measure. Neither group demonstrated a significant difference in reducing their writing apprehension, nor did they demonstrate a significant difference in improving their attitude toward writing. The native speakers made more revision changes than non- native speakers in the two writing samples.

Researcher/Title	Purpose	Population Sample	Instrumentation	Duration	Treatment	Research Design	Statistical Technique	Findings
Sailor (1996) The Effects of Peer Response Groups on Writing Apprehension, Writing Achievement, and Revision Decisions of Adult Community College Composition Students	To investigate the effects of peer response groups on students' writing apprehension, writing achievement, and revision decisions.	110 freshman in community college composition courses	1. Faigley and Witte's Taxonomy of Revision Changes 2. Daly-Miller Writing Apprehension Measure	One semester	Both Eng. 1101 and 1102 participated in peer response groups for thirty minutes per week during the same time period. Instructor used Diederich Essay Rating Scale.	Pretest- Posttest (Control Group Design)	1. ANOVA 2. Chi-square statistics	Eng. 1101 demonstrated a higher degree of writing apprehension and writing achievement than students in Eng. 1102. Age showed a direct positive correlation with both apprehension and achievement. Findings were consistent with prior research which suggest that apprehension is associated with writing achievement and that freshmen students revise at the surface level.

| **Shepherd-Wynn (1999)** The Effects of Collaborative Learning on English Composition Students' Writing Anxiety, Apprehension Attitude, and Writing Quality | To investigate the effects of collaborative learning on English composition students' writing anxiety, apprehension, attitude, and writing quality. To develop a collaborative writing model for teaching English composition courses. | 440 English composition students enrolled in fifteen sections of Freshman Composition 101 and 102 courses. | 1. Writing Apprehension Test (WAT) 2. Writing Attitude (Anxiety) Survey (WAS) 3. Writing Attitude Scale for Students(WASS) | One semester | Students wrote five essays. The first and last essays were used as pre and posttest writing samples. The second, third and fourth essays were written utilizing peer editing, peer tutoring and peer authoring. Instructors used holistic scoring to grade essays. Students used peer editing and peer tutoring checklists. | Ex post facto design within the context of multivariate framework. | Descriptive statistics; Univariate relationship between students' combined scores on the analytical writing techniques within the context of paired-sample t-tests and independent sample t-test. Spearman Brown's Intercorrelation Coefficient and Pearson's Product Moment. ANOVA/ANCOVA, and multivariate procedures with emphasis on discriminate analyses/MANOVA /MANCOVA, multiple regression analyses/stepwise regression procedure) and path diagnostic procedure and path analysis. | There was a significant relationship between students' collaborative writing assignments and anxiety, apprehension, and writing quality. Meanwhile, writing attitude had only marginal effects on writing quality. Peer tutoring was most the preferred approach followed by peer authoring and peer editing. There was no significant difference between male and female means scores for writing anxiety and apprehension. There was a significant relationship with a direct path to writing anxiety and apprehension, a significant relationship between peer editing and writing quality, and an indirect effect between peer tutoring and writing attitude. There was a significant relationship between and a direct path between peer tutoring and writing apprehension and a significant relationship between peer tutoring and writing quality. There was a relationship between peer authoring and writing attitude, apprehension and anxiety, but not a significant relationship. However, there was a significant relationship between peer authoring and writing quality. |

biographical information had no significant correlation with the study's findings and that one of the possible reasons for the gains shown with these groups may have been their lack of skills on exiting from high school.

Clifford (1977) implemented an investigation to test the effectiveness of two methods of teaching writing to 92 college freshmen in a remedial composition class. Students were randomly selected from each third name from entering freshmen who received a raw score between 40 and 50 on the Cooperative English Test, Form 1A at Queens College of the City University of New York. Both students and teachers were then randomly assigned to classes. The students were randomly assigned to six classes: two classes each were taught by three instructors of comparable training and skill; each taught one class in the traditional manner and one class with a collaborative composing approach. For example, instructor one taught a collaborative class ($\underline{n}$ = 15) and an experimental class ($\underline{n}$ = 16) as well as instructor two ($\underline{n}$ = 13) and ($\underline{n}$ = 16); instructor three ($\underline{n}$ = 15) and ($\underline{n}$ = 17), respectively. Students were administered pre-posttests. A writing sample was used to determine the students' experiential writing performance scores and the Cooperative English Tests, Form 1A and 1B, were used to determine the students' mechanical knowledge and vocabulary knowledge scores. After the pretests, the experimental group followed an eight-stage sequence. First, students brainstormed about a particular topic and then wrote freely for fifteen minutes on assigned autobiographical, expressive and expository topics, and then they were required to sit in small groups reading and evaluating their first drafts. Students then revised their drafts based upon their peer's comments and brought five copies to class for more detail using feedback checklists. Students then gave their essays to another group to be evaluated. Finally, students with similar problems and concerns were grouped to teacher discussion.

Students in the control groups followed a five-stage sequence. First they sat together as a class with strictly teacher-led discussions on various grammatical concepts, punctuation conventions, usage questions and sentence patterns. Then, students discussed various rhetorical conventions led by the instructor which was followed by a lecture on rules, patterns, strategies, and conventions of traditional rhetoric. Next, students' writing samples were used to pinpoint various errors common to students' essays. Finally, the instructor explained correction symbols and comments made in students' essays at the end of each class.

Clifford (1977) employed a 2 x 3 factorial analyses of covariance to test the significance of the differences between two groups. The findings revealed that the experimental group showed greater advances in composition than those taught by the traditional grammar approach. The findings also revealed that both treatments were equally successful in reducing the mean number of errors on the writing sample. However, collaborative learning did not tend to increase either vocabulary or mechanical knowledge. Overall, Clifford's findings indicated that feedback from a small, socially appropriate audience given immediately is more likely to change writing behavior and that peer editing helps students feel more comfortable with the composing process.

Danis (1980) conducted a study to examine the role of student writers during the discussion of six peer groups enrolled in an English 213 writing workshop at Michigan State University. Twenty-four students participated in the nine-week quarter study; six weeks focused on a series of ten short papers and three longer essays in small peer groups. During the first six weeks, the students composed and discussed in-class writing on Mondays; discussed two or three writings as a whole-class on Wednesdays; and participated in small group discussions on Friday. Students worked on final papers during the seventh and eight weeks, and they were engaged in the presentation and criticism of the paper. During the class period before the workshop sessions, students exchanged copies of their papers; they were to write out comments and bring those to the next class. In addition, they were provided guided questions to follow as they read the papers.

The researcher tape recorded and conducted interviews during each session. Students were also required to complete three survey that made inquiries about their goals, about their evaluation and description of the sessions, and about their attitude towards their writing and peer criticism. Danis' findings revealed that participants' four main types of verbal activity concerning writing products. First, they asked questions regarding criticism, recommendations on specific sections, and suggestions and comments about their essays. Second, they proposed their own suggestions for revising their essays. Third, they expressed agreement or disagreement concerning the recommendations of their peers. Finally, they explained the intentions behind their stylistic choices. Danis concluded that it is extremely important that faculty prepare students in peer response groups by helping them understand the nature and importance of peer feedback.

Pfeifer (1981) implemented a study to determine whether writing anxiety influenced the writing performance and individual personality type of 92 volunteer freshmen enrolled in one of five classes of Freshman Composition and Rhetoric at Ablilene Christian University in the fall of 1980. The researcher also examined the effectiveness of peer evaluation of student composition as a treatment for writing anxiety. The researcher used a holistic scale to rate students' sample essays, the Writing Apprehension Test and a similar device constructed by the researcher to identify students' degree of writing anxiety and the Myers-Briggs Type Indicator (MBTI) to identify students' personality type.

Two experimental classes using peer evaluation and three control classes employing instructor evaluation with marginal notes were compared in this study. Pre- and posttest scores were gathered from both treatment groups. Then the researcher used analysis of covariance to analyze the posttest variable scores from both experimental and control groups. The Pearson product-moment correlation was also used to test the relationship among the variables of writing anxiety, writing performance, and personality trait characteristics.

Pfeifer's findings revealed that there was a significant relationship between writing performance and personality trait characteristics and between writing anxiety and personality trait characteristics. However, peer evaluation did not significantly reduce the students' level of writing anxiety or increase the students' level of writing performance in the experimental group. Consequently, the researcher suggests that other factors such as personality, motivation, and creativity should also be considered prior to examining the relationship between writing anxiety and writing performance.

In 1986, McBride conducted a study to determine the effectiveness of peer tutoring/editing and traditional instruction on the writing abilities of freshman composition students based on the numerical scores made on pre-posttest writing samples. Seventy Freshman Composition 100 students participated in the study, with 36 in the experimental group and 34 in the control group. Two instructors used the peer tutoring/peer editing method of instruction while two other instructors used a traditional method of instruction excluding peer-tutoring/editing. In the experimental group, students wrote eight essays including pre- posttests and participated in eight peer tutoring sessions and were required to visit the writing lab when recommended. On the other hand, the control group wrote eight essays including pre-posttests, visited the writing lab when recommended and attended two instructor/student conferences outside of class.

McBride (1986) used the holistic scoring device, Diedrich Analytical Scale, to evaluate students' essays in seven categories: ideas organization, wording, flavor, usage, punctuation, and spelling. In addition, the researcher used a one-way analysis of variance (ANOVA) to test for differences between the means of the experimental group and control group. A two-by-two ANOVA was used to compare differences between gain scores of the experimental and control group to determine whether they were significantly different from one another.

McBride reported that the incoming writing performances from a sample essay writing of the student, the F value revealed no significant differences and indicated that the students were regarded as essentially equivalent prior to treatment at the .01 level. There was no significant difference in the gain scores in the writing performance of students in the control and experimental groups on Posttest 1. It was concluded that writing performances of both groups were average to above-average level in competency and students performed according to the expectations of the instructors. It was further concluded, therefore, that the writing performance throughout the semester course stayed the same for both groups. However, when the experimenter examined the final course grades for students in both the experimental and control groups, a difference was evident. Students in the control group received the following final course grades: A = 2, B = 8, C = 19, D = 2, F = 5. Students in the experimental group received the following final course grades: A = 1, B = 21, C = 10, D = 5, F = 0. The final exam grade determined 40% of the grade for the composition course. The final exam was graded holistically by instructors of Freshman Composition who did not know the identity of the student writers. Students in both groups achieved an average to above-average level of competency and performed according to the expectations of the instructor.

McBride further reported that there was no significant difference in gain scores on the seven individual items of the Diedrich scale between treatment groups. However, there was a significant difference between male versus female on the individual item wording at the .05 level. It was concluded that males gained more in wording than females on Posttest 1. The difference had no connection to the treatments among the groups. Male scores on the pretest in the area of wording were lower than female scores on the pretest and males ACT and SAT scores in English were lower than female ACT and SAT scores in the sample population of this study.

There was no significant difference between gain scores of males and females as a result of the treatment curriculum between the two groups. It was concluded that students in both groups performed at the same level. However, there was a significant difference between male versus female gain scores on Posttest 1. Male gain scores were significantly higher than female gain scores. This difference had no connection to the pedagogical treatment among the groups. Pretest scores, ACT, and SAT scores were lower for males than females in the study.

Overall, although the effect of the treatment curriculum did not show a significant difference among the groups' gain scores on the posttest, the experiment did indicate that peer tutoring/editing was equally as effective in the composition classroom as traditional instruction techniques based on students performance on the posttest and final course grades; therefore, the peer tutoring/editing workshop approach was an effective alternative to the traditional approach of teaching the writing process and should be used to improve student writing abilities.

Swift (1986) directed an investigation to identify whether writing attitudes, writing performance, and retention improved using the combined techniques of peer review and self-evaluation in teaching ENG 1101 at Broward Community College. The sample consisted of 176 freshmen in eight sections of ENG 1101, four experimental and four control sections. The study was conducted in the consecutive terms of 1985-1986 on the Central Campus of Broward Community College.

A Solomon four-group design was used with the level of significance set at .05. Peer review was employed the first half of the term while self-evaluation was employed during the last half of the term. Control groups were taught without the techniques of peer review or self-evaluation. Data consisted of pretest and posttest essays, retention rate, Writing Attitude Scale, and an informal survey. Differences in mean scores of posttest essays were considered with two-way analysis of variance which resulted in a significant "*F*" for the treatment group. However, neither pretest nor interaction was significantly different. A major finding was a greater increase in pretest to posttest essay scores using Difference between Proportions in classes receiving treatment than in control classes, although the retention rate was not significant in difference. Ten attitude items of concern were stated in positive terms on the Writing Attitude Scale. Using Chi Square to consider the ten items, three were found to show better attitude in greater observed frequency of response from the experimental group. An informal survey of reactions to experimental techniques indicated students' desire to be able to revise their writing before it wass evaluated.

Finally, Swift maintained that the combined techniques of peer review with self-evaluation had a modest effect in improving better writing performance. The experimental techniques had a significant effect in improving freshman writing performance from pretest to posttest essay scores. Moreover, the study implied a need for increased attention to writing process in the classroom.

Hart (1991) investigated two groups of 20 students ($\underline{N}$ = 40) to determine whether peer editing and critiquing techniques helped to improve their writing skills during a semester at Gloucester County College. He randomly selected two English Composition classes and placed them into an experimental and control group. Both groups took a 50 minute in-class pretest (Essay I). The experimental group utilized collaborative learning activities, including peer editing, peer criticism, reading aloud and peer interviewing. Meanwhile, the control group received instruction through the traditional lecture approach. Twelve weeks later, both groups took a 50 minute in-class posttest (Essay II). Using the Educational Testing Service guidelines, two members of the English Department simultaneously evaluated both the pre- and post- tests using the holistic evaluation method. Although each evaluator read the pretest and posttests, there was no discrepancy in scores which ranged from one through six. The means and standard deviations of the pretest were determined and analyzed using a one-tailed t-test at a confidence level of .01. Since the determined value of t for the analysis of the pretest was 2.00, there was no significant difference between the pretest mean scores of the experimental and control groups. The means and standard deviations of the posttest were calculated and analyzed by also using the t-test analysis, which showed t was 4.83. Hart's findings indicated that there is a positive relationship between peer editing and the improvement of college students' writing skills.

Shrewsbury (1995) developed a study to determine the effect collaborative learning strategies have on writing apprehension, writing attitude, and writing skills of basic writers, native speaking (N = 11) and non-native speaking (N = 5), enrolled in Developmental English 090. The developmental course emphasized effective paragraph and essay writing, revision, development of topic sentences, support sentences, concluding sentences, traditional rhetorical modes and the writing process. Students operated in a collaborative environment: They followed a writing process and arrived at a consensus within their group at each stage of writing. During the first class meeting, the students were administered the Daly-Miller Writing Apprehension Test (WAT) and the Emig-King Writing Attitude Scale for Students (WASS). The students also wrote a one-page essay which was photocopied for holistic evaluation. During the second class meeting, the researcher returned the students' essays and asked them to revise without specific directions. Afterwards, the researcher photocopied and filed the revised papers.

Students were then grouped and began brainstorming on their topic for writing. After the groups had reached a consensus, they discussed their freewriting strategies and then created a paper for homework. During the next class meeting, the groups shared copies of their work with each member of the group by either reading, their peers' papers and making comments on a Student Response Sheet or each student reading his or her own paper to the group. Each group reached consensus about how to improve the papers. The students revised for homework and returned the revised copies of the next draft. This process was followed on two other occasions. The students compiled five pieces of preliminary writing and a final draft including prewriting, a first draft, revision notes from their group consensus with more prewriting if necessary, a second draft, revision notes from the group, and the final draft, all of which were stapled. Students wrote a total of seven papers throughout the semester using the rhetorical modes, two personal narratives, two descriptions, two definition papers and a persuasive paper. Students began with paragraphs and were introduced to the essay by mid-semester. The final exam, a 500-word essay was written and revised during the two and one-half hour final exam scheduled and required by the college. Meanwhile, the students participated in a thirty minute to one-hour interview session during the first three weeks and the last three weeks of the semester. In a collaborative environment, students followed a writing process and arrived at a consensus within their group at each stage of writing. All writers still worried about their writing, but they collectively agreed that they spent more time on writing and rewriting. At the end of the semester, students were administered the Daly-Miller Writing Apprehension Test, the Emig-King Writing Attitude Scale for Students and a final essay for holistic evaluation and revisions for revision analysis.

Shrewsbury used both qualitative and quantitative measures in this study. She used two qualitative measures (interviews and journals) to determine the effects of collaborative learning on writing apprehension, writing attitude and writing skills of native and non-native college students in a developmental course. The researcher interviewed the students and examined their journals (individual and group) to analyze their revision changes. Both groups seemed to have made more surface changes during the first writing sample, yet the number of text-based changes increased by the last writing sample. Moreover, both groups seemed to focus on spelling, punctuation, and tense for formal changes while they focused on additions, deletions, and substitutions for the microstructure changes and additions, substitutions and consolidations for the macrostructure changes.

For the quantitative analysis, the researcher used analysis of variance (ANOVA) to determine the differences in pre and posttest scores of the Daly-Miller Writing Apprehension Test and the Emig-King Writing Attitude Scale for Students. The findings revealed that the means for writing apprehension on the pretest for natives (X = 88.181), non-native (X = 90) and the group mean was 88.75 while the means for the posttest for natives (X = 90.818), non-native (X = 97.40 and group mean was 92.875. The analysis of variance showed that there was not a significant group effect on the writing apprehension of the students: $F = 2.011, p = 178$; therefore, $p > .05$. A t-test revealed that as a whole the group's writing apprehension was slightly higher at the posttest, but at 10 significance level the mean difference is not statistically significant because p > 10. The means for writing attitude on the pretest for natives (X = 3), non-native (X = -8.2) and group mean was -.5 while the mean for the posttest for natives (X = 6.818), non-native (X = -.3) and group mean was 3.75. The analysis of variance revealed that there was not a significant group effect on writing attitude: $F = 1.921, p = 0.186$; therefore, $p > .05$. A t-test revealed that the difference in writing attitude between the pre and posttests for the whole group was not significant, $P = 151$, but with a significance level of .10, the mean difference was not statistically significant. Consequently, the results of the t-test revealed that the students' attitude improved toward writing.

On the pretest, students' writing skills were reported as follows: 15 students scored "F," and 1 scored "D." However, on the posttest, 1 scored "A," 3 scored "B," 7 scored "C," 4 scored "D," and 1 scored "F." In order to compute the weighted mean for holistic scoring, the researcher assigned each "A" a "4," each "B" a "3," each "C" a "2" each "D" a "1." The reported pretest means for the writing skills of the natives ($X = .09$), non-native ($X = 2$), and group mean was ($X = .125$) while the posttest mean for the natives ($X = 2.09$), non-natives ($X = 1.6$) and group mean was ($X = 1.562$). An analysis of variance revealed that there was no significant group effect on writing skills: $F = 822, P = 38$; therefore, $P > .05$. A t-test performed on the pre and posttest of the holistic scoring showed a statistically significant difference which indicated that the writing skills of all students improved.

In summary, Shrewsbury (1995) reported that during the treatment both native and non-native groups did not significantly differ in their writing skills; however, by the end of the treatment (posttest), both groups' writing skills improved. Her findings further revealed that neither group showed a significant difference in reducing their degree of writing apprehension nor their degree of negative writing attitude.

Sailor (1996) implemented a study to determine the effect of peer response groups on freshman composition students' (N = 110) writing apprehension, writing achievement, and revision decisions. The students (over age 25) were administered two survey questionnaires as pretest and postest. The Daly-Miller Apprehension Test was administered to measure the students' writing apprehension level while the Faigley and Witte's Taxonomy of Revision Changes to measure the students' revision decisions. The Diederich Essay Rating Scale was used to measure composition students' writing achievement in pre- and posttest writing samples. During the sixteen week study, students utilized peer response for thirty minutes per week during the same time period.

Sailor found that the English 1101 students demonstrated a higher degree of writing apprehension and writing achievement than students in English 1102. Age showed a direct positive correlation with both apprehension and achievement. Findings were consistent with prior research which suggested that apprehension is associated with writing achievement and that freshmen students revise at the surface level. Overall, Salior's findings were consistent with previous research.

In summary, the aforementioned studies are representative of the research that has been conducted on collaborative learning in the college classroom over the past twenty years (Clifford, 1977; Danis, 1980; Ford, 1973; Hart, 1991; McBride, 1986; Pfeifer, 1981; Sailor, 1996; Shrewsbury, 1995; Swift, 1986). The studies' findings indicate that collaborative learning improves students' writing skills; nevertheless, they are limited in scope. For example, the studies employed only one of the collaborative writing features prevalent in the literature, either peer editing, peer tutoring, co-authoring, or workshopping on a sample less than 200, an average of 73 students per investigation. Similarly, the studies employed either one or none of the three primary psychological behaviors (writing anxiety, writing apprehension, and writing attitude) that were often linked to collaborative learning and how they impact culturally diverse college students' writing skills. The experimental research design (pre- post control group design) was the primary design utilized in the studies. Finally, the studies used one or in some cases two of the statistical techniques including ANCOVA, ANOVA, descriptive statistics, chi-square statistics, one-tailed t-test, paired sample t-test, and Pearson Product-Moment Correlation.

A Comprehensive Collaborative Writing Study on
Black English Composition Students' Writing Quality

In order to broaden the database in this area, the author conducted a comprehensive study which employed three commonly used collaborative writing instructional methods (peer editing, peer tutoring, and co-authoring) and three psychological constructs (writing anxiety, writing apprehension, and writing attitude) to investigate the effects of collaborative learning on English composition students' writing anxiety, writing apprehension, writing attitude and writing quality.

The research literature suggests that writing is one of the most important components in the English curriculum. Nevertheless, the writing skills of college freshmen are steadily declining. Some researchers argue that because the teaching of writing is time consuming, not enough time is spent on teaching college students how to write effectively. Other researchers argue that the ineffectiveness of the traditional instructional approach has caused the writing skills of college students to diminish (Elbow, 1973; Emig, 1971; Koch & Brazil, 1978). Brandt (1987) argued that the traditional approach to teaching writing in the classroom tends to employ an organizational structure developed a century ago; thus, he posited that instructors using the traditional approach "probably do not prepare students very well for today's team-oriented world" (p. 3). Since the traditional instructional approach seems to be the major drawback in teaching writing, this study was particularly significant for several reasons. First, its findings should provide college instructors with an opportunity to consider collaborative learning, a nontraditional approach, as an alternative instructional technique to utilize in teaching writing. Moreover, this study was significant because it should help to further verify whether collaborative learning is an effective instructional approach in reducing writing anxiety and writing apprehension as well as improving writing attitude and writing quality. The studies identified in the literature search investigated the effects of collaborative learning on the writing quality of English composition students employing one or two of the following approaches of collaborative writing (peer editing, peer tutoring, or peer authoring). Therefore, this study should prove to be significant because it employed three of the most commonly used collaborative writing approaches (peer editing, peer tutoring, and peer authoring) individually as well as synergized the three collaborative writing approaches for the treatment.

The sample for this comprehensive study was drawn from a population of approximately 3,000 English composition students enrolled during the 1998 Fall semester at Grambling State University in Grambling, Louisiana. The 440 English composition students were enrolled in fifteen sections of Freshman Composition 101 and 102 courses. Both courses are mandatory for students entering the university with an ACT score of 17 or a SAT score of 620 and above. However, students with less than the required ACT or SAT score must enroll in Basic English courses, Basic English 092 (scores of 0-12) or Basic English 093 (scores of 13-15). Once students have successfully completed all developmental course requirements, they may enroll in Freshman Composition 101 and Freshman Composition 102 successively. Both courses emphasize the application of the rudiments of English grammar combined with practice in speaking, reading, listening, and writing paragraphs with emphasis on the longer composition.

This study employed three survey instruments to collect the data. The first survey, the Daly and Miller Writing Apprehension Test (WAT, 1975), was a 28-item instrument designed to identify students who are highly apprehensive about their writing (Faigley, Daly & Witte, 1981; Daily & Miller, 1975). The second survey, Thompson's Writing Attitude (Anxiety) Survey (TWAS, 1979), was a 30-item instrument designed to identify students' degree of anxiousness. The Emig-King Writing Attitude Scale for Students (WASS, 1979), the third survey employed in this study, was a 40-item instrument designed to identify students' writing attitudes (Shrewsbury, 1995) based on their preference for writing, perception of writing, and process of writing. A demographic information form was also employed to collect personal background data including gender and classification of students enrolled in the Freshman Composition courses.

Procedural Details

Procedures for this study were implemented in three phases. During the first phase, six English instructors administered the English composition students' pre-tests: a writing sample and three survey instruments. Students wrote a 50 minute in-class narrative essay which was used to measure their writing quality while the survey instruments were used to determine the students' writing apprehension, writing anxiety, and writing attitude. During the second phase of the study, the instructors presented lectures discussing the benefits of collaborative learning followed by a discussion on essay guidelines and holistic grading so that students would fully understand the criteria by which their essays would be evaluated. The English instructors discussed how students could write an essay utilizing peer editing, peer tutoring, and peer authoring, during a two-week period respectively. Students were also provided peer editing, peer tutoring and peer authoring, checklists during the appropriate time to help them with their assignments. Although some researchers recommend using one specific group throughout a semester, Bushman (1984) recommends that instructors should vary the group approach to meet the needs of the assignment. He suggests randomly assigned groups for short-term evaluation of student work and selected groups for longer revision (pp. 47-48). Since this study was conducted during the entire semester, each group was comprised different members for each collaborative assignment. The primary criteria that each English instructor used in establishing heterogeneous groups included gender, verbal ability, and what he or she knew about the students' writing skills based upon the pretest writing sample.

The English composition students were assigned code numbers for identification purposes. Throughout the study, students made revisions outside of class and submitted the edited copy (rough draft) and two typed copies of the revised essay (final draft) to the English instructor for evaluation. Essays were evaluated holistically by the instructor and one other instructor to determine the students' essay grade. If more than a one-point discrepancy existed between the scores from the two instructors, a third instructor evaluated the narrative essay. In all cases the instructors were required to reach more than 87% agreement. After each English instructor evaluated the sets of essays using holistic grading, he or she returned the essays to the writers and conferred with them prior to assigning the next essay. During each collaborative writing assignment, the English instructors monitored the activities but were not involved in the actual peer critiquing of the essays. They were, however, involved in explaining materials and/or advising about procedures in a facilitative role. Hawkins (1976) argued that the most important role for English instructors is to facilitate the collaborative activities by listening, observing, and questioning. Prior to each class meeting, the instructors preassigned English composition students to collaborative groups whose writing ability levels ranging from low, middle, and high.

The English composition students wrote three essays using collaborative writing instructional approaches in two week intervals. Peer editing was the first collaborative writing assignment. Students were assigned in groups of two to write a descriptive essay. Each peer editor was responsible for marking the errors using a peer editing checklist and adding any comments which he or she believed to be constructive and beneficial to the author of the paper. After each essay was edited and returned to the original author, recommended corrections were discussed between the author and the peer editor. The second collaborative writing assignment was peer tutoring. Students were assigned to groups of three to write a definition essay. Each English composition student brought three typed copies of his or her essay to class so that each member of the triad would be able to discuss the essay orally and complete the peer tutoring checklist. They spent a minimum of fifty minutes of the peer tutoring session reading aloud and discussing the strengths and weaknesses of each essay following the prescribed checklist until all members of the triad received feedback. Peer authoring was the third collaborative writing assignment. Students were assigned to groups of four. Each quartet wrote an exemplification essay jointly both in and outside of class. Students were informed that they could meet as many times as they desired outside of class. Peer authoring also required the students to implement strategies they learned during the peer editing and peer tutoring exercises. The students completed the essay as a group for which one grade was assigned with each member receiving the same grade.

After phase two of the study, the instructors administered the English composition students' posttests: a writing sample and three survey instruments. Students wrote a 50 minute in-class persuasive essay which was used to measure the writing quality of the students after the collaborative writing assignments. They were also administered the survey instruments to determine to determine whether collaborative writing changed their writing anxiety, writing apprehension, writing attitudes, and writing quality.

In summary, the first and fifth essays were used as a pre- posttests respectively, while the second, third and fourth essays were written using three collaborative writing instructional approaches (peer editing, peer tutoring, and co authoring respectively) to reduce the students' writing anxiety and writing apprehension and to improve their attitudes towards writing and consequently, to improve their writing quality. The differences in the scores assigned to Essays One and Five depicted the amount of gain experienced by the English composition students in regards to their writing quality. The survey instruments were used as pre- postests to determine whether collaborative writing caused a decrease in English composition students' writing apprehension and writing anxiety and an improvement in their writing attitudes and writing quality.

In order to determine the effects of collaborative writing on the English composition students' writing apprehension, writing anxiety, writing attitudes, and writing quality, the author employed a number of research designs (pre- posttest design, predictive design, and comparative design) in the study. Since this threefold design is rather complex, it employed univariate analytical analyses techniques within the context of descriptive statistics, stepwise regression, and path analyses. These statistical techniques were used to determine the differential effects of peer editing, peer tutoring, and peer authoring on writing anxiety, writing apprehension, writing attitude, and writing quality.

Results

The author employed descriptive statistics to describe the distribution of the sample under investigation. The sample consisted of 330 freshmen, 87 sophomores, 16 juniors, and 7 seniors. The gender distribution included 201 male and 239 female students who were enrolled in Freshman Composition 101 and 102 courses. Two hundred and sixty-seven students enrolled in Freshman Composition 101 and 173 enrolled in Freshman Composition 102. Although Freshman Composition 101 is a prerequisite for Freshman Composition 102, some students, however, enroll in Freshman Composition 102 prior to enrolling in Freshman Composition 101. As a result, students who enrolled in courses out of course sequence did not have the benefits of Freshman Composition 101 instruction. Consequently, these students in many cases were not as prepared as students who actually took Freshman Composition 101 prior to enrolling in Freshman Composition 102. Moreover, upperclassmen who enrolled in these courses in most instances had taken Freshman Composition 101 and or 102 previously and were repeating for a number of reasons. In most cases, they were more experienced at writing because they had been exposed to the academic environment.

Descriptive statistics was also used to analyze the English composition students' pretest, posttest and composite scores to determine the results of the three survey instruments (WAT, TWAS and WASS). With respect to gender, this study's sample could be considered as marginally low apprehensive and highly anxious. The male students were as apprehensive as the female students while the female students were more anxious than their male counterparts. Therefore, gender was more significant for writing apprehension than it was for writing anxiety. The comparison from pre- to posttest average scores indicated that there was no significant difference between male and females in their writing anxiety and apprehensive mean scores.

The comparison from pre- to posttest scores further indicated that:

(1) both the underclassmen (freshmen and sophomores) and the upperclassmen (juniors and seniors) were different in their writing anxiety as well as in their writing apprehension mean scores; (2) with regards to writing anxiety, English composition students were as anxious as the sophomore students, and juniors were more anxious than the seniors; (3) with respect to writing apprehension, the sophomore students were the most apprehensive, followed by the freshmen, the junior, and the senior students; and (4) students' writing anxiety and writing apprehension did not improve by classification.

The English composition students were then grouped into one of three categories (low, moderate, high) depending upon where their individual composite average scores fell on the writing continuum. For example, the average score for both pre- and posttest for writing anxiety was computed for the entire sample of English composition students. Therefore, the aggregated (or composite) score for anxiety was compared to the mean score for anxiety for all students in the sample. The same procedure was repeated for writing attitude and apprehension. The sample can be described as homogeneous with more moderate anxious and apprehensive writers than low-anxiety/low-apprehensive and high-anxiety/high-apprehensive writers. The estimated sample parameters were within the limits of marginal sampling errors.

A significant proportion (at least 67%) of the sample were moderate-anxious-apprehensive writers. The distribution of the sample within their respective categorization in the writing connection is as follows: 73 and 78 students were low-anxiety and low-apprehensive writers; 295 and 297 were moderate-anxiety and moderate-apprehensive writers; and 72 and 65 were high-anxiety and high-apprehensive writers, respectively. Furthermore, of the total 440 students in this study, 54 were low-anxious-apprehensive, 256 were moderate-anxious-apprehensive, and 50 were high-anxious-apprehensive writers; and students who were classified as low-anxiety and low-apprehensive can not be considered high-anxiety and high-apprehensive writers. However, students can be improperly classified as either low- or high-anxiety (apprehensive) or moderate-anxiety (apprehensive) writers.

Of the 73 low-anxiety and 78 low-apprehensive student writers, 54 were identified as low-anxiety and low-apprehensive writers; none was high-anxiety (apprehensive); and 19 were moderate-anxiety and moderate-apprehensive writers. Of the 65 high-apprehensive and 72 high-anxiety student writers, none was low-anxiety (apprehensive); 22 were moderate-anxiety (apprehensive); and 50 were properly categorized as high-anxiety and high-apprehensive writers. Of the 295 moderate-anxiety and 297 moderate-apprehensive students, 256 were properly categorized as moderate-anxiety (apprehensive) writers; and 24 and 15 were improperly categorized as low-anxiety (apprehensive) and high-anxiety (apprehensive) writers respectively.

It is important to note that during the analysis for writing anxiety and writing apprehension, English composition students' level of anxiety and apprehension was reported as either increasing or decreasing. However, English composition students' attitude toward writing was reported as either positive or negative. When their attitudes were positive, the students were more willing to self-disclose, more receptive to the instructors' evaluative comments about their writing, and were more likely to view writing as enjoyable. On the other hand, when students' attitudes were labeled as negative, they tend to fear the act of writing; therefore, they avoid writing situations. In general, students who possess negative attitudes believed that they could not write well.

The level of students' writing attitudes (low, moderate, and high) within the aggregated score indicated that 62 students were low, 306 were moderate, and 70 were high attitude writers. The breakdown of the 438 English composition students who completed the Emig-King Writing Attitude Scale for Students showed that 62 were low attitude writers, 307 were moderate attitude writers, and 69 were high attitude writers. A significant proportion of the sample (70%) was moderate attitude writers. The distribution of the English composition students within their respective categorization in writing attitude showed that: (1) 40 (64.5%) students enrolled in Freshman Composition 101 and 22 (35.5%) enrolled in Freshman Composition 102 possessed low-attitudes while 31(50.0%) female and 31

(50.0%) male students were categorized as low-attitude writers, (2) within the moderate-attitude English composition writers, 182 (59.3%) and 125 (73.1%) were enrolled in Freshman Composition 101 and 102, respectively. Of this number, 168 (54.7%) were females and 139 (45.3%) were males. The high-attitude writers included 45 (65.2%) and 24 (34.8%) students enrolled in Freshman Composition 101 and Freshman Composition 102 of which 39 (56.5%) were females and 30 (43.5%) were males.

The descriptive measures for the comparison of the pre- and posttest writing samples and the collaborative writing assignments by students' course enrollment and gender revealed that the average for the pretest writing sample ($\bar{x} = 66.39$) was less than the average for the posttest writing sample ($\bar{x} = 77.69$) with a difference in mean scores of 11.3 (77.69 - 66.39). This significant difference can be attributed to the collaborative writing instructional approaches administered before and after the writing samples.

In regards to every comparison across students' gender and course enrollment status, female students scored higher (on average) than male students; and the average scores for students enrolled in Freshman Composition 101 were consistently lower than the average scores for those enrolled in Freshman Composition 102. These comparisons were consistent when the scores for the three collaborative writing instructional approaches were computed together. Overall, peer authoring ($\bar{x} = 81.44$) appeared to be the most preferred method of teaching. However, peer tutoring ($\bar{x} = 76.50$) proved to be a better approach than peer editing ($\bar{x} = 73.73$) when teaching students writing. There was significant improvement in the English composition students' writing quality based on the average differences between pre- and posttest writing sample scores.

The author further examined four research questions using stepwise multiple regression and path analyses. Research question one explored the relationship between peer editing and writing anxiety, writing apprehension, writing attitude, and writing quality of English composition students. Results revealed that there was a significant relationship between peer editing and students' writing anxiety, writing apprehension, and writing quality. Peer editing strengthens the critical skills of the peer editor and provides immediate feedback for peers being evaluated. Peer editing makes the evaluation process less threatening; therefore, students who would normally react negatively to criticism from their instructors are more willing to accept it from their peers. The analysis also indicated that there was no relationship between peer editing and English composition students' writing attitude. Since this was the first collaborative writing assignment in the treatment, this finding is not surprising.

Research question two examined the relationship between peer tutoring and writing anxiety, writing apprehension, writing attitude, and writing quality of English composition students. Peer tutoring was significantly related to students' writing attitude but had no direct effect on it. Peer tutoring also had a significant indirect relationship with students' writing anxiety and was significantly related to writing apprehension. This collaborative writing instructional approach also had an indirect effect of peer tutoring on students' writing quality. Peer tutoring helps English composition students become better judges of their own writing. Reading and listening to a variety of peers' essays help them distinguish between good and poorly written essays. Because peer tutors spend a great deal of time being critical of their peers' essays, they learn how to become better writers. Meanwhile, tutees also become better writers since they tend to imitate the writing pattern of their peers.

Research question three investigated the relationship between peer authoring and writing anxiety, writing apprehension, writing attitude, and writing quality of English composition students. The analysis indicated that peer authoring had a significant correlation with writing quality and a significant effect to students' writing quality. Because peer authoring involves producing a single text with two individuals or a group, the collaborative writing approach provides opportunities for students to challenge each other by clarifying, reasoning, and supporting ideas during the writing process. In other words, peer authoring allows productive cognitive conflict to play out during the collaborative writing exercise. The success of peer authoring is also influenced by social factors. The peer groups that tend to benefit the most from collaborative writing were those that engaged dialogically with each others' ideas and words. These results did tend to support the view that peer authoring is most effective when the instructor models the behavior prior to the collaborative writing approach. Therefore, students need to observe and understand the negotiations that take place during the peer authoring process.

Research question four examined the analyses of the three collaborative writing methods when the scores were computed together in relationship to the writing anxiety, writing apprehension, writing attitude, and writing quality of English composition students. The students' scores for the three collaborative writing instructional methods when computed together tended to provide the most plausible treatment effects in the study. The collaborative writing approaches computed together were interrelated to students' writing attitude but did not have a direct effect on writing attitude. The collaborative writing instructional approach also had a significant relationship with and a direct path to students' writing anxiety. The scores of the collaborative writing assignments when computed together were also significantly related to students' writing apprehension. It was concluded that the scores of the collaborative writing approaches (peer editing, peer tutoring, peer authoring) when computed together were as effective as the individual collaborative writing approaches in reducing English composition students' writing anxiety and writing apprehension, with both having marginal effect on writing attitude. Although writing anxiety and writing apprehension had a significant effect on writing quality, it is not surprising that writing attitude had only marginal effects on writing quality.

Overall, the effectiveness of collaborative writing (peer editing, peer tutoring, peer authoring) on English composition students' writing quality was evident in the distribution of final course grades. The employment of collaborative writing in Freshman Composition 101 and 102 courses showed significant gain in the English composition students' final grade by improving their writing quality. With an effective sample of 392, students earned an average or above-average final course grade: A = 22, B = 109, C = 173, D = 70, and F = 16 as a result of the collaborative learning instructional approach.

Moreover, 314 of the English composition students received a C or better.

Recommendations and Implications for Improving Students' Writing in the New Millennium

Recommendations

Based on the results of this study, the author recommends that when collaborative writing is used as an instructional method, the first two or three weeks should be used to prepare students for working in collaborative groups (Ellman, 1979). Many English composition students are not trained to provide critical and objective feedback. This does not imply that students cannot be effective peer editors, peer tutors or peer authors but rather the fact that they have neither prior experience nor training in peer critiquing procedures. In order for this instructional method to be effective, training must be structured, sequential, and deliberate because the instructor cannot expect students to have the necessary skills in the peer critiquing process.

During the first week, students should receive instruction on the nature and role of collaborative writing. English instructors should model the behaviors they expect their students to practice when evaluating their peers' essays. Modeling such behaviors helps students to work in critiquing groups to peer edit, peer tutor, and peer author each others' essays more effectively. In addition, videos may also be used to teach students how to become effective peer editors, peer tutors, and peer authors. During the second and third weeks, English composition students should practice peer editing, peer tutoring, and peer authoring techniques with the aid of checklists to provide a greater sense of focus while critiquing their peers' papers. During the sessions, English composition students should practice their exchange in dialogue. Finally, collaborative writing is most productive when students have a thorough understanding of how to effectively critique their writing and the writing of their peers.

A longitudinal study utilizing a cohort group should also be conducted to determine the effects of collaborative learning on composition students' writing anxiety, apprehension, attitude, and writing quality. The longitudinal study should follow these cohort students through the completion of Freshman Composition 101 and 102 and Advanced Composition.

It is further recommended that English composition instructors participate in peer coaching. Peer coaching is a technique where instructors coach instructors. This should result in more effective interactive relationships with their students. The research suggests that peer coaching encourages collaborative learning. The research further suggests that instructors who receive training in peer coaching tend to have greater success when utilizing collaborative learning in the classroom. Moreover, peer coaching enables instructors to focus on the way they learn from their interactions with their peers. Therefore, teaching becomes a collaborative rather than an individual enterprise.

English departments should adopt the holistic grading system which is more subjective than the quantitatively-oriented and objective ratings traditionally found in English departments. Moreover, English departments should design and implement effective intervention programs such as collaborative learning to improve the students' writing quality. Finally, the author recommends that inservice workshops be conducted on language awareness to help English instructors become aware of both social and cognitive dimensions of language. Awareness of the double function of language can be useful to instructors as a background for guiding collaborative learning in the writing process.

<u>Implications</u>

English instructors should become knowledgeable of emergent research regarding the teaching of writing using collaborative learning as an instructional method. The following implications are derived based on the study's findings:

1.   There is a need for longitudinal studies to establish cohort groups that can remain together for extended periods of time

since research shows that time is necessary to build a trusting environment in which groups can collaborate. Longitudinal studies following these students through the completion of Freshman Composition 101 and 102 and Advanced Composition 213 would present a clearer picture of the effects of collaboration upon students and their learning processes.

2. There is a need for further research to investigate the effectiveness of collaborative learning using different modes of discourse. A study that tests the interaction effects of various modes of discourse would provide useful information on the value of matching the various collaborative writing approaches with different modes of discourse to enhance English composition students' writing quality. Educators should be able to determine the interaction between the collaborative writing approaches and the modes of discourse.

3. There is a need for longitudinal studies which observe English composition students throughout their academic career to determine the effect that collaborative learning has on these students in terms of preparing them for advanced level writing courses and in reducing their attrition.

4. There is a need for further research to parallel a study of English and mathematics students using both control and experimental cohort groups to compare the effectiveness of the collaborative learning instructional approach and the traditional approach on determining writing quality.

5. There is a need for further research to replicate this study in mathematics to determine the effect of the collaborative writing on mathematics students' math competency.

CHAPTER 5

Understanding the Issues: A Study of African American First Generation College Students

Neari F. Warner

Introduction

> Each of us, because our biographies, our projects and our
> education differ, encounters the social reality of everyday
> from a somewhat distinctive perspective, a perspective of
> which we are far too often unaware. (Greene, 1978, p. 14)

Given that no one factor is usually accepted as explaining a phenomenon, it is problematic to me that inequalities associated with the educational and life experiences of African American students are explained by reducing their plight to a single cause or issue. Mainstream and radical sociologists have attempted to do just that in regard to the persistence of racial inequality in schooling and in society (McCarthy, 1988b).

Mainstream sociologists of education reduce the complexities associated with racial inequality to the issue of the educability of minorities. The issue is articulated differently by the various groups of mainstream theorists (Clark, 1983; McCarthy, 1988b). For instance, conservative mainstream theorists attribute racial inequalities to innate cognitive inferiority (Jensen, 1967; Shockley, 1969). African American educators and theorists, however, argue that African American children demonstrate cognitive abilities and a very early readiness for learning, albeit for a different kind of learning than European American children. They suggest that this readiness is in direct relationship to their backgrounds. African American educators feel that African American children are prepared for tasks that are quite different from

European American children. They maintain that African American children are prepared early for survival rather than for academics (Clark, 1983; Cummings, 1977; Glasgow, 1981; Hale-Benson, 1986; Miller, 1974; Robinson, 1973).

Another group of curriculum theorists, mainstream liberals, accounts for the inequality in education by grounding their position in the theories of cultural and verbal deprivation (Birch & Gussow, 1970; Burling, 1973; Devin & Greenberg, 1972; Haskins & Butler, 1973; Horner, 1966; Leichter, 1973; McCord, 1969; Scanzon, 1971).

In brief, one perspective suggests that the experiences of African American students in impoverished environments cause permanent personality traits that inhibit their opportunity for success (Birch & Gussow, 1970; McCord, 1969; Scanzon, 1971). In similar manner, the other perspective focuses on the failure of the child to interact verbally within the home (Burling, 1973; Haskins & Butler, 1973; Horner, 1966; Leitcher, 1973). However, African American educators maintain that society fails to acknowledge that with African Americans, a variety of factors indigenous to their experiences affects their language development (Clark, 1983; Hale-Benson, 1986).

In sum, mainstream educational theorists fail to consider the conditions that limit and regulate the lives of African Americans by focusing on abstracting such as values, beliefs and tastes as dictated by European Americans. On the other hand, radical sociologists, the neo-Marxists, declare that racial domination is grounded within the nature and structure of capitalism. Racial antagonism, they suggest, is the residue of the discontinuities between labor and capital. Neo-Marxist theorists relegate humanity and consciousness to a subordinate position in favor of an economic ideology (Apple, 1979; Bowles & Gintis, 1976).

Nonetheless, regardless of their differences, mainstream and neo-Marxist theorists share the common bond of not having examined the adversarial relationship that marginalized groups experience within society. I suggest that neither perspective gives attention to the interaction of the

African American child with the oppressive, dominant society.

In the past several decades, proponents of multicultural education have tried to address issues of racial inequality in schooling. Multicultural education reformulates philosophies and curriculum such that it recognizes the omissions in education and advocates teaching ethnic histories–the problems, the issues, the contributions and the heritage–not as history for minorities alone but as history for all Americans. McCarthy (1988b) maintains that "multicultural education must be understood as part of a curricular truce, the fallout of a political project to deluge and neutralize Black rejection of the conformist and assimilationist curriculum models solidly in place in the 1960s" (p. 267). African American educators of today assert that "the changes, adding bits of black history and biography, amount to window-dressing on a Eurocentric perspective" ("Educators Debate," 1990).

Regardless of the posture, each of these groups of theorists neglected to examine African Americans in a more in-depth context. It is, perhaps, this negligence that inspired Hicks (1981) and McCarthy (1988a; 1988b) to suggest that it is important to understand the dynamics of race, class and gender in settings inside and outside of school when attempting to provide explanations for the experiences of African American students in educational institutions. Hence, McCarthy proffers a theory of non-synchrony through which he asserts:

> The patterns of the social stratification by race, class, and gender emerge not as static variables but as efficacious structuring principles that shape minority/majority relations in everyday life. (1988b, p. 275)

The oppressiveness of racism, then, is rarely considered when theorists profess to understand why many African American children seem unaffected by school instruction. Theorists fail to acknowledge that the life structures and values molded by poverty and racism are in direct conflict with those of the European American controlled schools. Many minority youth, particularly

African American youth, conclude that the school system was not designed to teach them. Somehow many of these students decide early that they are in an oppressive educational system. While some develop a variety of defenses to protect themselves, others become discouraged and drop out (Clark, 1983; Miller, 1974; Rashid, 1981; Robinson, 1973).

The large percentages of African American youth dropping out of educational institutions underscore a need for sensitizing and assisting theorists in understanding that by necessity African American youth relate mainly to their daily environment and much of their socialization is geared to survive in that setting. This research is intended to assist theorists in acknowledging that African American youth must maintain a dual existence–as part of a larger society yet separate from it.

W. E. B. DuBois (1903) described this phenomenon as African American people having two warring souls. Hale-Benson (1986) explains: "On the one hand, Black people are the products of their African American heritage and culture. On the other hand, they are shaped by the demands of Euro-American" (p. 178). Rashid (1981) adds that "the cultural and biological history of African Americans has resulted in an essentially African group of people who must function in 'essentially' European schools" (p. 58).

A survey of pertinent literature suggests that schools maintain the status quo–that schools are, in fact, designed to instill the values and attitudes of the dominant society and to promote the cultural orientation of the European American power structure. In very traditionally designed schools, learning experiences are teacher-oriented rather than student-oriented. Methods of teaching are restrictive; the teachers tend to lecture and demonstrate rather than permit the students to engage in discovery, inquiry and laboratory experiences. The organizational structure is rigid; there are strict grade lines, stigmatic grouping and orthodox lines of authority and supervision. The curriculum is limited to subject matter that is familiar to the masses; it does not lend to curriculum experimentation and innovation that would foster creativity and independent thinking for correlating ideas, experiences and expressions.

Macdonald (1988) suggests that as the schools replicate the social structure, employing the discourse of meritocracy, they are convincing the so-called "winners" and "losers" that they deserve the status they achieve. Accordingly, the curricula of the schools are designed to support and reinforce inequality such that schools with predominantly African American students emphasize vocational and general course programs whereas schools with predominantly European American students emphasize a college preparatory curricula. In racially mixed schools, the African Americans are disproportionately assigned to the general and vocational programs. After a while the African American students "learn and accept their place in life" (Cumming, 1977, p. 38).

In the American educational system where the slogan "education is the key" (Weis, 1985) resonates throughout the country, African American youth have been treated unequally. Whereas the school experiences of youth are expected to be meaningful, enjoyable and productive, marginalized youth, particularly African Americans, have experienced alienation, hostility and a general feeling of disengagement from a system that purports to educate all of its citizenry equally.

When theorists and educators appear perplexed as to the reasons for these reactions, I maintain that the conditions for their lives as well as the urban school systems to which these youths have been subjected are plausible areas in which to seek answers. I further maintain that some answers may be found in the wisdom of the students themselves; particularly the non-traditional student; for more than ever before, these disillusioned, marginalized students are returning as adults to the educational system which they abandoned as youths.

As these students return to the educational system, it is imperative that theorists and educators recognize the significance and importance that their life histories play in their present station in life, that is, to understand the "landscapes" (Greene, 1978) from which they have grown and in which they have attempted to prosper. Even for the most discerning scholars, it is not an easy task to understand another's life structures. Illustrative of this is the fact that findings of two major ethnographical texts, *Between Two Worlds* (1985) and *The Next Generation* (1974) result in contrasting, even oppositional theories, to explain the school activities and experiences of African American youth.

On the one hand, Weis' *Between Two Worlds* (1985) explores the educational culture at a predominantly African American two-year community college which she names Urban College. African American student culture is not allowed to exist on its merits; it is not accepted as having its own historical and developmental foundation. Instead, Weis chose to subordinate African American student cultural forms by studying them with preconceived theories defined by European American working-class male culture as found in Paul Willis' *Learning to Labour* (1977). European American working-class male culture is made the criterion by which African American student culture is delineated and understood (more appropriately–misunderstood). Weis does not consider the nuances of being African American in America. She does not consider the dynamics of race, class and gender and their relationship to the economic, political and cultural facets of the school. Weis' one academic year exploration of the elements of African American student culture lacked the perspective of a participant in the total experience of the students of Urban College. She neglected to examine the students in relating to the social, cultural and political underpinning that structure their daily existence. Weis never acknowledged that the dynamic of race is a significant factor in the culture produced by the students (Solomon, 1986). Weis never attempted to explore the production of differences–the nonsynchronous (Hicks, 1981; McCarthy, 1983a; 1988b) relations present in society. She provides no insightful clues into their lifestyles or never even considers that for Urban College students, mainstream culture is not necessarily the center of their orientation. In effect, Weis' study reflected a micro level of the social worlds of the African American students at Urban College. Thus, it led her to conclude that students collude in their own oppression and encourage their own continued super exploitation. Weis ignores or denies the racial antagonism created by the institution's agents and practices.

In contrast, Ogbu's *The Next Generation* (1974) portrays a relatively complete picture of the families, school life and community groups associated with the education of hundreds of fifth through twelfth grade students in the Burgherside school system. Ogbu's "thick description" (Geertz, 1973) included interviews with those who taught the youth and any significant others who had direct or indirect impact on education in the community. He utilized spatial maps, demographic graphs and charts to situate the community in terms of its cultural, political and economic reality.

Ogbu obtains generational information about education in Burgherside not only from the children but also from and about the education of their parents and their parents' parents. Analysis of these data of three generations revealed that for the oldest generation education was not as important as it was for the second generation. For the third generation, education was viewed as indispensable. However, as parents emphasized the importance of a good education on the one hand, they neutralized that value with verbal statements and personal experiences that were translated to mean that education does not really pay if one is African American. The message is tacit, but the impact is insidious. The Burgherside youth, therefore, think that there is no use trying to make it in school since they cannot succeed when they leave school regardless of their achievement. Ogbu concludes that Burgherside youth fail in school not because they cannot do the work or do not have the ability but because they are not serious about their work and make no serious effort to try to succeed. Ogbu accepts this view of children's failure as being more valid than the three explanations (cultural deprivation, inferiority of schools, and genetic inferiority) that are so pervasively used to explain the failure of African American and poor students.

As an added dimension, because Ogbu created the text out of the real life experiences of these students, he was able to unveil some positive elements of the Burgherside community. Through his immersion in the culture, Ogbu revealed that, despite their environmental limitations and the societal obstacles, the Burgherside families are still as normal in many aspects. He showed that the families spent time together, that there were patterns to their lives and that they enjoyed each other's company. In Burgherside, friends visited; children played and people helped one another. Ogbu implies that the families of Burgherside are optimistic about their children's future as they continue struggling and surviving against the backdrop of racial inequalities.

Ogbu's text is a strong contribution toward understanding how the experiences of African American students are shaped and molded. Research of this depth must be continued and expanded. Unless and until more research is conducted and its findings deployed, theorists will continue to devalue and ignore the cultures of marginalized groups. This study is intended to provide an in-depth view into how the life experiences of African American students affect all aspects of their lives. Because this study is created out of the real life experiences of African American students, theorists will be provided with practical and empirical evidence that show these African American students, in fact, do aspire to improve the quality of their lives despite the voluminous body of literature suggesting otherwise and that their school experiences are impacted in a myriad of ways by the structural constraints imposed on their culture.

Historical Underpinning

Historically and systematically, African Americans have been denied equal access to quality education. Weinberg (1977) reports:

> during the days of slavery, those in power acknowledged that laws prohibiting the education of blacks were intended to perpetuate "compulsory ignorance." Even five years after the Civil War, 90% of school-age blacks were not in school. As recently as 1940, public schools in the south operated on an average school year of 175 days for whites and 156 days for blacks. (pp. 1, 3, 5)

Ogbu (1978) believed that from emancipation from slavery in 1863 to the present almost all changes in education for African Americans have been responses to changes or anticipated changes in the social and political climate of the nation. Interestingly, President Abraham Lincoln, author of the Emancipation Proclamation, anticipates Ogbu's premise: "I claim not to have controlled events, but confess plainly that events have controlled me" (Foster, 1954, p. 255).

The inequalities noted and documented in educational opportunities for African Americans are grounded in the perceptions of many of the early educators and the early curriculum movements. For example, Edward L. Thorndike, a founding theorist of American behaviorism, has been noted by historians of education as one of the most influential persons in determining the form that American education took in the early nineteenth century (Franklin, 1986; Kliebard, 1986; Schubert, 1986). A salient feature of Thorndike's thinking was his acceptance of an hereditarian view of individual differences. He advocated a one-to-one relationship between an individual's social traits and behavior (Franklin, 1986; Kliebard, 1986). His major emphasis, however, was on heredity as it relates to intelligence. Generally, he believed African Americans were not as intelligent as European Americans. This assumed inferiority, he felt, was problematic to the point that he maintained that the presence of African Americans in a community diminished the quality of life within that community.

Other educators held different views of African Americans' intellectual ability and the American educational system. One of the pioneers in curriculum development was Werrett W. Charters who migrated from Canada and earned the Ph.D. at the University of Chicago in 1904. For Charters, human behavior was grounded in both heredity and environment. Consequently, he rejected the hereditarian thinking of many of the sociologists and educators of his day. Instead, he argued that other qualities such as character, personality and efforts were greater determinants of success than intelligence. He questioned:

> What right has any person to predict a failure because an
> intelligence quotient is somewhat low? To be sure, three

percent of the pupils in the school may be so defective as to be hopeless, but the other ninety-seven percent may possibly be able to develop compensating traits of personality which far outweigh mediocrity in mental ability. We of the classroom are inclined to feel sorry for the industrious child with a comparatively low mental score, who by dint of hard work keeps abreast of his class. . . . In making an inventory of the assets of a man industry, forcefulness, leadership, sympathy and ambition are major headings, which combined yield nothing in importance to brains and mental brightness. (qtd. in Franklin, 1986, p. 101)

In 1945, while addressing the graduates of Fisk University, a historically African American higher education institution in Nashville, Tennessee, Charters said to those graduates that America was entering a period in which the social, educational and economic promise of democracy would be realized by all, irrespective of racial distinctions (Franklin, 1986).

The major African American educators of the early 1900s held conflicting views on the most appropriate educational focus as well as the educational prospects for them. Booker T. Washington, the well-respected founder of Tuskegee Normal Institute in Alabama and a disciple of Samuel Armstrong, founder of the normal school in Virginia, championed the practical value of menial labor. He contended that "through manual training, the 'downtrodden child of ignorance, shiftlessness and moral weakness' would be converted into a 'thoroughly rounded man of prudence, foresight, responsibility and financial independence'" (qtd. in Kliebard, p. 133).

W. E. B. DuBois, a noted intellectual, historian and first African American to be awarded a Ph.D. from Harvard University, strongly maintained that the manual labor being promoted at Tuskegee was outdated and counterproductive. Washington's philosophy, DuBois contended, denied African Americans the intellectual training and professional skills that the changing industrial society demanded at that time (Kliebard, 1986).

Inappropriate education was a barrier to African Americans' opportunity for equal status in American society.

In addition, the historical exclusion of African Americans from equal education is evident in the textbooks of the nineteenth century. They systematically promoted inequality. Through suggestive, negative depictions and illustrations, racial difference and inequalities were portrayed. The widespread acceptance of such literature carrying the tacit messages of racism was an indication that twentieth century America supported a racially stratified society. During that era several major publications, read both in the North and in the South, intimated that Blacks were undesirable, inferior and socially unequal (e.g., *The Passing of the Great Race* (1921) by Madison Grant, *The Picturesque Geographical Readers* (1892) by Charles King and *The Leopard's Spots* (1902) by Thomas Dixon, Jr.).

Now, early in the new millennium, it is a reality that African Americans, who Ogbu (1978) characterizes as caste minorities, those who the dominant group regards as inherently inferior in all respects, are still searching for new directions– politically, culturally and educationally. Given the historical facts and development of African American people, this is not a startling revelation. African Americans were victims of a four hundred year period of bondage and servitude. They were not brought to this country to be given an education, citizenship or democracy; they were brought to this country to serve, labor and obey. Nevertheless, due to various social, economic and political pressures throughout history, African Americans have been given semblances of freedom. Their freedom came in various stages–not so much out of genuine concern for their liberation but more out of what Freire (1986) refers to as "false generosity." Freire declares:

> In order to have continued opportunity to express their 'generosity' the oppressors must perpetuate injustice as well. An unjust social order is the permanent fount of this generosity which is nourished by death, despair and poverty. (p. 29)

African Americans have been the recipients of many false, generous gestures. The Emancipation Proclamation proclaimed their freedom; the Thirteenth Amendment of the Constitution secured that freedom; the Fourteenth Amendment made them American citizens, and the Fifteenth Amendment provided penalties for any state that denied their rights of citizenship because of race, color or previous conditions or servitude. All of these stages of freedom, including the more recent congressional acts targeted toward improving the quality of life of African Americans did not guarantee real freedom. The freedom is a facade, and the schools are one of the social institutions by which society attempts to perpetuate and maintain the facade. Thus, the educational system has not been effective for all segments of the nation's citizenry. In the area of education in the American school system, the social class inequalities are too evident to be denied (Bowles & Gintis, 1976). For large segments of European Americans, the educational system has been an effective vehicle to achieve middle-class status. However, for far too many poor minorities, it has been an abysmal failure (Bowles & Gintis, 1976; Glasgow, 1981; Robinson, 1973). Rather than ameliorating the socioeconomic conditions of the poor and minorities, the formal U. S. educational system has aggravated their conditions (Cummings, 1977; Glasgow, 1981; Hale-Benson, 1986; Rashid, 1981; Robinson, 1973; Sedlacek & Brooks, 1976). The National Alliance of Black School Educators (1984) concludes:

> The institutionalization of deprivation and disenfranchise-ment among schools has permitted race and socioeconomic status to function as the chief determinants of access to quality treatment for children. The public schools often represent an integration of society's most crippling diseases—indifference, injustice and inequality. (p. 37)

Society's failure to seek solutions and to adequately educate African American students has produced monumental disdain and distrust of the public educational system, particularly schools serving primarily African American youths in large city schools. That there is a crisis in urban school settings has finally been acknowledged. The 1984 Report of the National Alliance of Black School Educators corroborates: "The notion that this nation once had good schools for the masses of African American students but has since let them deteriorate is inaccurate" (p. 37).

The Voices of First Generation College Students : A Qualitative Study

The failure of society to acknowledge that the non-synchronous relationship that African Americans experience in the larger society affects their school experiences is the basis of this research. It was with this premise in mind that I researched and subsequently sketched the life histories of four non-traditional African American first generation college students. My experiences as an African American educator at an historically African American postsecondary institution were the catalyst for my interest to go beyond the phenomenological descriptions to explain and understand the actions of African American students from the point of view of those students who, themselves, left the public schools disenchanted and returned to school settings after extended periods of absence.

The purpose of this research is to provide insights into the processes, pressures and people that have shaped the lives of these students. The study examines the contradictions, paradoxes and ambivalence in the lives of marginalized groups that prompt their leaving the educational system, particularly the urban school setting, and subsequently motivate their seeking empowerment through the same system. This research also reveals the commonsense ways and understandings of African American students that move them to return to the educational system which they rejected years before. The study reviews the historical, political and ideological backgrounds of African American students in the urban school environment in an attempt to improve the quality of their lives. However, this study is most important and unique because it draws on the background of first-hand experiences of African American college students. Thus, it gives a perspective of history and ideology in schooling, family and racial inequality not readily found in much of the published literature. The lucid, candid commentary of the research participants demonstrate their perceptions of their real world problems, challenges and satisfactions. Their vivid and realistic reflections provide a more balanced, albeit personal, account of what African American youth experience in settings inside and outside of school.

Methodology

My interest to do research in this area was strengthened by studying ethnography. Proponents of school-related ethnographies believe that ethnographic research allows for a more concrete understanding of the problems of urban students and urban schools (Blase, 1985; Dabney & Davis, 1982; Filling, 1980; Fordham, 1987; Hess, 1988; Rist, 1981; Semons, 1989; Sleeter & Grant, 1985). These proponents acknowledge that while ethnographies do not offer specific remedies to the problems of inequality in urban education, they do, in fact, provide understanding in such areas as:

> (1) the futility of dealing with issues improving or equalizing urban education in terms of only academic achievement; (2) establishing important relationships among societal factors, classroom behaviors and output variables such as academic achievement; (3) investigating the interaction between cultural characteristics and classroom behaviors as powerful or salient variables. (Filling, 1989, p. 273)

There are debates within ethnography regarding the nature of this research. For example, Roman (1988) contends that "naturalistic ethnography affirms a social world that is meant to be gazed upon but not challenged or transformed" (p. 55). It is, perhaps, this "unnatural" detachment of the researcher attempting to maintain a "natural" environment that was the impetus for researchers to consider the need for a different kind of ethnography–a critical ethnography where emphasis is on raising and disclosing issues where the research methodology is empowering for the group being studied, one that is emancipatory for the group under study. Hammersley and Atkinson (1983), for example, challenge the ethnographer's responsibility of merely describing the social world by suggesting that the researcher has a transformational responsibility to the group which she/he is studying.

In naturalistic ethnography, the primary goal is the description of cultures. On the contrary, the task of the critical ethnographer is that of going beyond phenomenological descriptions. "In order to get beyond the phenomenal level of analysis," says Roman, "ethnographers need to explain the underlying social relations that set objective limits on the 'appearances' of peoples' practices and their accounts of the social world" (p. 56). Thus, the characteristic nature of critical ethnography makes it ideal for this research.

> (1) It is a dialectical method, allowing the research to gather data in a way that recognizes the problematic nature involved; (2) It responds to semiotic analysis; (3) It generates a sensitivity to ethnocentrism in forming questions and interpreting observations; (4) It offers a means for examining the relationship between ideology, social behavior, and social structure; and (5) It provides a means for analyzing social structure by examining the fabric in which behaviors are embedded. (Thomas, 1983, pp. 485-487)

Warren (1982) endorses the life history/autobiography as an appropriate tool for this research:

> One could argue that adult education in American, with its roots in such a community studies tradition, has had a long

pragmatic tradition. One direct consequence of this pragma-
tism in adult education has been the recognition that
the experiences of individuals are the starting point for
determining the nature and design of any educational
endeavor. Autobiographical methods are but one way in
which researchers in adult education may obtain insights not
readily assessable by quantitative methods. . . . Indeed, this
seems important if an aim of adult education is to extend
educational programs and opportunities to new consumer
groups as well as to develop programs to reach those who
view the present array of programs as irrelevant to their lives.
(pp. 215-218)

Thus, rather than hear these stories told by me, this research is
designed to have students tell their own stories. It is only then that they
become "the best of all stories" for they provide data that experimental data
can not (Birren, p. 91).

In order to have their stories told, I approach this research as a critical
ethnographer because I know, from first-hand experience, the necessity of and
the benefits of going beyond the surface when attempting to assist or
understand those persons or situations that are different from another's span
of experiences and frame of reference. As a critical ethnographer, I will
attempt to bring the experiences of these research participants into the span
of experiences and scope of reference of all who read this study. Indeed, from
my perspective, this can be done only through qualitative methods.

Research Setting

The research was conducted in a four-year postsecondary institution
with an enrollment of ninety-eight percent African American. Geographically,
this University is situated in the heart of a beautiful, serene African American
middle-class residential development. The neighborhood residents, however,

are not the clientele of the University. The University is predominantly attended by students from low-income families and communities throughout the large metropolitan city in which it is located. Many of the students grew up in and still inhabit the low-rent housing projects that are within close proximity to the University. Because this University offers comparatively low tuition, has an open admissions policy, and espouses a mission of uplifting the disenfranchised, most of the students perceive it as their first step toward improving the quality of their lives. The passage reported below, taken from the University's catalogue, demonstrates this perspective:

> The institution was established primarily, but not exclusively, for the education of African American citizens of the Greater New Orleans area and the state of Louisiana in general. While the University admits and actively recruits qualified students without regard to race, color, origin, religion, age, sex, or physical handicap, it maintains its strong commitment to serving the higher education needs of the socio-economically disadvantaged of the Greater New Orleans Metropolitan area. (Southern University, 1989, p. 25)

Using demographic data of the entering freshman class for the past two academic years, I have provided a profile typical of the University's student population. A unique feature of this University is that it has an Evening/ Weekend College which enrolls the non-traditional student. Statistics on these students indicate that they are returning to this university in record numbers. Data also show that these students comprise forty percent of the total enrollment at the University but at least fifty percent of each year's graduating class. The University also serves as the major institution to which students from the city's two-year community college transfer. The community college student is, more often than not, a non-traditional student. Upon entry into the community college, the student is over the age of twenty-five and has had a break in his or her education of five years or more (Prager, 1983).

University data indicate that at least twenty percent of each semester's new enrollees are from the area community college. Consistent with that is the graduation rate for students who transferred into the University from the area community college. University records document that at least twenty percent of the graduating class for the past three years were non-traditional transfer students.

Identifying and Selecting Participants

Having worked in this setting for twenty-three years, I had a large pool of students from which to select. Very early in my career, through their own autobiographical voices, I learned that for most of these students the decision to return to school was a long, difficult, painful decision. In their own words, they admitted to approaching the educational setting with timidity, lacking self-confidence, harboring feelings of hopelessness, but clinging to the hope that their move back into the educational system will guarantee that the quality of their lives will improve because of it. Despite the many academic weaknesses most of them brought to the classroom, I concluded as Taylor and Dorsey-Gaines(1988) did as they studied the families and lives of achieving African American first graders.

> Their optimism about the future and their ability to imagine
> what life would be like if conditions were better seemed to
> keep them going, struggling and surviving, albeit precarious-
> ly, against the odds and without the support of the society to
> which they belong. (p. 192)

My selection of the four non-traditional African American first generation college students was not random. Fischer (1983) explains: "the amount of data needed from each subject requires high commitment from potential respondents, a factor which almost inevitably means using non-random sampling" (p. 31). She also suggests that "because the cost of data collection tends to be extremely high per student, the number of subjects is likely to be small in order to offset the per capita expense"(p. 30). For example, Willie (1990) researched the life histories of five outstanding African American scholars to provide insights into how significant events in their lives interconnected to facilitate their success. Semon (1989) selected five multi-ethnic urban high school students to compare his findings with the findings from the ethnographic studies of students from court order desegregated schools several decades ago. Goodson (1981) investigated one teacher's professional life history to explore the evaluation of a school subject in the changing educational system. Scheinfield and Messerschmidt (1979) investigated the lives of two teachers (young/old) to examine the differences in teaching styles as related to different life stages. Sarris (1978) studied five participants when researching the process of maturation of youngsters who grew up in housing projects and achieved some degree of success. For this study, I used four subjects. I selected four as the number of participants based on a simple, intuitive formula I created. I used the average of the total number of subjects used in the aforementioned life history studies. For me, this average of 3.6 translated into 4. Thus, I chose to research the life structures of four African American students who met the following criteria: (1) attended the University where the research is set, (2) considered non-traditional as defined by Prager (1983), (3) attended an urban public school for a large part of their schooling, and (4) potentially the first of the family to graduate from college.

Because of my position in the University, I was able to meet potential participants on a daily basis. As I would sit and chat with students, I listened closely for a signal that provided me with the opportunity to invite their participation in the project. Certain comments prompted me to solicit their participation, such as: "If people only knew what my life has been like;" or "I wish that I could tell these young students a thing or two;" or " If I knew then what I know now, I would never have stopped school;" or "Nobody would believe what has happened to me;" or "I'm so glad to be here after all I've been through."

Somewhere later within the conversation, I would cautiously and casually indicate to potential participants that I was working on a project where they would be able to tell other people their stories. My instincts, at the time, were accurate in that of the ten persons whom I solicited for the project, all were very excited and agreed to participate. Knowing that I needed to prepare for and should expect that some students would withdraw from the project, I began preliminary field work relative to the project in early Spring of 1990. All of the participants were very excited early in the project, but as time moved on, I lost most of them. I lost them at various points which I describe in a later section of this chapter. Hence, after the preliminary stages of the project were completed (the withdrawal of participants), I was left with four students who willingly and diligently completed the project–two males and two females.

I gave each of them a pseudonym although each expressed the desire to use his/her own name. According to Langness and Frank (1981), this is not unusual:

Many life-history informants <u>want</u> to use their actual names. Sometimes these are marginalized individuals who by setting their own stamp on the life-history written about them make a statement to the world, offering testimony, or bearing witness, about events that shaped their lives. (p. 126)

Nonetheless, realizing the importance of anonymity, I was able to convince them to accept the pseudonyms I had selected when they realized that the names represented an inversion of their initials. As such, the four students described below provide the data for the research in this study.

When I began interviewing participant Patricia Dawson, she was forty-one years old. She is the third of nine children. She grew up in a two-parent family, where the father is an excessive drinker. Pat, as she is affectionately known by her family, has separated from her husband and has moved back into her parents' household. She is the mother of two children, ages fourteen and twelve. Pat obtained a GED after having been out of school for seventeen years. Patricia is pursuing a baccalaureate degree along with three of her sisters who also delayed college enrollment. Patricia Dawson aspires to become an independent woman who can offer her children and herself a better life.

Participant Daniel Kelley was twenty-six years old when I began his interviews. He is the last of eight children. Daniel is from a single parent home, his father having died when he was ten years old. After the death of his father, Daniel attempted to assume much of the male responsibilities of the household. At age fifteen, he perceived himself head of the household when his mother left for extended periods of time. Although others of his siblings have attended college, none persevered. Daniel had pledged to improve his position in life and has decided that he will be the first among his siblings to graduate from college.

Participant Shirley Franklin is the first of four children; she is the offspring of a sickle cell anemia carrier and is one of two of the four children who contacted the disease. Although Shirley was reared by her mother and stepfather, she always had close contact with and enjoyed a pleasant relationship with her father. Shirley was twenty-nine years old at the onset of this project and was determined to live her life as fully as possible, despite the odds that predict that she will not live through full adulthood.

Participant Richard Allen comes from a two-parent home and is the second of four children. He felt anonymous and alienated by being the middle child. His parents sacrificed to send him to the parochial school system, feeling that it was the perfect "fit" for him. Richard was twenty-eight years old when these interviews began and had enrolled in college.

Voices From the Past

I have inferred throughout this chapter that the American educational system reneged on its responsibility to give all children the opportunity to engage in something meaningful that would prepare them for a better life.

Using the voices of the students, I demonstrate that the experiences of African American youth have not always been pleasant and have served primarily to alienate them from the system which purports to assist them in building productive, successful lives. These students, whose success in attaining a baccalaureate degree will mean that they are the first in their families to graduate from college, are also the high school students of the 60s and 70s who attended schools in a large urban school district. Throughout this chapter, I use the voices of these students to provide an insider's perspective into their urban schools, typical of most in the country, and into the culture from which students who attend these schools come. I examine the school and family experiences of these students in anticipation that their memories will provide linkage to the literature reviewed in this chapter while also providing a realistic perspective of how African American youth think and feel about their lives, how they see their world and how they have interacted with their environment.

I began my examination with school experiences. As you shall see, the diversity of the ages of these participants gives insight into the social, political and economic context which surrounded public education in this urban district where they each attended a different school within the district. Accordingly, participant Patricia Dawson attended school during the time that segregated school systems were the norm throughout much of the country. In contrast, participant Daniel Kelley attended school during the period when integration had been "accepted." However, European American flight had become the phenomenon, and previously all-European American schools began to take on a different look. No change was visible in the student population of the previously all-African American schools. Daniel's elementary school, formerly all European American, had a Euro/Afro ratio of 70/30. The population ratio of the magnet middle school which he attended was approximately 60/40, Euro/Afro. For senior high school, Daniel attended the college prep school whose population was 100% African American although it was open to all and had an excellent academic reputation. In the case of participant Shirley Franklin, she attended elementary school in the rural setting of her hometown. Incidents that affected her personality as well as her schooling prompted the family to move to the city. There she attended the integrated school of this urban district. Participant Richard Allen's educational experiences alternated between parochial and public schools. In each of these settings, the schools were integrated, with this public urban setting being more fully integrated.

The comments and memories, hence the data, provided by these participants suggest that regardless of the time and space perspective of education, there have been some basic unmet needs of the youths attending schools in this district. I used the voices of the participants to illustrate statistics and to illuminate issues brought forth in the literature. I first summarize the commonalities that permeate the experiences of these participants. Secondly, I discuss specific elements in the experiences of each participant in an attempt to point out the inconsistencies that existed in their home and school culture. I then draw conclusions as to what appeared to have been problematic in the experiences of these first generation students.

In general, the compilation of their experiences suggests that these participants attended schools where their actions, their teachers' action and the classroom activities were perfunctory. The participants were expected to play the appropriate role of eager, contented, submissive youth. They were expected to be self-motivated with a burning desire to learn. On occasions, the participants stepped out of their roles to send signs and signals of distress such as inattentiveness, misbehavior and apathetic attitudes. Their signs and signals were to no avail. They went unheeded or misinterpreted. The totality of their experiences provided a portrait of the urban school teacher. The picture they painted was of an individual who was distant and detached; the teachers demonstrated no warmth, kindnesses or gestures of nurturing. The attitudes of their teachers were nonchalant and minimally tolerant. Their approaches to the lesson were less than stimulating, and creativity was never apparent in any meaningful way. Their portrait was completed by the revelation that some teachers were individuals whose lack of interest or understanding of the culture prompted them to be insensitive, exploitive or condescending toward it. All of the experiences of these participants seem to be undergirded by the reality that their teachers appeared only to understand middle-class values and behavior.

In regard to culture, the compilation of the family experiences of the participants revealed that there is a culture among African Americans that is distinct and different from middle-class America, that is, European Americans. Most important, their stories demonstrated that their culture is not dysfunctional. The lives of these participants revealed that the most salient characteristics of the culture are the extensive network of kinships and the flexibility of self-help and survival skills. The participants painted a picture of a culture where relationships were nurtured, where day-to-day life was set within a maze of personal problems, where their homes and their mothers were the center of their orientation, and where educational empowerment was advocated but not necessarily anticipated. Most decidedly, it is safe to conclude that the manner in which the youth interacted with their parents, sibling and other relatives shaped their relationships, their perception of themselves and their ideas about life.

In view of these generalizations, I looked specifically at each participant in an attempt to make sense of their experiences and to offer explanations for their disdain of their school experiences. Participant Patricia Dawson's early dislike of schooling seemed to stem from the inconsistency she detected between home and school. At home, Patricia felt loved, wanted and needed by all. At school, Patricia felt unloved and unwanted by all, especially her teachers. When the activities in these two situations were inconsistent, Patricia had the normal, natural reaction of a child—to dislike the one which caused her pain and unhappiness. Thus, the conflict between home and school is established when Patricia is unable to receive the same nurturing and gestures of love and affection at school as she receives at home. Patricia had no reason to believe that everyone would not love her as her mother, her siblings and her grandfather did. Therefore, when she experienced feelings of alienation, she began developing a dislike for school very early in her experiences. Knowing that she had done nothing to warrant the teachers' dislike for her, Patricia created reasons and decided that teachers disliked her because she was "the poorest child in the class and couldn't wear pretty new clothes." Her mother's declaration that "the most important thing was that she was clean" had no impact on her attitude as she moved from year to year. In fact, at each juncture of her schooling, her early assessment was reaffirmed. At each juncture of her schooling, Patricia was subjected to situations that were of personal embarrassment.

When she entered junior high school, Patricia "hated school even more." The one incident that could have changed her attitude toward teachers and schooling actually solidified it. When Patricia was whipped by her mother "in the middle of the playground in front of all of the children for shooting hooky," she thought that the teachers should have actively attempted to lessen the embarrassment she felt. Patricia attributed no blame to her mother for this incident. She knew that her mother loved her; therefore, she knew that this act was precipitated by that love. Her mother was completely exonerated because Patricia knew that her mother had the right to discipline her when she had been disobedient. In the interview, Patricia explained:

> When I was a little girl, I decided then that my mother was the head of our household, although she was always telling us that our father was. I knew that was not true because all that my father did was bring home the money; anything else that happened in the house or the family was controlled by her. . . .

Thus, Patricia shifted the blame to her teachers. She said, "They didn't seem to care or even try to make me feel better about the incident."

Finally, the ultimate confirmation of Patricia's early hypothesis and the most extreme embarrassment came at the point when she was beginning to have a more positive attitude about schooling. When Patricia was pulled from the graduation practice line for lacking two units, she lost all faith and trust in teachers, counselors and the school itself. She dropped out of school and relegated herself to working and to helping the family. For Patricia, her home and family were a refuge from the frustrations and embarrassments of school. With her family, she felt safe, received love and experienced personal worth and satisfaction. Thus, Patricia was one student for whom the educational system did not work because it was unable to provide her with the nurturing and supportive environment she needed to feel as worthy and as wonderful at school as she felt at home.

The voice of Patricia Dawson becomes the voice of one of college campuses' fastest growing populations–the re-entry woman. She stated:

> . . . I remember very vividly my mother constantly told us
> throughout our childhood that she wanted us to go to school
> and get an education so that we, as females, wouldn't have
> to go through and put up with the things that she had to.

Literature suggests that in addition to some commonalities, the reasons for women's return are as varied and different as one woman is to another (Doty, 1965; Henry, 1985; Saslow, 1980). However, not much of this literature has focused on the African American woman. Patricia Dawson is a highly suggestive example of the re-entry African American perspective; it is extremely likely that many of the African American women returning to the campuses will have shared in some experiences similar to Patricia Dawson's. As Patricia and others like her enter postsecondary settings, it is important to know that the curriculum can not be void of support services and efforts that will facilitate the success of these students.

Unlike Patricia, participant Daniel Kelley felt welcomed, wanted and well-liked in the school setting. Daniel was obviously a very bright student whose academic potentials were recognized by his teachers, his family and persons within the community. By his own admission, that of "double agent," Daniel acknowledged the dualism that existed in his life.

I was ten years old when my father died. I cried only when

I was told about it. At the funeral, I didn't cry because I knew that he was a good man and that he was going to heaven. I also knew that he would not want me to be sad and that he would want me to go on with my life and be strong like his "little man." My childhood seemed to end with the death of my father.

. . . I vowed to myself and promised my father through a secret prayer that I would not be a burden on her [mother] and that I would help her all that I could. However, my mother seemed to be making me into a mama's boy. She would not let me play with the older boys, and she kept me close to her. I was always getting beat up and other children were always taking things from me. The day that I decided to take control of my life was the day that I named myself a double agent. It happened after a boy from another neighborhood beat me up and took ten dollars from me. I was really angry because I had saved that money after working endlessly for my brother and doing odd jobs in the neighborhood. I knew that if I went to my mother, she would say not to worry about it and that the Lord would take care of that person. I knew also that if I went to the police, they would not believe that I had ten dollars or, perhaps, would not even listen to my story. I decided, then, that I would get my money back so I started stealing. I didn't perceive it as stealing. I felt like I was getting back what so many people had been taking from me. . . . I got to be really good at stealing. Other children used to get me to steal things for them. My brothers and sisters knew what I was doing, but my mother didn't. I gained the respect and admiration of all the children in the neighborhood. This was, of course, among the children. . . .

Daniel's need to be the man of the house after his father's death seemed to have been the catalyst for the contradictions that characterized his life. Daniel appeared to be a happy, well-adjusted youth when in reality he was a despondent youth who needed his school activities to provide his life with meaning and personal satisfaction. However, school activities, that is the curriculum, became problematic for Daniel when he was unable to find personal success and accomplishment or immediate solutions for the situations that plagued his family.

Despite his aptitude and capabilities, Daniel found no sense of achievement in classroom activities. He did just enough to pass, constantly worked below his potential and literally took "an in-school vacation" through most of his schooling. Daniel's early motivations and competitive drives were soon diminished by a curriculum that was homogenized, diluted and geared toward masses; for Daniel, "school work was boring," and he was unchallenged. He used those unchallenged energies to effect pranks, "get rid of the teacher schemes" and ingenuous intellectual annoyances.

The curriculum presented other paradoxes for Daniel. For example, even though the school work was "boring" for him, "his brothers and sisters were doing poorly in school." He was not able to help them with their work because he was taking care of the critical situation they faced at home. Realizing that it "was getting harder and harder" for him and his siblings to survive as their mother left for extended periods, Daniel decided that his school activities were irrelevant to his real concerns. He was turned off by school because the activities "didn't teach how to survive once (he) left school each day." Daniel's disappointment in not having his needs met manifested in depression and thoughts of suicide. Thus, it seems safe to conclude that not only was the curriculum irrelevant to Daniel's real life concerns but also that Daniel was in need of sensitive, intuitive teachers who should have detected that the underachievement and apathy that he displayed were symptomatic of something deeper. As Daniel's voice, his story is prototypical of many urban students, it is important to realize that their entry into the postsecondary setting must be complemented by programs and activities that will enhance their experiences.

In manner similar to that of Daniel Kelley, participant Shirley Franklin needed sensitive, intuitive teachers. When her family moved to the city, Shirley found that the environment in the urban school was quite different from the school in her rural hometown. Shirley decided very early in her attendance at the urban school that "no one seemed to care." She reached this conclusion when the behavior she displayed did not provide her with the same kind of attention that it did in her rural hometown school. Shirley was fighting a deadly disease and as such felt the need to constantly defend herself against those who ridiculed her about it.

> The cause of many of my fights was my physical appearance. I was very, very skinny; I had an exceptionally large protruding stomach, and I was "sway-backed" (as my grandmother called it). While in fifth grade, I had a fight with a boy who told all of the children that I was pregnant. We fought after school. (Most times, I didn't win the fight but I would never give up.) I went home crying and told my mother what had happened. My mother explained that I was not pregnant and explained how girls get pregnant. (At that moment, I knew that I was going to fight that boy again for thinking that I was doing that.) My mother also explained why my stomach was large. She tried to explain why I had this disease. She explained that she was a carrier of a disease called sickle cell anemia.

When Shirley's behavior became unruly previously, she was handled with a sympathetic, yet, firm hand. However, in her new school, the city school as she called it, she was "sent to the office to sit until the next class." There were no counseling efforts, no attempts to investigate a possible cause of the behavior, and no real attempt to modify her behavior.

Continuing to acknowledge that "city schools" were different, Shirley felt that her teachers were also different. Her idea of the teachers being "more willing to talk about interesting things (such as the aspirin between the knee birth control pill) equates to a teacher's insincerity to his/her students and to his/her job. Teachers in the urban school also allowed Shirley to misuse her illness and "she took full advantage of this situation to get away with a lot."

> I spent my seventh and eighth grade years at the high school in the town. The teachers seemed to treat me much better than my elementary school teachers. With some of the teachers, I used to get special favors. For example, I made the basketball team and the cheerleading squad. I wasn't very good at either. I had very little athletic skills, and I couldn't dance well or keep a simple rhythm. Regardless of the reasons for my selection, I enjoyed being given special treatment.

This suggests that teachers were not fully aware of the physical and mental limitations of students with special health concerns. Given that "one in every 400 black newborns in the United States suffers from sickle cell anemia or a variant of the disease" (Sickle Cell Anemia, 1971), it is important that educators are knowledgeable of certain diseases, particularly since demographic projections indicate that the American public educational system will serve primarily African American and other minority youths. Thus, consciousness-raising programs and services are mandatory as more of these students enter postsecondary settings.

Contrary to other participants, Richard Allen's dilemma regarding school was fueled by his family. Richard's negative perception of public school was formed by his mother's insistence that public schools were not for him and by his brother's characterization of public school as being nothing but fun. When Richard's mother consented to his going to public school, he went with very low expectations.

Richard constantly compared his experiences in public school to those in Catholic school. Of the two, Richard preferred to go to public school because he "had more fun and didn't have to do much homework." He preferred public school because he felt "comfortable and among friends . . . like (he) belonged there." He preferred public school because he "didn't have to put out much academic effort. The lessons were easy because (he) had already had them in Catholic school."

> After completing ninth grade, my mother again allowed me
> to return to the public school. I was happy to be with my
> brother and my friends. I tried out for the football team. I
> made it but had to sit out for the first year. I had a very
> uneventful time at school. I liked being with my people, but
> I found that I didn't have to put out much academic effort.
> Much of the lessons we were having were easy to me because
> I had already had them in the Catholic school, especially
> English, math and science.

However, what seems to have been overlooked by Richard's mother and his teachers was his constant need to fight. Richard could never explain the reasons for the fights. According to him, "(he) had to fight and liked to fight." Neither his mother nor his teachers were willing to admit that the fighting, perhaps, was symptomatic of something deeper. Neither was willing to acknowledge that changing schools was not the answer. Thus, here again, a student needed the benefit of sensitive, intuitive teachers. The absence of such made school problematic for Richard.

Apparently, Richard was a troubled youth, searching for answers. Seemingly, his only release was through fighting. Regardless of the school setting, Richard was always fighting. In the Catholic school, his fight was not only physical, but he also fought "the burden of acting white" (Fordham, 1985). He explains:

> When I was in the Catholic schools, I always felt like I

couldn't be myself. I had to act normally, even different from the way I acted at home. It was like I had to act white for the teachers . . . and it seemed as though I had to act white in order for my classmates to like and befriend me.

Although Richard found some superficial peace in public school "among his own cultural community" (Perry, 1988), he was unable to resolve the issues that attributed to his constant fighting.

As Richard and others such as he return to postsecondary settings, many of them have not resolved their inner problems. Thus, it is imperative that colleges and universities provide programs and services that will assist non-traditional students in resolving academic and personal issues and problems.

Advocacy for Change

It seems safe to conclude that the lived experiences of the marginalized groups, particularly African Americans, coupled with current data infer that issues that have most affected and impacted the education of their youths- - poverty, language barriers and physical and emotional handicaps - - have been historically and systematically ignored in the normal system of American education. The following research support the voices of this study that further establish the need for the program recommendations and, in fact, serve as advocacies for change.

A 1989 study conducted by the National Academy of Science concluded that "Blacks in America trail Whites in all aspects of quality of life - - from economics and health to education and housing - - because of persistent discrimination and the lagging economy of the past two decades" (p. 1). The study found that the chasm between African Americans and European Americans is as wide as ever, despite the gains of the 60s and 70s.

Other findings of the study showed that economically, the median income (1986) for African American families was $17,604 and $30,809 for

European Americans making the poverty rate of African American families between two and three times that of European Americans. Educationally, African American high school youths dropped out at twice the rate of European American youths and are likely to attend college at less than half the rate of European Americans. The probability that African Americans will abuse alcohol and drugs is greater than that for European Americans. Socially, African Americans are twice as likely to be victims of crimes, while African American men particularly, have a six time greater chance of being victims of a homicide.

Added to this, Harold Hodgkinson's (1986) projections for the youth who will begin the decade of the 90s as ten year olders reveal that one third of them are nonwhite; twenty-four percent will live below the poverty line; eighteen percent were born out of wedlock; and twenty percent of the girls will experience pregnancy as teenagers.

Unfortunately, the numbers and the percentages maintain the same flavor at the state, local and school district levels throughout the country. In Orleans parish, for instance, a study from the New Orleans Council for Yououng Children in Need reported the following: that forty-five percent of children under five live in poverty, failing to receive proper nutrition or education; that one out of five births is to a teenager; that the infant mortality rate is highest in the state; that fewer than half of poor children attend preschool; that one out of five first and seventh grade students are held back; and that fewer than half of the students graduate from high school (New Orleans Council, 1988). In fact, the entire graduation rate for the state from public high schools was "49th of the 50 states and the District of Columbia. The state's rate was 60.1 percent compared to 71.1 percent in 1987" (State Graduation, 1989, p. 8).

The level of minority underachievement in basic computational skills was revealed in a study, "Everyone Counts," (1989) conducted by U.S. mathematicians and scientists. For Louisiana, a dismal picture was painted: more than half of the state's college freshmen must take remedial courses, the average math ACT score is 15.2 as compared to the national average of 17.2.

Finally, in an eight southern state region, Louisiana ranked last in mathematics performance of eleventh grade students. In addition to the aforementioned facts, other data suggest that the educational system has gone awry because of various other reasons and influences.

Giroux (1988; 1989) offers insights into the problematics of the educational system as influenced by the last two presidential eras. On the Reagan era, he purports that education, particularly school curriculum, has been manipulated by corporations under the guise of investing in our children. "For students," he writes, "learning is often reduced to the exercise of lifeless paperwork, the 'mastery of knowledge that has little to do with their own experiences'" (1988, p. 8). His research of the Reagan era led him to conclude that education and "learning were defined in ways that ignored the diversity of experiences, traditions, voices, histories and community traditions that students bring to school" (1989, p. 729).

Educators, parents, theorists and business-people are now acknowledging the reality of what has happened in education with powerfully profound statements. A national education advisor comments, "the country's educational system has operated on the faulty premise that a certain number of students are destined to fail" (p. B-2). An education analyst adds, "The whole system is biased against kids who don't already know what teachers are trying to teach" (Pierre, April 6, p. B-4). A group of educators from an urban school district notes the importance of apprizing the public of two fundamental lessons:

> (1) the future of our country depends upon the strength of our city schools; the city schools are as essential to the national welfare as America's military bases are to the national security; and (2) our country can not afford to write off and child's future; all children can larn. (Green, et al., 1988, pp. 1-2)

William Spady, director of the High Success Program on Outcome-

Based Education, said "educators should rethink some 'sacred cows' of education such as the grade structure and the nine-month calendar, both entrenched in this country's education system" (Pierre, 1991, April 6, p. B-4). The local superintendent, Thomas Tocca, commented, "restructuring entails a willingness to change, a fundamental change which strikes at the heart of our cherished assumptions and time-honored paradigms" (Pierre, p. B-2).

I submit that one facet of the renaissance has to be in the area of curriculum. There needs to be a change in curricula direction—one that prepares for the demographic predictions of a minority majority and one that must go far beyond the superficial gestures of including a few African American studies programs or courses in the curriculum. McCarthy (1990) observes:

> Continued Anglocentric dominance in the content and organization of American school curricula underscores the fact that educators have merely paid lip service to minority demands for greater inclusion of knowledge about the history and culture of Hispanics, blacks and Native American. (p. 130)

This becomes the challenge for educators—to understand how the experiences of African American students have affected them, to learn from them and to work through those lessons to make the school activities meaningful. Will it happen? Will education for the twenty-first century become sensitive to the diverse needs of students or will it continue to be standardized by a curriculum designed to maintain the status quo? However, there have been warnings to the consequences of maintaining the status quo. A perspective from corporate America is reflected in the words of Owen Bradford Butler, retired chairman of Proctor and Gamble: "As poverty, crime and related ills tear at the fabric of American life, taxpayers are faced with two choices: Raise a generation of children who will contribute to the country's growth or be prepared to watch them destroy it" (Woods, 1989, p. B-1).

Hodgkinson (1986) echoes that position in these terms: "if they (minorities) succeed in life, non-minorities will benefit. If they fail, all of our lives will be diminished" (p. 174).

Theoretical perspectives within the literature suggest that whatever is decided relative to curriculum policies and classroom practices today will determine the direction of education and its students for the twenty-first century (Apple, 1983; Beckum, Zimmy & Fox, 1989; Ediger, 1989; Grant, 1989; Wells & Morrison, 1985). Apple (1983) comments:

> It is crucial that we debate now the questions of what we should teach, how it should be organized, who should make the decisions, and what educators should and can do about (and in) a society of large and growing disparities in wealth and power. (p. 325)

In this debate, I suggest that the critical theorists have the most realistic perspective.

Challenge for Curriculum

Glenn (1989) feels that it is essential that curriculum and pedagogy be culturally sensitive and show respect for human diversity. He suggests that the society needs "an approach to education that takes seriously the lived culture of children and their families" (p. 779).

Glenn's (1989) proposition that two kinds of schools fail to serve poor and minority students well.

> (1) . . . segregated schools in which drill is stressed and expectations are low, schools in which a dismal miasma of failure hangs over students and teachers alike; (2) . . . integrated schools in which they are an unwelcome foreign presence - - schools that make no pedagogical adjustments

to respond to their strengths or to meet their needs. (p. 777)

Grant (1989) adds:

> In order to help as many urban students as possible, the
> curriculum must be neither sterile nor remote from the lives
> of urban students. It must be relevant to their lives, but it
> must also provide a range of possibilities for the future, if it
> is to encourage students to pursue positive goals and dreams.
> (p. 769)

To achieve this end Giroux (1988) advocates:

> A type of critical pedagogy fundamentally concerned with
> student experience: it takes the problems and needs of the
> students themselves as its starting point. This suggests both
> confirming and legitimating the knowledge and experience
> through which students give meaning to their lives. (p. 257)

If there is any chance of such a paradigm, one of critical praxis, coming to
fruition, MacDonald (1988) prescribes the manner in which it must begin:

> Our activities, efforts and expectations should be focused
> upon the ideas, values, attitudes, and morality of persons in
> school in the context of their concrete lived experiences; and
> our efforts should be toward changing consciousness in these
> settings toward more liberating and fulfilling outcomes.
> (p. 161)

Proponents of critical praxis, of which I am one, emphasize the
importance of personal experiences and maintain that reflection and revelation
of the private life activities of students will ultimately lead to education.

"Schooling, they believe, is not likely to provide intellectual experience that becomes internalized unless students participate in the formulation of their goals" (Eisner, 1985, p. 71).

Similarly, the personal relevance orientation to curriculum supports the theory--

> that for experience to be educational, students must have some investment in it–must have some hand in its development–and that without actual participation or the availability of real choices within the curriculum schooling is likely to be little more than a series of meaningless routines, tasks undertaken to please someone else's conception of what is important. (Eisner, p. 69)

These curriculum concepts allow the student to become his or her own person. Dr. Asa Hilliard, a noted professor of urban education who recently supervised a major university's curriculum revision asserts that "everyone needs to see themselves (sic) as a participant, not just a spectator. It motivates them to do more, to study, to read where they had not read before" ("Educators Debate," 1990, p. A-13).

Recent literature proclaims that teachers can not help urban students learn to empower themselves and take care of their lives if the curriculum focuses on raising test scores and ignores or marginalizes the history, culture, lifestyles and structural constraints that surround urban students (Adler,1900; Alter & Denworth, 1900; Fulghum, 1990; McCormick, 1990; Morganthau, 1990; Wyman, 1990). Nonetheless, to challenge the existing historical system and attempt to move into a different curriculum direction will be a monumental task, to say the least. Doll (1988) describes it best:

> Developing a curriculum based on instability and uncertainty is frightening. It requires a major attitudinal change. At the practical level this means a willingness to open the curri-

culum, as well as methods of instruction, to public scrutiny and debate. It means the curriculum must undergo change as it is being delivered; that ends must be ends-in-view, not absolutes. It means that a major change must occur in the teacher-student relationship, particularly as each gropes to understand the other. (pp. 128-129)

This study and other studies have shown that these critical perspectives are valid and must be given consideration if there is any hope of students experiencing success. For example, a study which surveyed GED candidates reported that the factor cited most often for their dropping out of school was a feeling of "disengagement" from school (American Council on Education, 1991). Directors of that study said, "The results of this study suggest that adult educators should examine previous schooling experiences in order to recommend appropriate educational strategies for adult learners" (American Council on Education, p. 3). In similar manner, I submit that the findings of this study have certain implications for curricula reform for non-traditional students. Therefore, the following recommendations will enhance the experiences and facilitate the success of non-traditional African American first generation college students.

Recommendations

A Census Bureau survey found that 3.3 million college students were thirty years older in 1989–double the figure fifteen years ago (Older students, 1991, p. G-11). Hence, college and universities must make some changes to meet the challenges of these non-traditional students. These students, manipulating families, jobs and school assignments, face challenges that most of their younger classmates could never imagine. Therefore, it is important that curriculum planner possess the vision to establish programs that are consistent with the life situations and personal experiences of these students.For example, it is highly likely that as these students return to school, they are accompanied by the duties and responsibilities of parenting. Clearly, then, child care programs are needed as co-curricular to academics. An associate director of a university based Center for the Education of Women reports that "the way financial aid is calculated doesn't provide support for child care" (Older students, p. G-11). With this being a reality, I recommend that colleges and universities establish child care facilities which are campus-based or at least under their jurisdiction. Child-care facilities associated with the university would mean that parenting responsibilities would not necessarily interfere with school attendance. I recommend that such a program would have two specific components: one designed for care of pre-school children and one designed for school-age children. In the child care program, pre-schoolers would receive general physical, hygienic care while the school-age child would receive tutoring and assistance in home assignments.

I submit that this recommendation is very practical and would be in tune with the needs of participant Patricia Dawson and the many others like her. According to an Associated Press survey, "one in every five women in college was 35 or older in 1989" (Older students, p. G-11). This is significant considering that fifteen years before, the figure was only one in eight. Many of these women who return to school with commitment and dedication could very easily become detracted by their need for babysitters and their desire to assist their children with home assignments. Thus, I propose that the experiences of non-traditional students will be greatly enhanced by child care programs associated with the college or university which these students attend.

Closely aligned to the students described above are the many non-traditional students who return to educational settings with many unresolved personal issues. As such, it becomes important that schools provide services that will help students to resolve or, at best, cope with their situations. Therefore, as non-traditional students return to school, I recommend that colleges and universities establish counseling programs focusing specifically on mental health services. A campus-based mental health service will be a supportive service to those non-traditional students who enter with personal problems ad those who may be experiencing stress in their current life situations as well. These students need professional assistance to effectively confront their life situations and personal environment. A campus-based counseling program would be readily accessible to students and could enhance their ability to effect a balance in their lives and their ability to remain in school.

Such a program should begin as a free service and may be staffed by faculty and/or graduate assistants with the appropriate expertise. Also, the fear of and stigma that people usually attach to mental health services may mean that the program will have to be advertised creatively–not to deceive the students, but also not to discourage their patronage. The directors and advocates of the program will also need to sensitize the campus to the goals and objectives of the program as well as appraise them of the signs and symptoms of a student in distress, such as those which were displayed by participants Daniel Kelley and Richard Allen–behavior which regularly interfered with effective classroom management; high levels of irritability including unruly, violent and abrasive behavior; and poorly prepared work inconsistent with previous work.

I propose that if students avail themselves of services that assist them with stressful, problematic areas of their lives, they are more likely to experience academic success and more likely to persist in school. Thus, I strongly recommend that colleges and universities establish mental health counseling programs to assist their students during their difficult times.

In addition to the aforementioned program, I propose that colleges and universities should establish monitoring programs specifically for non-traditional students. A dean of admissions suggests that most non-traditional students "demand a personal relationship with their professors, unlike their younger classmates who may sit in the back of the class to escape notice" (Older students, p. G-11). In contrast, these students are searching for teacher relationships. They need relationships that engender a strong sense of understanding and appreciation and that will continue to motivate them. Such a relationship can increase the effectiveness of the curriculum by helping students focus on the connection between their life, career and personal goals.

The university should carefully select mentors who will provide supportive and nurturing experiences for non-traditional students. The mentors should be persons who will serve as consistent and reliable sources of encouragement and inspiration. Within the structure of this mentoring program, non-traditional students should be able to build self-confidence, should become creative problem solvers and should be able to minimize their weakness while building on their strengths. Because non-traditional students usually return to school consumed with fear and anxiety, a mentoring program will make their transition less frightening. Thus, the mentoring program is my last but most important recommendation, for it is this program that will make students feel comfortable as they return to educational settings.

To be sure, these are just a few programs that address the challenges issued by the critical theorists. I submit that the continuing challenge for educators and theorists is to make a difference in the lives of urban high school students and non-traditional, first generation college students by assisting them to empower themselves and to improve the quality of their lives through education. I submit that learning for empowerment can happen only by providing students with a meaningful curriculum transmitted by a cadre of dedicated, sensitive educators. I maintain that if the messages deployed, both explicitly and implicitly, through this research and that if these recommendations for curriculum-related programs are given serious consideration for implementation, there is a ray of hope as we enter the new millennium.

CHAPTER 6

Attitudes and Attribution that Influence the Academic Performance of Students of Color

Gwen Spencer

Introduction

Despite the challenges to academic achievement – economic, cultural, emotional, familial, and social –and despite overt and covert acts of prejudice, there are students of color who are persisting and succeeding. Although these challenges can not be minimized, understanding the attitudes and beliefs that contribute to the *successful* academic achievement of ethnic minority students is critical to nurturing and supporting ethnic minority educational achievement. This chapter explores causal attribution and self-efficacy tendencies among African American, Native American and Hispanic college students. Implications for educational support and intervention are discussed in light of the ethnic minority student's attribution belief patterns.

"Causal attribution" is defined as the explanation that an individual uses to understand his or her circumstances and experiences. It is not necessarily a factual or scientific explanation but rather "…how it seems to me" (Weiner, 1986). Academic achievement is inextricably linked to the causal attributions that an individual makes about her learning success or lack of success. A student who believes she can manage her academic success is more likely to persist when facing obstacles. Once successfully negotiating obstacles, that same student is more likely to believe that she can manage future educational challenges (Smith & Price, 1996).

Research to date indicates that academically successful Caucasian university students tend to attribute their achievement to both their "effort" as well as their "ability" (Pintrich & Schunk, 1996; Platt, 1988; Weiner & Kukla, 1979). In other words, the student's success is credited jointly to personal abilities (intelligence, creativity, and artistic or physical strengths) and to hard work or discipline. This attribution pattern appears consistent with the values of self-reliance and individuality historically characteristic of the cultures within Western Europe and the United States.

However, African American, Hispanic and Native American cultures, when compared to the majority Caucasian American culture, are considered to be more "collective" with an orientation to the group, the family, or the tribe. This orientation to the "collective" has potential implications for the attributional beliefs of ethnic minority individuals who may more strongly identify with community and family. Because the aggregate of African American, Hispanic and Native American students has not academically achieved at rates comparable to Caucasian and Asian American students, there is the question of whether culture and the educational legacy of ethnic minority students impact attributional beliefs and motivation. The question for exploration in this chapter is "How academically achieving ethnic minority students attribute their success in ways that parallel or differ from achieving Caucasian students?"

This chapter is organized into three primary sections. Section One is a general discussion of attributional beliefs as related to achievement particularly, academic achievement. The Second Section examines critical differences and similarities of attributions and self-efficacy for ethnic minority students. Finally, Section Three offers strategies for assessing and addressing attributional issues with ethnic minority students.

Academic Motivation and Attribution

Motivation to learn is critical to the acquisition of skills, concepts and academic disciplines. It is the process that sustains goal-directed activity and it is demonstrated in the choice of task, the level of persistence, and the achievement level or mastery of a task (Pintrich & Schunk, 1996). Motivation impacts new learning as well as the application of previously acquired knowledge. According to Ugurolglu and Walberg, the correlation between learning and motivation is unequivocally positive (Wlodkowski, 1985).

How a student attributes her academic successes or failures has implications for the direction and degree of motivation that she expends toward her course work. The student that excels educationally is more likely to attribute academic achievement to her effort and abilities than the student whose achievement is marginal or inadequate. Weiner and Kukla (1979) demonstrated in their research that the individual high in achievement motivation is "...more internal with respect to success..." and perceives that she has "...more ability and (can) expend more effort, than subjects low in achievement motivation" (p. 5). As might be expected, there is some motivational benefit to maintaining a sense of ownership and pride over one's achievements. Even when faced with a crisis, the academically achieving student is motivated because she believes that she can handle the challenge by expending a commensurate amount of energy or effort.

Conversely, evidence suggests that "underachievers" may not seek out help because they strongly attribute their failures to uncontrollable factors and may believe that it is unlikely that support can make any difference in their achievement level. The underachieving student, clearly in need of an "academic life jacket," often continues to flail when there are many educators waiting and wanting to assist.

Motivational researchers have observed that the student who fails academically tends to ascribe his lack of achievement to external factors far more frequently than the student who succeeds academically does. This "self-serving bias" permits the individual student who is experiencing failure a way to maintain some sense of self-esteem and hope for the future (Arkin & Maruyana, 1979, p. 85). The student can thereby escape culpability for failure because the outcome was created by something that "happened to me" rather than something that "I created." The student who attributes her failures exclusively to lack of ability is likely to escape a negative reaction from others who believe that the failure is due to the student's uncontrollable limitations. However, this same attributional belief frequently creates a fatalistic "What's the use of trying?" attitude within the student who believes that no amount of trying can alter her inevitable failure. Attributing academic failure exclusively to a lack of effort allows the student to "save face" in the short term and to hold out the option that success is possible in the future. To believe that poor grades are not due to poor cognitive abilities or preparation allows the student to continue to believe that her success is still attainable with more effort.

There appears to be an inverse negative relationship between academic achievement and the ethnic minority student's attribution to external variables like "luck," "difficulty of classes," and "events outside of the student's control" (Spencer, 1998). A student who attributes his grades to external factors is more likely to share problems like, "This professor rambles when he lectures and nobody can figure out what's important" or "The bookstore ran out of textbooks for the class and my book won't arrive for at least another week." This external attribution may cause a student not to fully accept his failing grade on a first exam because he believes that "I can still Ace the class because the professor said we can throw out our worst test grade and this is the one that I am going to throw out."

There is evidence that a college freshman who believes that academic achievement is a reflection of *both* ability and effort is more likely to succeed than the student who primarily attributes achievement to either effort or ability (Platt, 1988). Attributions to effort and ability are optimal for academic achievement. By ascribing academic success only to personal effort, the student creates a serious dilemma when he experiences setbacks or failures. At these junctures, the student may believe that he does not have what it takes to master college coursework. On the other hand, the student who ascribes her academic success only to her ability has a tendency to become too confident and therefore does not expend the necessary effort to maintain consistent college achievement. Thus it appears that the "...most desirable state of affairs for students is that they leave high school with a balanced perception of both their ability and effort as causes of academic achievement" (Platt, p. 577).

Academic Motivation and Attribution for Students of Color

Understanding the issues related to attribution and self-efficacy for African American, Hispanic, and Native American College students is critical to their persistence and success. Since so many ethnic minority students must overcome so many academic and social obstacles, it would be anticipated that there is a need for greater resolve and motivation to achieve educational goals among this group (Geraldi, 1990). But the attributional beliefs and motivation for ethnic minority students may differ significantly from the beliefs that fuel academically achieving Caucasian students. Research conducted during the last two decades suggests a number of motivational differences between ethnic minority students and Caucasian students. However, within this relatively small body of research, there are conflicting results that may be caused by the differences in ethnic and linguistic perceptions as well as socio-economic variables. .

African American, Hispanic, and Native American students attribute their academic success to their ability, their effort, the time they spent on their studies, and their "willingness to keep on trying even in the face of disappointment or failure" (Spencer, 1998). A Multiple Regression Analysis demonstrates a significant and positive relationship between academic achievement, as measured by the student's Grade Point Average, and the student's attribution to "ability." In other words, the better the student's academic achievement; the more likely the student is to attribute his success to his abilities and competence. Identification of one's "ability" as essential to academic achievement is an attribution that is apparently shared by both Caucasian students and ethnic minority students.

There is a notable difference between the attributions of ethnic minority women and men with regard to the importance of their achievement attributed to the help or assistance of university faculty and staff. Ethnic minority female students were much more likely to attribute their academic achievement to the support from others than ethnic minority male students were (Spencer, 1998). This gender difference may be linked to the dominant American cultural belief that it is more acceptable for women to request or value professional support and assistance regardless of ethnicity. Additionally, there may be cultural expectations particularly among African Americans and Hispanics men that they should remain self sufficient and strong (Jenkins, 1994; Olivas, 1994). This situation may be exacerbated by the hesitancy of some Caucasians to offer assistance to African American males who are perceived to be potentially confrontational and aggressive. Closer examination of each ethnic minority cohort, African American, Native American, Hispanic, further elucidates similar and differing attributional and self-efficacy issues for student achievement.

For African American students, the research on motivation and attribution does not validate the notion that for African Americans, self-concept and academic achievement are somehow interdependent. African Americans appear to sustain beliefs about their personal control and have a high expectancy and a positive self-regard. This perception in light of the underachievement of many African Americans appears to be a somewhat unrealistic and exaggerated attitude (Graham, 1994, p. 108). It would seem likely that personal success and academic achievement would influence an individual's self-esteem. Yet this does not reflect the African American experience. This apparent disparity has generated a number of hypotheses among educators.

According to Steele many ethnic minority students, particularly African Americans, are able to maintain a sense of positive self-concept by discounting the importance or relevance of academic evaluation (Pintrich & Schunk, 1996). In other words, the African American believes that his worth can not be measured by what is largely an Euro-American educational system. Instead, the American educational system measures what a Western culture values and strives to perpetuate. For some ethnic minority students, there may be a sense that the educational benchmarks of achievement should more accurately measure their own cultural values and standards. Steele (1992) captures this dilemma in his statement describing the African American student's perception that "... you must first master the culture and ways of the American mainstream, and since that mainstream (as it is represented) is essentially white, this means you must give up the particulars of being black..." (p. 77).

Still another viewpoint is articulated by Crocker, Voelkl, Testa and Major (1991) who believe that African Americans may discount negative evaluation believing that their assessment reflects racially biased attitudes toward Blacks. Even positive academic evaluations may be discounted because the African American student believes that the grade is a tempered by the (Caucasian) educator's desire to appear unprejudiced. Thus, African American students may minimize the importance and credibility of both the negative or positive evaluations that they receive.

Ogbu submits that the African American may be inclined to discount academic achievements as a measure of self worth because good grades and diplomas do not necessarily result in occupational and economic benefits of the Caucasian American (Jenkins, 1995). National comparative salary tables illustrate a wide gap between annual salaries of educated Caucasians and educated African Americans particularly with males would certainly validate this perception. This assumption is reflected in the following, "Doing well in school requires a belief that school achievement can be a promising basis of self-esteem and that belief needs constant reaffirmation even for advantaged students (Steele, 1992, p. 72). Educators have observed that some African Americans may maintain their self-esteem by de-emphasizing school achievement and giving more credence to peer-group relations where there is a sense of more personal control to negotiate positive outcomes.

A study conducted by Taylor and Olswang (1997) reveals that African American students, attending a predominantly white university, believed that certain personal characteristics are necessary to academic success. Fifty-nine percent believed that self-confidence, cultural pride and determination were essential to their achievement academically. On the other hand, only 14 percent of the African American students believed that study skills and academic preparation were necessary for success. A strong majority of the students believed that they were as qualified as any other student and that their success was within their personal control.

Inherent in all of these hypotheses, the African American students appear to have disengaged their academic achievement level from their intellect or abilities. Rather, how the students consider non-cognitive variables, like effort and external evaluation are seen as determinants of their academic achievement. The attributional research does not confirm that African Americans' achieve less success due to a negative self-concept of their ability.

Educational researcher, Graham, who reviewed sixty-three cogent studies on motivation, observed that African Americans appear to have scores that are more external than Whites on the internal-external continuum. Graham notes that the "...patterns of externality and perceived uncontrollability may actually be adaptive, not maladaptive..." (Pintrich & Schunk, 1996, p. 144). The African American who ignores the realities of educational and economic disparity might be unable to access and address his current, albeit difficult, realities. When the differential of economic conditions is taken into account, the research is inconclusive regarding any differences between Caucasians and African Americans regarding attribution to external versus internal causes.

The research literature is even more limited for Hispanics than African American's achievement motivation and attribution. Nonetheless, a few attributional studies among Latino students are worth citing. For Hispanics, there appear to be differences in attribution patterns between male and female students. Valencia (1991) noted that attributions of academically successful Hispanic females were more likely to credit their success to their family while Hispanic males were more likely to attribute their success to their own ability and effort. Research conducted by Granada indicated that Hispanic women in particular note that the willingness of their parents to encourage independence and autonomy was highly beneficial to later academic and professional achievement (Valencia, 1991).

Hispanic students appear to share several attributional attitudes with Caucasian students. Dalah's (1988) study showed evidence that Hispanics and Caucasians make dispositional attributions for positive behavior leading to success with members of the same ethnic group (1990). At the same time, Hispanics and Caucasians make fewer negative behavior attributions for members of the same ethnic group (Dalah).   Also, Powers and Rossman (1984) observed that Hispanics, like Caucasian students, tend to attribute their failure to the context of the task, an uncontrollable event.

Minimal research has been coring the attributional beliefs of Native Americans and Alaskan Natives.   Powers and Rossman (1984) observed that Native Americans tended to attribute their educational failure to a lack of effort, a pattern that parallels the attribution patterns of African Americans.

Hispanic, Native American and African American students may share a perception that one way to reconcile their "lower" grades and test scores is to discount the importance of their ability in achievement.   Herein lies a critical point of reconciliation for many ethnic minority students.   In order to achieve successfully, ethnic minority students must believe in their ability to compete successfully.   Yet the potential for receiving negative evaluation of their academic work is quite likely for many students of color.   This results in students downplaying the significance of their innate ability to achievement. It is less threatening to the student's self-perception to attribute the inevitable "ups and down's" of academic performance to a proportional amount of effort and time extended by the student.

Implications and Interventions With Students of Color

Ethnic minority students who are achieving most successfully are those who attribute their achievement to their academic ability and not just to their effort.   Therefore, it is critical that, beginning in elementary school, students of color hear from others and then internalize a self-respect for their capability and competence.   Believing that it is only the time they spend studying and their effort that translates into academic achievement is likely to result in discouragement and futility when they are faced with setbacks and failures.

Research points to the importance of hardiness and self-efficacy to the ongoing achievement of ethnic minority students. Educators, family members and community persons, can facilitate a student's success by helping students deal with their failures and disappointments. By encouraging the ethnic minority student and debriefing his failures, the student can enhance his own sense of inner strength and stamina. Highlighting role models and identifying mentors who have overcome obstacles and failures offer students of color the hope and skills to deal with their own downfalls and disappointments. Whether it is a personal reality or not, students of color more than Caucasian students, do not believe that they are prepared for a four-year university experience. Even among those ethnic minority students who are generally succeeding academically and have set high educational aspirations, there appears to still be some feeling of academic underpreparedness or shortcomings (Spencer, 1998).

Even when an ethnic minority student is experiencing marginal academic achievement, it may be advantageous to focus on what she did "right" and not focus exclusively on her shortcomings. The academically struggling student is frequently already focused on her "failures" and therefore tends to dismiss her ability and skills. Initially, the exploration of the student's strength may seem incongruent in light of the academic performance but ultimately it is the student's belief in her capability that will result in persistence. Assessment of what contributed to a poor academic performance should include not only "what do you need to do differently?" but also "what did you do well last term?" and "what have you learned from this experience?"

One area in need of further exploration and research is the role that religious beliefs may have the lives and learning of ethnic minority students. Without a better understanding of the role of religion, a strong reservoir of inner direction and strength for ethnic minority individuals has frequently been overlooked by educators (Blaine & Crocker, 1995; Jenkins, 1995; Stevens-Arroyo, 1995). Not only may religion be influential to the individual students but partnerships between churches and schools may also facilitate improved educational success of ethnic minority students.

Without question, ethnic minority students have a better chance of succeeding educationally, emotionally, and economically if obstacles to access and achievement can be addressed. At the same time, it is critical to identify and to encourage the cultural and personal beliefs that ethnic minority students use to mitigate their obstacles and maximize their opportunities. Understanding the motivation and the causal attribution beliefs of ethnic minority students can result in improving their educational persistence and success. Since ethnic minority students will become the new majority in the 21st century, educators are challenged to not simply address the academic deficiencies but also affirm the strengths within each student.

CHAPTER 7

The Relationship of Achievement and Academic and Support Services for Native American College Students

Frances Swayzer Conley

Introduction

Education for Native Americans in the United States has almost always been fraught with difficulty. Harvard, William and Mary, and Dartmouth made early attempts to provide education for indigenous peoples, according to the Carnegie Foundation for the Advancement of Teaching (CFAT) (1989). These early attempts appeared to have as their real motive the procurement of funds for the institutions, not the education of native Americans. These efforts were aimed at inculcating European values into the American Indian experience (CFAT; Wright & Tierney, 1991). Such early attempts failed because they ignored or negated the peculiarities of Native American cultures (CFAT; Tierney & Kidwell, 1991; Wright & Tierney, 1991).

In 1825, a unique cooperative effort among the Choctaw Tribe, the Baptist church, and the federal government led to the founding of Choctaw Academy near Georgetown, Kentucky. Choctaw was a significant institution for 20 years (Oppelt, 1990). Oppelt described its academic programs as advanced. Among its offerings were such courses as arithmetic, astronomy, English grammar, geography, history, moral philosophy, natural philosophy, practical surveying, vocal music, and writing. Manual training was added some years after the founding, Oppelt reported. Financial exiguity, shifting tribal attitudes and support, changing political arrangements and federal policies, and loss of local support led to the demise of this institution.

Then in 1880, Baptists founded Bacone College in Oklahoma with a land grant from the Creek Tribe (Wright & Tierney, 1991). Its founding purpose was to train Indians for the clergy, a purpose parallel to Harvard's founding mission with respect to the dominant American culture. There were three initial enrollees, but that figure had risen to 56 within 5 years. Wright and Tierney also reported that by the turn of the last century only a few Native Americans had entered institutions of higher education. As of the early 1930s, only 385 Native American college graduates had been identified.

By the end of World War I, approximately 2,000 native Americans had enrolled in some form of higher education. Although their numbers continued to grow, as late as 1966 only 1% of the Indian population was enrolled in college (Wright & Tierney, 1991). However, the ideal of a postsecondary education institution to involve Native Americans on a large scale had been envisioned by August Breuninger, a college educated Indian, as early as 1911:

> A University [sic] for Indians is the greatest step that we educated Indians could make in uniting our people. . . . It would eliminate the general conception–that an Indian consists of only feathers and paint. It would single us out as REALLY PROGRESSIVE [sic]. It would give us a better influence with the rising generation, by setting out our character in such a conspicuous manner as to be. . .observed and imitated. (CFAT, p. 23)

However, it was more than one-half century before this ideal became a reality. Providing for Native Americans to remain on their reservations and receive higher education in familiar settings did not appear to capture widespread interest beyond Native American cultures (Tierney & Kidwell, 1991).

The Inception of Tribal Colleges

In 1969, Navajo Community College in Tsaile, Arizona, opened--

making an important first in culturally oriented, reservation-based tertiary education for the Indians (Boyer, 1989-90; Oppelt, 1990; Raymond, 1986). Today there are 30 such institutions in 13 of the 48 contiguous states. Almost all are located on or near the reservations which they serve (Washington, 1993). Haskell Indian Nations University attracts students from 39 states and territories (*Peterson's Guide to Two-Year Colleges*, 1992). All of these institutions are public except D-Q University in Davis, California, and Bacone College in Bacone, Oklahoma. All are members of the American Indian Higher Education Consortium (AIHEC) except Bacone. Two institutions- -Haskell and Southwest Indian Polytechnic Institute (SIPI)- -in Albuquerque, New Mexico, have 100% Native American enrollments. All others, except Bacone, have majority native American enrollments.

Most tribal colleges are two-year institutions, according to *Peterson's Guide to Two-Year Colleges* (1992), and they are among the top 50 producers of native American associate degree graduates ("Special Report," 1995). Most of these colleges accept 100% of their applicants. These institutions enroll approximately 11,000 Native American students. Although these institutions are vital entities, Badwound (1991) suggested in his study of the influence of American Indian values on tribal college institutional life that tribal colleges were not effective in promoting tribal culture. He listed lack of financial support as a barrier to institutional efforts to transmit tribal culture.

Unmet Needs of Tribal College Students

Native American postsecondary students have an extensive record of cultural disjunction, poor academic performance, and attrition in the college environment (Beaty & Chiste, 1986; Beaulieu, 1991; Benjamin, Chambers, & Reiterman, 1993; Bold Warrior, 1992; Boyer, 1989-90; Browne & Evans, 1987; CFAT, 1989; Charleston, 1994; Coladarci, 1983; Falk & Aitken, 1984; Guyeth & Heth, 1983; Hill, 1991; Hoover & Jacobs, 1992; Huffman, Sill, & Brokenleg, 1986; Idaho Committee on Indian Education, 1993; "Indian Nations at Risk," 1992; Jensen, 1993; Lin, LaCounte, & Eder, 1988; Mooney, 1988; Pavel, 1992; Pego, 1994; Pottinger, 1989; Raymond, 1986; Reyhner, 1991; St. Pierre &

Rowland, 1990; Tippeconnic, 1988; Wright, 1990; Wright & Tierney, 1991). Houser (1991) reported that upon entering higher education institutions, Native American students have found the campuses to be too large and too unreceptive, creating feelings of loneliness and isolation (Hornett, 1989; Hurlburt, Gade, & McLaughlin, 1990; Pottinger, 1989; Reyhner, 1991; Wright, 1985) and subsequently leading to substantial attrition (Houser, 1991). Pottinger estimated Native American attrition to be as high as 75-85% in the Southwest. Tierney and Kidwell (1991) concurred with Pottinger with respect to the general tribal college population.

American Indian students are the least successful ethnic group in higher education (Benjamin et al., 1993). For example, less than 60% of the Native Americans who enter high school graduate; of those who graduate, only one third enter college. Of those who enter academe, only 15% receive baccalaureate degrees (Tierney & Kidwell, 1991). These statistics indicate little variance from those reported by Beaulieu (1991), Browne and Evans (1987), Hoover and Jacobs (1992), Kleinfeld, Cooper, and Kyle (1987), Red Horse (1986), and Wright and Tierney (1991).

Moreover, poor education is assumed to be a significant factor associated with other challenges to quality life among indigenous peoples. For instance, the extremely high rate of unemployment- -estimated to be as high as 80% (CFAT, 1989; Tierney, 1991)- -is a well documented reality of Native American life (Bold Warrior, 1992; Boyer, 1989-90; CFAT, 1989; Cohen, 1989; Mooney, 1988; Pottinger, 1989; Raymond, 1986; Tierney, 1991; Wright & Tierney, 1991). Elevated levels of alcoholism, tobacco use, and other forms of substance abuse, as well as other health issues, continue to plague Indians (Ben, 1992; Bold Warrior; 1992; Boyer, 1989-90; Cohen 1989; Flannery, 1992; French, 1992; Hodgkinson, 1992; Jensen, 1993; Lamarine, 1993; Noar, 1981; Raymond, 1986; Reyhner, 1991; Sanderson, 1980; Weibel-Orlando, Weisner, & Long, 1984; Wiley, 1989). In view of these problems besetting Native Americans, it appears that lack of adequate education is their most pervasive obstacle (Appleson, 1994; Beaty & Chiste, 1986; Beaulieu, 1991; Benjamin et al., 1993; Browne & Evans, 1987; Charleston, 1994; Coladarci, 1983; Falk &

Aitken, 1984; Guyeth & Heth, 1983; Hoover & Jacobs, 1992; Huffman et al., 1986; Idaho Committee on Indian Education, 1993; "Indian Nations at Risk, 1992; Jensen; Lin et al., 1988; Mooney, 1988; Pavel, 1992; Pego, 1993, 1994; Pottinger, 1989; Raymond, 1986; Reyhner; 1991; St. Pierre & Rowland, 1990; Tippeconnic, 1988; Wright, 1991; Wright, 1990; Wright & Tierney).

If Native American college students are to minimize the preponderance of the negatives for themselves and for posterity, they must have the empowerment of an appropriate education in an appropriate setting. Yet when these students have sought postsecondary education, certain conditions associated with tribal life have made it extremely challenging for them to persist. For example, because unemployment and its concomitant poverty are so prevalent among Native Americans, the vast majority of tribal college students quality for need-based financial assistance (Boyer, 1989-90; Houser, 1991; Wright & Tierney, 1991). Therefore, without financial aid, these students would not be able to enter college or to remain if the aid were withdrawn (Steward, 1993).

Another serious barrier for many tribal college students is that they are academically underprepared to master college-level work. Many reservation high schools do not have the resources to prepare students to succeed in college (Beaulieu, 1991; Hill, 1991; Raymond, 1986). In addition, high school drop-out rates among tribal students are the highest in the nation (Coladarci, 1983; Dehyle, 1992; Eberhard, 1989; Latham, 1985; Reyhner, 1991; Swisher & Hoisch, 1992; Tierney & Kidwell, 1991; Wright & Tierney, 1991). According to Mooney (1988) and Houser (1991), 40% of the students in tribal colleges have not earned a high school diploma. This statistic underscores the need for developmental courses to give these students the basic skills which they need to succeed in the regular curriculum.

Developmental courses alone, however, might not be sufficient. Other services critical to the support of underprepared students are the services provided by learning assistance centers. Typically, these services include developmental courses, as well as other essential components- - academic, career, intercultural, peer, and personal counseling services; learning skill development; tutorial services; diagnostic and placement services; and a resource or materials center (Hodgkinson, 1992; Osborne & Cranney, 1985, 1985; White & Schnuth, 1990). Prior to the college years, Native American students receive inadequate counseling services (Hoover & Jacobs, 1992). Generally, they have low motivation and aspirations (Falk & Aitken, 1984; Guyeth & Heth, 1983; St. Pierre & Rowland, 1990; Swisher & Hoisch, 1992; Tippeconnic, 1988), a present-time orientation (Hornett, 1989), and an external locus of control (Beaty & Chiste, 1986). Learning assistance center services would therefore give students appropriate out-of-class academic reinforcement, counseling, and goal-getting support.

Quite often students enter tribal colleges without being proficient in organizing and prioritizing their activities, in managing time wisely (Farabaugh-Dorkins, 1991; Osborne & Cranney, 1985), or in using effective study strategies (Falk & Aitken, 1984; St. Pierre & Rowland, 1990; Swisher & Hoisch, 1992). Further, they need help in budgeting their resources wisely (Falk & Aitken). Many of them have no experience with credit or credit cards and bank accounts (Cohen, 1989). They need assistance in wending their way through the college bureaucracy (Boyer, 1989-90; Kleinfeld et al., 1987). Consequently, college survival skills represent another acute need of tribal college students.

Since the typical tribal college student is a nontraditional student with children (Boyer, 1989-90; CFAT, 1989; Falk & Aitken, 1984; Farabaugh-Dorkins, 1991; Houser, 1991; Mooney, 1988), child care services are another critical issue. Just as critical are transportation assistance services because long distances, extreme climatic conditions and scarcity of vehicles are serious impediments to student transportation to and from college (Benjamin et al., 1993; Boyer; CFAT, 1989; Houser, 1991; Mooney). This situation is compounded by the small number of tribal colleges which have residence halls (Oppelt, 1990; Wicks & Price, 1981).

A recurrent theme surrounding tribal or nontraditional students' matriculation is their need to feel connected to institutional life without having to relinquish their cultural connectedness (Benshoff & Lewis, 1992; Browne

& Evans, 1987; "High Risk," 1992; Houser, 1991; Lin et al., 1988; Pavel, 1992; Wright, 1985, 1990). Commuter center services would provide a collegial, supportive environment for students to fraternize and form social enclaves (CFAT, 1989; Oppelt, 1990). Since many tribal college students must be away from their residences all day, a commuter center would ideally include provisions for students to have food (CFAT). Courses in students' tribal languages would also help students to feel connected (Boyer, 1989-90; Hodgkinson, 1992; Huffman et al., 1986) because they would help students to perpetuate their heritage in a casual comfortable environment.

Most students at tribal institutions come from communities where alcoholism and its related menaces are the highest in the nation (Bold Warrior, 1992; Boyer, 1989-90; Cohen, 1989; Dick, Manson, & Beals, 1993; Hodgkinson, 1992; Lamarine, 1993; Leung, Kinzie, Boehnlein, & Shore, 1993). Alcohol and substance abuse is prevalent among college students in general (Hodgkinson, 1992; Schuckit, Klein, Twitchell, & Springer, 1994); but Hodgkinson has identified Native American young people as being at greatest risk. A wellness/substance abuse program would enable tribal college students to have better access to information and services to address a number of health issues. Such a program would be significant in view of the high rates of fetal alcohol syndrome, diabetes, tuberculosis, suicide, homicide, spousal and child abuse, fatal automobile accidents, and shortened life expectancy among Native Americans (Bold Warrior, 1992; Boyer, 1989-90; Cohen, 1989; Hodgkinson, 1992; Noar, 1981; Raymond, 1986).

The compounded onus of these Native American phenomena makes college persistence especially difficult. Red Horse (1986) indicated that the educational attainment of Native Americans has remained unchanged over the years. Hoover and Jacobs (1992) estimated the Indian college student persistence rate to be 25%. Pego (1993) referred to a survey reported by Kidwell in which 79 postsecondary institutions tracked the success of their Native American students. These institutions also indicated that only 25% of the students persisted beyond the first year. This plight signals some specific implications for tribally controlled colleges, since they were established "to meet very specific tribal needs" (Pego, p. 18). The imperative for tribal institutions is to change the direction of education for Native Americans in two specific aspects: by implementing programs successful in attracting Native American students and by effecting substantive developmental education programs to support the students' college achievement and thereby curtail the high attrition rate among tribal college students.

A Synthesis of the Literature

Factors Affecting Achievement Among Tribal College Students

Huffman, Sill, and Brokenleg (1986) used two questionnaires to collect data for their investigation and comparison of the social, cultural, and aspirational factors related to college achievement among Sioux and Caucasian students. The random samples consisted of 38 Native Americans from a population of 128 and 48 Caucasians from an estimated population of 4,500. Both samples were drawn from students at the university of South Dakota and Black Hills State College. Because the dependent variable, college achievement, was operationalized to mean college GPA, no freshmen or graduate students were included in the study. These investigators used a combination of t-test and chi-square as their statistical techniques and tested their hypotheses using both a parametric and a nonparametric test, the Pearson R and the Spearman Rho, respectively.

The researchers grouped the independent variables into three sets of factors. Analysis if the results showed that two of the social factors--family income and parents' educational level--had no significant relationship to college achievement in their group of participants. However, high school GPA was significantly related to achievement for the Caucasian group, but not for the Native Americans. Among the cultural factors, neither college integration nor participation in college environment was significantly related to college GPA in either group of students. Native American traditionalism was significantly related to college GPA. Finally, among the aspirational factors--which used the Spearman Rho- -parents' educational aspirations were related to college achievement for the Caucasian sample. This finding, however, was not confirmed among the Native American sample. Students' educational aspirations did not appear to be related to college achievement for either group.

Huffman et al. (1986) reached two major conclusions. One was that among Caucasian students high school GPA and parental encouragement--which may show that factors leading to academic success are in preparation for college--were found to be related to higher educational attainment. Another was that among Sioux students success in college appeared to be related more to cultural identity. The implication was that where Indians perceived institutional disinterest in their cultural identity and heritage, they were less likely to experience a strong sense of self-identity and confidence. Mattering has also been cited by Schlossberg, Lynch, and Chickering (1989) as an important factor in keeping students involved in education. Considering the small sample size, one must exercise caution in generalizing these findings to larger populations.

In a similar study, Lin, LaCounte, and Eder (1988) sought to examine the effects of school environment on the academic performance and graduation expectation of Indian students in comparison to Caucasian students. Data were collected through questionnaires administered in regular classes at a four-year, mid-sized, predominantly Caucasian college in Montana and through questionnaires handed out at the Indian Career Service Center, where a sealed questionnaires receptacle was placed. The sample consisted of 632 students, 87 of whom were American Indians. There were 508 Caucasians, 21 other minorities, and 16 who did not declare their racial identity. The Indian sample size was basically representative of the general institutional Indian population. All academic classifications from freshmen to graduate students were included. The researchers used factor analysis on SPSS-X to reduce the ten Likert-type questions to four factors: (a) the feeling of hostility against Native Americans on campus, (b) attitude toward college, (c)attitude toward professor, and (d) feeling of isolation. These researchers ran the *t*-test to compare and contrast Native American and Caucasian students with respect to the perception of college environment, GPA, and the probability of obtaining a college degree.

Analysis of the findings of the Lin et al. (1988) study indicated significant differences between Native Americans and Caucasians on all four factors. The former group showed a lower GPA, but a more positive attitude toward college. Perceived hostility against them and sense of isolation were reported to be more pronounced among Native Americans. No statistically significant differences were reported between the groups in their perception of the probability of obtaining a college degree or their attitude toward professor. Interpretation of the results yielded two conclusions worthy of the attention of all tertiary-level educators: that despite the perceived hostility and isolation, Native Americans remained respectful of their professors--a reflection of their traditional upbringing--and that even in such an adverse environment these students displayed an awareness of the significance of a college education to their future. The authors of this study recommended high administrative support, specialized faculty, closely monitored courses, and an academic advisement office to improve campus environment for indigenous students. One possible flaw of this investigation was the seemingly unstructured distribution of questionnaires at the Indian Career Service Center. The researchers did not explain the procedure in this aspect of data collection. If there were no controls for the number of questionnaires a participant could complete, the integrity of the findings could be compromised. The t-test was the appropriate statistical technique for assessing differences between two groups (Isaac & Michael, 1990).

Tribal College Response to the Needs of Native Americans

Wicks and Price (1981) completed a qualitative study of the tribal college movement. This movement had been in effect only about a decade, and only 11 tribal colleges had been founded at the time that the study was conducted. Beyond Native American communities, not very much was known about these institutions; and not many researchers conducted their studies on this subject. Wicks and Price collected data for their report through on-site interviews with executive heads of 9 of the 11 tribally controlled colleges identified by the Bureau of Indian Affairs (BIA). They also collected data by examining status reports, Title III proposals, catalogues, handbooks, newsletters, and general brochures provided by the colleges under study. These investigators presented the overall mission of these colleges and the common institutional features revealed in their study.

Examination of data collected showed five general categories of purposes served by tribal colleges: (a) addressing tribal needs and concerns; (b) preparation for transfer to four-year institutions; (c) perpetuation of tribal culture, heritage, and history; (d) occupational education; and (e) adult and continuing education. However, Oppelt (1990) observed that at some tribal institutions there were discrepancies between espoused objective and actual programs. The researchers identified more than a dozen features common among the institutions. The first five centered upon administrative aspects:

1.   The tribal colleges were established by legal tribal charters.
2.   Most of the institutions existed under paternalistic control of sponsoring accredited institutions.
3.   The majority of the tribal colleges came into existence without any prior needs assessments or long-term plans for development.
4.   All except one were established in the early 1970s (1970-1973).
5.   Native Americans comprised the vast majority of the administrative and institutional personnel.

The remaining eight features, with the exception of the last one, shared a curricular theme:

1.   None of the institutions had student residence halls or athletic programs. However, Oppelt (1990) reported that by the time this datum was published one of the tribal colleges did have residence halls.
2.   Students at tribal colleges were older than their dominant-society cohorts, and there were more part-time than full-time students.

3.   The serious problems confronting the tribal colleges lay in the areas of facilities, financial resources, personnel, regional accreditation, and student services.

4.   The curricula mirrored academic requirements and cultural contributions and philosophies.

5.   Lack of public and private transit systems, long distance, poor roadways, and severe weather conditions created transportation problems.

6.   Tribal colleges employed an open-door admission policy.

7.   Instructional delivery was achieved under a dispersed or outreach concept of decentralization.

8.   All of the tribal colleges were members of AIHEC. The researchers concluded that though the tribal college movement was rather nascent, Native American institutions were attempting to respond to tribal needs. They further concluded that these institutions would likely become closely identified with American higher education, a prediction that has already materialized.

While the data reported in this study are useful to researchers, their usefulness may be limited by the absence of certain identifying data regarding the report itself. For instance, the investigators did not specify when the data were collected. Another possible limitation is that there was no obvious mechanism for including data on student progress and achievement. The researchers were silent on the data analysis procedures employed in their study.

Persistence Among Native American College Students

A study with significant implications for the present study was conducted by Martin (1993). He used the Student Adaptation to College Questionnaire (SACQ) to investigate factors that influence persistence and graduation among a special population at Little Big Horn College. The self-selected sample was limited to members of the Crow Tribe living on or near the reservation at Crow Agency, Montana, and concurrently enrolled at Little Big Horn. Martin examined five major areas of adjustment: (a) academic adjustment, (b) social adjustment, (c) personal emotional adjustment, (d) institutional attachment, and (e) full scale adjustment. In all five areas, Martin reported, these participants were generally below the norm for college freshmen and sophomores whom other researchers had sampled. He cautioned against viewing these results with alarm or negativity, and he described them as outcomes related to an educational process still in its infancy.

Martin also reported that in the college's 13-year existence 87 students had received Associate of Arts degrees and that nine students had earned professional certificates. Moreover, enrollment had risen to 200 by the spring of 1993. A full-time counselor had been employed to increase persistence and graduation rates. Further, he reported continued field-related faculty development. Another significant finding was that Little Big Horn had instituted a curriculum to strengthen institutional goals and to remain true to is founding mission. Administrators and faculty indicated willingness to network with external sources to improve educational services to students. This type of commitment and support is among Roueche (1984) 11 elements critical to a successful program for low-achieving students (Carbone, 1987; Osborne & Cranney, 1985).

Developmental Education and Tribal College Students

Osborne and Cranney (1985) carried out a study among 19 experienced full-time faculty members in the Indian Education Program at Brigham Young University. Their purpose was to examine the success of the program by comparing it with the 11 elements which Roueche (1984) had identified as critical to a successful program for low-achieving students. These elements were strong administrative support, mandatory assessment and placement, structured courses, award of credit, flexible completion strategies, multiple learning systems, volunteer paid instructors, use of peer tutors, monitoring of student behaviors, interfacing with subsequent courses, and program evaluation. These researchers collected data by means of interviews and questionnaires.

They organized their findings into three categories: (a) administrative support, (b) teaching-learning styles, and (c) monitoring student progress. Analysis of the data regarding the first category showed that all respondents singled out administrative support as the key element in the success of the program. They ranked the selection of faculty to teach basic skills and general education courses for Indian students as an important element. Also, all respondents cited control of courses as another key factor in the Indian students' success. The respondents ranked as salient features a financial aid office and an academic advisement office. Eighty percent of the participants listed as being vital a tutorial lab which focused primarily on basic skills. Other services, such as summer programs for high schoolers, a campuswide Indian club, annual observance of Indian week, leadership development activities, a quarterly news magazine, and funding a development program were also listed as essential to Native American students' success.

Analysis of the findings with respect to teaching-learning styles and the Native American revealed that most participants viewed Native American students as typically visual learners who approach learning holistically. Most also indicated that Native American students process information differently from the way that non-Native Americans do. However, the respondents showed no consensus regarding which teaching style was most effective for Indian students. Most respondents allowed for special help sessions and individualized office conferences, and they reported that students relied heavily on peers in the tutoring labs and in other support sessions.

Regarding the final category, analysis of the data indicated other significant points. Faculty were directed to report to the Advisement Center such student behaviors as excessive absenteeism, poor test scores, and homework delinquency. The Advisement Center, in turn, contacted these students to offer assistance through counseling and laboratory or personal counseling. The Advisement Center monitored students' progress through computer linkage to identify problem areas.

Most of the foregoing findings confirmed the 11 points of the 1984

Roueche study. Other findings confirmed some enduring assumptions among Indian educators. Those findings were the following:

1. Seventy percent of the participants indicated concern with Indian students' lack of English proficiency.
2. Almost all participants commented on student and faculty adjustments needed to accommodate culturally appropriate, effective learning environments, as well as some Native American characteristics regarding time management, self-dependency, non-competitive learning, the importance of a college education, and tribal differences.
3. Some respondents expressed concern about many parents' limited ability and proclivity to provide encouragement for their sons and daughters in college.
4. The majority of the faculty participants identified poor study habits, inadequate time management, and absence of long-range goals as serious barriers to the success of Native American students.

Osborne and Cranney (1985) made the following recommendations: (a) better preparation to empower prospective teachers to understand cultural diversity; (b) better predictive tests; (c) curricular refinement; (d) comprehensive orientation to college life and services; (e) better techniques and programs to foster self-esteem; leadership qualities, motivation, and encounters with role models; (f) effective bridge programs with college-bound high school students; and (g) improved monitoring programs to track student progress and to intervene as needed. These researchers conceded that the small sample size might limit the generalizability of their findings to larger populations. However, they cited the experience of the faculty- -for the most part, more than 12 years' tenure; the size and extended record of the program--one which had grown from 40 to 500 students in less than 20 years; and its retention as features that lent credibility to the findings. The survey method was an appropriate technique to employ in this status study.

A study by Rowland (1994) pointed out the significance of culturally relevant education as crucial element for self-determination among indigenous peoples. According to Rowland, the Northern Cheyenne people of Southeastern Montana had experienced little access to such education. In his study, he sought to examine tribal leaders' knowledge and current reservation experience to conceptualize the traditional Cheyenne definition of education and use the elders' perspective as a basis for recommending ways to adapt educational practice to the needs of the Northern Cheyenne. Rowland used a semi-structured interview format to elicit responses from 19 elders regarding these four areas: (a) tribal definition of wisdom and knowledge, (b) characteristics of Cheyenne teachers and students, (c) learning environment, and (d) role of education in the Northern Cheyenne community. Examination of the data gleaned from these interviews showed a marked difference between tribal and non-tribal views of education. Because of the oppressive nature of reservation life, the elders expressed the view that non-tribal government and Christian boarding schools had ignored and violated the Cheyennes' holistic learning environment. This finding seemed to confirm an earlier finding by Osborne and Cranney (1985) that faculty in the Indian Education Program at Brigham Young University believed that Native American students approach learning holistically. The Cheyenne view knowledge as a gift from the Creator which assumed a moral quality to benefit the community and which contrasts with the non-Native practice of using education to assimilate and to control, Rowland reported.

The researcher also presented two other significant results of his investigation: The first phase of Cheyenne education must address the oppression of and the internal strife among the tribal members and tribal spirituality and memberships should be utilized in tribal education to make learning meaningful and purposeful for the tribe. Rowland (1994) said that it was significant for Dull Knife Memorial College, which serves the reservation, to play an important role in using the elders' perspective to empower the Cheyenne community. This recommendation, as well as others relating to the Cheyenne holistic system, provides a framework from which relevant culture-sensitive tribal education may evolve. Rowland's use of Cheyenne elders was significant because it is compatible with the belief of tribal educators that tribal members are instrumental in helping tribal colleges to transmit Native American culture (Manzo, 1994). Also, the interview was the appropriate forum for generating candor and spontaneity of participants' responses and for gauging the tenor and spirit of their responses.

Native American Languages Courses

In the final report of *Indian Nations at Risk: An Educational Strategy for Action* (1992), the authors identified erosion of native languages and culture as one of the four reasons that Indian nations are at risk as a people. One of the major strategies for alleviating the problem was promotion of tribal language and culture. Task force members went further to expound a rationale for including native languages in the curriculum:

> Use of the language and culture of the community served by schools forms an important base from which children are educated. If a Native [*sic*] language is to be retained for use and continued development, it must be used in the home and reinforced in the schools. (p. 15)

Pego (1994) has said that among Native Americans their primary tribal languages are the primary forms of communication. Manzo (1994) has referred to the main mission of the member institutions of AIHEC to "promote and encourage the development of language, culture, and traditions of the American Indian, Eskimo, and Alaskan Natives" (p. 6). The Idaho Committee on Indian Education (1993), in its goals and recommendations for improving American Indian education, called for the creation of a learning environment in which American Indians' values, languages, and traditions are respected, maintained, and promoted. Charleston (1994) also listed this goal as a benchmark of true Native education.

Academic and Personal Counseling Services

Hoover and Jacobs (1992) performed an assessment of Native

American students' perception regarding four areas crucial to their successful completion of college: (a) high school preparation, (b) quality of college course instruction, (c) personal views toward attending college, and (d) study skills abilities. The sample for this study was 320 members of the American Indian Science and Engineering Society (AISES) who attended their 1990 fall conference. Two hundred fifty-seventy (80%) students responded to the survey. They provided demographic data, as well as responses to 45 items on three Likert-type subscales. The instrument had been field reviewed twice by professionals and had been field tested by AISES students and education students in a large research university. The subscale items had a .88 Cronbach Alpha rating. The researchers analyzed demographic data related to high school preparation by computing frequencies. They used ANOVA to compare means computed for the subscales and the Tukey Multiple Compression Test to analyze differences among the subscale means.

Analysis of the results of this investigation indicated that the respondents expressed favorable impressions of their high school college preparation and slightly favorable impressions of their college instruction and their attitudes toward attending college. However, the students expressed less favorable sentiments about college academic and career counseling received in high school. This finding is relevant for tribal colleges because it establishes the urgency for these institutions to help students to clarify their college and career aspirations, especially during their first semester of enrollment- -the period when students are at greatest risk of not persisting (Hoover & Jacobs, 1992). Also students were only slightly positive about their study skills abilities. This finding suggests a need for tribal college to provide study skills/college life supports for students to bolster positive attitudes about their abilities. Favorable attitudes about ability showed a positive correlation with academic achievement, according to Hoover and Jacobs.

The statistical techniques employed were appropriate in that they permitted the researchers to observe both between-group and within group variance. Further, using a reliable instrument and Indian subjects- -44% of whom were 100% Native American- -constituted strengths of the study. The caveats are that these students did not represent the typical tribal college student and that they participated by self-selection. Random sampling of the AISES members would have scaled down the possible bias associated with using only those participants who were available and cooperative. In addition, the respondents were atypical of many tribal college students, who have been described as underprepared. This atypicalness limited the generalizability of the findings to underprepared tribal institution populations. Moreover, if these AISES students- -most of whom reported college GPAs of 2.6 or better- - expressed unmet academic and career counseling needs and only marginally positive opinions of study skills/college life services, it appears to follow that underprepared students enrolled in college need these services even more if they are to maintain acceptable academic standing and thereby persist.

Personal counseling has been described as a means of enhancing self-esteem ("Counseling to Enhance Self-Esteem," 1991), which has been cited as a major factor in achievement. In fact, self-esteem and achievement have been assumed to have a reciprocal relationship. Hornett (1989) pointed to low self-esteem as characteristic of many tribal college students. She said that once these students perceive that others hold low expectations of them, the students begin to collaborate with their naysayers by performing at low levels. Wetsit (1994-95) observed in her study of Native American college students that effective counseling was a way to convey trustworthiness, empathy, and understanding. These supports are significant for students trying to believe in their self-worth.

Kleinfeld et al. (1987) presented their observations of the value of a postsecondary counseling program, whose purpose was to guide Native American students through their college years. This program was housed in an Alaskan school district, but its services extended into students' college experiences. The counselor tracked students, visited them in college, joined them in outings, and generally helped them to make adjustments to adulthood. These authors reported that the college attrition rate decreased from 50% to 16% following the inception of the program. Coalitions between school districts and tribal colleges might help to maximize the benefits of such personal counseling services for underprepared students.

Wellness/Substance Abuse Services

In her 1992 study, Flannery sought to identify the prevalence, patterns, and ceremonial practices of smokeless tobacco use among indigenous students attending tribally controlled postsecondary institutions. In November 1990, she used the Tobacco Use Questionnaire to collect data from 337 American Indian students at eight institutions. Three of the institutions were located in South Dakota; two were located in Montana; and one each was located in California, New Mexico, and North Dakota. The instrument called for responses to (a) demographic items; (b) ceremonial tobacco use items; (c) cigarette, moist snuff, chewing tobacco, nasal snuff, and dry snuff items; (d) dental health care items; and (e) family and peer use items.

According to Flannery (1992), analysis of her findings showed a high incidence of tobacco use among the respondents. Slightly more than 50% of the participants indicated that they were current smokers; 17.1% said that they were current moist snuff users, 6.7% were current users of chewing tobacco. None of the subjects reported that they currently used nasal snuff or dry snuff. These figures represented an overall current tobacco use rate of 64.4%. Slightly more than 8% (8.3%) said that they had never used tobacco in any form. However, some respondents reported that they used more than one form of tobacco. More than one third of the moist snuff users also smoked cigarettes, and 36.4% used chewing tobacco.

The Native American students in this investigation showed regional differences in their tobacco use. Subjects in Montana, North Dakota, and South Dakota (the Northwest) indicated that they were more inclined to smoke cigarettes than those from New Mexico (the Southwest) were. This latter group showed a greater likelihood to use smokeless tobacco than their counterparts in the Northwest did. Moreover, the students reported tobacco use in conjunction with Native American ceremonial or religious practices.

They indicated that pipe tobacco was most commonly used (35%) for such purposes. They also reported use of cigarettes (21.3%) and smokeless tobacco (5.4%).

Flannery (1992) interpreted her findings to mean that Native American college students are a population at risk with respect to tobacco use. She recommended tobacco prevention programs, as well as greater culturally appropriate tobacco education and cessation efforts among Native Americans of all ages. Flannery identified dentists, health educators, physicians, and researchers as parties responsible for effecting the appropriate measures for reducing health and behavioral risks from tobacco consumption of all forms.

One caution regarding this study is that it elicited responses from students only. Some researchers have suggested that self-reporting of some abusive substances usually results in underreporting and therefore constitutes bias (Embree & Whitehead, 1993; Lamarine, 1993). Nevertheless, the study represents an important contribution to Native American health and education research. It has significant implications for tribal communities, tribal health providers, and tribal college educators.

Wilson and Lamarine (1990) engaged in a research project whose purpose was to study the relationship between sources of information and their effect on adolescent behavior. They used a nonrandomized sample of 311 students enrolled in semester-long university health courses in California and Georgia. The close-ended questionnaire was designed to gather data about adolescents' sources of accurate information about alcohol, tobacco, drugs, and sexuality. Participants were self-selected, and their responses were reported anonymously. The average age of the sample was 22.4. The researchers analyzed their data using chi-square tests of significance, with an established alpha level of .05.

Examination of the data collected revealed no significant regional differences between respondents from the two states. The participants reported the following average ages at which they had had their first experiences with the variables under study: (a) 14.0 for alcohol, (b) 13.1 for tobacco, (c) 15.7 for drugs, and (d) 15.8 for sexuality. The investigators reported the following average ages at which participants had received accurate information about variables: (a) 15.3 for alcohol, (b) 15.5 for tobacco, (c) 15.8 for drugs, and (d) 15.1 for sexuality. In reference to the sources of accurate information, the respondents indicated that schools were the main sources of their information. This finding has particular significance for the current study. It emphasizes the need for tribal colleges to promote wellness education for their students. Flannery (1992) also emphasized this need in her study.

Wilson and Lamarine (1990) employed appropriate statistical techniques in their investigation. Their study, however, was not without limitations. The volunteer subjects enrolled in health courses during a given semester may not have been representative of the subjects in this study. Furthermore, these students may not have been competent judges of what constitutes accurate information. Also, their recall of what they had received and when they had received it may not have been accurate. Limitations notwithstanding, the results of this study are credible. One of the researchers, Lamarine (1993), conducted a similar investigation using Native American high school seniors. Analysis of the data also showed that the school was the primary source from which students had required information about substance abuse and related wellness issues.

A more recent study with relevance to this investigation was done by Arnold (1994) to identify ethnic identity and perceptions of tribal problems, potential tribal problem helpers, reasons for occupational choices, and potential obstacles to attainment of career goals among Native American tribal college students. Arnold also measured students' achievement, affiliation value/expectancy disjunction, knowledge of mental health professionals, training, general level of psychological distress, and prior contact with mental health professionals. This study used a descriptive/correlational design involving a sample of 128 Native American tribal college students–93 females and 35 males.

The researcher employed a member of instruments to assess the variables. One was the Native American Multi-factor Ethnic Identity Continuum (NAMEIC). To gather data relative to perceived tribal problems, reasons for occupational choice, and potential obstacles to career goals, he used a fill-in-the-blank format. For data relating to potential tribal problem helpers and disjunctions, he employed forced-choice Likert-type rating scales. He used a 12-item questionnaire to collect data regarding knowledge of mental health professional training and the Brief Symptom Inventory (BSI) to gather information about participants' psychological distress. Participants also provided yes-or-no answers to questions related to their prior contact with mental health professionals.

Analysis of the results of this study appeared to indicate that Native Americans believed that alcohol, drug abuse, loss of cultural identity, unemployment, and education were serious tribal problems. Also, the findings suggested that Native Americans perceived the following helpers to be most instrumental in solving Native American problems: (a) creator/God, (b) family, (c) friends, (d) tribal holy people, (e) medical doctors and mental health workers, (f) teachers/professors, (g) ministers, (h) politicians, and (i) lawyers, respectively. These entities were also viewed as having greatest utility in addressing mental health problems. The participants said that ethnic identity was medially associated with marginally increased ratings of clinical psychologist helpers for mental health problems. A significant correlation existed between general psychological distress and increased achievement and disjunctions. Further, the participants identified desirability of job and ability to help others, especially other Native Americans, as major considerations in their occupational choices. Finally, the participants viewed personal, financial, and family matters as critical barriers to attaining career goals.

This study represents an important augmentation of available research material pertaining to Native Americans. It reflected the need for tribal educators to expand the kinds of services which tribal students need to remain well and to remain in college. The findings should inform decision making by tribal leaders and educators, health care professionals, lawmakers, legal professionals, and tribal members. The fact that Arnold (1994) used a number of assessment instruments is an indication of diligence in producing a full-bodied report with utilitarian value. Using Native American participants constitutes another strength of the study.

Other Student Services

An exhaustive search yielded no empirical studies devoted exclusively to the role of learning assistance center services, tutorial services, college survival services, financial aid services or child care services in promoting academic achievement among tribal college students. Yet the preponderance of data presented in the introduction has documented the conviction of many researchers and authors of the importance of these services. Furthermore, reports by Boyer (1989-90), Houser (1991), O'Brien (1990), Wiley (1989), and Wright and Tierney (1991) and studies by Arnold (1994), Falk and Aitken (1984), Osborne and Cranney (1985), and Steward (1993) have shown that financial aid is crucial to tribal college student persistence. Aside from providing funds for tuition, books, and supplies, financial aid has been shown to provide money for child care services and transportation- -two serious needs of many parenting tribal college students.

Likewise, studies by Falk and Aitken (1984), Martin (1993), and Osborne and Cranney (1985) have indicated the impact of learning assistance center services- -including tutorial services and study skills development- -on achievement and persistence among tribal college students. Also, the Kleinfeld et al. (1987) study and the Osborne and Cranney (1985) study have documented the relevance of college survival skills assistance for Native American college matriculants.

The paucity of research studies which have specifically addressed these services illuminates the need to validate their impact on tribal college student achievement. In addition, Pavel (1992) has called on researchers to develop indicators that measure Native Americans' progress in achieving sustained retention in higher education. This study has contributed to the development of such indicators.

Outcomes Assessment and Tribal Colleges

According to Wright and Weasel Head (1990), very few studies have assessed educational outcomes of tribal institutions. One must bear in mind that outcomes assessment at tribal colleges has its own set of unique circumstances. Therefore, traditional outcomes measures may not be applicable to Native American colleges (Houser, 1991). According to Houser, many students at tribal institutions have families and therefore may not be able to pursue their studies full-time, uninterrupted to completion. Likewise, many students desire to pursue only a course or two to improve job skills or to satisfy general interests. Special populations- -such as Native Americans- -participate in programs designed just for them.

Because of the geographical and social isolation of tribal communities, it is not unusual for tribal colleges to be the only source of such services as adult and community education, skills enhancement, professional development, or recertification (Houser, 1991). Houser offered these circumstances to support his observations that not all tribal college students wish to earn a degree and that not all degree-seeking students are able to attain their goal within the minimum time expected. These observations are not unlike observations made by Chaney and Farris (1991) in their national study of retention with respect to the mainstream postsecondary student population. However, because of the extent of underpreparedness among tribal college students, it is not uncommon for them to exhaust their financial aid eligibility before they attain their educational goals (Tippeconnic, 1988). Consequently, if tribal institutions are judged by mainstream outcomes criteria, the results would not present an accurate account of the effectiveness of tribal colleges.

This scenario must not be viewed as resistance to outcomes assessment among tribal colleges. In fact, available research- -albeit scant (Wright & Weasel Head, 1990)- -has documented the existence of outcomes assessment data for tribal institutions. For instance, Houser (1991) has referred to a 1990 AIHEC study which contained data collected from six accredited tribal colleges. These institutions- -Oglala Lakota, Sinte Gleska,

Standing Rock, Turtle Mountain, Salish Kootenai, and Blackfeet- -provided data extending over a six-year period (1983-1989). During the period under study, these institutions graduated 1,575 Native Americans. Among these graduates were 210 who earned one-year vocational certificates; 1,198 who earned associate degrees; 158 who earned bachelor's degrees; and 9 who earned master's degrees in education.

Moreover, approximately one third of these graduates- -mostly those with vocational certificates and associate degrees- -continued their education, while others looked for employment in their communities. A substantial majority of those who pursued further study outside their communities returned to those communities after they had completed their studies, according to Houser. Eighty-three to 88% of the graduates of these six institutions had succeeded in finding employment, Houser (1991) indicated.

Similarly, Wright and Weasel Head (1990) presented the results of a study carried out by the Center for Native American Studies at Montana State University. The objectives were to ascertain (a) the success of tribal college students in obtaining gainful employment or in continuing their education, (b) the success of tribal institutions in preparing graduates for employment or further study, and (c) the level of student satisfaction with the quality of educational services provided by tribal colleges. The researchers used survey instruments mailed to the 418 associate degree graduates of the seven tribal colleges in Montana.

Analysis of the data collected showed that 62% of the 122 respondents said that they were employed, 10.8% indicated that they were unemployed, and 23.4% responded that they were not seeking employment. Forty-six percent of the 52 who were not in the labor force were full-time students. Seventy-five percent of the participants reported that they had found employment in fields related to their degrees. The percentage of graduates who have secured employment has been cited by Nolte (1994) as an important indicator of institutional effectiveness. The statistics reported by Wright and Weasel Head (1990) were especially significant in view of the fact that many of the new hires were Native American female heads of households who were former recipients of public assistance (Houser, 1990).

Further, results of the Wright and Weasel Head (1991) study indicated that 33% of the survey participants rated their preparation for additional study as excellent, with 38% rating it as good. Eighty-six percent of the graduates said that the preparation of the instructors was excellent or good. A very significant finding of the study was that the graduates gave the quality of the education which they had received a mean rating of 3.36 on a scale of 4.00. Findings such as these appear to be comparable to outcomes reported among mainstream higher education institutions (Haeuser, 1993; Kasworm & Marienau, 1993; Williford & Moden, 1993).

Wright and Weasel Head (1990) did not discuss the statistical techniques used to analyze their data. By their own admission, they collected data by means of an instrument which did not permit comparison of pre- and post-graduation data. Such comparison would have shown the impact of the students' college experiences on their employment and earning power. While these limitations must be acknowledged, the study should be well received for its significance in establishing the role of outcomes assessment in Native American higher education.

The review of literature related to the significance of tribal colleges and particularly to the academic and support needs of Native American students in postsecondary education confirmed the need for further research to increase the database in the area. Most of the literature reviewed attributed the low achievement and persistence among Native American college students to a number of factors- -poor academic preparation and lack of adequate financial support most serious among them. In addition, the literature review illuminated the importance of determining the relationship between specific components of academic programs and support services available to underprepared tribal college students and student achievement- -the focus of the present investigation.

A Study of Achievement and Academic and Support Services for Native American Students at Tribally Controlled Colleges

Finally, an extensive investigation was conducted by the author in 1997 to determine the relationship of achievement and academic and support services at tribally controlled colleges. The specific purposes of this investigation were to identify the components of developmental education programs at tribally controlled colleges in the United States and to investigate the relationship between each component and achievement among underprepared students at the institutions under study.

The major foci of this investigation were to identify the component of tribal college developmental programs and to observe the predictability of these variables on achievement among underprepared students. The variables were gender, developmental courses, Native American languages courses, learning assistance services, academic counseling services, personal counseling services, tutorial assistance services, college survival services, child care services, commuter center services, financial aid services, transportation assistance services, and wellness/substance abuse services. The sample consisted of 626 participants, the entire underprepared student population enrolled at three tribal institutions in the United States between the fall of 1991 and the fall of 1992.

Extensive research data have well documented the need for Native Americans to receive culturally appropriate education to minimize myriads of negatives that impact their lives (Hornett, 1989; Hurlburt, Gade, & McLaughlin, 1990; Pottinger, 1989; Reyhner, 1991; Wright, 1985). A significant accomplishment in meeting that need was the inception of the tribal college movement in 1969 with the opening of Navajo Community College in Tsaile, Arizona. The movement proliferated in the 1970s and 1980s. These institutions were founded "to meet very specific tribal needs" (Pego, 1993, p. 18). Numerous researchers (Appleson, 1994; Beaty & Chiste, 1986; Beaulieu, 1991; Benjamin, Chambers, & Reiterman, 1993; Bold Warrior, 1992; Boyer, 1989-90; Browne & Evans, 1987; Charleston, 1994; Coladarci, 1983, Falk & Aitken, 1984; Guyeth & Heth, 1983; Hoover & Jacobs, 1992;

Huffman, Sill, & Brokenleg, 1986; Idaho Committee on Education, 1993; "Indian Nations at Risk, 1992; Jensen, 1993; Lin, LaCounte, & Eder, 1988; Mooney, 1988; Pavel, 1992; Pego, 1993, 1994; Pottinger, 1989; Raymond, 1986; Reyhner, St. Pierre & Rowland, 1990; Tippeconnic, 1988; Wright, 1990; Wright & Tierney, 1991) cited lack of adequate education as the most pervasive obstacle confronting Native Americans. Yet Badwound (1991) noted that because of exiguous budgets, tribal institutions were not maximally efficacious. Still others, however- -such as Boyer and Houser (1991)- -have suggested that these institutions have fomented almost miraculous positive results among their Native American populations. Also, Wright and Weasel Head (1990) indicated in their study that tribal colleges had a positive impact on their communities.

A plethora of studies have centered on various aspects of Native American life and education. The foci of the current empirical inquiry were to identify the components of developmental programs at tribal institutions and to determine the relationship of those components to achievement among underprepared students enrolled at these colleges and universities. There were 12 components hypothesized to comprise a comprehensive developmental program for a tribal college. Among tribal institutions, only 11 components were identified: developmental courses, Native American languages courses, learning assistance center services, tutorial assistance services, academic counseling services, personal counseling services, college services, child care services, financial aid services, transportation assistance services, and wellness/substance abuse services. These components and the pre-collegiate attribute of gender were independent variables.

Three of the eleven elements identified by Roueche (1984) as critical components of a developmental program were in place at all institutions: (a) structured courses, (b) award of credit, and (c) peer tutors. A fourth element, mandatory assessment and placement, was in place at two of the institutions. Moreover, college survival services- -cited by Boyer (1989-90), Cohen (1989), Falk and Aitken (1984), Farabaugh-Dorkins (1991), Kleinfeld et al. (1987), Osborne and Cranney (1985), St. Pierre and Rowland (1990), and Swisher and

Hoisch (1992) as a crucial need among tribal college students--were offered by all three institutions. Additionally, Native American languages courses, a means of maintaining cultural connectedness, were provided by each of the institutions. Benshoff and Lewis (1992), Browne and Evans (1987), Houser (1991), Lin et al. (1988), Pavel (1992), and Wright (1985, 1990) have pointed to the importance of tribal connectedness among Native American college students.

Further still, learning assistance center services–advocated by Hodgkinson (1992), Osborne and Cranney (1985), and White and Schnuth (1990)--were available to all participants in this study. Academic counseling--whose value has been described by Hoover and Jacobs (1992) and Wetsit (1994-95–and personal counseling--shown by Beaty and Chiste (1986), Falk and Aitken (1984), Guyeth and Heth (1987), Hornett (1989), St. Pierre and Rowland (1990), Schlossberg et al. (1989), Swisher and Hoisch (1992), and Tippeconnic (1988)--were other components of programs at each of the institutions.

Among the results whose definitiveness was more cogent, being female was shown to have both a direct and an indirect effect on achievement among underprepared tribal college students. The indirect effect occurred by way of the academic service developmental courses. The direct relationship was a positive one (.09). The indirect effect, however, was negative (-.03 and -.01, respectively). The total effect of gender on GPAl was .06; for GPA2 it was .10. The results showed that overall the effects of gender (female) on achievement were positive. Since females were the referent group, the data pertaining to gender were interpreted to mean that females earned higher grades than their male counterparts. The observation also showed that for the first term, females achieved a mean GPA of 1.54, compared to 1.11 achieved by males. Similar results occurred for the subsequent term during which females showed a mean GPA of 1.83 and males showed a mean GPA of 1.35.

This finding paralleled findings reported by Houston (1993), who concluded that females have a proclivity to learn by the concrete sequential cognitive style. This style, she asserted, is associated with academic success.

She found that females who processed information using the concrete sequential style earned higher course grades than males and other females who learned through a medium other than the concrete sequential style. Other studies have indicated that factors related to biology, heredity, and environment impact the learning process and influence gender differences (Buteyn, 1989). In a related investigation, Scalley (1993) observed that males were more likely than females not to persist. Lower academic achievement and higher attrition among males may be assumed to be associated with the societal expectation that in their traditional head-of-household role, males should be income producers rather than saunterers about the halls of academe. Also, Gold, Burrell, Haynes, and Nardecchia (1990) have said that males were less likely than females to self-refer for services which may support their success.

Why males and females perform differently academically has been the subject of voluminous research, according to Reeves (1993). Yet she observed that not much has been done to interpret the implications of this research. She, Jones (1992), and Scalley (1993) have recommended that further research be conducted to bring more specificities to the entity of gender differences.

In the analyses regarding financial aid, the referent group was students who had access to a financial aid program with a student loan component. With direct effects of .35 and .43, respectively, financial aid emerged as the variable more critical to achievement than any other variable was. Specifically, the referent group outperformed their peers who only had access to financial aid which did not require repayment.

This finding was reminiscent of similar findings by other researchers. Arnold's (1994) and Falk and Aitken's (1984) studies demonstrated the absolute indispensability of financial aid to achievement among Native Americans. Arnold found in his study that Native American students cited financial matters among the most crucial barriers to the attainment of their career goals. The Falk and Aitken (1984) study identified financial aid as the most serious factor in attrition among American Indians. In fact, even students who persisted listed adequate financial support as the factor most responsible for their persistence. This finding of the current study also confirmed the observation shared among Boyer (1989-90), Houser (1991), and Wright and Tierney (1991) that the vast majority of tribal college students qualify for need-based financial assistance.

Many tribal institutions do not offer a student loan program (R. Beaver, personal communication, November 21, 1995). Nevertheless, given the results of the present investigation, perhaps tribal college decision makers might consider including student loans as an alternative for students who have exhausted all other pecuniary resources before they attain their education goals. Some loan programs have a "special circumstances" clause (United States Department of Education, 1996-97) which might be applicable to tribal college students. The current investigation has added an illuminating and contemporary dimension to the findings of precedent researchers.

Developmental courses showed a direct negative effect on achievement for both terms (-.29 and -.10, respectively). The referent group was students who were required to enroll in developmental courses. These students did not perform as well as those who received the service via another course or who had the option of enrolling in developmental courses. Students in the referent group had a mean GPA1 of only .35, while their counterparts who received the services via another course or at their own option attained a mean GPA of 1.75. For GPA2, the mean GPAs were 1.11 and 1.87, respectively.

This finding did not corroborate the findings of previous studies. Griffin (1990), Patty (1989), Purvis and Watkins (1987), and Stone (1992) reported a positive association between completion of developmental courses and achievement and persistence among underprepared college students. Results of the Pattty study pointed out that completion of developmental courses was positively associated with GPA and persistence. An outcome of the Purvis and Watkins study indicated that underprepared students who enrolled in developmental courses performed better initially in the regular curriculum and that they persisted longer than students who did not enroll in them. Findings of Stone's study showed that arts and science majors who were identified via assessment as having skills deficits and who enrolled in developmental courses persisted at a higher rate than students who did not have skills deficits and those who did have them but did not enroll in the courses. The present investigation did not substantiate among Native American student populations findings which have been disclosed about other student populations.

A number of factors help to explain this seemingly anomalous outcome. First, Patty Grant (personal communication, November 22, 1995) noted a high turnover rate among tribal college instructors because some use the tribal college setting mainly as a means of gaining entrance and facilitating their upward mobility as higher education professionals. Second, Houser (1991) reported that tribal college instructors are not always familiar with cultural and social aspects of Native American life or the Native American learning behaviors. Third, he implied that tribal college students might view placement in developmental courses as punitive. Fourth, Native American students have been characterized by low motivation and aspiration (Falk & Aitken, 1984; Guyeth & Heth, 1983; St. Pierre & Rowland, 1990; Swisher & Hoisch, 1992; Tippeconnic, 1988), a present-time orientation (Hornett; 1989), and an external locus of control (Beaty & Chiste, 1986). Another consideration is that perhaps students who opted to complete developmental courses were students who were most likely to succeed and who believed that such courses would support their success. Finally, some students are required to complete- - and possibly repeat- - as many as five developmental courses simultaneously before they are able to advance to the regular curriculum. The presence of any one or any combination of these conditions could limit the effectiveness of the courses in terms of short- and long-term achievement.

Moreover, the fact that the negative correlation between developmental courses and achievement weakened for the second term may suggest that Native American students' apparently deferred tendency to benefit from these courses may be a function of their acculturation to the college milieu. Martin's (1993) research seems to support this conjecture. He used the Student Adaptation to College Questionnaire (SACQ) to observe factors that influence persistence and graduation. Members of the Crow Tribe enrolled at Little Big Horn College ranked below the norm on all five of the major adjustment factors: (a) academic, (b) social, (c) personal, (d) institutional attachment, and (e) full scale adjustment. According to Martin, his finding stood askew to the findings of other researchers who had sampled college freshmen and sophomores from other populations. His results and those of this study perhaps should give impetus to future studies to document a possible association between developmental courses and adjustment as they relate to student achievement. These findings might also suggest to tribal educators that students' adjustment to college life could be more crucial initially than developmental courses. Perhaps the sooner students succeed at adjusting, the sooner they will be able to succeed academically.

The findings produced by additional data analyses showed an important association with student achievement. For example, females–the referent group–had a considerably higher mean GPA (1.82) two terms following completion of the last developmental course than they had the previous term (1.54). Males did not perform as well as females either term; yet they, too, showed a comparable increase in GPA2 (1.35) over GPA1 (1.11). These improvements across the gender line indicated that the services which tribal colleges offered for underprepared students were beneficial to all students generally.

Likewise, when developmental courses, native American languages courses, personal counseling services, and college survival services were involved, students consistently showed higher achievement for the second term than for the first. More precisely, students who opted to complete developmental courses earned mean GPAs of 1.75 and 1.87, in that order, compared to .35 and 1.11, respectively, for those who were required to complete the courses. The mean GPA differences between students who completed native American languages as an option and those who completed them as a requirement were only slight for the first term, 1.48 and 1.35. However, for the ensuing term, the respective differences were more pronounced, 1.97 and 1.43. Marked differences were also shown for the first term between students who received optional personal counseling services and those who received required services, 1.75 and .35, respectively. Similar results were evident for the second term, 1.87 and 1.11, respectively. An intriguing observation was that, except for college survival services, wherever a service was required, the referent group did not perform as well as the cohort which had an option to receive the service or which received it through some other medium. These results seemed to echo Native Americans' aversion to what they view as arbitrary assimilation. As early as colonial times, Native Americans have not responded positively to receiving education that has not been motivated by their own volition (Wright, 1989). Also, the lower achieving group might possibly fit the profile of Native American students previously described by Beaty and Chiste, (1986); Falk and Aitken, (1984); Guyeth and Heth, (1983); Hornett, (1989); St. Pierre and Rowland, (1990); Swisher and Hoisch, (1992); and Tippeconnic, (1988).

Students who were required to complete a college survival course earned mean GPAs of 2.64 for the first term and 3.07 for the second, substantially higher than the scores for students who received the services via another course (1.35 and 1.43, respectively). Hoover and Jacobs' 1992 study suggested a need for tribal institutions to provide college life supports to foster positive attitudes among students about their abilities. These researchers reported that favorable attitudes showed a positive correlation with academic achievement. Also, this finding that a compulsory college survival course resulted in the highest mean GPA was an important response to Pavel's (1992) call for researchers to develop indicators that measure Native American students' achievement and persistence.

Numerous studies have established the role of academic services in influencing student achievement and persistence. The findings of the current investigation have enhanced the work of previous researchers. For instance, the present findings have documented that the extent of the services provided for underprepared tribal college students, as well as the means by which these services were delivered, was more critical to achievement than was their mere availability. Perhaps tribal educators might revisit their delivery systems to discover optimally efficacious strategies by which to provide academic services.

The pattern of improvement regarding academic services also prevailed for support services. Without exception, students who had access to the more extensive services performed better than students who had access to limited or no service. For instance, students who had access to a financial aid program with a student loan feature attained a mean GPA of 2.64 for the first term and 3.07 for the second, compared to 1.03 and 1.33, respectively, for those who had financial aid which did not require repayment. First- and second-term mean GPAs reported for students having access to financial aid (with loan) recurred with those having access to frequent interreservation transportation assistance and with those having access to wellness/substance abuse services which included both seminars and a course. The students who had access to thrice daily intrareservation transportation assistance had mean GPAs of 1.35 and 1.43, respectively. Those with no access to transportation assistance had respective mean scores of .35 and 1.11. Finally, the students who had access only to wellness/substance abuse seminars achieved mean GPAs of 1.03 and 1.33. One may assume that the more comprehensive the service, the higher students achieved academically. This finding should be taken under advisement by tribal college administrators whose purview entails support services for underprepared students. Inasmuch as most tribal institutions do not have comprehensive support programs (Houser, 1992), it is critical that they broaden their collaboration and partnerships with external agencies until such time that they are able to provide comprehensive, centralized, campus-based student support services. Falk and Aitken (1984) proposed multiple manifestations of institutional commitment to support Native American students. Osborne and Cranney (1985) also espoused a comprehensive approach to providing student services.

In regards to the serendipitous findings, numerous regression analyses were executed to demonstrate diligence in capturing variance among the variables under study. In one of the analyses, institutional type emerged as a variable with statistical significance to achievement among underprepared tribal college students, that is, whether students attended a two-year or four-ear institution appeared to have a bearing on academic achievement. This finding was serendipitous, since institutional type was not among the independent variables assumed to be related to student achievement. The results were not revealed because to report them would be to breach a condition under which data were collected: that all data would be reported in aggregate form only. Nonetheless, this finding should prompt future researchers to investigate the role of institutional type in gauging student academic achievement and persistence.

Future Directions for Developmental
Educators in Tribal Colleges

With respect to the results of this research study, these conclusions may be deduced. The independent variables accounted for 28% of the variance in achievement among underprepared tribal college students for the first term following completion of the last developmental course. For the next term, these variables accounted for 24% of the variance. These findings suggest that the major portion of the variance in student achievement was attributable to variables not included in prediction model.

The unexplained variance in the prediction models intimated that there were other variables not in the models which may have helped to explain the variance in achievement among underprepared tribal college students. Carstens (1994) reported in his investigation that college admissions models which rely solely on cognitive measures to identify at-risk students may not be effective in identifying skills-deficit students who have the potential to succeed. Therefore, his suggestion that a combination of noncognitive and traditional variables be used as valid success predictors among special populations appears to have merit for students admitted to college through alternate provisions. This combination of variables may more fully account for the unexplained variance.

A greatest-to-least ranking of the independent variables exerting direct effects upon achievement included financial aid (with loan), developmental courses (required), and gender (female) respectively, for both one and two academic terms following completion of the last developmental course. Gender also had indirect effects on achievement mediated via the academic service developmental courses both terms. Tribal educators and decision makers might consider exploring other variables that may be more success predictive regarding achievement. Also, tribal educators might devise counseling and college survival models that focus more on encouraging males to become more active participants in their own success. Yet, another consideration is that tribal institutions may opt to direct monies generated by the 1994 Equity in Land-Grant legislation toward strengthening the existing components of their developmental programs through centralization or other appropriate means.

The results also revealed that the typical tribal college developmental program was a decentralized one comprising these academic and support services: developmental courses, Native American languages courses, limited decentralized learning assistance center services, tutorial services, academic counseling services, personal counseling services, college survival services in some format, financial aid services, and wellness/substance abuse services. Child care services and transportation assistance services had not become institutionalized among all colleges, and commuter center services were not a part of any of the programs. These findings showed that, in the main, tribal institutions had in place programs whose components were consistent with those recommended in relevant research literature pertaining to developmental education. Mean score comparisons showed consistent rise in achievement of the second academic term over the first.

Also, the results of this study suggest that the profile of the typical successful underprepared tribal college student was one who is female, who is not required to complete developmental courses, and who has access to a financial aid program that includes student loans. One may surmise from this portrait that underprepared students who do not fit this prototype are less likely to perform as well academically as the cohort. This portrait may serve as a base upon which tribal educators may structure more success-predictive models for their students. Of course, one must bear in mind the caveats uniquely associated with tribal education. Therefore, educators should consider the following recommendations:

1. Based on a limitation of this study, an imperative recom-mendation is that further efforts be made to conduct more expansive research encompassing all tribal institutions in the United States. Such studies would continue to update the database of what is known about tribal education in this country.

2. Since tribal institutions have begun to receive funds authorized by the Equity in Land-Grant Status Act of 1994, another recommendation is that research be conducted to measure the effects of these new monies in terms of critically needed improvements in facilities, technology, library holdings, and employment of additional personnel, the lack of which has been cited as a major factor in the inability of tribal institutions to participate in research studies.

3. Some of the land-grant money which tribal institutions receive will come in the form of grants (J. McDonald, personal communication March 11, 1997). Therefore, the next recommendation is that tribal educators use their grantsmanship to procure funds to collaborate with reservation high schools to develop bridge programs for prospective college students. These programs may be effective in curtailing the number of underprepared students who enter tribal institutions under the "ability-to benefit" provision. While it is laudable as a means of access, this provision no doubt contributes to the high attrition rates reported among Native Americans. Collaboration such as that reported by Kleinfeld et al. (1987), Martin (1993), and Osborne and Cranney (1985) in which there is an interfacing of secondary and postsecondary experiences would lessen attrition. In the same vein, it is recommended that when tribal college students complete their final developmental course, there be similar interfacing of developmental and regular services to help students become acclimated to the rigors of regular curricular requirements.

4.   A further recommendation is that longitudinal studies be conducted to measure institutional effectiveness among tribal colleges. Such studies would not only document success but also identify areas needing improvement. Relevant data such as these could inform tribal decision makers in matters of planning and development. They could also form the basis upon which monies from both the private and the public sectors could be awarded to these institutions.

5.   Results of studies by Benjamin et al. (1993), Huffman et al. (1986), Pavel (1992), and Pottinger (1989) have intimated that pre-collegiate attributes may not be meaningful predictors of success among Native American student populations. Nonetheless, it would be beneficial to discern whether these characteristics do in some way have a bearing on the achievement of underprepared tribal college students. Therefore, another recommendation is that more definitive research be undertaken to observe the relationship between students' demographic characteristics and achievement.

6.   Also, future researchers should investigate gender differences among tribal college students as they relate to academic attainment.

7.   Moreover, replicate studies should include other variables which may explain more filly the factors which may impinge on student achievement, in view of the fact that the variables in the prediction model in this study accounted for 28% of the variance in achievement for the first term and 24% for the second term following completion of the last developmental course.

8.   Further, the serendipitous finding of this study that institutional type may be a significant consideration in tribal college students' academic performance and retention should provide the foundation for further empirical investigation.

Finally, the research has shown that tribal colleges admit students each year who are not prepared to succeed in regular curricula. Not only do these students require developmental courses, but they also need other services to support their successful matriculation. Because underpreparedness among tribal college students, together with its concomitant attrition, generally exceeds that among other student populations, tribal college decision makers have the intricate challenge of meeting the needs of culturally diverse students, at the same time that they contend with exiguous budgets. Consequently, a crucial undertaking for tribal institutions in the new millennium is to devise success-predictive frameworks for meeting students' needs, stringent budgets notwithstanding.

CHAPTER 8

Tribal Colleges: Meeting the Needs
of American Indian Students

Laura D. Browne and Gordon Kitto

Introduction

This chapter will share ideas from conversations between the authors, Gordon Kitto, a Santee Sioux educator and Laura Browne, a non-Indian educator. Concerned with facilitating the success of American Indians students in higher education, it is our hope this chapter will help educators understand why so few American Indian students attend and graduate from our institutions of higher education and how tribal colleges are changing the face of American Indian higher education. We begin with statistical information regarding enrollment trends. This is followed by a review of the major events in the history of American Indian education.

With this background, we move to a discussion of American Indian students as "minorities" and higher education's response to their needs. We will then endeavor to show how self-determination has forever changed the face of America Indian education and how tribal colleges are attempting to meet the needs of their students through various programs with roots in the dominant educational milieu.

Demographics of American Indian
Participation in Higher Education

According to the American Council of Education (1992), approximately two million people self-identified as American Indian in the 1990 census, representing 0.8 percent of the total U.S. population. Of that two million, 103,000 enrolled in higher education. This represents less than one percent of all higher education students. In addition, these students are concentrated in two-year institutions: "more than half (53 percent) enrolled at two-year colleges in 1990 (only Hispanic students, at 55 percent, had a higher proportion of students attending two-year colleges)" and they are "more likely than any other racial/ethnic group to attend public colleges or universities. In 1990, 88 percent of Indian students enrolled in public institutions, compared with 78 percent of all students and 81 percent of minority students" (O'Brien, p. 5). Using statistics based on data provided by federally recognized tribes and the Bureau of Indian Affairs, Dr. Dean Chavers (Lumbee) provides a different statistical profile. He believes "these figures are more accurate because they include only those individuals who are one-quarter or more Indian and enrolled in a tribe" (*Indian Country Today*, p. A12). Dr. Chavers, President of the Native American Scholarship Program in Albuquerque, N.M. continues:

> The[se] results seem to indicate that Indians are overrepresented in college enrollments. In fact, Indians are underrepresented. The truth is that only 55,000 Indian were enrolled in college. The rest of the 103,000 were wannabes. . . non-Indian people who want to be Indian, and pretend they are Indians, distorting data collection by the colleges, the U.S. Census and other agencies. [In addition,] only 50 percent of American Indian young people finish high school, 17 percent of these graduates go on to college, only 19 percent of these students graduate from college which means only 1.6 percent of the Indian population is earning a college degree. In comparison, 80 percent of non-Indian students finish high school, 40 percent go on to college, 54 percent graduate in six years and 17.3 percent earn college degrees. With a college drop out rate of over 80 percent, non-Indians are earning 10.8 degrees for every Indian who earns a degree. (p. A12)

History of American Indian Education

In the beginning, "the hundreds of tribes, bands, clans, and extended family groups of Native Americans who inhabited North America in the late 15th century had their own forms and concepts of education. The focus was to facilitate a child's acquisition of environmental and cultural knowledge necessary to (1) survive in a subsistence lifestyle and (2) contribute meaningfully to the overall socio-economic welfare of the group" (Bureau of Indian Affairs, 1988 qtd. in Utter, 1993, p. 194). But the government of the United States used education to [convert and] acculturate Native Americans (Kidwell, 1994).

Tribal leaders recognized the need to understand the ways of their new neighbors and many encouraged the exchange of ideas; some even allowed young men from their tribes to attend white schools. This exchange was not without it's problems, as Canassatego, an Iroquois chief, noted in his reply to an offer from the Virginia Legislature to send six youths to be educated at the Williamsburg College of William and Mary:

> Several of our young People were formerly brought up in the College of the Northern Provinces; they were instructed in all your Sciences; but, when they came back to us, they were bad Runners, ignorant of every means of living in the woods, unable to bear neither cold or hunger, knew neither how to build a Cabin, take a deer, or kill an enemy, spoke our language imperfectly, were therefore neither fit for Hunters, Warriors nor Counsellors; they were totally good for nothing. (Irving, 1971, p. 19)

As the colonists pressed further westward, "the government agreed to provide payments and services, including education. That relationship is the basis for educational services for Native Americans to the present day" (Kidwell, 1994, p. 241). Vine Deloria Jr. (Standing Rock Sioux) noted that:

> Treaty records and related correspondence in the nation's archives relate only to a fraction of the nearly 400 treaties

negotiated from 1778 to 1781. Records that do exist show conclusively, however, that Indian nations ceded their lands to the federal government with great reluctance and that they did so...largely on the basis of federal promises to educate their children. (Deloria, 1979, qtd. in Olivas, 1997)

Historical Perspective: Major Events and Personalities

1515   The first Indian education: the Spanish Laws of Burgos provided the opportunity to "work into God's grace" (Utter, 1993).

1565   Jesuits took The People to Havana to learn reading, writing and farming (Utter, 1993).

1618   The Henrico Proposal, also known as the East India School in Richmond VA., was the first school established to teach Indian children (Stein, 1992).

1636   "Indian Colleges" at Harvard, William and Mary and Dartmouth established based on Eleazor Wheelock's belief that effective civilization efforts required removal of "selected young men from the influence of family and home" (Oppelt, 1990).

1819   The Civilization Act allocated $10,000 to support Christian missionary schools whose desire to teach reading, writing and arithmetic coincided with their desire to convert (Kidwell, 1994).

1830   The Removal Act authorized and established the conditions for boarding schools funded by government, church and Indian annuity payments (dollars given in exchange for ceded tribal lands) (Reyhner, 1992).

1830   Treaty with the Choctaw Nation provided for Indian higher education but money not used until 1841 for scholarships to white colleges and the Hampton Institute (*Report on Indian*

Education, 1976, qtd. in Goodchild & Weschler, 1997).

1879–   Carlisle Indian School, established in Carlisle, PA by Civil
1912   War veteran Capt. Richard Pratt, was the most comprehensive educational system to date. It focused on academics,
agriculture, manual arts, homemaking skills, athletics and
`outings'. Once these students returned home, their skills
weren't needed and their language/ways were foreign to their
relatives (Oppelt, 1990).

1887   Dawes Severalty Act, or the General Allotment Act, allocated
160 acres per family and 80 acres per individual living in
Indian Territory. The government purchased surplus land
for $1.25 per acre and the proceeds were placed in trust for
supplies and education (Utter, 1993).

1911   August Breuninger, a mixed blood Menominee, called for the
creation of an Indian controlled university where American
Indians could "hold onto their Indianness" while learning to
accept and live in the white world (Crum, 1989 p. 20).

1911   Arthur C. Parker, noted Seneca scholar from New York
who, with the help of other college educated Indians,
established the Society of American Indians (SAI) (Crum,
1989).

1912   Jim Thorpe, graduate of Carlisle Indian School, won the
Olympic gold medals in the pentathlon and decathlon
(Oppelt, 1990).

1924   The Snyder Act granted citizenship to American Indians
(Banks, 1975).

1928   The Meriam Report, critical of boarding, private and mission
schools, recommended adequate funding of scholarship and
loan programs to support American Indian attendance at
colleges and universities (Utter, 1993; Kidwell, 1994).

1928   Students at the Haskell Institute in Lawrence, KS formed the
Junior College Club which later became a short-lived junior

college program (Crum, 1989).

1934   The Wheeler-Howard Act, also known as the Indian
        Reorganization Act, established an Indian Bill of Rights and
        dispensed with the allotment system. This was the first step
        to tribal self-sufficiency and identity (Oppelt, 1990).

1934   The Johnson-O'Malley Act provided state/federal coopera-
        tion in the delivery of services, especially education (Utter,
        1993).

1935-   25,000 American Indian people went to war. Included were
1945   the Navajo Code Talkers and one of the three soldiers
        raising the flag at Iwo Jima (Oppelt, 1990).

1944   The National Congress of American Indians was organized
        by Native Americans (Banks, 1975).

1944   Tony Lujan, a Taos Pueblo from New Mexico and Solon
        Sombrero, Mescalero Apache, advanced the idea of an
        Indian college to "help young Indians...bridge the gap
        between the Indian world and the larger dominant society"
        (Crum, 1989 p. 22).

1945   Archie Phinney, a college educated Nez Perce anthropologist
        from the University of Kansas, added his voice to the called
        for Indian higher education (Crum, 1989).   1949--The
        Confederated Indian Tribes of Nevada organized to request
        that Stewart Indian School near Carson City become an
        Indian junior college (Crum, 1989).

1950s   Raymond Nakai, later chairperson of the Navajo Nation, and
        Stanley Red Bird, Rosebud Sioux leader, unsuccessfully
        advanced the call for the establishment of Indian colleges on
        their respective reservations (Crum, 1989).

1954   Supreme Court decision banned school segregation (Oppelt,
        1990).

50s-   The Civil Rights movement, Black activism and the
60s   American Indian Movement (AIM).   Despite Johnson-

O'Mallley, by 1964 educational opportunities remained almost non-existent (Utter, 1993; Oppelt, 1990).

1961 Dr. Jack D. Forbes (Delaware-Powhatan), Assistant Professor of History at San Fernando Valley State College, and Carl Gorman, Navajo artist, organized the American Indian College Committee (Crum, 1989).

1963 Orville Lane (Pawnee), established the American Indian College Foundation and, with Eva Nichols (Lakota Sioux), sought funds to establish an Indian college. They appealed to Korczak Kiolkowskio of the Crazy Horse Monument for assistance, but were unsuccessful (Crum, 1989).

1964 Lakota Sioux relocated to the San Francisco area "occupied Alcatraz Island, claiming `abandoned' federal land in the name of Native America and requesting the creation of an Indian university" (Crum, 1989, p. 23).

1965 Title III of the Higher Education Act allocated funds to assist developing institutions of higher education (Oppelt, 1990).

1968 President Nixon signed the Indian Civil Rights Act which formalized "self-determination" policies begun by Presidents Kennedy and Johnson (Utter, 1993).

1970 Tribal autonomy, first acknowledged in the Wheeler-Howard Act of 1934, was strengthened while continuing the unique relationship with the federal government (Utter, 1993).

1972 Indian Education Act-the first legislation designed to move to resolve the lack of Indian control/management of Indian education (Utter, 1993).

1975 Indian Self-Determination and Assistance Act—transferred control of American Indian education from the Bureau of Indian Affairs (BIA) to local tribes (Utter, 1993).

1978 Indian Child Welfare Act, American Indian Religious Freedom Act and Tribally Controlled Community Colleges

Act (Stein, 1992).

1990   Native American Languages Act

1992   Indian Nations at Risk task Force Report and the White House Conference on Indian Education (Reyhner, 1992).

1994   Tribally controlled community colleges recognized as land-grant institutions (Bigart, 1997).

American Indian Students as "Minorities"

For over 400 years, "Native American students throughout the United States have experienced school failure in educational systems organized, administered, and controlled by members of a predominantly white society" (Wenzlaff and Biewer, 1996, p. 40). These schools were designed to convert, acculturate, and assimilate Indian people into the dominant culture. Despite promises made in the Dawes Act and the misappropriation of Indian land, the federal government never allocated adequate funding for Indian education. "American Indian communities remain isolated, chronically neglected places that benefit little from the nation's wealth. Unemployment and alcoholism are persistent problems¼ and statistics on life expectancy, family income, and educational opportunities among Native Americans can parallel those of Third World countries" (Carnegie, 1997, p. 2). Today, according to the National Congress of American Indians (1999):

> Median household income for American Indians on reservations was $19,897 in 1989, compared with $30,056 for the entire U.S. population according to the U.S. 1990 census. At that same time, 31.6% of American Indians lived below the poverty line, compared with 13% for the U.S. In addition, unemployment hovers around 50% on most Indian reservations, rising as high as 90% on some. The rate for the U.S. population as a whole is now 4.2%. (www.ncai.org)

Miller (1990) notes that the "pervasiveness of economic and racial inequality accounts in large part for why so many of the educationally disadvantaged are students of color" (Miller, 1990, p. 6). Therefore, it comes as no surprise that American Indian students are considered minority, at-risk or underprepared students. Yet tribal leaders today, as their grandfathers before them, recognize the need for education as a means of tribal economic development and autonomy. "Problems arise when Native American students try to maintain their cultural customs and values in educational systems that do not recognize the customs and values of the Native American culture" (Wenzlaff and Biewer, 1996, p. 40).

As noted earlier, 53% of American Indians seeking higher education enrolled in community colleges. With their emphasis on vocational training, general/transfer programs, remedial services and flexible admission standards and delivery systems (Oppelt, 1984), community colleges seems to be ideal institutions for part-time attendance by "educationally disenfranchised" students (Boyer, 1989). Yet only a handful of Asian, Pacific Islander and American Indian students "participate in higher education generally or in developmental education in particular" (Boylan, Bonham, & Bliss, 1994, p. 3). These same researchers also note that "community colleges...may not be the best choice for promoting educational opportunity for students of color until serious efforts are made to enhance the retention" (Boylan, Bliss, & Bonham, 1993, p. 3).

According to Miller (1990), a comprehensive approach to improve minority achievement would include effective retention strategies such as "administrative commitment, financial resources, student services, curricula, personnel, and timeliness of intervention and progress (p. 6).

Frances Swayzer Conley, in a summary of research titled "The Relationship of Achievement and Academic Support Services for Developmental Students at Tribal American Colleges" (Barham and Farmer, 1998) concluded "...that...tribal colleges had in place programs in which components were consistent with those recommended in the research pertaining to developmental education" (p. 1).

In 1984, Oppelt referred to tribal colleges as "higher education's best kept secret." After an unprecedented second visit by the Carnegie Foundation for the Advancement of Teaching and Learning in 1997, Boyer writes: "In a movement still hidden from most of the nation, hope and a sense of renewal has emerged in American Indian communities" (p. 1).

Self-Determination and Tribal Colleges

The idea of Indian postsecondary education was not a 20th century phenomenon; it dates back to the indigenous Aztecs, Incas, and Mayans (Crum, 1989). "Nobody but Indians really wanted to see Indian colleges come into being in the first place" (Belgarde, 1994, p. 9). Yet Indian postsecondary education would be realized when a complex set of political events converged to create an atmosphere conducive to American Indian educational self-determination. Those events included: a) the age of democratic reforms; b) the government's policy shift to Indian self-determination; c) tribal access to federal dollars; d) tribal leadership's prioritizing of education (especially higher education); and e) preservation of Indian culture through Indian-oriented courses (Crum, 1989).

First advanced by Dr. Jack Forbes (Delaware-Powhatan), Professor of History at San Fernando Valley State College,

> the creation of an Indian university...Indian-controlled and Indian-centered would help perpetuate Indian tradition and culture by offering native-oriented courses, including native American history, anthropology, religion, folklore, tribal law and dramatic arts...[and] regular college level courses to educate and prepare young Indians to become future tribal leaders and teachers. (Crum, 1989, p. 22)

Elsewhere in the educational world, the community college movement was gathering momentum. With their emphasis on vocational training, general/transfer programs, remedial services and flexible admission standards and delivery systems (Oppelt, 1984), community colleges became the model for tribally controlled community colleges.

Tribally controlled community colleges, located on a reservation and chartered/controlled by a federally recognized Indian Tribe (Carnegie Foundation, 1989; Stein, 1992), have the following missions:

1.   Provide comprehensive academic and occupational education which is culturally relevant to the tribal community;
2.   Establish learning environments which encourage participation by and builds self-confidence in students who have come to view failure as the norm;
3.   Celebrate and help sustain/preserve rich Native American traditions through cultural values and tribal languages;
4.   Provide essential services which enrich the surrounding community including: socio-economic programs, adult education/literacy tutoring, GED, vocational programs and leadership management. (Oppelt, 1984)

The first tribally controlled community college, Navajo Community College, was established in Shiprock, AZ in 1968. Two years later, Oglala Sioux Community College was established on the Pine Ridge Reservation in South Dakota and Sinte Gleske Community College was established on the Rosebud Reservation in South Dakota in 1971 (Stein, 1992; Oppelt, 1990). Currently, there are 31 tribal colleges in the United States and Canada. Paul Boyer, former editor of *Tribal College: American Indian Journal of Higher Education*, suggested several goals for tribal colleges in the Summer, 1990 issue of the *Journal*. One was a campus "climate of concern and support that is promoted by all its members". This climate of concern must include "academic and social support offered to all students" (p. 14). In addition, "reflect[ing] the surrounding culture in courses and the larger campus climate is perhaps the single most important role a tribal college can play in encouraging student achievement" (p. 15).

According to the second Carnegie report (1997):

Tribal colleges have proven their ability to enroll students who were not served by higher education, to graduate students who dropped out from other institutions, and to sponsor successful community development programs. Indeed, the tribal college is often the most stable institution on a reservation. [But] one institution alone cannot break down all the barriers Indians face. But after years of physical hardship and cultural neglect, Indians themselves are gaining the confidence and skills needed to lead their nations. (p. 2)

Conclusion

"For the past 500 years, tribes have survived despite the odds because they retained their cultural values and their spiritual beliefs" (Ambler, 1997 p. 10). Current research, accreditation reports and government audits indicate that "tribal colleges, with their culturally-infused curriculum and commitment to comprehensive academic and social programming, are effectively meeting the needs of their students and stakeholders creating a new mood of optimism and self-respect among native people" (Carnegie, 1997, p. 2).

CHAPTER 9

Critical Thinking Ability and Success on the National Counsel Licensure Examination for African American Nursing Students

Betty J. Farmer

Introduction

These are changing times. Technological advances and the discovery of new knowledge provide daily opportunities for learning. This is also true in the professional world. No longer can professionals be expected to learn all the "job skills" needed for a lifetime in any educational preparation program. Instead, it becomes important to learn to think creatively and critically and to have the ability to modify learning to apply it to situations as they are encountered. According to Glaser (1985) and McPeck (1981), the development of critical thinking skills is an indispensable component of higher education (Miller, 1992). In fact, as higher education has focused more on measurable outcomes, critical thinking skills have been among those outcomes. Nursing education has also been concerned with measuring educational outcomes.

No doubt, critical thinking skill is considered an essential outcome for nurses' preparation in the different types of nursing programs including associate degree, bachelor's degree, and master's degree. Miller and Malcolm (1990) suggested that because of the broader range of clinical practice assumed by the bachelor's and master's degree nurse, greater emphasis should be placed on critical thinking at this level.

No doubt, critical thinking is an integral part of decision making for nurses. In day to day practice, nurses encounter multiple patient situations in which they must define problems accurately and make the best possible choices from among the available solutions. They must then implement these choices in the form of nursing interventions and evaluate effectiveness of their actions. In 1984, the American Nurses' Association (ANA) established the Standards for Professional Nursing Education to guide expected student outcomes for baccalaureate nursing programs. According to ANA:

> The baccalaureate nurse graduate will perform in a certain way because of her educational preparation. If the needs of the people are to be met, the focus of the baccalaureate nursing program must be on intellectual skills, such as problem solving, critical thinking, and making nursing judgments based on interpersonal and technical skills. The nursing major in the baccalaureate degree program in nursing is concentrated in the upper division and is built upon a broad general education base. The general education base contributes to a knowledge of man and the world, as well as providing the content base for nursing intervention. The baccalaureate nurse is an educated person capable of thinking, of self direction, of problem solving, of self fulfillment and self evaluation. Hence, baccalaureate nurse's role is fulfilled through the nursing process. (pp. 7-8)

The nursing process, once considered simply a problem solving process, now includes a broader scope of complex thinking process. Yura and Walsh (1983) purported that the nursing process was the core and essence of the nursing profession. The nursing process is important to all patient related nursing decisions and should be learned in all types of nursing programs. Yura and Walsh pointed out that the flexibility and adaptability of the nursing process enable nurses to use judgment and creativity in caring for patients in varied situations. These nursing educators believe that the nursing process is sufficiently structured to serve as a blueprint and to systematically guide all nursing decisions.

The nursing process consists of a number of phases including, assessment, analysis, planning, implementation, and evaluation (Beare, 1991). The first phase, assessment, is the establishment of a data base from which to derive a decision regarding the client's needs. The second phase, analysis, serves to identify the actual or potential health needs based on the assessment phase. In the third phase, the planning phase, goals are established and strategies are developed to achieve the goals. The fourth phase, implementation, involves the initiation and completion of actions necessary to achieve the goals. The final phase of the nursing process is evaluation. Evaluation involves determining the extent to which the patient's goals have been met.

Problem solving and decision making are routine parts of nurses' responsibility in applying the nursing process. Nurses utilize critical thinking skills to identify and apply the appropriate solution from several possible alternatives in delivering safe, quality health care. Thus, nurses must be skilled in critical thinking to be competent health care professionals.

Critical Thinking Defined

Numerous attempts to define critical thinking were identified in the literature. There is much discussion and very little consensus regarding the definition of critical thinking. McPeck (1990) stated that critical thinking is important to the context of the knowledge within disciplines. McPeck (1981) postulated that individuals can develop their critical thinking abilities through immersion in the discipline. Yinger (1980) stated that critical thinking should be regarded as "the cognitive activity associated with the evaluation of products of thought....this cognitive activity, more accurately called critical or evaluative thought, is an essential element of problem solving, decision making, and creative production" (p. 14). Perry (1981) concurred with Yinger's definition and went on to state that critical thinking is the process of constructing individual meaning by employing learning strategies for reaching one's goals. Halpern (1984) described critical thinking as thinking that is intentional and goal directed in that it solves a problem, makes an inference, or arrives at a decision. Ennis (1985) described critical thinking as a broad concept which extends beyond an individual using reflective thinking and deciding what to believe or do. Ennis argued that critical thinking is closely connected to creative thinking and problem solving, and is, therefore, a rational process.

Glaser's (1985) definition five characteristics of critical thinking: (1) listening or reading carefully to understand the beliefs of others, (2) examining evidence to determine if it supports the stated beliefs of others, (3) discovering unstated values and assumptions in an argument, (4) drawing independent conclusions, and (5) modifying the individual belief system as needed. Siegel (1988) argued that critical thinking is based on logical reasoning. He stated that "a critical thinker has a propensity and disposition to believe and act in accordance with reason, as well as the ability to assess the force of reason in the many contexts in which reasons play a role" (p. 23). Siegel's (1980) definition suggests a close relationship between critical thinking, rationality, and problem solving. Kurfiss (1988) argued that critical thinking is a mental process used "to explore a situation, phenomenon, question, or problem to arrive at a hypothesis or a conclusion...that integrates all available information that can therefore be convincingly justified" (p. 2). She also argued that the conclusion and justification provided to support an investigation are the outcomes of critical thinking. Therefore, critical thinking is a defined problem solving mental process (Kurfiss, 1988).

Paul (1993) described critical thinking as "disciplined, self directed thinking that exemplifies the perfections of thinking specific to a particular mode or domain of thinking" (p. 462). Paul also viewed critical thinking as the art of thinking about an individual's own thinking in order to make it more clear or accurate. Moreover, Paul related an individual's ability to think critically to the development of insight into egocentric and ethnocentric thinking, the tendency toward self deception, and the formation of moral character.

Although these definitions have been used to describe critical thinking, the most commonly referenced definition of critical thinking in nursing education was provided by Watson and Glaser (1980). Watson and Glaser considered, " critical thinking to be a composite of attitudes, knowledge and skills, which includes the following: (1) attitudes of inquiry that involve an ability to recognize the existence of problems and an acceptance of the general need for evidence in support of what is asserted to be true; (2) knowledge of the nature of valid inferences, abstractions, and generalizations by which the weight or accuracy of different kinds of evidence are logically determined; (3) skills in employing and applying the above attitudes and knowledge" (p. 1).

Watson and Glaser believed that attitudes suggest a frame of mind that recognizes the existence of a problem, while knowledge, on the other hand, involves weighing the accuracy and logic of evidence. These researchers believed that knowledge represents an understanding of the nature of valid inferences, abstractions, and generalizations and that the skills must be acquired by individual students.

Watson and Glaser (1980) used their definition to develop the WGCTA to measure critical thinking ability. Specifically the WGCTA was designed to assess how students are able to reason analytically in five subtest areas. These subtests include: (a) inference: discrimination among degrees of truth or falsity of inferences draw from data; (b) recognition of assumptions: recognizing unstated assumptions in given statements; (c)   deduction: determining if conclusions follow from information in given statements; (d) interpretation: weighing evidence, and deciding if conclusions based on given data are warranted; and (e) evaluation of arguments: distinguishing between arguments that are strong and important and those that are weak or unimportant.

Watson and Glaser (1980) reported that the WGCTA yielded a total score with internal consistency reliabilities in the .69 to .85 range, and test-retest reliabilities in the .70 to .75 range. The WGCTA also yielded five sub scores with test-retest reliabilities ranging from .45 to .69. The sub scores are weighted equally in deriving the total score. They further reported that content validity was established by expert consensus. The instrument has undergone approximately 30 years of study, research, experimental analysis, revision, and refinement by both Watson and Glaser and users of the test.

A Critical Review of the Literature

Critical <u>Thinking</u> <u>Ability</u> and <u>Academic</u> <u>Performance</u> in <u>Nursing</u> Education

There have been many researchers who have advocated the need for development of critical thinking skills in nursing students (Bandman & Bandman, 1988, Creighton, 1984; Jenkins, 1985; Levenstein, 1981, 1983, 1984; Rubenfeld & Scheffer, 1995). But only a few studies attempted to measure the impact of nursing education on the development of critical thinking skills in students. Richards (1977), Gross, Takazawa, and Rose (1987), and Miller and Malcolm (1990) each conducted research comparing posttest performance on the WGCTA to pretest performance. These researchers sought to measure the effect of a nursing curriculum on the development of critical thinking skills in students.

Felts conducted an ex post facto design study to determine which selected cognitive variables most effectively predicted successful performance in nursing courses, and the relationship between selected cognitive and demographic variables and performance on the NCLEXRN. First time NCLEXRN examination writers (297) from five NLN accredited associate degree nursing programs in a Midwestern state comprised the study subjects. The dependent variables in the study included nursing courses GPA and NCLEXRN. Stepwise multiple regression was used to select variables which provided the best prediction. The ACT composite score was a significant predictor ($p < .001$) of nursing GPA. This variable accounted for 27% of the variance ($F = 35.867$) in the nursing GPA. Further, the support courses (nonnursing courses required in the program) and microbiology were significant predictors ($p < .001$) for the nursing GPA. Together, these accounted for 47% of the variance. Finally, the pass/fail rate on the NCLEXRN was addressed. Three discriminant analyses were utilized with admission criteria, college course grades and college GPAs. The admissions variables of the high school GPA and ACT social studies score yielded significant discrimination ($p < .001$) between the pass/fail groups on the NCLEXRN. The canonical correlation coefficient (.403) indicated that 16% of the variance could be explained by this variable (Felts, 1986).

The next discriminant analysis was applied to grades obtained in the college courses. Variables that yielded significant discriminations between the successful and unsuccessful examination writers were microbiology, anatomy, physiology, sociology, child psychology and English I. The canonical correlation coefficient (.541) indicated that 29% of the variance could be explained by this group of variables (Felts, 1986).

The final variables used in the discriminant analysis were grade averages in sciences and humanities, support and nursing GPAs, and cumulative grade point average. Of these, the variable which yielded significant discrimination between the successful and unsuccessful examination writers was the cumulative GPA. The canonical correlation coefficient (.478) indicated that 23% of the variance could be explained by this group of variables (Felts, 1986).

Felts concluded that ACT composite score is the best admission criteria predictor for nursing course success and the support courses GPA and microbiology are the best college variable predictors. Performance in college courses predicts passing or failing status on the NCLEXRN more accurately than does performance in high school. For the purpose of this study, a significant conclusion was suggested. Grades in the biological sciences, social sciences, and humanities were differentiators for pass/fail on the NCLEXRN (Felts, 1986). The fact that these courses are differentiators may, according to Felts, be related to the content of these courses and the integration of the problem solving process. The role of the nursing courses in relation to the NCLEXRN was not identified. These courses contain information which has been determined imperative for nursing practice by educators and regulatory agencies. This suggests that the licensure examination, as well as the nursing curriculum, bears investigation. Felts recommended additional research by nursing educators to identify essential knowledge and skills for basic nursing practice.

Whitley and Chadwick (1986) used a systems framework to study the failure rate on the NCLEXRN experienced by 1983 graduates of a northwestern Bachelor of Science in Nursing (BSN) program. The study group included 176 graduates (28 unsuccessful exam writers and 148 successful candidates). NCLEXRN performance was the dependent variable in the study, while 12 demographic variables were used for comparison purposes. The analysis of the data indicated that unsuccessful candidates, when compared to the successful candidates, had significantly lower SAT verbal and math scores, entry science GPAs, cumulative entry GPAs, nursing major test scores, and exit GPAs. Pearson's correlations were computed with all variables and then tested for significance using student's t-test. The stronger predictors of later success on NCLEXRN were science and prerequisite entry GPAs, senior school of nursing exams, the actual exit GPA, the number of academic warnings and the difference between the entrance and exit grade point average. All these variables showed robust causal differences between the successful and unsuccessful examination writers (Whitley & Chadwick, 1986).

A second part of the study included an interview using a structured protocol that was analyzed by content analysis. All faculty and 20 students were interviewed. In general, the data pointed to a bimodal distribution. Faculty believed that students had low scholastic potential (64%) and that clinical/theory mismatch existed (59%) while the students felt that the curriculum lacked essential content (65%) and that they needed more practice in clinic/skills labs. Students also stated (50%) that they needed more review before NCLEXRN. In general, both the faculty and the students identified dissatisfaction with the curriculum and the teaching methods. Whitley and Chadwick (1986) pointed out that the study results indicate an overall concern with the curriculum and teaching methods and whether these meet the needs of the learners in preparing them for success on the NCLEXRN.

Gross, Takazawa, and Rose (1987) conducted a study to determine the impact of nursing curriculum on students' critical thinking ability. A sample of 108 associate (AS) and baccalaureate (BS) students were tested by the WGCTA when they entered the program and just prior to graduation. The research findings indicated comparable improvement in critical thinking skills of AS and BS degree nursing students. The findings suggested that students who demonstrated higher cumulative GPAs also demonstrated higher levels of critical thinking skills. This was even more prevalent for students in the baccalaureate nursing program. The demographic variables of age and the number of years in college for BS nursing students were shown to be related to critical thinking scores and academic performance. The findings also indicated that the measure of cumulative GPA is perhaps more important than the critical thinking score in predicting NCLEXRN success. However, the researchers indicated that better performance by the BS nursing students than the AS nursing students may be due to the criteria used in admitting students to the new curriculum and may have had some impact on the findings of the investigation. For example, students entering the BS program may have been selected from students who already had the proven ability to obtain a BS degree in nursing. Moreover, the data also suggested that the cumulative GPA at the time of graduation was more important in predicting NCLEXRN success than critical thinking scores (Gross, Takazawa & Rose, 1987).

Miller (1987) implemented a study to determine the impact of a baccalaureate degree nursing (BSN) program on the critical thinking skills of students as measured by the WGCTA. The sample for this study consisted of 137 students from a BSN program in Colorado who completed the WGCTA pre and posttest. Descriptive statistics were employed to determine if there was a difference in critical thinking skills of nursing students at the beginning of the freshman year compared to their critical thinking skills after graduation. Correlational statistics were then applied to identify whether there was a significant relationship between the posttest and the cumulative GPA in the nursing major courses. Miller's research findings indicated that the nursing student performance on the WGCTA pre and posttest showed a significant difference ($p < .05$ level). Further, the findings revealed that a significant relationship ($p < .05$ level) existed between the total score on the posttest and the GPA in the nursing major. It can be argued then that the nursing students' critical thinking skills did improve as a result of the nursing curriculum. Findings from these research studies should prove useful to nursing faculty in their efforts to facilitate critical thinking in the nursing curriculum.

Miller (1992) stated that higher education is being held accountable for educational outcomes. Nursing education is obligated to focus on educational outcomes, and critical thinking is one of these outcomes. Miller's study addressed the impact of a baccalaureate nursing program on the critical thinking skills of students using the Watson-Glaser Critical Thinking Appraisal (WGCTA). The ex post facto study used a pre and posttest design to investigate the relationship between the independent variable (college curriculum, including nursing courses) and the dependent variable (posttest performance on the WGCTA). The sample included 137 participants (Miller, 1992).

The pretest mean (70.00) and posttest mean (72.50) were compared. The difference was significant at the .05 level. Each of the five subtests of the WGCTA showed posttest scores that were higher than the pretest scores. Only the recognition of assumptions and deductions subtests showed gains that were significant at the .05 level. When the posttest WGCTA score was correlated to the GPA in the nursing courses, the Pearson product moment correlation coefficient produced a significant r (.05 level) which accounted for 4% of the variance. The overall GPA correlation coefficient was not significant. Finally, a t-test was applied to investigate whether there was a difference between the gain scores on the WGCTA and the type of generic nursing program, either associate degree or diploma. The t-value for diploma graduates was significant (.01 level), but was not significant for associate degree graduates.

Miller concluded that the overall results obscure the individual performance of the students. Some made large gains, others small gains and others, no gain. Miller called for more emphasis on engaging students in solving nursing problems rather than finding a "correct" answer. Miller challenged nursing educators to include more problem solving experiences, case studies, discussion and reflection, and position papers rather than traditional activities and testing strategies.

Saarmann, Freitas, Rapps, and Riegel (1992) formulated a study to examine the influence of student exposure to faculty on critical thinking skills. It was hypothesized that the greater the length of exposure, the higher the level of critical thinking ability and values would be. A cross sectional survey was used with a convenient sample of faculty from four schools of nursing in southern California. All participating faculty had at least a master's degree in nursing. Baccalaureate nursing student seniors and entering sophomore students were included along with ADN graduates. One hundred twenty eight subjects were used in the analysis (faculty = 32; BSN = 32; ADN = 32, sophomore = 32). The Watson Glaser Critical Thinking Assessment was used. The differences among groups in critical thinking ability was analyzed using analysis of covariance. When the scores were controlled for age, the difference between the scores of faculty and that of sophomore nursing students was not significant ($F = 1.97$, df = 1,123, $p = .163$). The scores of ADN nurses and graduating BSN nurses were comparable (Saarmann, Freitas, Rapps & Riegel, 1992). Only two values were significantly different among the various groups. Faculty members valued achievement more highly and goal orientation less than the other respondents. Interestingly, there was great similarity between the values of all three groups. This suggests that socialization into the nursing role may occur both in the educational and work settings.

Hartley and Aukamp (1994) also studied the difference between the critical thinking ability of nursing students and nursing educators using the Watson Glaser Critical Thinking Appraisal (WGCTA). The sample included 50 nurse educators from 10 nursing programs. Values on the WGCTA (obtained by Sullivan in 1987) were used to represent baccalaureate nursing students in the study. The nurse educators had a higher level of critical thinking ability than did the students ($t = 3.13$, df = 94, $p < .05$). This researcher cautioned the use of these study results. The report of the study did not state that the scores for the faculty were age adjusted and the small size of the sample did not permit the results to be generalized to all nursing educators.

In summary, a number of research studies addressed critical thinking in nursing education. Studies by Felts (1986), Gross, Takazawa, and Rose (1987), Whitley and Chadwick (1987) revealed that students who had higher cumulative GPAs achieved higher levels of critical thinking skills. Miller (1992) found that the overall GPA was not significant in explaining the variance in critical thinking skills for students in associate degree, diploma, or baccalaureate degree nursing programs. Several studies focused more on faculty input in the process of developing critical thinking skills in nursing students. Saarmann, Freitas, Rapps and Riegel (1992) found that there were no significant differences in the critical thinking abilities of students, as measured by the WGCTA, when they were exposed to the faculty for longer time frames. The scores of ADN and BSN graduating nurses were comparable. Hartley and Aukamp (1994) compared critical thinking skills of nursing students and nursing educators and found a statistically significant difference, with educators scoring higher. This finding, however, was not age adjusted. All the researchers addressed the need for nursing educators to more fully understand and incorporate critical thinking skills development in nursing preparation.

In regards to critical thinking and academic performance, Berger (1984) surveyed 137 sophomore nursing students in a baccalaureate school of nursing to determine whether there was a relationship between critical thinking ability and GPAs in nursing and science courses. The WGCTA was employed to measure the critical thinking ability of these students. Pearson's correlation coefficients were computed to analyze the data. The research findings suggested that there was no significant relationship between nursing students' GPAs and their critical thinking scores in either nursing or science ($r = .219$ and $.139$ respectively). However, the Berger (1984) study revealed a positive relationship between science and nursing grade point averages ($r = .357$).

Berger (1984) argued that these findings suggest that nursing students who were successful in science courses were also successful in nursing courses. This longitudinal study also demonstrated that nursing students' critical thinking ability increased as they moved through the curriculum, although GPAs were not correlated with this increase. Thus, Berger suggested that the findings might be important in helping to develop teaching strategies as well as in designing curricula to facilitate the critical thinking skills of nursing students.

Yocom and Scherubel (1985) conducted a retrospective study to examine student performance prior to and after admission to a baccalaureate nursing program compared to passing or failing the State Board Test Pool Examination (SBTPE) and to their performance on the individual sections of the SBTPE. The study sample included 139 graduates from the baccalaureate nursing program at the University of Illinois in 1980. Data related to course grades, grade point averages, credit hours earned prior to admission, school attended prior to admission, previous academic degree, race, and all SBTPE scores were used in the study.

Pearson's product moment correlations were utilized in the Yocom and Scherubel study. Correlations were demonstrated between the two preadmission liberal arts GPAs and preadmission cumulative GPA, and the psychiatric nursing subtest of the SBTPE ($r = .40$, $p < .001$). Correlations were demonstrated between all post admission GPA categories and the five subtests of the SBTPE and the SBTPE pass/fail rate ($r = .43$ to $.68$, $p < .002$). With the exception of clinical practicums in obstetrical, psychiatric, and public health nursing, statistically significant correlations ($p < .05$ to $p < .001$) were found between individual course grades and all SBTPE categories (Yocom & Scherubel, 1985).

In relation to the SBTPE pass/fail the Yocom and Scherubel study, the senior year clinical nursing theory GPA had the highest correlation. For almost all courses taken throughout the nursing program, there was a significant difference ($p. 01$) between mean grades for students who were successful on the SBTPE and those who were not (Yocom & Scherubel,

1985). According to Yocom and Scherubel, there appeared to be an interaction between the school attended, race, and SBTPE pass/fail. However, since minority students accounted for only 10% of the population, caution must be used in interpreting these results. Yocom and Scherubel also stated that they were unable to find other studies describing minority student performance on SBTPEs (Yocom & Scherubel, 1985).

Sullivan (1987) implemented a longitudinal study of registered nurses who completed the BS degree in nursing to determine the relationship between critical thinking skills, creative thinking ability, academic achievement, and clinical performance. In order to measure the critical thinking ability of the 51 registered nurses, the WGCTA pre and posttest was administered upon entering and exiting the baccalaureate nursing program. The Torrance Test of Creative Thinking and the Stewart Evaluation of Nursing Scale were also administered to the sample population to determine if critical thinking, creativity, and academic and clinical performance improved while students were in the nursing program.

Sullivan's findings indicated that critical thinking scores revealed no significant differences between the registered nurses' entry and exit scores. Clinical performance and mean GPA were higher, while creativity scores were lower. The GPAs were significantly higher. The findings further suggested that the longer it had been since these registered nurses completed the first nursing degree or diploma, the higher the critical thinking score was upon entering the BS degree nursing program. This finding suggested that more experienced nurses had higher scores when they enrolled in the program when compared with the less experienced nurses. These data showed; however, that at graduation, few differences were found in the scores of the more experienced and less experienced registered nurse graduates of the BS nursing program (Sullivan, 1987). Sullivan's study was important since he found that there may be a relationship between high school performance and critical thinking skills. The GPA may be more important than test scores for admitting students in nursing programs. The study finding suggested that additional experience may increase students' ability to think critically. These variables may help nursing faculty in developing teaching strategies for nursing students.

In summary, several studies have addressed critical thinking ability and academic performance. Berger (1984) found that there was no significant relationship between students GPAs in either science or nursing courses and their critical thinking ability. Yocom and Scherubel (1985) found that there was a statistically significant difference between mean grades for baccalaureate nursing students for almost all courses taken throughout the nursing program and their scores on the State Board Examination. As a result of a 1987 study, Sullivan concluded that there may be a relationship between high school performance and critical thinking skills. A commonality between all these studies was the call for nursing faculty to place additional emphasis on critical thinking skills within all nursing education programs.

Critical Thinking Ability and the National Counsel Licensure Examination for Registered Nurses (NCLEXRN)

The literature search revealed that few studies have been conducted to determine the relationship between critical thinking ability of nursing students and performance on the NCLEXRN. The existence of such a relationship would support the need to develop and facilitate critical thinking abilities among nursing students.

Bauwens and Gerhard (1987) conducted an investigation with the WGCTA to determine its effectiveness when used as a potential predictor of success for registered nurses on NCLEXRN. Participants of the study included 145 nursing student graduates who completed the WGCTA. These nursing student participants allowed their NCLEXRN scores to be used in this longititudinal study. The GPA and the WGCTA were used as predictor variables. Findings from this descriptive correlational study indicated that critical thinking scores contributed to NCLEXRN success. These data suggest that the GPA and WGCTA scores tend to be good predictors of NCLEXRN success for nursing students (Bauwen & Gerhard,1987). In Bauwens and Gerhard's study, the correlations among the variables suggested that the cumulative nursing GPA at graduation is highly predictive of NCLEXRN success when compared to the entry GPA. Interestingly, the data also suggested that the WGCTA score upon entry is a much better predictor of NCLEXRN success than the WGCTA upon program completion. The findings indicated that the WGCTA scores were effective as preadmission screening criteria for baccalaureate degree nursing programs.

McKinney, Small, O'Dell, and Coonrod (1988) conducted an ex post facto correlational study to determine which measures of academic success predicted success on NCLEXRN. The study sample consisted of 136 baccalaureate nursing graduates from a private liberal arts college. The purpose of this investigation was to determine the relationship between predictor variables, as well as identify baccalaureate nursing students in an integrated curriculum who might have developmental needs in order to progress academically. The researchers argued that the study was significant to develop teaching strategies and counseling intervention. Descriptive statistics and simple regression analysis were employed to identify whether the NCLEXRN score was predictable by any of the variables. Correlation analysis was also employed to measure the correlation between the NCLEXRN score and independent variables in the study. The study results indicated that each of the independent variables, Scholastic Aptitude Test, mathematics subtest; Scholastic Aptitude Test, verbal subtest; Scholastic Aptitude Test, total; prenursing grade point average, nursing clinical grade point average; nursing theory grade point average; and nursing total grade point average, were positively correlated ($p < .001$) with NCLEXRN scores.

In 1989, Rachel conducted a study which was designed to determine the critical thinking ability of baccalaureate nursing students in relationship to their subsequent performance on the NCLEXRN. The study also sought to determine whether age upon program completion and previous educational experience made a difference in the NCLEXRN scores. The sample population for the study included 155 nursing students who were administered the WGCTA and the NCLEXRN between 1983 and 1988. The researcher employed a stepwise logistics regression procedure to determine the relationship between the critical thinking ability of baccalaureate nursing students and their performance on NCLEXRN.

The findings of the study revealed that there was a significant relationship between nursing students' critical thinking skills as measured by the WGCTA and their performance on NCLEXRN. NCLEXRN performance increased as WGCTA scores increased. There was no significant relationship with age upon graduation and previous educational preparation when coupled with critical thinking ability on NCLEXRN performance, which is incongruent with research that demonstrates the positive effects of age and previous educational experience on critical thinking ability. However, Rachel's study did provide support for the positive relationship between critical thinking and NCLEXRN success. These findings further showed that other variables when coupled with critical thinking abilities had no significant impact on NCLEXRN performance (Rachel, 1989).

A study was undertaken by Dell and Valine (1990) in an attempt to determine multivariate relationships among the college GPA, SAT/ACT scores, age, and performance of new baccalaureate degree nursing students on the NCLEXRN. The sample for this study included 90 senior generic nursing student volunteers scheduled to graduate and take the NCLEXRN during the 1990 academic year. These students were enrolled at four small undergraduate institutions. Seventy eight (78) of the 90 nursing students completed the consent forms and the instruments, and actually participated in the study. Dell and Valine used multiple regression to analyze the data. The multiple R between the NCLEXRN and the independent variables was .80 ($F(6,43)$, 12.58, $P < .001$). GPA, SAT/ACT/ACT scores, self-esteem, and age accounted for 64% of the variance in the scores on the NCLEXRN. GPA accounted for the greatest amount of the variance (58%, $R = .76$, $F(1,48)$, 66.44, $p < .001$). The R square change for GPA and SAT/ACT scores did not significantly explain the variance of the NCLEXRN beyond the GPA. Three measures of self-esteem were entered into the equation. The multiple R was .78, ($F(5, 44) = 13,68$, $p < .001$). The R square change was insignificant indicating that self-esteem did not contribute to the variance in NCLEXRN scores. Dell and Valine (1990) argued that this is understandable since predicting cognitive scores with noncognitive measures is a difficult task.

Finally, age was considered in the equation. The multiple R was .80 $(F(6,43) = 12.58, p < .001)$. The R square change was insignificant at the .05 level. Age did not contribute to the variance of NCLEXRN scores beyond the other study variables. Although the study predicted almost two thirds of the variance, one third of the variance remained unaccounted for. The authors suggested that sex and race may account for some of the variability. They called for additional studies using larger samples and including more minority students.

Wold and Worth (1990) conducted a study with 155 nursing students in four successive classes. Four predictive instruments were used, including the Within's Group Embedded Figures Test, Extended Range Vocabulary Test, Inference Test, and the SAT Verbal score. These instruments were intended to measure three attributes: verbal ability, convergent thinking, and field independent perceptual style. Results were correlated with cumulative nursing clinical GPAs, cumulative nursing theory GPA, average cumulative faculty clinical evaluations, and seven prerequisite course GPAs. Pearson product moment correlations revealed measurements between the predictors and three criterion measures. The largest single correlation (.83, p < .001) was between the cumulative clinical ratings. The largest intercorrelation among the predictors was between the SAT verbal test and Extended range Vocabulary Test (.72, p < .001). The Inference Test was found to significantly predict the theory course GPA at the .05 level. The seven prerequisite course GPAs along with the SAT verbal score were the best predictors of course performance, accounting for 46% of the variance.

The results of the study did not support previous research that had identified the four instruments as predictive of student success utilizing the nursing process. The authors concluded that the problem of identifying predictor sets for nursing student success remains unsolved.

Horns, O'Sullivan, and Goodman (1991) conducted a study to

explore predictors of NCLEXRN success. The study looked at both input (preadmission) and process (second, third, and fourth year) variables. The screening sample (N = 208) included students completing the NCLEXRN in 1985.

Forward regression analyses, using the NCLEXRN score as the dependent variable, were performed. Variables were entered hierarchically, eliminating those that were not significant before continuing to the next progression. At preadmission, the significant predictors were GPA and race which together accounted for 33% of the NCLEXRN variance. In the second year, the NCLEXRN prediction equation was improved by 15% by adding the two nursing course theory scores. In the third year, the adult health course explained an additional 11% of the variance and in the final year, the grade for one nursing course and the percentile ranking on the National League for Nursing (NLN) assessment examination explained an additional 9% of the variance. In the final equation, 67% of the NCLEXRN score variation was explained by admission GPA, race, NLN assessment score, and three nursing courses (Horns, O'Sullivan & Goodman, 1991).

The study findings paralleled other research which related preadmission GPA and SAT to NCLEXRN variance. The authors suggested that "it may be useful to conceive of race as a proxy variable for other skills necessary to success on the NCLEXRN such as SAT scores or reading ability" (p. 13). Thus, this study strongly advocates additional research utilizing varied racial and ethnic populations.

In summary, a few studies have addressed the relationship between critical thinking ability and performance on the NCLEXRN. Bauwens and Gerhard (1987), McKinney, Small, O'Dell, and Coonrod (1988), and Rachel (1989) all supported the finding that critical thinking skills, along with various other variables, is statistically significant in predicting success on the NCLEXRN. Dell and Valine (1990) found that almost 60% of the variance in NCLEXRN could be explained by GPA. Horns, O'Sullivan, and Goodman, in their 1991 study, supported other's findings that GPA and SAT were predictive of the NCLEXRN success.

Minority Student Success on State Board Examinations

Although numerous research studies have attempted to identify predictors of academic success in higher education, the literature is limited regarding research that focuses on predictors of success of minority baccalaureate nursing students on the State Board Test Pool Examination (SBTPE). The SBTPE was responsible for the licensure examination for registered nurses prior to the establishment of NCLEXRN. Earlier research studies often focused on the use of preadmission examinations as predictors of success on the SBTPE (Katzell, 1970). A number of research studies have shown the Scholastic Aptitude Test (SAT) to be a good predictor of academic success, however, considerable controversy exists surrounding the use of the SAT as a predictor of minority student success. Several studies have demonstrated that the SAT, when used with other variables, can predict for blacks as well as it predicts for whites (Dell & Halpin, 1984; Outtz, 1979; Sharp, 1984).

Outtz (1979) conducted a study to identify the relationship between black nursing students' performance on the SBTPE and their high school background. The investigation also sought to determine the relationship between selected GPAs of black students in high school and college. The sample of the study consisted of 110 black nursing students who graduated from baccalaureate degree nursing programs between the period from 1973 to 1977. The participants were taking the SBTPE for the first time. Outtz used stepwise regression analysis to examine the relationship between the variables. Pearson Product-Moment Correlation Coefficients were also computed to help determine the relationship between performance factors on the SBTPE and high school background factors of black graduates of the baccalaureate degree nursing program. The relationship between SAT scores and cumulative GPAs in high school and college was examined using multiple regression analysis, and then the multiple R for the prediction of the SBTPE scores was computed.

Outtz's findings revealed significant correlations between high school cumulative GPA and college cumulative GPA. These data showed that the GPA in high school science courses and the GPA in college science courses had a positive relationship ($r = .29$, $p = .01$). Also, in using the stepwise multiple regressions, it was revealed that the cumulative college GPA was found to be the best predictor in all five areas (medical surgical nursing, obstetric, pediatric, and psychiatric nursing) of the SBTPE ($r = .58, .47, .53, .54$ and $.54$; $p = .01$). The second best predictor discovered was the SAT Verbal examination. There was a significant difference found in the correlation between the cumulative college GPA and the SAT Verbal ($r = .165$). In summary, according to Outtz in the 1979 study, the SAT would not be the best predictor of success for black nursing students on the SBTPE. Rather it was found that the cumulative GPA in college was the best predictor of success for black nursing students on the SBTPE.

Dell and Halpin (1994) conducted an investigation to identify variables that best predict success of black nursing students on the SBTPE at a predominantly black baccalaureate degree nursing program. The investigation also sought to determine if these predictors were identical for both program success and SBTPE success. The population for the investigation was composed of 456 black students admitted to the institution between 1970 and 1974. The sample was limited to those nursing students who completed the nursing program and took the SBTPE for the first time. The sample included 181 nursing students who graduated with a bachelor's degree and wrote for the SBTPE.

Dell and Halpin computed two separate discriminant analyses to measure the relationship between the independent variables and the dependent variables. When computing the first discriminant analysis, four variables (SAT verbal, SAT quantitative, high school GPA, and the NLN Prenursing Examination) were utilized to differentiate between black nursing students who graduated from those who did not successfully complete the nursing program. The analysis revealed that there was a significant difference between black nursing students graduating and not graduating on each dependent variable. The findings revealed that the high school GPA and

NLN Prenursing Examination possessed the strongest significant predictive relationships. The second discriminant analysis indicated that the four variables in the first discriminant analysis, plus the college GPA, significantly differentiated between those who were successful on the SBTPE and those who were not. The findings demonstrated a significant difference between black nursing students who passed the SBTPE and those who failed on each independent variable. The data revealed that the college GPA possessed the highest discriminating weight followed by the SAT verbal and then the NLN Prenursing Examination.

Sharp (1984) conducted a study to determine the predictive relationship of a number of selected high school and college performance variables, using stepwise discriminant analysis to determine the best combination of the selected variables predictive of nursing student performance on the SBTPE. The seven variables addressed by Sharp were high school grade point average (HSGPA), nursing grade point (CNGPA), and five ACT standard scores, English score (ENG), Mathematics score (MA), Social Studies score (SS), Natural Sciences score (NSC), and ACT composite score (COMP). The sample for this study consisted of 322 baccalaureate degree nursing students during the period between 1974 and 1979. The sample was selected from a population of 572 baccalaureate degree nursing students and was limited to graduates whose records included ACT scores, high school GPA, cumulative high school GPA, and SBTPE scores. The sample was also limited to nursing students who were taking the SBTPE for the first time. Sharp used multiple regression analysis to determine the relationship between the independent variables and the dependent variables.

The framework for Sharp's study was provided by 13 research questions. The findings of the study showed a predictive relationship between the ACT English score, the ACT social science score, and the composite ACT score. The data revealed that the best possible combination of predictors include GPA, mathematics, and natural science courses. The first seven questions were concerned with the predictive relationship of each of the selected variables to SBTPE performance. The results for each variable were significant at the p = .0001 level. F-values for each of the variables were HGPA 11.77; CNGPA 21.68; ENG 23.15; MA 37.51; SS 28.12; NSC 43.31 and COMP. 56.40. The last five research questions examined the interactive relationship of the sleeted variables that were predictive of performance on each of the SBTPE subexaminations (MED, SURG, OBS, NCH, PSY). Multiple regression analysis was used to identify the predictive combinations. F-values were computed for four combined groups: HSGPA, CNGPA, ENG, MA, SS, NSC = 10.43; CNGPA, ENG, MA, SS, NSC = 12.54; CNGPA, MA, SS, NSC = 15.57; CNGPA, MA, NSC = 20.20. All results were significant at the p = .0001 level.

Boyle (1986) studied the effectiveness of admissions criteria in successful selection of minority students in a baccalaureate nursing program as evidenced by successful program completion, final GPA, and SBTPE scores. Study subjects included 145 minority students (blacks (n = 111); other (n = 34)) admitted to a baccalaureate nursing program at a large Midwestern university. An exploratory statistical approach was used to test various models. Multiple regression and stepwise multiple regression was used to predict GPA and SBTPE performance for the students completing the program. A full model and a reduced model were examined.

The full model included the five predictors: entering GPA (ENTGPA), ACT, high school rank (HSRANK), age and number of college credit hours prior to admission to the nursing program (HRSPTA). The F-values were significant at the .05 level and accounted for 25% to 55% of the explained variance for the total group and the black subgroup. The F tests of the full versus the reduced model were not significant indicating that the models that were not retained in the reduced model did not significantly explain additional variance. The ACT was the most significant predictor for each test score within the SBTPE. ACT was the only predictor in the reduced model for the medical, psychiatric, and surgical scores on the SBTPE.

In Boyle's study, the best indicators of academic success as measured by final GPA were the ACT and ENTGPA for all groups. But for the black subgroup, the ENTGPA and ACT were somewhat less predictive. The

ENTGPA was predictive of program completion ($p < .005$). It was found to more accurately predict completion than incompletion. Boyle concluded that the size of the nonblack minority subgroup sample hampered the explanatory power of the study for the other groups. Since the ENTGPA did not accurately predict the individuals who were not successful in the program, these study findings differed from the previous findings of Dell and Halpin (1984). Boyle called for additional students to determine factors which impede program completion.

Rami (1992) conducted a retrospective pilot study to evaluate the predictive ability of four variables on NCLEXRN success. These included prenursing GPA, ACT scores, comprehensive examination scores, and scores on the Basics I, NLN Achievement Test. Subjects for the convenient sample included 35 African American baccalaureate nursing students. Multiple regression analysis was used to evaluate the contribution of the four predictor variables in the NCLEXRN success. The NLN Basic I test score was the single significant variable ($r = .5327$, $p < .001$) for NCLEXRN success. All the other variables were nonsignificant at the .05 level. The multiple R indicated that only 33% of the NCLEXRN score variance could be predicted from the examined variables. Rami concluded that the study was inconclusive in predicting NCLEXRN success with only the NLN Basic I test being significant as a predictor. Rami recommended replication of the study using a larger sample.

A more recent investigation was conducted by Frierson, Malone, and Shelton (1993) to assess the effect of an intervention procedure on African American nursing students on the NCLEXRN. The sample consisted of a class of eight African American, senior, nursing students attending a predominantly black university. The nursing students in this sample participated in a special intervention program that emphasized instruction concerned with effective test taking, the utilization of learning team method, and faculty reinforcement.

Frierson, Malone, and Shelton's study demonstrated that the special intervention procedure was effective in improving African American nursing student performance on NCLEXRN. The researchers indicated that the academic records of the nursing student participants were very similar to nursing students in previous classes. However, the research findings revealed that the mean NCLEXRN score and the passing percentage were significantly higher for African American nursing students who received the intervention. Frierson, Malone, and Shelton argued that a larger number of students can be successful in nursing programs when effective intervention procedures are available to them. This is especially significant for African American nursing students, given their history of lower test performance and limited access to professional nursing programs due to many societal factors.

Finally, only a few studies were found that dealt with minority student success on RN licensure examinations. Outtz (1979) reported that cumulative college GPA was the best predictor of success for black nursing students on the SBTPE. Dell and Halpin (1984) stated that the high school GPA and the NLN Prenursing Examination were the strongest predictors of SBTPE success. Both Sharp (1984) and Boyle (1986) identified the predictive relationship between the ACT scores and SBTPE success. Frierson, Malone, and Shelton (1993) added an intervention in their study and found that minority students' success on the licensure examination was improved when effective intervention procedures were added to the nursing curriculum.

Study of African American College Students' Critical Thinking Ability and Success on the NCLEXRN for Nurses

A 1997 study conducted by the author is the first extensive investigation of the relationship between critical thinking ability and success of African American nursing students on the National Council Licensure Examination. The problem of this study was to investigate the critical thinking ability of African American baccalaureate nursing students at five selected historically black colleges and universities (HBCU's) located in the southern region of the United States. The study also examined whether relationships existed between their critical thinking ability, age, gender, cumulative grade point average (CUMGPA), marital status, health related work experience, educational experience, and success on the National Council Licensure Examination for registered Nurses (NCLEXRN). In addition, the study also investigated the relationship between the demographic variables, and critical thinking ability included five subtests from the Watson-Glaser Critical Thinking Appraisal. The sample included 124 students from five baccalaureate nursing programs at historically black colleges/universities in the southern United States.

This study was significant for a number of reasons. The review of the literature revealed that virtually nothing had been done to determine the relationship between critical thinking ability and success on NCLEXRN for baccalaureate African American nursing students. The nursing profession has been committed to the provision of equitable services to a diversified population. In order to do this, nursing educators have sought to assure a heterogeneous provider population (Boyle, 1986; Claerbaut, 1978; de Tornyay & Russell, 1978; Snead, 1983). Minorities continue to be under represented in the nursing profession (Boyle, 1986; Philpot & Bernstein, 1978). This has been blamed on a number of factors, including high attrition. Bower (1976) reported an attrition rate for minority students that was four times the attrition rate for white students. The development of critical thinking skills may decrease the attrition of minority students, and increase their success in program completion and licensure examination.

As patients have become "sicker" and hospital days have become fewer, nursing students must also be more astute at diagnosing patient needs and intervening expediently. They must possess a strong knowledge base coupled with the ability to think critically to become effective problem solvers. These two factors must coexist if the educational process is to prepare nurses to meet the health care challenges of the future. A strong educational preparation, which includes both development of an adequate knowledge base and critical thinking ability has the potential to enhance the nursing student performance on NCLEXRN. Thus, all nursing students, including the baccalaureate African American nursing student would benefit from this preparation

In 1991 the National League for Nursing (NLN) Criteria and Guidelines for evaluation of Baccalaureate Nursing programs included critical thinking as one of the five elements in measuring outcome criteria for reviewing baccalaureate nursing programs. Also, accreditation requirements of the NLN demand that all nursing graduates use the nursing process as a basis for guiding their decisions practice (Justus & Montgomery, 1986). The concern for investigating the critical thinking ability of African American baccalaureate nursing students emanates from the complexity of professional nursing which requires cognitive skills beyond memorization of medical disease facts and procedures.

It is believed that identification of strength and weaknesses in critical thinking abilities of nursing students will enable nursing programs to focus on critical thinking in a more structured manner. This concerted effort could improve the student's ability to use critical thinking skills, and apply the nursing process. Subsequently, nursing students would have increased success in professional nursing programs and be better prepared to pass the NCLEXRN. Furthermore, when faculty members are aware of students' strengths and weaknesses in critical thinking, they can adapt and develop teaching strategies to impact the effectiveness of critical thinking skill development in nursing education.

Additionally, the information gathered in the study also helps to identify the extent to which present baccalaureate nursing programs impact the critical thinking ability of their graduates. It provides new information for schools of nursing from which they can examine the role of critical thinking within their curricula. Moreover, the data collected provides evidence that certain demographic variables significantly impact student performance on NCLEXRN. The research findings did provide additional insight into the role of faculty in designing and developing teaching strategies to facilitate the development of critical thinking skills and the application of those skills in the nursing profession.

Two instruments were employed to collect data for this study: the Background Information Survey (BIS) and the Watson-Glaser Critical

Thinking Appraisal (WGCTA). The Background Information Survey was designed to capture descriptive information from each member of the sample. The items collected from each individual were age, gender, marital status, years worked in health and nonhealth related fields, and previous post secondary education. The Watson-Glaser Critical Thinking Appraisal (WGCTA) is considered the instrument of choice in nursing education for measuring critical thinking ability (MacMillan, 1987). Therefore, with five subtests identified as Inference, Recognition of Assumptions, Deduction, Interpretation, and Evaluation of Arguments which define critical thinking, the WGCTA was used to measure the critical thinking ability of the participants in the study sample.

Prior to administering the WGCTA and the demographic survey, a consent form, which described the intent and use of the data, was signed by all participating students. Students also permitted the researcher to obtain their cumulative GPAs and NCLEXRN results from the universities. These authorizations executed by each participant enabled the collection and subsequent analysis of the data. Although all of the graduating nursing students at each universities' request, completed both instruments, only those students who had given written permission were included in the study population. Student anonymity was maintained by using coded numbers in place of names. No other personal identifiers were used in the study.

To adequately answer the research questions, many methods were used to analyze the sample data. Descriptive statistics, z-test, and regression techniques were used to analyze the data. In this study, the outcome on the NCLEXRN exam was thought to be dependent upon demographic factors. Of the 124 students taking the NCLEXRN examination, 83.1% passed while 16.9% failed. There were two major types of variables used in the analysis, continuous and categorical. For the continuous variables, various descriptive statistics revealed that, in the WGCTA, the lowest possible score on each section was 0 and the highest possible was 16. Meanwhile, students scored highest on the Evaluation of Arguments section of the WGCTA (10.38). However, this section also had the second highest variability in scores as measured by the standard deviation (3.34).

Most of the categorical variables were demographic. The data contain frequency counts and sample percentages for each level of each demographic categorical measure. Some levels of highest education and health related work experience contain small cell sizes. Therefore, these two variables were dichotomized. The variable, highest education, was dichotomized by grouping together those with a high school education and those with beyond a high school education. The variable, health related work experience, was dichotomized by grouping together those with no health related work experience and those with at least some health related work experience.

The exploration of factors important in determining the outcome of the NCLEXRN examination was analyzed. Mature, experienced, goal oriented students are perceived to pass more frequently than those who are not. Age was perceived to be an important factor in determining the passing of the NCLEXRN. Age was dichotomized by grouping together younger students, 20 to 29, and older students, 30 to 49. Among the proportion of students in each of these age groups, older students passed the exam at a higher rate (94%) compared to younger students (79%). However, a two sample z-test revealed that the proportion of older students passing the examination was significantly higher than that of younger students ($p < .05$).

Marital status was perceived to be an important factor in determining the passing of the NCLEXRN. Among the proportion of single and married students that passed the NCLEXRN, married students passed the exam at a higher rate (91%) compared to single students (80%). However, a two sample z-test revealed that the proportion of married students passing the examination was not significantly higher than that of single students ($p > .05$).

Among the three two-way combinations of marital status, highest education, and health related work experience. All students, single and married, with more than a high school education passed the NCLEXRN examination. Of the 31 married students, 28 passed the NCLEXRN, which is 90% of the married students.

A higher percentage of students with health related work experience passed the NCLEXRN than students with no health related work experience. Finally, all students having more than a high school education with and without work experience passed the NCLEXRN, yielding a 100% passing rate. Only 74% of the students with a high school education without work experience passed the NCLEXRN.

Logistic regression was used to analyze five research questions addressing items that influenced NCLEXRN outcome. On research question one, the author investigated whether or not there was a significant relationship between the critical thinking ability of African American baccalaureate nursing students and their success on the NCLEXRN. The analysis revealed that there was not a significant relationship between the critical thinking ability of African American baccalaureate nursing students and their success on the NCLEXRN.

Research questions two and three are involved with the relationship between critical thinking components and NCLEXRN outcome within generic and nongeneric groups. Generic students are those having, at most, a high school education and no health related work experience. Nongeneric students are those having more than a high school education and health related experience. The nongeneric students passed the examination at a higher rate compared to generic students. A two sample z-test revealed that the proportion of nongeneric students passing the examination was significantly higher than that of generic students.

On research question two, the author examined whether or not there was a significant relationship between the generic African American baccalaureate nursing students' critical thinking ability and their success on the NCLEXRN. The analysis showed that there was not a significant relationship between the critical thinking ability of generic African American baccalaureate nursing students and their success on the NCLEXRN.

On research question three, the author examined whether or not there was a significant relationship between the nongeneric African American baccalaureate nursing students' critical thinking ability and their success on the NCLEXRN. The data revealed that there was not a significant relationship between the critical thinking ability of nongeneric African American baccalaureate nursing students and their success on the NCLEXRN.

On research question four, the author investigated whether or not there was there a significant relationship between the African American baccalaureate nursing students' critical thinking ability, age, gender, CUMGPA, marital status, health related work experience, educational experience and their success on the NCLEXRN. The data revealed that all males and all students with more than a high school education passed the NCLEXRN. This data indicates that there was not a significant relationship between the critical thinking ability of nongeneric African American baccalaureate nursing students and their success on the NCLEXRN. However, CUMGPA and HRWEXP had a practical impact on the passing of the NCLEXRN. Also, for every increase in unit for CUMGPA (based on a 4.0 scale) a student was 9.37 times more likely to pass NCLEXRN.

On research question five, the author investigated whether or not there was a significant relationship between the African American baccalaureate nursing students' age, gender, CUMGPA, marital status, health related work experience, educational experience and their critical thinking ability as measured by the WGCTA. Regression analysis was performed to investigate the significance of the relationships. The results of the regressions showed that the dependent variable was statistically significant, $F_{[6,110]} = 4.32$, p , < .01. Age had a significant negative relationship with inference, $p < .01$. However, CUMGPA had a significant positive relationship with inference, p < .01. All other models were insignificant at the 0.05 level of significance. The model relating WGCTA components with INF had the largest R^2 of any of the models, $R^2 = .19$.

For Research Questions One, Two, Three and Four, there was no statistically significant relationship between critical thinking ability as measured by the Watson-Glaser Critical Thinking Appraisal and the passing of African American baccalaureate nursing students on the NCLEXRN (p>.05). However, the z-est revealed that the proportion of students with other postsecondary education and other health related work experience, passing the

NCLEXRN examination was significantly higher than that of generic students (p< .01). The generic students are those who began their college education within a year following graduation from a high school and had no health related work experience.

The demographic data were similar to that which was expected in relation to age, CUMGPA and critical thinking ability. Gross, Takazawa, and Rose (1987) found that both age and number of years in college for baccalaureate nursing students related positively to critical thinking scores and academic performance. In this study, the z-test revealed that the older student pass rate was significantly higher (p=.02) than that of the younger student rate.

On the research question, "Was there any significant relationship between African American baccalaureate nursing students's age, gender, CUMGPA, marital status, health related work experience, education experience and their critical thinking ability?", the only component measure that demographic factor, CUMGPA, had a greater impact on inference versus the other WGCTA components. The higher the CUMGPA, the better the student was able to correctly discriminate among degree of truth and falsity of inferences drawn from given data. It is also important to note, that a students' ability to infer from the given data decreased as age increased.

This study focused on demographic and WGCTA factors and their influence in effecting the outcome on the NCLEXRN examination. Data were presented showing demographic makeup of the students. Calculations were made concerning particular differences in NCLEXRN passing percentages among age, generic status, and marital status groups.

Five research questions were analyzed using the data. Four of the research questions sought to find items which influenced NCLEXRN outcome. Logistic Regression was used in calculating models involving factors affecting NCLEXRN outcome. One research question sought to find demographic factors which have an impact on critical thinking skills. OLS regression was used in calculating models involving factors affecting WGCTA components.

The cumulative GPA, with a p value of .06, marginally statistically significant, demonstrated a practical impact on the nursing students passing the NCLEXRN. However, there was no statistically significant relationship found between critical thinking ability as measured by the WGCTA and the passing of African American baccalaureate nursing students on the NCLEXRN. Inference was the only component measure that only one demographic factor (CUMGPA) statistically significantly related to.

Prognosis for the Future: Conclusions, Implications, and Recommendations

As a result of the findings of this study, the following conclusions were derived. (1) Success in passing the NCLEXRN is dependent on the student knowledge base, and subtle other factors, and student success on the Watson-Glaser Critical Thinking Ability Appraisals did not contribute to the ability to predict success or failure on the NCLEXRN at any significant level. (2) Maturity contributes to the likelihood of success on the NCLEXRN. Again, although not directly derived from the study findings, two elements were considered which may have contributed to this conclusion. First, it is generally recognized that time is a major factor in the mastering of many life skills as well as academic requirements. Second, it is thought that with maturity often come fewer distractions. (3) Being married contributes to an element of success on the NCLEXRN. While not directly derived from the study findings, it was surmised that those who were married may be highly motivated and/or more goal oriented. (4) A cautious conclusion was that male nursing student participants may bring greater motivation to the study of nursing and to performance on the NCLEXRN. While caution is called for, one could speculate that since nursing has been dominated by females, those males who make a decision to enter the profession are those with only the highest motivation.

The findings from this research are significant to the nursing profession, in general, and to nursing educators, in particular. Because this research dealt with an essentially unstudied group of individuals, it represents an attempt to describe relevant variables which impact the success of African

American baccalaureate nursing students in attaining licensure as registered nurses.

Nursing, as a profession, is committed to providing an ample supply of practicing professionals and to addressing the needs of a diverse population. It behooves nursing educators, therefore, to determine how best to prepare nurses who will represent diversity. There is no shortage in the number of minority students who seek to enter a nursing preparation program. But as minority students are accessing education more readily, it is important that the revolving door syndrome (high attrition) is prevented and that educators do everything possible to assure their success in achieving professional status.

In this study, the pass rate for NCLEXRN licensure among the participants was 83%. This number is below the national average of approximately 90% and well below the average for Louisiana which was 95.8% in 1994 (the last year for which the data is available) according to The National Council of State Boards of Nursing (Louisiana State Board of Nursing, 1994). This indicates that there is a need for educators to address this area in order to achieve a higher pass rate for the African American nursing students on the NCLEXRN. It might also be argued that generic baccalaureate nursing students are not being adequately prepared in their prerequisite courses prior to entering nursing professional programs. In this case, nursing educators must look at all curricula of nursing programs and ensure that students take the appropriate courses which will provide strong foundations from which to build.

The finding that previous health related work experience was associated with success had implications for nursing education as well. As early as within the high school setting, prospective nursing students could be appropriately counseled to participate in health occupation courses in which practicums are offered. Additionally, nursing educators could provide for a transitional course prior to entering the professional curriculum. This finding might also point out the need for nursing education to include more clinical experience to simulate clinical setting so that the students reap the benefits of previous health care related work experience.

Finally, since inference was identified as the most influential of the subtest scores for NCLEXRN success, nursing educators must focus additional attention on assisting students to develop this skill. This might include the development of additional teaching strategies which focus on attaining this skill. The finding that had negative statistically significant relationship with inference is perplexing and bears additional study.

The conceptual model allowed for prediction of success or lack of success on the NCLEXRN. However, the findings of the analyses of the study suggested that critical thinking ability as measured by the WGCTA did not predict African American baccalaureate nursing students' performance on the NCLEXRN. Therefore, additional research is recommended. It is important to investigate further to determine the latent variables which might account for the outcome.

One possibility for further research might be to utilize an instrument which is likely to accurately measure critical thinking ability for African American baccalaureate nursing students. Although the Watson-Glaser Critical Thinking Appraisal has been widely used, its use with African American nursing students has not been sufficiently large to validate it as a true indicator of what it purports to measure.

None of the research which was reviewed addressed the influence of the WGCTA subtest scores on NCLEXRN success. Additional research is recommended in order to further investigate and/or validate the strength of this relationship and to determine how to utilize this information.

A number of years ago, baccalaureate nursing educators came together with nursing service personnel to look at the total curriculum of nursing education programs. At that time, the issue was the lack of technical skills in baccalaureate educated nurses. Since that time, nursing education has done a creditable job in assuring that the graduates can perform with technical skill. But has the pendulum swung too far? Baccalaureate nursing educators must remember that they are, first preparing an individual who has a knowledge base equivalent to other individuals with a like education, and second, preparing a professional nurse, skilled in both the art and science of nursing. Nursing education should develop stronger partner relationship with other disciplines in order to derive whatever benefits are available in relation to strengthening critical thinking abilities.

With the daily changes in health care, nurses are moving out of the hospital and into the community at an alarming rate. This requires more independent practitioners, individuals who can apply theoretical concepts, and make appropriate inferences from these concepts, in order to derive a valid conclusion. Nursing education must be ready to prepare this practitioner.

CHAPTER 10

Goal Orientation, Cognitive Tool Use, and Achievement: Preferences and Behaviors of African- and Latina-American College Women During Hypermedia Instruction

Heather A. Katz

Introduction

Increasingly, college students are being exposed to interactive hypermedia (IHM) as educators integrate it into their course curriculum. IHM is an associative environment comprised of links and nodes that requires learner control of computer-based applications to access multimedia information resources (e.g., text, graphics, video, audio, animations, interactions, etc.) via non-linear, user-determined, navigational paths (Burton, Moore, & Holmes, 1995; Kommers, Grabinger, & Dunlap, 1996). Serving as either stand alone or ancillary instruction it bypasses some of the bandwidth and access barriers of internet connectivity, allows for user controlled and self-paced learning, and offers substantive interactivity.

Both educators and researchers espouse that the nature of IHM holds great promise for instructional programs that can accommodate and adapt to the unique learning needs and characteristics of variant learners. Cognitive tools are one attribute that when embedded within IHM programs can assist learners with specific cognitive tasks such as information processing, and in general, comprehension (Lajoie, 1993). Cognitive tools can include advance organizers, bookmark, find, glossary, help, index, notebook, and map. Investigating how learner characteristics (e.g., goal orientation) influence adaptive or maladaptive patterns of cognitive tool use can help to understand how these characteristics influence not only the learning process, but also learners' performance in achievement situations within interactive hypermedia environments. Furthermore, it can assist educators to effectively integrate IHM instruction into the college curriculum in ways that are not only engaging and educative, but also appropriate for students having both unique and diverse learning needs that are not only shaped by racial/ethnic characteristics but are influenced by one's present learning environment and past learning experiences.

This chapter reports on the empirical research that investigated the interrelated and combined effects of African American and Latina American women's goal orientation (GO) on their cognitive tool use (CTU) and achievement in an interactive hypermedia environment (IHME). The treatment used in this study *HIV & AIDS Prevention Education for Women of Color* is an IHM program that was specifically developed for the undergraduate African American and Latina American women. It accounts for individualized learner characteristics, gender, age, race/ethnicity, and the college milieu while providing HIV/AIDS prevention education and interactive skills-building information for this population. Investigating the interaction effects between GO and race among college students within an IHME begins to answer the call for further research to study GO with diverse populations across variant educational settings (see Middleton & Midgley, 1997).

Results from this study can assist in understanding how college students learn in an IHME, and can help to facilitate research-based integration of IHM programs into the college curriculum that takes into account learners' unique characteristics and instructional needs, differences in learning environments, age, gender, race/ethnicity, and socio-economic status. This can produce learner- as opposed to media-centered IHM instruction that can positively influence learners' behavior and achievement outcomes.

Research Questions

Investigating the interrelated and combined effects of learners' goal orientation (GO) on their cognitive tool use (CTU) and achievement in an interactive hypermedia environment (IHME) was fueled by five research questions: (1) What is the effect of learners' GO on CTU in an IHME? (2) What is the effect of learners' GO on learner achievement in an IHME? (3) How does learners' CTU predict and affect learners' achievement in an IHME? (4) What is the combined effect of learners' GO and CTU on achievement in an IHME? (5) Does race—African American and Latina American—affect learners' GO in an IHME?

Literature Review

Hypermedia

Interactive hypermedia environments have the possibility to elicit significant performance outcomes when used to (a) disseminate instruction to different learners across various disciplines; (b) meet the needs of variant learner characteristics, styles, and behaviors; and (c) increase learners' performance outcomes. Research that focuses on empirical results concerning hypermedia-based instruction and its relevance to cognitive learning theories provides evidence of such outcomes. Several experimental studies have reported (a) significant gains in learner performance (Borsook & Higginbotham-Wheat, 1992; Crosby & Stelovsky, 1995); (b) increased course completion rate (Hardiman & Williams, 1990); (c) decreased demand on teaching time (Higgins & Boone, 1992); and (d) a positive attitude toward hypermedia instruction (Janda, 1992). Overall, when hypermedia is integrated into instruction it has the following five potential outcomes: (a) provides rich and realistic contexts for multichannel (e.g., auditory and visual) learning (Cunningham, Duffy, & Knuth, 1993; Moore, Burton, & Myers, in press); (b) content is accessed non-linearly and instructional order and pace is learner determined (Cunningham et al., 1993); (c) focuses learner attention on the relationship of facts and multiple perspectives of information (Jacobson & Spiro, 1995; Spiro & Jehng, 1990); (d) encourages active student-centered learning to create individualized learning environments (Grabe, Petros, & Sawler, 1989); and (e) promotes collaboration and cooperative learning for learners to jointly construct new knowledge (Ambrose, 1991; Nelson & Palumbo, 1992; Park, 1991; Vanderbilt, 1992; Yang & Moore, 1995-6).

Knowing which type of goal oriented learners use what type of cognitive tools during interactive hypermedia (IHM) instruction can lend further insight as to how learners of different epistemic beliefs fair in an interactive hypermedia environment (IHME) and how these beliefs influence learning. This knowledge can assist educators to successfully transition college students from traditional instruction to IHM instruction and to devise appropriate instructional methods to ensure successful and appropriate integration of instructional IHM into their existing course curriculum. Instructional designers can benefit in their design of IHM programs creating environments that meet the variant cognitive needs of individual learners. As a result, IHM programs can deliver maximum instructional effectiveness and assist learners to reach maximum achievement levels.

Cognitive Tools in an Interactive Hypermedia Environment

When learners self impose actions and processes (i.e., learning strategies) to acquire information or skill that involve agency, purpose, and instrumentality perceptions (to include methods such as organizing and transforming information, seeking information, and rehearsing, or using memory aids), they are using self-regulated learning strategies (SRLS) (Zimmerman, 1989). Research reports that the use of SRLS can foster active cognitive engagement in learning and increase academic performance (Weinstein, 1996; Weinstein & Mayer, 1986; Winne & Hadwin, 1997). Park (1995) concludes that it is extremely important to include learning strategies [e.g., cognitive tool use (CTU)] into the design and development of computer-assisted instruction (CAI) for they not only require learners to think but to write down what they think. He suggests, "future research should collect empirical evidence of the efficacy of the learning strategies in CAI settings even though the effectiveness of learning strategies has been well established in a non-CAI environment" (Park, 1995, p. 452).

Similar to SRLS in traditional learning environments, cognitive tools have the potential to assist learners to acquire, process, and comprehend information within an IHME, giving learners a more active role in constructing their own knowledge. Cognitive tools can act as structural aids to assist learners in managing new information. They can provide the scaffolding needed for learners' to free up lower level cognition so that concentration is focused on tasks that require higher-order cognitive skills, which can develop effective forms of self-regulated learning (e.g., CTU) (Lajoie, 1993; Winne & Stockley, 1998). Research has reported that CTU during computer-assisted instruction can assist learners to construct knowledge and support cognitive processes, such as memory and monitoring one's learning experience, and allow learners to engage in otherwise unattainable cognitive activities (Lajoie, 1993).

Consequently, it is theoretically deduced that the function of cognitive tools within IHMEs is similar to the function of SRLS within traditional learning environments—they provide learners with actions and processes to elaborate, rehearse, and organize when acquiring, processing, and comprehending information. This analogous relationship between SRLS in traditional learning environments and cognitive tools in IHMEs lays the theoretical foundation to investigate cognitive tools in an IHME. Table 2 highlights the cognitive tools investigated in this study, and theoretically frames the parallel relationship between them and SRLS.

Goal Orientation

This study adopts the goal orientation (GO) ideology of Dweck and Leggett (1988), Pintrich and Schunk (1996), and Wolters, Yu, and Pintrich (1996)—a reflection of individual differences that learners bring with them to a learning task; and, is empirically conceptualized and measured as individuals' personal characteristics. Researchers posit a significant relationship between learners' GO, self-regulated learning strategies (SRLS), and achievement within traditional learning environments. Learners can elicit the following three GOs during achievement situations, which can affect their direction and regulation of thought and behavior, use of SRLS, and level of academic performance within traditional learning environments: (a) task (T)—having a purpose or goal in an achievement setting, seeks to develop competence and extend one's mastery and understanding, and tends to use more effective SRLS that result in positive performance outcomes; (b) performance-approach ($PAPP$)—having a focus on self, strives to demonstrate competence, and uses SRLS for the attainment of successful achievement outcomes; (c) performance-avoid (PAV)—having a focus on self, seeks to avoid the demonstration of incompetence, and generally demonstrates ineffective and inefficient SRLS or limited to null use of SRLS, resulting in a negative achievement outcome (Ames & Archer, 1988; Hagen & Weinstein, 1995; Nicholls, 1984; Pintrich & Garcia, 1991; Pintrich & Schrauben, 1992).

Contradictory results are evident from research that exclusively investigates the approach tendency of the performance GO, while excluding the avoidance tendency. Anderman and Young (1994) found that a $PAPP$ orientation was negatively correlated with the use of deep cognitive strategies and positively correlated with surface level strategies. Similarly, Nolen (1988) and Meece (1988) found that an ego orientation goal (approach tendency) was positively related to surface level cognitive strategies, but unrelated to the use of deep cognitive strategies. Whereas, Kaplan and Midgley (1997) found that ability goals were positively related to maladaptive strategies, and uncorrelated with adaptive learning strategies.

Although goal theorists have continually described the performance-avoidance component, only recent studies have investigated the avoidance tendency in conjunction with both the $PAPP$ and T components. Investigating all three goals, Middleton and Midgley (1997) reported that both the $PAPP$ and PAV tendencies were not facilitative to SRLS, whereas Elliot and Harackiewicz (1996) found that only the PAV undermined intrinsic motivation. Moreover, it is important to note that some research has indicated that learners can simultaneously pursue multiple goals, and that there might be approach and avoidance tendencies within both the task and performance

Table 2: Implications of Self-regulated Learning Strategies (SRLS) for Cognitive Tools in Hypermedia Environments (IHMEs)

Cognitive Tool	SRLS	Implication	Significance of Cognitive Tools Within IHME
Bookmark	Bookmarking Organizing Information Environmental Structuring	Organization and structuring of information is a learning strategy employed in traditional learning environments and shares similar characteristics to the bookmark tool in hypermedia environments	The bookmark tool allows learners to organize their information according to categories, and add or delete bookmarks, thus structuring their learning environment, and freeing up cognitive resources that would otherwise attempt to remember where information is located.
Find	Organizing Information Seeking Information	Cognitive style was significantly related to achievement, tool use, and attitude when using an index/find tool to search hypermedia programs (Leader & Klein, 1996). This is similar to traditional learning environments where cognitive style learners use, such as index use.	During hypermedia database searches a field-independent learners performed significantly better than field-dependent learners when using an index-find cognitive tool (Leader & Klein, 1996). Leader and Klein call for further research that investigates how learners with variant learning characteristics use hypermedia.
Glossary	Seeking Information	Cognitive style was significantly related to achievement, tool use, and attitude when using an index/find tool to search hypermedia programs (Leader & Klein, 1996). This is similar to traditional learning strategies style affects which learning strategies learners use, such as seeking information.	During hypertext reading learners declared they usually did not read the glossary terms; however, observation showed that learners accessed the glossary (Altun, 1999). Students in computer-optional definition conditions were much more willing to read word definitions than students in a printed text condition (Reinking & Rickman, 1990).

Table 2 Cont'd: Implications of Self-regulated Learning Strategies (SRLS) for Cognitive Tools in Hypermedia Environments (IHMEs)

Cognitive Tool	SRLS	Implication	Significance of Cognitive Tools Within IHME
Help	Seeking Assistance Seeking Information	Performance-avoid learners tend not to ask for help in traditional environments for fear of looking "Dumb" (Middleton & Midgley, 1997). In a hypermedia environment, the anonymity allows learners to seek help without such fear of looking incapable.	The pilot study of the study discussed in the Chapter indicated a significant interaction between GO and the use of the help tool. Spatial maps are effective in facilitating navigation and conceptual maps are effective in facilitating learning; thus, "the constraints imposed on navigation by a conceptual map not only reduce the time spent exploring the document but also significantly enhance learning" (McDonald & Stevenson, 1999). Students who use hypermedia programs with an embedded instructional map performed significantly better (p<.01) than students without an embedded instructional map (Barba, 1993).

Table 2 Cont'd: Implications of Self-regulated Learning Strategies (SRLS) for Cognitive Tools in Hypermedia Environments (IHMEs)

Cognitive Tool	SRLS	Implication	Significance of Cognitive Tools Within IHME
Map	Concept Mapping Vee Diagram Advance Organizers	Navigational aids reduce learners' cognitive load (as do concept maps, Vee diagrams, and advance organizers)-to not only process information but to monitor one's progression through hypertext-on their working memory by helping them with the task of orientation (McDonald & Stevenson, 1999).	Disorientation in hypermedia can have detrimental effects on learning resulting in learners wandering through hypertext without monitoring their cognition or employing SRLS, and are unaware of what material has been viewed or not viewed (Hammond & Allinson, 1989). This can result in the learner having to focus on reorientation and possibly compromising learning (Kim & Hirtle, 1995).
Notebook	Note taking Organizing Information Summarization Monitoring	Reading and writing are largely interrelated, interactive; and, these two processes should be integrated and connected (Tierney & Shanahan, 1991). The design of notebooks in interactive multimedia systems can allow learners to use strategies that assist in rehearsing, organizing, and elaborating information to make the learning task more personally meaningful (Schroeder & Kenny, 1995).	Readers brought to the hypertext environment their expectations and beliefs about the interrelated nature of reading and writing and would print out pages of the hypertext and make notes in the margins. Overall, experienced computer users emphasized the need for hypertext environments that allow one to take notes as well as read (Altun, 1999).

goal conceptualizations; however, literature only referents the such combinations of GOs, and, how they might influence learners' patterns of behaviors (Kaplan & Midgley, 1997).

It is evident that different GOs yield variant adaptive or maladaptive patterns of affect, cognition, and behavior within traditional learning environments. The GO, SRLS, and achievement relationship within a traditional learning environment is clearly documented and thus provides the theoretical foundation to investigate GO, CTU, and achievement within an IHME. This investigation goes beyond current goal research and can assist in understanding how GO affects learners' perceptions about their reasons for CTU within IHMEs. Furthermore, this study provides the opportunity to further the GO research to a non traditional learning environment—IHME, using a different learning domain—HIV/AIDS education, with diverse races—African American and Latina American, in a different educational setting—college. This speaks to the need to explore GO with diverse participants, using other disciplines, and with age groups beyond the K-12 realm (Middleton & Midgley, 1997).

The Interactive Hypermedia Instructional Treatment

Content Relevance

The program's instructional content was derived from HIV/AIDS public domain information disseminated by the United States Centers for Disease Control. Subject matter experts[p] in the areas of social and cultural implications regarding HIV/AIDS, and HIV/AIDS content accuracy

---

[p] Included a southwestern state university professor of Social Work who has conducted extensive research in the area of HIV and AIDS and women of color, and two health educators from a southwestern state university Health Services.

provided formative evaluation of the program. Macromedia Authorware 4.0 was used to create the interactive hypermedia (IHM) instructional program.

HIV/AIDS prevention education that is disseminated via a popular interactive medium, which has both culturally relevant and credible content, and represents the same race, cultural, and socio-economic status (SES) background of the target audience is purported to have not only a higher rate of viewer engagement and acceptance but improves the accurate perception of one's health risk (Pittman, Wilson, Adams-Taylor, & Randolph, 1992; Stevenson & Davis, 1994; Stuber, 1991; Wingood & DiCelemente, 1992). This IHM program can begin to answer the collective call to action for new and innovative ways to disseminate culturally appropriate HIV/AIDS intervention programs that are specific to the unique needs—age, education level, SES, and environment—of diverse sub-groups that exist within both the African American and Latina American communities (National Center for HIV, 2001). Collectively, research shows that various media—video (Stevenson & Davis, 1994), talking-computers (Staton, 1996), and hip-hop music therapy (Stephens, Braithwaite, & Taylor, 1998)—can be effective in delivering innovative HIV/AIDS prevention education.

Design Principles

This IHM program was developed according to Park and Hannafin's (1993) twenty design principles and respective implications for the design of interactive multimedia. These implications are derived from twenty principles that are theoretically grounded in psychological, pedagogical, and technological empirical research, respectively. For example, the program's cognitive tool availability supports Implication 2—*embed structural aids to facilitate selection, organization, and integration.* While the modules and sub-modules, which contain layers of instruction and interactive activities support both Implication 1—*layer information to accommodate multiple levels of complexity and accommodate differences,* and Implication 3—*organize lesson segments into internally consistent idea units* (Park & Hannafin, 1993, p. 68).

Instructional Modules

The hypermedia program consists of three core instructional modules: (a) *Facts*—includes two separate submodules: *HIV Facts* and *AIDS Facts*; (b) *Protection*—includes two separate submodules: *Abstinence*, and *Safer Sex* that has three submodules: (a) *What is Safer Sex?*, (b) *How Can I Protect Both Me and My Partner?*, and (c) *What Places Me at Risk*; (3) *Communication*—includes two separate submodules: *What to Say* and *How to Respond*.   The *What to Say* submodule includes videos and interactive activities that display how women can communicate to their partner about HIV/AIDS and the need to use protection to prevent against contracting HIV.   The *How to Respond* submodule includes audio clips/videos of potential excuses that men might use to avoid both safer sex and talking about HIV/AIDS.   Interactive activities allow woman to respond to such excuses by typing their own responses to the excuses (in the form of audio clips).   All modules include menus of information and interactive activities.

Cognitive Tools

The cognitive tools—bookmark, find, glossary, help, map, and notebook—are accessible from the lower navigation bar on all screens and from a drop down menu located within the program's top menu bar (see Figure 1).   The *Bookmark* tool creates links to screens to allow quick and repeated viewing of information deemed important/relevant by the user.   The *Find* tool allows the user to type in a word/phrase that they wish to find.   A listing of the word/phrase is returned in the *Page* box. The user can then click the page she wishes to access, and the page/screen is presented with the word/phrase highlighted in lime green.

The *Glossary* tool allows the user to read definitions of HIV/AIDS related terms found within the program, and also provides the opportunity to browse additional terms that are not contained in the program. To browse the *Glossary* the user clicks a letter contained in the top letter bar. This displays the letters' respective terms below the letter bar in the left hand *Term* box. Clicking a term displays its definition below the letter bar in the right hand *Definition* box. The user may also click on words contained within the

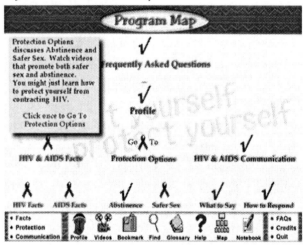

Figure 1: Screen shot of HIV/AIDS program displaying advance organizer for the Protection module, and cognitive tools in bottom navigation bar.

Definition box. If the word is not contained in the glossary, the user will receive the message *Sorry that word does not appear in the Glossary.*

The *Help* tool allows users to gain information as to the functionality of the program. Help topics include: *Bookmark Tool, Find Tool, Glossary Tool, Help Tool, Map Tool, Navigation, Notebook Tool,* and *Tool Bar.* Clicking a *Help Topic* in the right hand box displays its respective *Help Topic Description* in the left hand box.

The *Map* tool (see Illustration 1) serves as a navigational device, an advance organizer, and tracks users' module completion. Each module is represented by its respective module name and is accompanied by a red AIDS ribbon. When the user clicks either a ribbon or a module name, they are linked to that respective module. It also features mouse rollovers that summarize the modules' content, allowing the user to know what to expect from each module (i.e., advance organizer). A checkmark alerts the user that she has completed the respective module.

The *Notebook* tool allows the user to take notes and answer questions as she navigates through the instructional program. It is divided into sections that coincide with the program modules—*Facts*, *Protection*, and *Communication*—in which the user can append, add, or delete notes. The *Notebook* contents are written to three text files—*notesfacts.txt*, *notescomm.txt*, and *notespro.txt*, which can be printed upon program completion.

Having the program track the users' completion of the modules can assist the user to determine which ones she has completed or not completed. This can "free-up" the users' lower order cognitive processes (i.e., keeping track of module completion) allowing the user to concentrate on tasks that require higher order cognitive processes (e.g., relating program content to her own life experiences regarding the issues that surround HIV/AIDS, and reflecting on them as she answers questions and organizes her thoughts using the *Notebook* tool.).

Profiles

Profiles are intended to inform the user about the facts regarding HIV/AIDS and to provide a culturally and ethnically appropriate role model so that the user feels empowered to learn and communicate about HIV/AIDS and the options available to protect against contracting HIV. There are two *Profiles*—*Laqita's Profile*, an African American female and *Vivian's Profile*, a Latina American female. The *Profiles* highlight Vivian's and Laqita's attitudes and thoughts regarding HIV/AIDS with respect to the decisions and choices that they have implemented. Both Laqita and Vivian describe their teen years and their experiences with making choices that revolved around HIV/AIDS. This information is disseminated via QuickTime movies.

The *Profile* is randomly assigned at the beginning of the program after viewing the program instructions. After viewing the initial *Profile* the user clicks the *Close* button and is forwarded to the *Main Menu* where she chooses one of the three modules to begin the program.

Profile screens are only displayed if the assigned *Profile* has information relative to a respective module. For example, *Laqita's Profile* is viewed prior to the *Abstinence* module but not before the *Safer Sex* module. However, *Vivian's Profile* is viewed prior to the *Safer Sex* module but not prior to the *Abstinence* module. This is because Vivian and Laqita advocate different protection options. The *Profile* screens provide access to QuickTime movies that are relevant to the respective module/section. After the QuickTime movie ends the user is asked to use the *Notebook* tool to answer a few pre-module questions and reflect how her life is similar or dissimilar to that of the *Profile's*.

Methodology

Sample

A total of 50 African American and Latina American undergraduate women from two data collection sites constituted the sample population. Random sampling identified 2 African American and 2 Latina American participants from a large southwestern state university. Purposive sampling identified 46 African American participants from a small southern state Historically Black College and University. Participants from the southwestern university were traditional students, whereas their HBCU counterparts were non-traditional students in that most were older students—either married with children or single mothers, employed full and or part-time, and received financial aid. A professor from this HBCU described the academic competencies of the majority of the students as having "comparable levels to that of community college students who were in need of or had taken remedial courses prior to enrolling in their freshman undergraduate courses." The southwestern university participants owned their own computers and had access to the university's state of the art technology labs. The majority of the students at the HBCU did not own computers and relied on the computers provided by the one computer lab that was open 7 days a week, 24-hours a day. The southwestern university participants had extensive computer and hypermedia experience, while the majority of the HBCU participants had minimal computer and hypermedia experience.

Grouping Variables

Goal Orientation: Independent Variable. The independent variable is goal orientation (GO). Participants were grouped [as determined by the Pattern of Adaptive Learning Survey (PALS) (Midgley et al., 1997)] at the ordinal level into an appropriate GO—task *(T)*, performance-approach *(PAPP)*, and performance-avoid *(PAV)*. The PALS is a Likert-type self administered survey having a five-point forced-choice scale, with 1 representing "NOT AT ALL TRUE" and 5 representing "VERY TRUE." Exploratory factor analysis was used to assist in the development of this PALS scale and internal consistency for *T*, *PAPP*, and *PAV* were assessed using Cronbach's alpha, yielding .83, .86, and .75, respectively.

Achievement and Cognitive Tool Use: Dependent Variables. Dependent variables included learner achievement[pp], and cognitive tool use[ppp][pppp]. However, for Research Question CTU is both a predictor and an independent variable; and, in Research Question Four it is a predictor variable. The 42-item True/False pre- and posttest instrument *HIV/AIDS Knowledge Questionnaire* used to assess participants' HIV/AIDS knowledge was comprised of two independent surveys: (a) the *HIV and AIDS Knowledge* (1994 - 1998) instrument created by the *Measurement Group*; and (b) The World AIDS Day Resource Book survey *How Much Do You Know About HIV/AIDS?* (1998) developed by the American Association for World Health organization. Combining the two instruments allowed for a thorough assessment of the

---

[pp] Achievement is measured by pretest to posttest gain scores.
[ppp] Cognitive tools include bookmark, find, glossary, help, map, and notebook.
[pppp] Use is measured by the number of times a tool is accessed and the amount of time (in minutes) it is used.

participants' HIV/AIDS knowledge, and accurately represented the content in the hypermedia program.

Procedures

First, participants signed the consent form and completed the PALS questionnaire and the HIV/AIDS Knowledge Questionnaire pretest. Second, the researcher explained the nature of IHM to the participants and inquired if there were any questions before they began the program; if so, the researcher answered the question(s) in a manner that did not jeopardize the validity or reliability of the study. The researcher then gave the participants their respective personal identification number and password to ensure their anonymity and confidentiality. Third, the participants began the self-paced IHM instructional program on either a PC or MAC computer. Participants self-terminated the IHM program at a point in which they deemed appropriate. Fourth, after participants terminated the IHM program they completed the HIV/AIDS Knowledge Questionnaire posttest and the Demographic Questionnaire, which queried the participants' age; race; undergraduate class and major; and self-perceived levels of HIV/AIDS and instructional design knowledge, and computer experience. Finally, the researcher debriefed the participants, which included answering any of their questions regarding the study and informed them that the HIV/AIDS information contained in the program was accurate and current according to the dates cited within the program. Immediately after the quantitative data was collected and analyzed the participant follow-up interviews were conducted. The participant interviews were conducted via telephone and taped recorded with the participants' consent.

Data Analysis

This mixed-methods study used quantitative investigation as the primary research method and qualitative as the secondary. To answer Research Question One, *What is the effect of learners' goal orientation (GO) on cognitive tool use (CTU) in an interactive hypermedia environment (IHME)?*, six one-way ANOVAs were calculated with GO—task *(T)*, performance-approach *(PAPP)*, and performance-avoid *(PAV)*—as the independent variable and the number of times accessing the tools—bookmark, find, glossary, help, map, and notebook as the dependent variables, respectively for each ANOVA. Additionally, five one-way ANOVAs were calculated with GO—*T*, *PAPP*, and *PAV* as the independent variable and the amount of time (in minutes) accessing the tools—bookmark time, glossary time, help time, map time, and notebook time as the dependent variables, respectively for each ANOVA.

To answer Research Question Two, *What is the effect of learners' GO on learner achievement in an IHME?*, a one-way ANOVA was conducted with GO—*T*, *PAPP*, and *PAV* as the independent variable. The dependent variable was achievement (pretest to posttest gain scores).

To answer Research Question Three, *How does learners' CTU predict and affect learners' achievement in an IHME?*, a multiple regression analysis was conducted with CTU—bookmark, bookmark time, find, glossary, glossary time, help, help time, map, map time, notebook, and notebook time—as the predictors and achievement (pretest to posttest gain scores) as the criterion variable. Additionally, a one-way ANOVA was conducted with the cumulative sums of the total number of times each tool was accessed as the independent variable and achievement (pretest to posttest gain scores) as the dependent variable.

To answer Research Question Four, *What is the combined effect of learners' GO and their CTU on achievement in an IHME?*, a multiple regression analyses was conducted with GO—*T*, *PAPP*, and *PAV*; and CTU—bookmark, bookmark time, find, glossary, glossary time, help, help time, map, map time, notebook, and notebook time—as the predictors and achievement (pretest to posttest gain scores) as the criterion variable.

To answer Research Question Five, *Does race affect learners' GO in an IHME?*, a one-way ANOVA was calculated with race—African American and Latina American—as the independent variable and GO—*T*, *PAPP*, and *PAV* as the dependent variable. Results were compared to research in traditional learning environments that found middle school African American females tended to adopt T GOs (Middleton & Midgley, 1997).

Participant Interviews

Patton's (1987) theory of depth interviewing, specifically the interview guide was employed to collect data from the participant interviews. The following eight interview questions constituted this study's interview guide: (a) In general what did you think about the *HIV & AIDS Prevention Education for Women of Color* program? Likes? Dislikes? Strengths? Weaknesses?; (b) Tell me about the cognitive tools that you did or did not use and why you did or did not use them.; (c) Did you have any specific strategies in mind when you were using the tools? Yes/No…Please elaborate.; (d) Did you find the tools a benefit or a hindrance? Yes/No…at what point in the program? Please elaborate.; (e) Do you think the tools helped you to retain and/or process the information in the program? Yes/No…Please elaborate.; (f) Do you use any strategies or study aids similar to the cognitive tools in this program when you study for your classes? Yes/No…Please elaborate. Please compare and contrast the two.; (g) Do you think that the program had or will have an effect on your knowledge, attitude, beliefs, and behavior regarding HIV and AIDS? Yes/No…Please elaborate.; (g) Based on the participants' quantitative data other probing questions were developed.

Interviewees were selected via purposeful sampling—theory based, maximum variation, and natural grouping. Respectively, the constructs were GO—T, $PAPP$, and PAV ; achievement—low, medium, and high; and race—African American and one Latina American. Inductive analysis (Patton, 1987) was used to conduct coding of the qualitative data. This allowed for the discovery of the issues that were relevant to the IHM study and its treatment to emerge from the participants' responses. Specifically, analyst-constructed typologies were employed to code the data. This allowed the researcher to describe and classify patterns and themes of the participants' learning behaviors for which the participants did not have any labels or terms to describe.

Results

Goal Orientation Identification

Forty-three participants were identified as task (*T*) oriented learners, 4 as performance-approach (*PAPP*), and 3 as performance-avoid (*PAV*). Further analysis of the goal orientation (GO) means revealed that seven of the participants had borderline GOs that were similar to another GO. One *PAV* participant's GO mean was very close to a *T* GO: $MEAN_{PAV} = 4.00$, $MEAN_T = 3.80$, $MEAN_{PAPP} = 3.67$; while, the other was close to a *PAPP* GO: $MEAN_{PAV} = 5.00$, $MEAN_{PAPP} = 4.67$, $MEAN_T = 3.80$. The GO mean of one *T* participant was similar to the mean of a *PAV*: $MEAN_T = 4.20$, $MEAN_{PAV} = 4.00$, $MEAN_{PAPP} = 3.67$. While, the means of three *T* participants were similar to a *PAPP* GO: (a) $MEAN_T = 5.00$, $MEAN_{PAPP} = 4.83$, $MEAN_{PAV} = 4.17$; (b) $MEAN_T = 4.20$, $MEAN_{PAPP} = 4.00$, $MEAN_{PAV} = 2.33$; and (c) $MEAN_T = 4.40$, $MEAN_{PAPP} = 4.17$, $MEAN_{PAV} = 3.17$. Likewise, the GO mean of a *PAPP* participant was similar to a *T*: $MEAN_{PAPP} = 4.17$, $MEAN_T = 4.00$, $MEAN_{PAV} = 2.17$.

Research Question One: Goal Orientations and Cognitive Tool Use

The ANOVA[ppppp] indicated that the *PAV* learners used the map significantly more times than both their *T* and *PAPP* counterparts: $F(2, 47) = 5.89$, $p = .005$, $MEAN_{PAV} = 22.33$, $MEAN_T = 9.40$, $MEAN_{PAPP} = 7.25$. The post hoc Tukey test indicated that the mean scores between the *PAV* and the *T* were significantly different: Tukey $= 12.94$, $p = .005$, as were the mean scores between the *PAV* and *PAPP*: Tukey $= 15.08$, $p = .01$.

Similarly, the cumulative number of times a learner used the tools was significant. Analyses indicated that the *PAV* learners cumulatively used an assortment of the tools significantly more than their *PAPP* counterparts: $F(2,$

[ppppp] Find time is not analyzed for Research Questions 1, 3, and 4 because when the hypermedia program calls in the computer system's "Find," it is prevented from tracking the time (in minutes).

47) $= 3.14$, $p = .052$, $MEAN_{PAV} = 40.00$, $MEAN_T = 23.60$, $MEAN_{PAPP} = 19.00$. The post hoc Tukey test indicated a near significant difference in the mean scores between the *PAV* and the *PAPP*: Tukey $= 21.00$, $p < .06$. Likewise, there was a near significant difference in the mean scores between the *PAV* and the T groups: Tukey $= 16.40$, $p < .06$. The results indicated that there were no other significant findings regarding CTU—bookmark, find, glossary, help, and notebook—among the three GOs. However, patterns of cognitive tool use (CTU) among the GOs are worth mention.

Though ANOVA results were not significant in other areas of tool use, descriptively it shows which GOs preferred which tools and for how long. The means indicated that the *PAV* used the notebook more than the *T* and *PAPP* groups, while the *T* used the notebook more than the *PAPP* groups: $MEAN_{PAV} = 17.00$, $MEAN_T = 12.73$, $MEAN_{PAPP} = 11.50$. The glossary and the bookmark were not used by the *PAPP* group, but were used by the *T* and *PAV* groups, having similar bookmark means—glossary: $MEAN_T = .44$, $MEAN_{PAV} = .33$; and bookmark: $MEAN_T = .03$, $MEAN_{PAV} = .02$. The help tool was used by both the *T* and *PAPP* groups but not the *PAV* group: $MEAN_T = .44$, $MEAN_{PAPP} = .25$; while, the find tool was used only by the *T* group: $MEAN_T = .21$.

Though not significant, there was a difference in the means for the amount of time (in minutes) each GO spent using the respective tools. Descriptively, the *PAV* group used the notebook and cumulatively used an assortment of the tools for a longer amount of time (in minutes) than both the *T* and *PAPP* groups—notebook: $MEAN_{PAV} = 21.88$, $SD_{PAV} = 10.57$; $MEAN_T = 18.82$, $SD_T = 17.86$; $MEAN_{PAPP} = 15.26$, $SD_{PAPP} = 13.44$. The total time of all tools used were: $MEAN_{PAV} = 23.91$, $SD_{PAV} = 11.41$; $MEAN_T = 21.15$, $SD_T = 18.06$; $MEAN_{PAPP} = 16.28$, $SD_{PAPP} = 12.84$. Descriptively, *PAV* participants spent more time (in minutes) in the program than the *PAPP* and *T* participants: $MEAN_{PAV} = 111.67$, $SD_{PAV} = 50.64$; $MEAN_{PAPP} = 89.75$, $SD_{PAPP} = 20.76$; $MEAN_T = 78.60$, $SD_T = 28.86$.

Research Question Two: Goal Orientations and Achievement

The ANOVA[pppppp] indicated no statistical significance between the participants' GOs and their gain scores. Descriptively, the *PAPP* group had greater gain scores than the *T* and *PAV* groups, while the *PAV* group had a negative achievement score: $MEAN_{PAPP} = 2.45$, $SD_{PAPP} = 0$; $MEAN_T = .45$, $SD_T = 4.64$; $MEAN_{PAV} = -.81$, $SD_{PAV} = 3.72$.

Research Question Three: The Relationship Between Cognitive Tool Use and Achievement

The multiple regression ($R = .56$, $F = 1.23$) did not reveal an overall significance between CTU and the GOs. However, there were two significant relationships and one descriptively worth mention. Analysis revealed a significant positive relationship between achievement and the amount of time (in minutes) the glossary tool was used: Glossary Time—$r = .56$; $t(42) = 2.46$, $p = .02$; $B = 2.42$; beta weight = .45. A significant negative relationship was found between achievement and the number of times the glossary tool was used: Glossary—$r = .56$; $t(42) = -2.26$, $p = .03$; $B = -3.84$; beta weight = -.51. No significant relationships were found between achievement and the number of times using or the time (in minutes) that the tools were used—bookmark, find, help, map, and notebook. However, one positive relationship is descriptively worth mention: Bookmark time—$r = .59$; $t(42) = 1.58$, $p = .13$; $B = 25.54$; beta weight = .49.

Additionally, a one-way ANOVA was conducted with achievement as the dependent variable and the learners' cumulative frequencies of using the cognitive tools (low = 0 - 25, medium = 26 - 51, and high = 52 - 75) as the independent variable. The grouping of the cognitive tool frequencies was based on the range of the frequencies occurring among the total number of times participants accessed the tools. The results did not yield significance. Though descriptively, achievement was shown to increase across all levels of cumulative tool access with high tool access having the most gain, followed by

---

[pppppp] An ANCOVA was conducted with the same independent and dependent variables as the ANOVA and yielded similar non-significant results.

low, and medium having the least: $MEAN_{High} = 1.22$, $MEAN_{Low} = .67$, $MEAN_{Medium} = .13$.

Research Question Four: The Relationship Between GO, CTU, and Achievement

Results from the multiple regression ($R = .59$, $F = 1.19$) did not yield an overall significance between GO, CTU, and achievement. However, there were two significant relationships, and three descriptively worth mention. A significant negative relationship exists between achievement and the number of times the glossary tool was used: Glossary—$r = .59$; $t(42) = -2.29$, $p = .03$; $B = -3.94$; beta weight = -.52. Yet, a significant positive relationship was found between achievement and the amount of time (in minutes) the glossary tool was used: Glossary Time—$r = .59$; $t(42) = 2.39$, $p = .02$; $B = 2.37$; beta weight = .44. No significant relationships were found between achievement and GO and the number of times using or the time (in minutes) that tools were used—bookmark, find, help, map, and notebook.

However, three relationships are descriptively worth mention: (a) A positive relationship between achievement and the number of times the bookmark tool was used: Bookmark—$r = .59$; $t(42) = 1.34$, $p = .18$; $B = 2.84$; beta weight = .37; (b) a positive relationship between achievement and the amount of time (in minutes) the bookmark was used: Bookmark time—$r = .59$; $t(42) = 1.58$, $p = .13$; $B = 25.54$; beta weight = .49; (c) a negative relationship between achievement and the amount of time (in minutes) the map was used: Map time—$r = .59$; $t(42) = -1.43$, $p = .16$; $B = -.74$; beta weight = -.37.

Research Question Five: Goal Orientation Preference of African Americans and Latina Americans

The intended one-way ANOVA with race as the independent variable and GO as the dependent variable was abandoned due to the disproportionate number of African American and Latina American participants. Instead, the frequencies of the different GOs within both race categories were analyzed. Analysis indicated that all of the Latina American participants ($N = 2$) were T

oriented as were the majority of the African American—41 *T*, 4 *PAPP*, and 3 *PAV*.

Participant Interviews

Initially, twelve participant interviews were identified using the constructs—GO, achievement, and race. However, due to the low participant number of Latina American participants, and the unavailability of the participants for follow-up interviews seven interviews in total were conducted: one *T* learner (Latina American), two *PAPP* learners (African Americans), one *PAV* learner (African American), two high achievement learners (both African American, *T* learners), and one low achievement learner (an African American, *PAPP* learner).

Themes. The following nine themes surfaced and were deemed relevant: Supported Information Processing, Fostered Problem-Solving, Navigation Assistance, Attention Getting, Classroom Connections, Real Life Connections, Educational/Informative, Change in Knowledge, Attitude, Beliefs, and Behavior (KABB), and No Need...Don't Use. For a detailed analysis, explanation, and implications of the themes see Katz (2001; 2002).

Discussion. This study investigated the relationships between learners' variant goal orientations (GO) and their CTU and achievement in an interactive hypermedia environment (IHME). Both positive and negative relationships demonstrate the importance to consider both the number of times that cognitive tools are accessed and the length of time that they are used. It is also important to consider both the form and function of cognitive tools and their interdependent relationship with learners' GO and achievement. The occurrence of participants' atypical GO behavior demonstrates the need to consider learners' adoption of borderline and multiple GOs. Moreover, it was apparent that learners can change their GO during a single learning task dependent upon the context of the learning task at hand and the variant situated tasks contained within the overall learning task. Explanations of these findings are addressed and implications for future GO and interactive hypermedia (IHM) research/design are discussed.

Cognitive Tool Use and Goal Orientations

Understanding the behaviors of variant goal oriented learners in an IHME can help educators to facilitate the integration of hypermedia instruction into the curriculum. Results from research question one indicated that the relationship between CTU and GO elicited somewhat atypical behaviors as compared to the GO and cognitive strategy relationship reflected in traditional learning environments.

Participants Adoption of Borderline/Multiple Goal Orientations

First, it is important to indicate that some participants adopted borderline (having similar means) GOs. This resulted in participants eliciting behavior that was atypical of their assigned GO—task (T), performance-approach ($PAPP$), or performance-avoid (PAV). For example, PAV learners used more cognitive tools than T learners who typically use more cognitive strategies than their PAV cohorts. Similarly, others adopted multiple (having identical means) GOs, which made it impossible to assign them to one GO. Participants' adoption of borderline/multiple GOs yielded results that are atypical of most traditional GO research (see Ames, 1992; Deci & Ryan, 1985; Elliot & Harackiewicz, 1996; Wolters et al., 1996). Yet, their occurrence is documented (see Kaplan & Midgley, 1997) and is becoming more prevalent within GO research.

Performance-avoid Goal Orientation Elicits Adaptive Behavior

Participant's who adopted a PAV GO accessed the map tool, and, all of the cognitive tools significantly more times than their T and $PAPP$ counterparts. The PAV learners preferred to access the notebook tool more times than the T or $PAPP$ learners. Moreover, the PAV's notebook entries revealed that they used the notebook in a manner that is more characteristic of a T or $PAPP$ learner—longer entries having a higher quality of writing. These results are uncharacteristic of a PAV goal oriented learner that typically demonstrates maladaptive behavior and outcomes. However, several reasons can account for these phenomena.

First, the *PAV*'s demonstration of adaptive learning behaviors can possibly be attributed to the fact that 2 of the 3 *PAV* learners had borderline GOs. One *PAV* learner borderlines with a *T* GO, while the other borderlines with a *PAPP*. This could explain why the *PAV*'s atypical behavior is more characteristic of behavior elicited by *T* and *PAPP* GOs. Similarly, learners having *T* GOs that borderline with *PAV* and *PAPP* GOs can explain their atypical behaviors of accessing fewer tools than their *PAV* counterparts.

Second, it is possible that the hypermedia environment that provided easily accessible cognitive tools and instruction on their use may have influenced the *PAV* learners to use more cognitive tools more often. Cognitive tool use within hypermedia instruction can free up learners' lower level cognitive strategies (e.g., monitoring task completion via the map) to employ higher level cognitive strategies (elaboration and association via notetaking in the notebook) (Lajoie, 1993). This could possibly explain the *PAV*'s adaptive behaviors to access both the map and the notebook more times than the *T* and *PAPP* groups.

Third, it is interesting to note that as participants approached a self-assigned time limit (due to classes, work, etc.,) they reported that their focus shifted away from the learning process to task completion. Hence, this can account for maladaptive behaviors and explain why the *T* group accessed fewer tools than the *PAV* group. This might be especially relevant for participants having a *T* GO that borderline a *PAPP* or *PAV* GO.

Why? Adopting Borderline/Multiple Goal Orientations

It appears that participants' borderline GOs, which resulted in atypical behavior is similar to previous research that found learners' adoption of multiple goals can result in the use of adaptive or maladaptive strategies (Kaplan & Midgley, 1997). This adoption of multiple GOs requires further research in that variables such as age, gender, or domain content can account for such atypical behavior (Kaplan & Midgley, 1997). Additionally, manipulation of the GO variable for a situated task verses a reflective task might influence the adoption of borderline/multiple GOs as well as the use of a laboratory setting as opposed to a field setting (Kaplan & Midgley, 1997).

Since the variables—gender, domain content (HIV/AIDS), and a public laboratory setting—applied to this study they might have impacted participants' adoption of borderline/multiple GOs, resulting in atypical behavior. For instance, it has been purported that self-regulated learning strategies (SRLS) might be best suited for college-aged learners since their college academic environment requires them to be self-regulators of their class schedule and learning and study processes (Pintrich & Garcia, 1994). It is possible that this study's population of undergraduate students adopted a *T* GO and self-regulated extensive use of cognitive tools because such adaptive behavior is characteristic of undergraduate students whose purpose is to acquire knowledge in order to succeed in college. There is also evidence that women are more *T* oriented learners than their male counterparts, thus, use a greater amount of cognitive tools (see Middleton & Midgley, 1997), as reported in the findings of this study.

The study's domain content—HIV/AIDS—and its relevance to women of color might also have influenced the participants' behavior. The participants might have viewed various public media reports (e.g., television, newspapers, and billboards), which advertise that young adult African and Latina American women are disproportionately affected by HIV/AIDS and have a greater chance of HIV infection. This heightened awareness could have influenced the participants to acknowledge the relevance that HIV/AIDS prevention education has in their lives, thus, taking a greater interest to learn from the program. Such an interest could have influenced the learners to adopt a *T* GO and elicit adaptive behaviors (e.g., greater CTU) and positive achievement outcomes.

Moreover, the study's investigation of learners' GOs within the situated task of participants viewing the *HIV & AIDS Prevention Education for Women of Color* program in a computer laboratory setting might have influenced the learners to adopt borderline/multiple goals. Similarly, it is possible that learners' GOs were dynamic and changed as the situated tasks within the hypermedia program changed. For example, a learner might have adopted a *T* GO when viewing videos and adopted a *PAV* orientation when filling in blank content matrices, and a *PAPP* GO when viewing the map and calculating where next they would navigate to in the program. This could have resulted in participants' eliciting both adaptive and maladaptive behaviors and achievement outcomes.

Since this study was conducted under the confines of a computer laboratory setting it did not offer participants an extended amount of time to reflect on the task at hand as would have an actual classroom setting or a series of classroom settings. Additionally, participants' academic and work schedules could have influenced participants' to self-impose time constraints. Such constraints might have forced participants to concentrate more on completing the situated task at hand as opposed to having more time to reflect on the program's content when viewing the program and answering the pretest and posttest. Realizing the value and relevance of the HIV/AIDS content, yet "feeling pressed for time" and "rushing" to complete the program and/or the posttest in order to "make it to" a class or a job was expressed during the participant interviews. As a result, regardless of the participants' adoption of a *T*GO, they might have simultaneously adopted either *PAPP* or *PAV* GOs. This simultaneous adoption of multiple goals might have influenced participants to elicit maladaptive behaviors (e.g., less use of cognitive tools and low achievement outcome).

Cognitive Tool Use and Achievement

Understanding the relationships between CTU and achievement within an IHME can assist designers to create learner- as opposed to media-centered instruction. Such instruction can help facilitate positive achievement outcomes. Results from Research Question Three and Four revealed both positive and negative relationships between CTU and achievement.

It is very interesting to report that both positive and negative relationships exist between achievement and the number of times a tool is accessed. The same positive and negative relationships exist between achievement and the amount of time (in minutes) spent using a particular tool. For instance, a significant negative relationship was found between achievement and the number of times that the glossary tool was accessed. However, a significant positive relationship was found between achievement and the amount of time spent using the glossary tool. Thus, for each time that the glossary tool was accessed achievement decreased, but the longer amount of time that the glossary tool was used achievement increased. Descriptively, the opposite relationship exists with the map tool. The more times a learner accessed the map tool their achievement increased, but for each minute that they spent using the map tool achievement decreased. Descriptively, positive relationships exist between bookmark and achievement, and bookmark time and achievement. Thus, achievement increased not only each time that the bookmark was accessed, but also with each minute that the learner used the bookmark. These results demonstrate that it is necessary to consider both the form and function of cognitive tools as well as how and if they assist learners' with their higher order cognitive strategies (e.g., elaboration of content in the notebook tool) or lower order cognitive strategies (e.g., using the help tool to understanding how to use the program), and in turn, how these relationships affect achievement.

Notably, it is worth mention that achievement increased across all levels—low, medium, and high—of the total number of times that a participant accessed the tools. Anecdotally, a participant in the high tool use level (having accessed the notebook extensively, and having the highest achievement gain score) corroborated this empirical result when she reported that using the notebook helped her to learn the information contained within the program.

There are several possible reasons for the occurrence of both positive and negative relationships. It appears that the purpose and function of each cognitive tool must be considered when trying to understand the occurrence of both positive and negative relationships between CTU and achievement. For example, accessing the glossary tool a few times yet spending longer periods of time in the glossary reading the definitions might have increased achievement because the learner acquired information from the definitions that assisted her to process and understand the program's content. However, accessing the glossary tool several times and quickly browsing the definitions instead of thoroughly reading them to gain insight into the program's content might have decreased achievement.

Moreover, achievement might have increased each time a learner accessed the map tool because it helped her to design a relevant learning path that prioritized the order in which she learned the content. This could have allowed her to skip over information previous learned and quickly navigate to "new" information. However, viewing the map for long periods of time might have prevented the learner from quickly acting upon (i.e., rehearsing or elaborating) the information stored in her short-term memory. This could have resulted in the decay of information that was stored in her short-term memory (Peterson & Peterson, 1959). As a result, her long-term memory never acquired the information, thus, resulting in decreased achievement.

In order to understand the interrelated effects of CTU on achievement it is imperative that the form and function of the cognitive tool, the number of times that a tool is accessed, and the length of time that it is used be considered simultaneously. The occurrence of both positive and negative relationships between CTU and achievement demonstrates that CTU is multifaceted and deserves further research. This can assist designers in their efforts to imbed cognitive tools within hypermedia instruction that can facilitate positive achievement outcomes.

Participants' Engagement With the Interactive Hypermedia Program

John Dewey's (1963) progressive curriculum theory states that education should be centered around the learner's experience. The culturally and gender appropriate hypermedia program used in this research entitled *HIV & AIDS Prevention Education for Women of Color* was centered around the target audiences' experience of being undergraduate women of color. Moreover, it acknowledges the environment that puts this population at risk for contracting HIV—the college milieu. This design proved effective in engaging the participants to learn about their risk factors regarding HIV/AIDS.

Interviews revealed that the participants were very responsive to the program and found the program to be very engaging—time spent on the program ranged from 21 minutes to 2 hours and 49 minutes. Additionally, the program was described as interesting, informative, and educational. Participants reported that they could relate to the program's characters that represented their own race, socio-economic status (SES), and college lifestyle. Moreover, they described themselves as feeling more informed of their HIV risk status and empowered about their protection options after having viewed the program. This is inline with research that finds HIV/AIDS intervention programs that are (a) disseminated via a popular interactive medium; (b) both culturally relevant and credible; and (c) representative of the same race and SES background of the target audience, to have a higher occurrence of viewer engagement and acceptance, and, an increase in learners' accurate perception of their health risk (Pittman et al., 1992; Stevenson & Davis, 1994; Stevenson, McKee Gay, & Josar, 1995; Stuber, 1991; Wingood & DiCelemente, 1992).

Conclusion

This study corroborates the documented relationship between learners' goal orientation (GO) and their use of SRLS and achievement in traditional learning environments. Results revealed significant positive and negative relationships between learners' GOs and their cognitive tool use (CTU) and achievement in an interactive hypermedia environment (IHME). It further acknowledges that learners can adopt borderline/multiple GOs, which can result in learners' demonstration of maladaptive or adaptive behaviors. It supports the notion that learners' GO is a dynamic and not static learner characteristic—one that can change depending upon the learning task at hand, the situated tasks within the learning task, the learners' level of interest/commitment to the task, and learners' self-perception of their academic competence or competence with the task at hand. For example, performance-avoid (*PAV*) learners who were borderline with both task (*T*) and performance-approach (*PAPP*) GOs demonstrated adaptive behaviors such as using the map and notebook cognitive tools more times and for longer periods of times than their *T* and *PAPP* peers. This is atypical behavior of a *PAV* GO that typically demonstrates maladaptive behavior (i.e., using less cognitive strategies than their *T* and *PAPP* peers). Moreover, the positive learning outcomes of IHM instruction that is both culturally and gender appropriate cannot be overstated.

These findings can assist educators and designers to understand the active roles GO and CTU within and for the design of learner-centered IHMEs that foster positive achievement outcomes. This can further assist in understanding how learners learn in an IHME, and can help facilitate research-based integration of instructional IHM into the curriculum.

Suggestions for Further Research

This study has several implications for future research in the areas of GO, and hypermedia research and product design. Yet, first it is important to note that of the 50 participants 41 were *T*-oriented learners and African American. This is inline with similar GO research that finds African American females to be *T*-oriented learners (Middleton & Midgley, 1997). It is also consistent with research that finds African American students to have more "positive" attitudes and self-beliefs then Caucasian students (Graham, 1994; Mickelson, 1990). However, it is important to recognize the unequal number of these groups with regard to both race and the three GO grouping as a possible limitation of this study. Hence, future research is encouraged to extend the GO research in both hypermedia and traditional learning environments with learners of variant academic, racial, ethnic, cultural and socio-economic backgrounds as well as larger samples to explore the natural grouping of learners' Gos.

Goal Orientation. Learners' adoption of borderline/multiple GOs and their resulting atypical behavior supports the need for future research to investigate how learners coordinate multiple GOs and actively switch from one GO to another as they engage in learning tasks. This study revealed that learners' GO is more dynamic than it is static. It lends evidence that learners' GO can change during a learning task depending upon the context of the learning task and the situated tasks contained within (i.e., different types of interactions and activities: videos, drop and drag, matrix completion, notebook use, navigation, and reading text). Thus, further research is needed to study the dynamics of learners' GO. This can include the investigation of how, why, and when learners' GOs change during a learning task. Likewise, it is possible that a learner's GO might change depending on the learners' level of enjoyment/commitment for the particular task. For example, learning how to derive physics equations as opposed to learning how to kick-box. The investigation of the dynamics of learners' multiple, borderline and changing GOs will require a dynamic assessment instrument—one with the ability to measure learners' management of multiple GOs—as opposed to the static instrument that was used to measure the three GOs investigated in this study. Suggestions for future research questions include but are not limited to: (a) What is the relationship between learners' race, self-efficacy, and GO?; (b) How do learners manage borderline/multiple GOs during learning tasks?; (c) What are the implications of variant learners adopting borderline/multiple GOs for the development of an assessment tool that measures borderline/multiple GOs?; and (d) How does learners' level of interest in/commitment to a learning task affect their GO?

Hypermedia. Hypermedia research has out grown its infancy stage to establish itself as a viable instructional medium, yet further research is needed to understand how it can meet the needs of variant learners who have divergent learner characteristic and behaviors. There is a need to further investigate learners' CTU in an IHME and how this CTU is affected by learners' GOs and in turn how they collectively affect learner achievement. The influence of variant leaner characteristics, which can elicit adaptive or maladaptive CTU and its affect on achievement in an IHME, requires further research.

Cognitive Tools. Specifically, the form and function of cognitive tools requires further investigation. It is apparent that participants used the notebook tool to assist with content elaboration and information processing, while the map tool was used for the purpose of navigation and not information processing. Clearly, the notebook tool assisted learners with their higher order cognitive strategies to elaborate on and process information. However, the map tool was more instrumental in assisting lower level cognitive strategies such as navigation and keeping track of one's place within the program. Likewise, the help tool could be described as a "house keeping" tool in that it explained the "what" and "how" of operating the program, rather than assisting with the processing or understanding of the program's content. Further research is needed to investigate "how" and "why" learners use cognitive tools. Additionally, future studies that investigate which tools assist higher order cognitive strategies and which tools assist lower level cognitive strategies can provide further explanation and understanding regarding the form and function of cognitive tools, and in turn their effect on achievement. This can also add insight to how learners' adoption of borderline/multiple GOs might be affected by, and, affect CTU.

Moreover, further research is needed to understand how learners' varying levels of computer competencies affect their use of cognitive tools and achievement outcomes. The majority of the participants in this study had minimal computer experience and almost no exposure to instructional IHM programs. Results indicated that learners' varying levels of computer competencies and experience with hypermedia programs can influence learners' behavior in that a learner with lower computer skills might expend their cognitive resources "figuring out" how to use the program. As a result, ones' cognitive resources are exhausted on the operation of the hypermedia program and cannot effectively and efficiently concentrate on the learning task at hand. This can result in learners' maladaptive behaviors—not effectively or efficiently using cognitive tools and low or negative achievement scores. For example, learner' might not use cognitive tools to help process information or assist with program operations—the notebook to elaborate, rehearse, or reflect on content, the help tool to learn how to operate the program, or the map to navigate the program and determine program completion. Such maladaptive behavior can result in negative achievement outcomes. This could possibly explain the negative achievement outcomes displayed by some participants in this study. Further research is needed to investigate how learners' variant levels of computer and hypermedia experience affect their GO, CTU, and achievement during IHM instruction.

Suggestions for future research questions regarding learners' use of cognitive tools during hypermedia instruction include but are not limited to: (a) How does learners' self-perception of their academic-competence affect GO, CTU, and achievement in an IHME?; and (b) How does learners' adoption of borderline/multiple GOs affect CTU and achievement in an IHME?

Culturally and Gender Appropriate Interactive Hypermedia Environments

There is also a need to further the development and investigation of culturally and gender appropriate instructional IHM programs. The unique characteristics of the rural HBCU population and the affects of these characteristics on learners' adoption of borderline and dynamically changing GOs during the course of the IHM program dictates the need for research to further investigate how different populations of undergraduate students use cognitive tools. Further research can investigate the effects of learners' variant characteristics across different academic environments on their behavior and achievement within IHM instructional programs. Such investigation can include a cohort comparison of students' from different types of academic institutions—for example, community colleges, state universities, private universities, rural, and inner city. Similarly, further investigation of learners' from different undergraduate class and socio-economic levels across various race/culture/and ethnicities can help to explain learners' variant CTU, behavior, and achievement during IHM instruction. It can also help to understand the unique needs of learners from different cultural backgrounds and how this affects their behavior, interest, and engagement within IHM instructional programs. Suggestions for future research questions include but are not limited to: (a) What effect does culturally relevant instructional hypermedia have on the learning behavior and achievement outcomes of learners from variant racial/cultural backgrounds?; (b) What are the effects of culturally/gender appropriate IHM programs that provide intervention education regarding race/gender-specific health risks?; and (c) How do learners of variant cultural backgrounds and academic environments behave, engage in, and respond to instructional IHM programs? What affects does this have for their learning experience and achievement outcome?

CHAPTER 11

Creating an Affirming Culture to Retain African American Students During the Post Affirmative Action Era in Higher Education

Lee Jones

Introduction

The 1999- 2000 Seventeenth Annual Status Report on Minorities in Higher Education, released by the Office of Minorities in Higher Education of the American Council on Education (ACE), summarizes the most recent data available on key indicators of progress in American higher education. The report touches on a number of areas like trends in high school, degrees conferred etc., but for our scope of interest we wish to reflect on college participation and educational attainment, college enrollment and college graduation rates.

Demographic Trends and College Enrollment

The 18 to 24 years old currently enrolled in colleges decreased during the 1980s but remained relatively unchanged at approximately 25 million during 1990s. Since 1990, the number of white college –age youths has fluctuated slightly around 20 million, while the number of African American college-age youths increased by nearly 8 % between 1977 and 1997 and by 3.7 % in 1990. The Hispanic college - population more than doubled during the past 20 years, in addition to a 31 % increase during 1990. High school graduates ages 18 to 24 increased in 1997.

College participation rates for whites in 1977 has increased by more than 13 percentage points, and the African Americans rates dropped during

1980 but outbalanced it with an increase of 10 percentage points during the past ten years. Hispanics 1997 college participation rates were significantly higher as indicated during the late 1970s and 1980s.

African American females registered at colleges varied from 36.4 % in 1996 to 43.6 % in 1997. The latter rate is the highest ever recorded by African American women. Meanwhile, the participation rate of African American high school graduate males remained constant between 1996 and 1997 at roughly 35%. It is worth mentioning that African Americans maintained the highest gender gap in college participation in 1997 in comparison with the three major ethnic groups.

Nationally, the proportion of adult ages 25 to 29 who completed four or more years of high school education was fairly constant during the past two decades. In 1997 more than 87% in this group had graduated from high school, which shows an increase of less than 2 percentage points over the 1988 rate of 85.7%. The percentage of African Americans and Hispanics with four or more years of high school was up slightly for 1997, while the corresponding percentages of white remained constant.

Although African American men in this group, ages 25 to 29, with four or more years of high school education decreased from 87.2% in 1996 to 85.2% in 1997, there was an increase of nearly 4 percentage points since 1990. African American women in this category increased by nearly 3 percentage points from 1996 to 1997, to 87.1%- - an increase of more than 5 percentage points since 1990.

According to the Current Population Reports (CPS) of the US Department of Commerce, 27.8% of all young adults ages 25 to 29 held a bachelor's degree or higher as of 1997. Approximately 29% of whites in this age group held at least a baccalaureate degree in 1997, compared with 14.4 % of African Americans and only 11% of Hispanics. The proportion of African American men with at least a bachelor's degree decreased slightly in 1997, to 12.1%, while the rate for women remained unchanged at 16.4%. Consequently, African American women indicated a higher completion rate than men.

Since the late 1980s, African Americans have shown great strides in college attendance. From 1988 to 1997 their overall enrollment in higher education increased to 57.2%, including a 16.1 increase during the past five years. Conversely, the number of white student enrollment has decreased by 3.1%, while total enrollment has increased by only 1.4%. Women of color increased 4% from 1996 to 1997, while men of color showed a 3.3% increase from 1996 to 1997.

Despite the enrollment gains at independent colleges and universities, lower-cost public institutions enrolled the vast majority of African American students. Furthermore, African American enrollment at historically blacks colleges and universities (HBCUs) continuous to decrease compared with other type of institutions. HBCUs enrolled 14.4% of all African Americans attending U. S. colleges and universities, down from 15% in 1996 and 17% in 1988. Hispanic enrollment in higher education increased 79.2% from 1988 to 1997, which was the highest among the four major ethnic groups. Asian American enrollment increased 73% from 1988 to 1997, and American Indians indicated a 54% increase in college enrollment during the past decade, including a 3.6 gain from 1996 to 1997.

College Graduation Rates

Sixty-five percent of Asian American students completing college had the highest graduation rate of all racial and ethnic groups. White students were second with 58%, trailed by Hispanics, African Americans and American Indians. The six-year graduation rates for African Americans at Division I institutions increased from 38% in 1966 to 40% in 1997. With a 6 percentage point increase, African Americans exhibited the greatest progress of all racial and ethnic groups in terms of increasing their college graduation rate. African American women graduated at a rate of 45% in 1997, compared to 34% rate for African American men. The gap in college completion rates of African American men and women is the largest among all racial and ethnic groups.

Relevant Terms Defined

An unavoidable dilemma when dealing with culturally diverse student learners is the issue of the terminology used to conceptualize them. It is evident that there is no consensus in the use of terms, particularly in the area of "labels for specific groups." In the development of many university's retention strategies, as is the case throughout the literature, there is bound to be some inconsistencies in the way some people utilize terminology. To assist the readers and users of this chapter, some terms have been defined for the purpose of clarity. Other definitions are also included in an attempt to make the reader aware of the diversity that exists within specific racial/ethnic groups. Common questions that exemplify the complexity of these situations include inquiries such as who are culturally diverse students, students of color, and minority students? Who are Asian Pacific Americans, Native Americans, African Americans, Chicano/Latino, Hispanic, and Mexican Americans? Therefore, for the purpose of this chapter, the following terms are defined.

Culture. The ideations, symbols, behaviors, values, customs and beliefs that are shared by a human group. Culture is transmitted through language, material objects, rituals, and institutions and are from one generation to the next.

Diversity. Recognition and acknowledgment of differences that are unique to each group that is part of the culturally diverse community.

Culturally Diverse Students. The four under-represented racial/ethnic groups: African American, Asian/Pacific American, Chicano/ Latino, and Native American.

Race. A socially and historically defined human grouping hereditarily assigned but not biologically defined. Refers to very large human groups comprised of diverse populations and ethnic groups.

Recruitment. The process of identifying and informing African American, Asian/Pacific American, Chicano/Latino and Native American populations in order to provide them with support systems that will facilitate improved and enhanced access to the university with the expectation of increasing enrollment of culturally diverse students.

Retention. The continuous process to create, maintain, and support ongoing strategies for meeting the personal, academic, social and financial needs of culturally diverse students to ensure academic success and graduation.

The University. The main campus of the home institution and any branches, which may comprise a multi-campus system.

The following terms are applied to specific groups.

African Americans. The terms Afro-American and African American reflect the identity of Blacks based on their origins in Africa and their presence in America. Today, different labels are used to refer to people of African descent residing in the US. In the Southern and Eastern parts of the US, people of African descent more often referred to themselves as Black than African American. In the Western part of the US, they usually referred to themselves as African American more so than Black. Mainly people outside of the group use the "African American label." For many people of African descent, the reference does not make much of a difference. The contexts in which the terms are being used determine their response to it.

Asian Pacific Americans. Many diverse groups make up the Asian Pacific Americans. These include, but are not limited to Cambodian, Chinese, East Indian, Filipino, Guamanian, Hawaiian, Hmong, Indonesian, Japanese, Korean, Laotian, Samoan, and Vietnamese cultures (Takaki, 1989). The 1980 US Census Bureau also includes smaller groups: Bangladeshi, Butanese, Bornean, Burmese, Celbesian, Cernan, Indochinese, Iwo-Jiman, Javanese, Malayan, Maldivian, Nepali, Okinawan, Sikkimese, Singaporean, and the Sri Lankan. Asian Pacific Americans are perceived as not only looking alike, but also being alike. The stereotype of the model minority for Asian American students also persists. A careful examination about who Asian and Pacific Islanders is needed. They represent many cognitive strengths and weaknesses, have diverse ethnic roots, live in many parts of the US, and range from newly immigrated to having roots of over 200 years in the US (Pang, 1995).

Chicano. The term refers to US born individuals with ancestry in Mexico. While the origins of the term Chicano is not clear, the often used explanation is that Chicano is a derivation of the "Mexican" people, a group of the Aztecs who inhabited Azltán, or what is the present day southwest portion of the United States. Chicano also reflects a political frame of mind and level of consciousness regarding this group's rights within the US society.

Chicano/Latino. The preferred label by the otherwise called Hispanics.

Hispanic. The US Census Bureau introduced this label to count individuals with Spanish surnames living in the United States. The terms encompass distinctly different populations such as Cubans, Puerto Ricans, Mexicans, Salvadorians, Haitians, etc. Many groups reject the term because it is too broad and it was given without consent. It is however, the most used term by government agencies and the media.

Latino. A self prescribed term used by anyone of Latin American descent residing in the United states, regardless of race.

Native Americans. Persons who are descendants of aboriginal/ indigenous peoples of North American prior to 1492 with cultural identification through tribal affiliation or native community recognition. There are between 330 and 430 federally recognized tribes (with 330 being the more common figure) and approximately 200 federally recognized Alaskan Native Villages. Currently, there are at least 200 additional tribes seeking federal recognition. These numbers do not include those tribes recognized only by the states, nor those groups not recognized by either. In all, there are well over 600 distinct Native American tribes and groups and at least that many Native Alaskan Villages. These approximations are very conservative. In the state of Washington there are at least 27 federally recognized tribes and over 60 Native American groups. Each of them has its own distinct culture, language, values, and beliefs.

Persistence and Success of African American Students: Critical Issues

A review of the literature is needed to determine critical issues affecting performance, persistence, and graduation rates of African American students attending postsecondary institutions. The literature suggests that students' likelihood of remaining through graduation depends on the level of social and academic integration into college life. Social and academic integration is dependent upon a number of cognitive and non-cognitive factors shared by many African American students.

A caveat is in order. For years, researchers have studied African American students as a single entity, making comparisons to majority students as a single group. The more recent trend is to study specific ethnic groups and subgroups and then compare various groups to the majority group. Acknowledging the need to understand the expectations and experiences of specific groups and subgroups in order to propose programmatic institutional changes to meet their unique needs, we suggest that there are factors common to various ethnic groups across campus which can guide efforts to encourage participation and success in the university experience.

Five student issues relevant to institutional climate emerge from the literature. First, as underscored by recent research, college for most majority students is a continuation of the next logical, expected step in an established set of family and sociocultural values and traditions. For most African American students, attending college represents disjunction - - not a rite of passage into one's cultural traditions, but often breaking away from family and cultural heritage. Research has only begun to examine the subtle effects of disjunction on the success of culturally diverse students as they separate from, yet try to maintain connection with their cultural heritage and identity.

African American students often bring to college a lack of understanding of the expected conventions of academic culture. Students are concerned about their academic preparation, yet they are often unaware of the skills needed to balance the multiple demands of the academic, social, cultural, and personal dimensions of their lives. In addition, conventional behavioral expectations of college classes (assertion, competition, and individualism) often conflict with the students' cultural norms and values. Self-doubt combined with issues of alienation enhances their sense of disjuncture, thus inhibiting the potential for success. Living on a predominantly white campus intensifies awareness of one's own ethnic difference. Differences in speech patterns, dress codes, and behavioral norms underscore the need to adopt to the novel - - and sometimes bewildering - - world of academe.

Second, financial aid is often the primary consideration in making the decision to continue or leave. Students consider not only the amount awarded, but also the proportion of grant to loan aid. Burdensome loan debt creates stress that effects student success and satisfaction with the college experience. Anxiety as a result of financial stress becomes even more pronounced when added to the student's general feeling of alienation and dissatisfaction.

Third, the influence of the campus climate on the persistence of culturally diverse students at predominantly white institutions is replete in the literature. The research is consistent in pointing out that, for example, African American students attending predominantly white campuses experience more stress, racism, and isolation and are less likely to persist than their counterparts at historically black colleges. Students' interaction with faculty, staff, majority peers, and the social environment of the campus affects their attitude, behavior, and perceptions, thus enhancing or diminishing their satisfaction, academic achievement, and persistence. Being a "Guest in Someone Else's House" (Sotello & Turner, 1994) means always being on one's best behavior. It also means being under scrutiny, having little or no history in the house, which makes the student feel that he or she does not belong. Feeling apart from the academic and social campus life is one of the main reasons culturally diverse students drop out.

In the classroom, students may find themselves isolated and ignored - - except as examples of stereotypes from often well-intentioned faculty. Large classrooms are perceived as impersonal and intimidating. Students encounter curricula designed with a monocultural perspective and faculty who discount their cultural views as irrelevant and ways of learning as inappropriate. Eurocentric curricula and traditional methods of teaching and testing imply one fixed truth and deny plurality of shifting interpretations based on different experiences. Classroom conversations dominated by majority students remind culturally diverse students of their guest status. If students do not succeed they are misunderstood as underprepared and unmotivated (Adams, 1992). Students know in which classes they will find a supportive atmosphere, a respect for cultural differences, high expectations, and positive role models.

Elatedly the research also points to the positive influence of informal faculty-student interaction on the success of African American students. With few African American faculty as role models and mentors, culturally diverse students tend to have litter interaction with faculty, instead reporting reticence toward approaching majority faculty.

Outside the classroom, culturally diverse students note the proportion of faculty, administrators, and staff who are persons of color. They are keenly aware whether enough African American students are recruited to create a community to which they can belong, and whether there are accessible programs and services that support but do not stigmatize them. They are sensitive to the climate in their classes, in the residence halls, as they walk down the mall, gather informally in the student union, and interact with their peers whether majority students or culturally diverse students.

African American students' interactions with majority peers are often fraught with tension. A lack of familiarity with the background and expectations of African American students account for infrequent socialization among students. While the official message from the institution may be "yes, we want you as part of our academic community," the community of majority peers can appear unsupportive, placing the psychological well-being of the culturally diverse student in jeopardy (Wright, 1987).

Four, adjustment for success requires congruencies between one's career plans, a selected academic program, and a realistic appraisal of one's own interests, strengths and weaknesses. African American students often share with majority students incongruencies in long and short-term goals, and the ability to achieve them. However, incongruencies between goals and realistic self-appraisal is particularly critical for the culturally diverse student whose models of careers or educational opportunities may be limited.

The final issue that effects culturally diverse student retention is students' personal characteristics. Student background characteristics found to correlate with successful achievement include family income levels, educational level of parents, and academic preparation. Positive self-image, self-esteem, and internal locus of control also influence students' successful experiences.

The relationship between family income, the educational level of parents, and student persistence is clear. A parent who herself has attended college and who is able to share in the experiences of her son or daughter attending college can provide invaluable psychological support and encouragement, offer informal suggestions on how to 'work' the system, and may be able to ease the student's financial anxieties. Although the student's socioeconomic background may aid in the transition and adjustment, a hostile and unsupportive campus climate may place the student in psychological jeopardy and at risk academically.

More so than the second generation African American college student, the first generation college student feels at odds with the expected conventions of the academic culture and the institutional climate if it is perceived as intimidating and threatening. Parents who are unable to assist their son or daughter financially contribute to the student's sense of uncertainty and anxiety.

For some non-traditional students, the personal and academic transition requires a redefinition of self and values. The importance of the role of self-perception in the transition process is significant. Institutional practices, academic regulations, and policies may contribute to undermining students' perception of self and sense of being in control. An inclusive climate, faculty involvement, positive interaction with peers, classroom practices and curricula which validate differences can combine with a student's positive self-image, and sense of being in control.

Jacqueline Rowser (1997) conducted a study of African American students at predominately white institutions and found that more than 90% of the students surveyed perceived their academic preparation for college as adequate. More than one-third of students in the study expected to earn "3.0" grade point average or greater during their first year in college, while more than 90% of the students expected to graduate in five years or less (Rowser, 1997). Despite the positive expectations of the African American students in the study, she found the expectations of these students disturbing. She pointed out that research indicated that (1) African American students earn fewer credits than white students in their first year; (2) African American students have poorer grades than whites throughout the college experience; (3) and African American students will flunk out at a significantly higher rate than white students, or will be more likely to drop out during their first two semesters than white students (Rowser, 1997).

As a result of these findings, Rowser (1997) determined that African American students' expectations were "unrealistic" because less than 70% of the students had a 3.0 grade point average or better entering college, yet 90% of the students expected a 3.0 or better. In addition, since African American students often begin college in remedial courses, where credits do not apply towards graduation or major requirements, it would be difficult to graduate in four years, as 50% of the students in the study expected. The gap between student expectations and outcomes allude to another misperception of African American students, that some perceive the college experience as an extension of high school (McNairy, 1997).

In the article "The Challenge for Higher Education: Retaining Students of Color," Francis McNairy (1996) indicates that inadequate high school preparation and inadequate study habits contribute to student attrition. Citing Crosson (1988) and McNairy (1996) further elaborates that this lack of student preparation is reflected on standard measures of academic performance in college, their overall performance, and retention rates. One reason for the lack of student preparation and inadequate study habits can be attributed to some students having attended high schools that lacked resources to properly prepare students, and as a consequence, they develop adequate study habits (McNairy, 1996).

In "Leaving College: Rethinking the Causes and Cures of Student Attrition" (1987), Vincent Tinto discussed the concept of commitment with regard to attrition, categorizing it into two types: student and institutional. Tinto (1987) indicates that the higher a student's goal (educational or occupational), the higher the chances that a student is willing to work to attain that goal. Given this position, it must be noted that the level (whether high or low) and the clarity of a student's goals can positively or negatively impact student attrition. McNairy (1996) indicates that most students of color tend to be first generation college students and generally have a generic goal: to obtain a good job. These students usually lack the best academic background and information that would allow them to select a lucrative field or even work through the system to achieve their goals (McNairy, 1996; Obiakor & Harris-Obiakor, 1997). This concept has a substantial connection to Tinto's (1987) idea, which indicates that an extended period of uncertainty in the student's intentions contributes to student departure.

Thus far I have attempted to highlight key concepts of student attrition as it relates to the student (i.e. student preparation, study habits, intentions and commitment, and goal setting patterns). Any reason or combination of the reasons mentioned can impact a student's stay in college. However student attrition is not solely a student problem, nor is it solely caused by students. Institutional factors have a tremendous influence on student attrition, which is the next factor I will examine.

Causes of Attrition: Institutional Factors

Institutional factors that impact student attrition can be viewed in two categories: organizational policies, and institutional or campus climate. Organizational policies extend throughout an entire college or university system, from student services and student affairs to academic areas and majors. McNairy (1996) highlighted financial aid as a difficult area given the students' unfamiliarity with financial aid applications, erroneous assumptions made by white financial aid staff members, and family emergencies that may affect the financial status of the student. Love (1993) had similar findings with regard to black students lack of information on financial aid, but notes cutbacks in funding; the shift from grant assistance to more loan assistance; and an assurance by the institution to the students for continuous financial support. In another study of black student attrition at a large predominately white northwestern university, Gary Sailes (1993) found that 45% of the participants in the study indicated that they received inadequate financial aid, while another 35% reported that they did not receive any aid. While the delivery of financial aid relies on sophisticated federal and state methodologies, it is one area of a vast number of areas that is crucial in determining student persistence and should be explored by institutions.

Campus, or institutional climate, is another area (and what I believe is a major area) that impacts student attrition. Barbara Love (1993) discusses the climate of most predominately white institutions, indicating that they were established under the law and / or practice that excluded black students (and other minorities), which was built into the structure and fabric of the institution. She further notes that there has been little discussion about white racism on campus, and even denial of it. Throughout time we have seen racism manifest in student to student interactions, staff and student interactions, and faculty and student interactions. It can be overt or subtle. For example, low expectations by white faculty based on presumptions of lack of preparation, lack of ability, and prior disadvantage can block communication with students of color (Love, 1993). In addition, the ignorance of the cultures and contributions, as well as the lack of professional role models for students of color all impact student retention (McNairy, 1996). This supports Tinto's (1987) theory that the lack of academic integration whether formal or informal can influence student departure.

As described in the causes of student attrition, both students and institutions are very much involved in the process. Students of color are completely responsible for their performance in school. However if they are placed in environments that are not welcoming (via organizational policies, or the formal and informal interactions with other students, staff, and faculty), chances of these students feeling alienated can increase, consequently increasing student attrition rates. The next section will explore characteristics of effective retention models, which will be followed by a discussion on quality in higher education, and how these strategies combined can positively influence student retention in the next millennium.

Characteristics of an Effective Retention Model

With the dramatic increase in culturally diverse learners and the de-emphasis on affirmative action, it has become increasingly important for universities to reaffirm their commitment to provide a quality education for all students. At many institutions it has become necessary to develop a university wide strategy specifically for African American students. Recognizing the considerable task a university has to attract, recruit, retain African Americans, all colleges, campuses and departments can profit from a concerted effort to share programs and resources.

To assist the university in providing ongoing retention initiatives to retain and ultimately graduate large numbers of culturally diverse students, it is important for universities to develop a comprehensive strategy that will guide the university and all of its units in developing and maintaining a climate that is conducive and reflective of the type of students enrolling at institutions of higher education. The strategy that I propose is not intended to provide all the answers to what is noted to be a very complex issue. Rather, the intent of the university's development of a recruitment and retention strategy is to provide a document that is a "work in progress." That is, although a strategy should be developed to cover a minimum of five years, it is beneficial to make yearly revisions to its specific objectives and strategies. Ideally, the president, the senior vice presidents will need to work with the "multicultural taskforce" to ensure that appropriate accountability structures are in place that will ensure responsible and timely implementation of this important initiative. In short, this retention strategy will be a living document for the university.

Given the multi-dimensional character of minority retention problems for most predominately white institutions, the retention strategy will need to use several different approaches. Four major objectives help define the tasks for developing this retention strategy: (1) to review actual retention and graduation data of the university and compare this with selected peer institutions; (2) to assess the various aspects of the university environment to determine factors that may lead to the attrition of culturally diverse learners; (3) to ascertain what specific multicultural retention initiatives are available, and (4) to develop a specific retention plan and time lines with built in accountability structures designed to increase the retention and ultimate graduation of culturally diverse students.

While the retention strategy will not necessarily identify cause and effect relationships between variables, it should offer a view of the latest retention literature, a statement of the problem, national recruit-ment, retention and graduation data by ethnic group and operational definitions. When adopting a retention plan, it will also be necessary to include an extensive audit of retention initiatives occurring throughout the university, a synopsis of the university's recruitment history, reten-tion graduation data, the university's athletic retention and graduation data, and retention and graduation data of selected peer institutions, etc.

A comprehensive retention strategy, by definition, must focus on the complete student (e.g. intellectual, social, spiritual, physical, and cultural). While there are some strategies that are generalizable to all underrepresented groups, it is important to recognize that the strategies that follow are meant to look at each underrepresented group as a separate entity.

There are many strategies that can be incorporated to develop an effective retention model. Of these strategies, models should: (1) have the support of administration, by incorporating retention / diversity into the strategic plan of the university; (2) recruit faculty for participation; (3) provide motivational lectures; (4) provide proactive financial aid counseling; (5) get students involved with programming activities; (6) maintain up-to-date knowledge on retention issues; (7) regularly assess program effectiveness; (8) incorporate early assessment and intervention; (9) develop faculty mentoring; (10) develop leadership seminars; (11) and develop and maintain a caring and competent staff (Carreathers, Beekman, Coatie, & Nelson, 1996). Carreathers et.al, (1996) highlight some or all of these characteristics in Texas A&M's Department of Multicultural Services, the University of Louisville's Center for

Academic Achievement's "Thriving and Surviving" program, and the University of Texas at Austin's Preview Program. These three models were initiated and are supported by the leadership of their respective universites and / or a governing bodies. Texas A&M's Department of Multicultural Services was initiated by the institution's Division of Student Services. The University of Louisville's Thriving and Surviving Program was mandated the U.S. Office of Civil Rights. Lastly, the Preview Program at the University of Texas at Austin is a part of the Office of the Dean of Students. Parker (1997) and Madison (1993) both indicate the crucial need for an institutional leader to support such efforts.

Suggestions for retention models are infinite. However other notable strategies include mentoring, peer advising, student leadership conferences, student skills workshops, and cultural events (Carreathers et al., 1996). Mallinckrodt and Sedlacek (1987) suggests policies to maximize usage of athletic facilities, and campus gyms; more union programming for specific groups; and usage of areas such as libraries and career and counseling centers also help retention. Lastly, Parker (1997) and Tinto (1987) provide suggestions which discuss retention from a systems perspective. Parker suggests the following: (1) the creation of positions dedicated to handling retention activities; (2) the recognition of the need for additional funding sources; (3) the establishment of mentoring programs for minority students – programs which have helped minorities see successful staff and students who can show them a path to success, and which give them confidence and support they need; (4) the reorganization of faculty / staff duties and responsibilities to assist in retention activities, especially for institutions with limited resources; (5) the development of a reporting system for identification and tracking so that institutions can have accurate data, and data processing capabilities on the different facets of their programs; and (6) the development of faculty or staff training to better understand minority populations (Parker, 1997, p.120). Tinto (1987) indicates that: (1) institutions should ensure that the new students enter with or have the opportunity to acquire skills needed for academic success; (2) institutions should reach out to become more personal with students beyond the formal domain of academic life; (3)

institutional retention actions should be systematic in character; (4) institutions should start as early as possible to retain students; (5) the primary commitment of institutions should be to their students; and (6) education, not retention should be the goal of institutional retention programs.

A review of the characteristics of effective retention models demonstrates that there is no shortage in concepts or ideas to assist universities in retaining African American students. However, even with the implementation of these models, African American students continue to leave higher education without accomplishing degrees, which is cause for concern by the higher education community. The advent of the new millennium presents many new challenges for the higher education enterprise, particularly with regard to issues such as diversity, quality, accountability, and productivity. Minority populations continue to increase and the need to do more with less continue to haunt institutions. Because of these pressing issues, it is imperative that institutions consider new, or maybe not so much new, but alternatives to address these concerns. The next section will examine two approaches that can, if properly applied to retention, improve retention, as well as improve quality in higher education.

Reframing African American Student Retention with Total Quality Management (TQM) and the Learning Paradigm

Over the past decade, two trends have gained the attention of the higher education community: Total Quality Management (TQM) and the Learning Paradigm. William Bryan (1996) defines TQM as:

> "...a comprehensive philosophy of operation in which community members (1) are committed to CQI and to a common campus vision, set of values, attitudes, and principles; (2) understand that campus processes need constant review to improve services to customers; (3) believe the work of each community member is vital to customer satisfaction; and (4)value input from customers." (p. 5)

Two key elements of TQM are improvement and customer orientation (Melan, 1993). Along with these elements, establishing a mission and vision are significant to TQM, as well as systematic analysis or assessment, participation, and viewing the university as a system (Lozier & Teeter, 1993). TQM's focus on processes, improvement, and saving costs is what attracts higher education particularly when legislators,

trustees, and industry demand accountability productivity (McDaniel, 1994). While TQM has experienced some success in student affairs administration, it has yet to be accepted in the academic arena. However the learning paradigm offers a transformation in pedagogy, with hints of quality and TQM.

The Learning Paradigm offers a complete change in teaching, as we know it. Robert Barr and James Tagg (1995) notes a change in instruction that will create environments and experiences that allow students to discover and construct knowledge for themselves. As opposed to teachers simply providing lectures, now professors will coach, counsel, and collaborate with students during the learning process (McDaniel, 1994; Barr & Tagg, 1995). Because funding for the learning paradigm will be outcome-based, Barr and Tagg (1995) indicate it will save money. At the same time they purport that the learning paradigm will promote success for diverse students as opposed to simply access. Overall, the learning paradigm presents several similarities to TQM because of continuous improvement through teaching methods, student roles changing to that of a teammate in the learning process, and the quality and accountability aspects since students will be responsible for their own learning.

In its application to the retention to African American students, TQM and the learning paradigm appear to offer bright prospects. TQM examines entire processes and how they relate to one another; therefore it would view retention models as a system within the university, as Tinto (1987) suggested in one of his six principles. The assessment/ systems analysis aspects of TQM would consider any deviations from that of the stated mission and goals, and allow for continuous improvement. Another aspect that is appealing to retention of African American students is the customer orientation of TQM. TQM allows for feedback from customers, therefore giving a voice to African

American students in colleges and universities. In addition, if universities view African American students as customers, an inherent reliance on these students intellectually, culturally, and financially by colleges and universities will develop as a means for survival. In its application to retention models, the primary benefit of the learning paradigm is the increased interaction between the student and the teacher. The fact that students and teachers will collaborate in the learning process will allow students to establish a rapport with faculty who would otherwise have not interacted with them as much. According to Tinto (1987), academic integration both formally and informally increases the likelihood that a student would remain in school. Of course the collaboration between African American students with white faculty does not remove any stereotypes, preconceived notions, or even racists acts by some faculty. However the clear and continuous statement of the institution's mission by leadership, and visible display of commitment to diversity could reshape the behavior, beliefs, culture of some racist faculty and staff in institutions.

A Culturally Diverse Student Retention Plan

Once the data have been collected and compared with the university's sister institutions and national retention data, frequently used terms have been operationally defined for the campus, and a review of the retention literature has been obtained, it is then time to begin with one's strategy - the most important part of the retention plan. Below is an outline of a Culturally Diverse Student Retention Plan. While I do not purport that the retention strategy below has all the answers, it is one which could provide a good start for those institutions that are serious about institutionalizing efforts to retain culturally diverse students.

The culturally diverse student retention plan should include a clearly articulated vision statement, statement of values, mission statement and goals, objectives and strategies.

Vision

The university seeks to develop a university-wide approach to increase the retention and graduation rates of culturally diverse students. The ultimate goal is to increase the retention and graduation rates of these students so that they equal or exceed that of majority students at the university.

Statement of Values

In the process of developing and implementing a strategy that aims at increasing the retention and graduation rates of culturally diverse students, the following principles must permeate all actions taken. First, an institutional commitment that communicates respect, inclusion, trust, a challenge for growth, and understanding of, and positive regard for all culturally diverse students is imperative. Second, students must be made aware of the importance of individual responsibility, the freedom to grow, self-confidence, and a sense of their own authorship of their destiny. Third, in order to meet culturally diverse students' needs holistically, student services and support will be based on a spirit of collaboration and cooperation across the university community.

Mission Statement

The university is committed to developing, implementing, and assessing a five-year plan to improve the retention and graduation rates of culturally diverse students.

Goals, Objectives, and Strategies

Finally, the university should outline its goals, objectives and strategies to effectively implement the retention plan.

I.   To create an inclusive university climate that supports the well being and enhances the total educational experience and ultimate graduation of culturally diverse students.

A.   To increase an awareness and appreciation of multiculturalism across the academic community.

    1.   Survey culturally diverse students to assess their needs, their concerns, and their recommendations for improving the campus climate.

    2.   Offer diversity education workshops to every advisor, faculty and staff member, and ensure that their efforts for diversity are included in performance evaluations.

    3.   Encourage student participation in multicultural/diversity training.

    4.   Develop and promote events that recognize diverse cultural heritage.

    5.   Project a positive multicultural image through publications related to the university.

    6.   Hold an annual multicultural convocation and reception.

    7.   Support and collaborate with a curricular diversity committee in its efforts to increase the number of courses that address multiculturalism and diversity.

    8.   Include presentation on the university's diversity and its enrollment management recruitment, and retention plans for culturally diverse students during orientation sessions for new faculty, staff and administrators.

    9.   Continue partnerships that will ensure the successful transition for students transferring from other colleges and universities.

    10. Continue and develop new working relationships with other minority offices, agencies, and organizations that provide support services for students.

B.   To increase incrementally each year the number of faculty and staff of color

    1.   The president will meet each year with deans and heads of major units to personally reaffirm multicultural hiring goals, with special emphasis on tenure track faculty.

        2.   Identify staff and financial assistance at the university level to provide
incentives for departments and units to hire a more diverse staff.

        3.   Produce an annual report documenting the number of faculty and staff of color employed by the university.

C.   To integrate the campuses and surrounding communities to improve the local racial climate.

        1.   Expand special living community opportunities to better support culturally diverse student populations.

        2.   Host teleconference presentations on campus that address racial issues that would include the university and the surrounding community.

        3.   Participate in city council meetings.

D.   To provide opportunities for faculty and staff of color to interact with culturally diverse students as the students adjust to the campus environment.

        1.   Implement a bi-annual reception for faculty, staff and students.

        2.   Implement activities that celebrate cultural heritage that comprises
faculty, staff and students.

E.   To provide opportunities for all faculty and staff to interact with culturally diverse students as the students adjust to the campus environment by establishing a professional mentor program for multicultural students.

F.   To provide culturally diverse students with a permanent space that they can call
their own and where they can see an immediate reflection of their cultural heritage.

        1.   Allocate spaces for a Multicultural Student Services Office on all campuses.

        2.   Provide more artwork across campuses.

II.   To provide an academic environment and support structure that is aimed at improving the retention and graduation rates of culturally diverse students.

A. To coordinate academic retention programs to maximize their effectiveness.

    1. Have each college and branch campus appoint a person to coordinate its retention initiatives, monitor the implementation of these initiatives at the college level, and serve as an active member of a Council on Retention.

    2. Provide this representative with the resources and authority to oversee services to culturally diverse students in the areas of advising, mentoring, and participation in academic clubs and activities.

B. To systematically assess the effectiveness of retention programs and use the results to improve them.

    1. Provide an accurate database to track all undergraduate students.

    2. Perform annual evaluations of existing retention programs by departments, offices and majors.

    3. Analyze the culturally diverse student demographic report in regard to retention data to identify trends.

    4. Survey non-returning culturally diverse students to identify the reasons why they leave the university.

C. To provide all incoming culturally diverse students with a pre-college experience by continuing to provide on and off-campus programs targeting culturally diverse students, in which they are introduced to the history of higher education, how the system works, and the demands and expectations of college life.

D. To develop culturally responsive classrooms that actively engages students in learning.

    1. Assess pedagogical needs of the faculty members.

    2. Encourage faculty members to utilize campus educational centers for the review of curriculum and teaching style for multicultural inclusiveness.

    3. Facilitate cross-disciplinary collaboration among faculty, administrators, and students in the development of culturally sensitive classrooms.

E. To assist culturally diverse students with their social, academic, and cultural adjustment to college.

    1.   Assess the academic needs of culturally diverse students and how the university is meeting them.

    2.   Monitor multicultural student academic progress.

    3.   Establish a comprehensive University Mentoring Program to assist culturally diverse students in adjusting to and maximizing on the university experience.

    4.   Highlight and recognize multicultural students' academic achievement and scholarship.

F.   To provide the ongoing information and guidance necessary to facilitate connecting culturally diverse students to educational and career programs that meet their needs.

    1.   Assist culturally diverse students to inventory their existing education skills and help focus their interest in selecting a degree program.

    2.   Provide culturally diverse students with sensitive and appropriate academic advising.

    3.   Assist culturally diverse students in accessing academic support services as their need for these services arises.

    4.   Promote culturally diverse student enrollment in the Four-Year Degree Agreement.

    5.   Provide options and information on post-graduate education and assist with preparation for the application process.

    6.   Publicize the academic support structure available to culturally diverse students.

    7.   Collaborate with student groups and other units across campus working in existing and future multicultural retention efforts to apply principles of career development and success to educational experiences.

    8.   Provide a multicultural perspective that enhances career development, employability, and preparation for graduate studies.

    9.   Provide opportunities for students to link their education with their cultural communities through service learning, observation of service delivery, internships, cooperative education and research.

III.   To assist culturally diverse students in securing adequate financial aid.

    A.   To assist students and their parents to understand and utilize the financial aid process and eligibility.

        1.   Include financial aid information in all publications and mailings to prospective students.

        2.   Include presentations on all types of financial aid as a regular of component of recruitment events and new student orientation.

        3.   Conduct workshops, assisting students in filling out financial aid applications.

        4.   Continue to assist students in the aid distribution process.

    B.   To assist students and parents in identifying suitable scholarships and grants.

        1.   Include scholarship and grant information in all publications and mailings to prospective students.

        2.   Include scholarship and grant information as a regular component of recruitment events and new student orientation.

        3.   Conduct workshops to assist students in filling out scholarship applications.

    C.   Increase scholarships available to culturally diverse students.

        1.   Create a multicultural scholarship endowment fund.

        2.   Increase allocations for multicultural scholarship support from ongoing fund raising efforts.

    D.   Inform students and parents on loan eligibility and how to apply for guaranteed student loans.

    E.   Inform students and parents on work-study eligibility and how to qualify and apply for work-study.

    F.   To obtain resources for an emergency loan program.

        1.   Provide interim financial support for students whose aid is delayed.

        2.   Provide emergency money for students not eligible for financial aid.

IV.   To monitor the implementation of the university's Five-Year Multicultural Student Retention Plan.

    A.   To provide an accurate database for all students.

B. To maintain periodic meetings to discuss the implementation of the plan, receive and provide feedback to various departments, and re-direct efforts as needed.

C. To provide the various departments with a format for the evaluation of their particular efforts regarding the implementation of this plan.

D. To make council members available as consultants to the campus in the development, implementation, and evaluation of specific retention plans.

E. To generate an annual report showing the overall impact of the plan and providing recommendations for improvement as needed.

Planning for the campus reorganization can be a very painful process. Although change is inevitable for many people participating in the development of a campus retention strategy, there will be some who would prefer to cling to the way things are. There must be clear and strong leadership from the president and provost of the institution. Another important feature of reorganizing the campus Office of Multicultural Affairs is to ensure that the university has invested financially to the structural changes. The Multicultural Retention Strategy is designed to provide structure to the retention strategy. Further, in recognizing the university's strong commitment to recruiting culturally diverse students, it is imperative that each academic department and academic support unit play a significant and ongoing role in formulating, implementing, and maintaining coordinated retention strategies and plans. The next section deals with providing an organizational structure that will be at the center for implementing the day to day activities of a university's multicultural office.

Recommendations for Retention Programs

In order to improve African American student retention in higher education, it is apparent that institutions must do more. Not only does retention require the design of elaborate models that include mentoring, financial incentives, and other support services for students, but also leadership and faculty must become and remain involved beyond what they have in the past. The following are some recommendations by which leaders in higher education institutions should follow in order to achieve improvement in the retention of African American students:

1.   Leadership in both the academic and administrative realms must establish clear missions and strategic plans. They must also support diversity initiatives and make themselves visible in efforts to retain African American students (Howard, 1996). Leaders must also know how to use identify relevant research and data to implement change in processes as well as organizational culture (Kinnick & Ricks, 1993).

2.   Assessment must be used in administration and the classroom to continuously improve quality and initiate change (Gray, 1997).

3.   Faculty must be encouraged to participate in retention efforts, which include establishing

4.   formal and informal relationships with students. Non-Black faculty should also become involved in retention efforts such as mentoring (Kobrak, 1992).

5.   Administrative units such as student service areas and academic areas should implement quality improvement teams (Holmes, 1996).

6.   Students should be viewed as customers in both the classroom and student service areas.

7.   African American and other diverse faculty and staff should be hired.

8.   "Zero" tolerance policies for racism should be established on college campuses (Madison, 1993).

9.   Faculty and staff should be continuously trained on multiculturalism and professional topics.

10. Encourage African American student involvement in campus activities and the usage of campus facilities and services.

11. View the institution as an entire system by which everyone has a role in the education of students.

If institutions consider these concepts, improvement in not the retention of African American students can be achieved, but also for other diverse groups.

Conclusion

Over the years African American students have increasingly enrolled in predominantly white institutions. However, despite their growing numbers, African American students have left predominantly white institutions without bachelor degrees in disproportionate numbers. Part of the reason for the early departures from school result from inadequate preparation by the students, inadequate study habits, poor goal setting and a lack of commitment by the student. However research indicates that a large part of these departures (which include the students' lack of commitment) is because of the poor institutional climates and instances of racism. Faculty play a large role in the perpetuation of these environments, in addition to retention models, which have not been maximized in terms of their potential. Total Quality Management and the Learning Paradigm are the latest trends in higher education. They both focus on quality, continuous improvement and assessment, and teamwork. Other aspects of TQM include strategic planning, clear goals and mission, and accountability. Leadership plays an important role in implementing these models. If leadership were successful in implementing these models, along with demonstrating a strong commitment to diversity, institutions would improve retention for African American students tremendously.

CHAPTER 12

Responding to Cultural Diversity: Developing Literacy Skills for Understanding Educational Research

Wilton A. Barham

Introduction

James Banks has indicated that the United States is a culturally diverse country which consists of a common overarching culture, as well as a series of microcultures (Banks, 1997). Banks has also indicated that the major goal of the school or college should be to help students acquire the knowledge, skills, and attitudes needed to function effectively within the national macroculture, their own microcultures, and within and across other microcultures. Multicultural education is now promoted as a concept and a series of programs that can promote the development of learning and other social and economic benefits for all members of our diverse populations (Banks & Banks, 1997; Grant, 1995, 1999; Timm, 1996). The intent of this chapter is to focus on the development of literacy skills related to the conduct of educational research that can benefit the growing diverse populations of students in our colleges and universities (Brown & Dowling, 1998; Crowl, 1996; Maxwell, 1996; Wolpert, 1991). A teacher's ability to assist students from diverse backgrounds in the development of adequate literacy skills has been recognized as a very important goal of an effective teacher preparation program. These literacy skills are also considered important tools for conducting research in the undergraduate and graduate curriculum (Bierhanzl, 1999; Craft, 1996). Basic literacy is the minimum but adequate ability to read and write. It can also describe a program designed to achieve such basic skills (Lingua Links, 1997). The literacy skills to which I refer include listening, speaking, reading, writing, and thinking (Brown & Dowling, 1998; Richardson, 1990).

As we learn to help students with diverse cultural backgrounds and experiences in developing adequate literacy skills and use these skills in presenting research reports, we must be aware of some of the contemporary writing issues. They are (a) historical, social and intellectual contexts of the social science which serve as frames for the questions we ask, and the answers we get; (b) every language has gram-matical, narrative, and rhetorical structures; (c) writing involves disclosure of forms of power and values; and (d) writing involves the use of authority and power to tell about the people we study. In science writing (a) we write a narrative and create some kind of narrative meaning (e.g., shape of research report reveals subsections that are narratively driven.); (b) narrative consists of facts, plain language, and objectivity; and (c) words are objective, precise, unambiguous, non-contexual, and nonmetaphoric.

In this chapter, I demonstrate how a model or theoretical framework of separate and integrated literacy skills are useful for promoting understanding in education research. I also discuss the common and different literacy skills and literary styles used in quantitative and qualitative research paradigms. These are skills and styles that all students from these diverse backgrounds and educational preparation lack. In describing these paradigms, common rhetorical devices such as metaphor and imagery are used.

Each particular field has its own set of literary devices and rhetorical appeals such as theorems and probability tables (Richardson, 1990). It is expected that both consumers from diverse cultural backgrounds and producers of educational research will be the beneficiaries of the ideas presented in this chapter.

Various models, chain of reasoning or research spectra, have been proposed (e.g., Krathwohl, 1993; Tuckman, 1988; Werthhamer, 1999) that relate to the development and conduct of the process of educational research. The authors have all indicated the importance of the various literacy skills that are integral to this understanding. However, emphasis has not been given to the development and integration of these skills as part of a systematic approach to assist students from diverse cultural backgrounds and experiences. The model presented in Figure 1 attempts to demonstrate the prominence of these skills in attempting to master the process of educational research. This model of literacy skills for understanding educational research consists of five major stages:

A Model of Literacy Skills for Understanding Educational Research

(1) Problem Development: This stage consists of links to previous studies, problem development, and relevant theories and concepts; (2) Critical Literature Review: Here, questions, hypotheses, models (theoretical frameworks), methods, results, conclusion, and limitations are discussed; (3) Design: The subjects, situations, treatment, observations or measurement, basis for sensing attributes or changes, and procedures are presented at this stage; (4) Findings: The results of data collection and data analysis are presented and discussed; and (5) Conclusions and Recommendations: Conclusions, recommendations, and link to the next study are the content of the final stage. To acquire these skills of research successfully, students will have to develop and integrate the literacy skills of reading, writing, thinking, and listening simultaneously. Teachers must also be trained in working with students from diverse cultures so that they can recognize and deal with deficiencies such as those related to English-As-A-Second-Language (Craft,

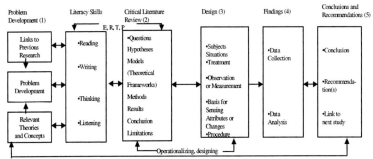

Reading, listening, writing, thinking and listening skills are integrated at all five (5) levels of this model.

Note: This model was developed with ideas from Krathwohl (1993, 1998) and Tuckman (1994, 1998)
    E=Explanation; R=Rationale; T=Theory; and P=Point of View
Figure 1: A Model of Literacy Skills for the Understanding of Educational Research

1996). These literacy skills must also be taught and applied within the process of educational research; each skill is utilized in varying degrees at the five stages of the research process. How could the development of these skills influence the understanding of the research process for consumers as well as producers of research? An explanation of the elements of this model will answer that question.

Problem Development

The problem development phase, the usual beginning stage of the process, is a very difficult undertaking for most individuals. It is not always very focused and precise. This is so because the conceptualization of the problem to be investigated is usually very broad and abstract. This is usually compounded by the fact that many students from diverse backgrounds lack sufficient knowledge of the use of the English Language. The researcher is expected to narrow the scope of the problem and provide more focus. The problem statement should indicate that a relationship exists between or among two or more variables, should be stated clearly and unambiguously in the form of an explicit or implicit question, and should imply the possibilities for empirical testing. This statement is usually embedded in a narrative discourse which is contextual, that is, the researcher describes the problem, describes the literature about the problem, and mentions deficiencies in the literature. The discussion of the context, establishing a sufficient amount of background information relating to the problem of interest requires that students undertake a review of the literature; they must be aware of past and present knowledge involving the topic of inquiry. In other words, a foundation upon which the study is based is established at this stage; this is the link to previous studies and the integration of relevant theories and concepts.

However, in order for the learner to present an acceptable discourse, he or she must apply the skills of reading comprehension effectively (Mitchell, 1989; Wassman & Rinsky, 1997). What are the levels and techniques of reading comprehension that should be taught at this step and throughout the research process so that the learner can develop an effective problem statement? (1) Literal level. At this level students are expected to (a) locate, recognize and identify explicitly stated information based on the information source that they have; (b) locate and identify information deemed important; (c) recall information once read; and (d) derive literal meaning from words, sentences and paragraphs. (2) Interpretive level. Here learners are expected to (a) go beyond an author's literal statements, that is, draw inferences from an author's statements; interpret an author's meaning (supported with evidence from basic information); and integrate new information with old; (b) weave together ideas from content; recognize an author's purpose, attitude, tone, or mood; demonstrate a sense of following the organization of the written material; and predict outcomes and solutions; (c) make summaries; sense relationship among variables, events, people, and ideas; paraphrase; and draw conclusions; and (d) examine statements and determine if they represent ideas which the author would support; and cite evidence from the text which supports or rejects the statement as an expression of the author's ideas.(3) Applied level. Finally, at this third level, the learner should be able to (a) synthesize an author's ideas with his or her own ideas and experiences and (b) formulate broad and specific principles or generalizations and then be able to express these principles or generalizations in written form.

It is clear that reading skills are intertwined with writing skills because much writing is required at the problem development stage and throughout the entire process. Students will be expected to write a problem statement (i.e., a statement of purpose), which consists of the main point, subpoints and supporting details (Mitchell, 1989). The class instructor should expose the learner to various writing approaches as he or she proceeds to develop this section of the research process: formulating a problem statement; organizing prewriting; writing a scratch outline; developing an outline from prewriting; subordinating ideas; traditional outlining; or using Warnier-Orr diagram (outlining scheme) (Mitchell, 1989). Depending on the ability and experience of the writer, some writing steps may need more development than others. Thinking skills or tools are necessary elements of the writing process. In the process of developing a problem statement we have to think about it. As Miles and Rauton (1985, p.1) reminded us, "Our minds are constantly active; we cannot help it. The first need is to learn how to observe our thoughts in action." To be more skillful thinkers we must become more aware of our thoughts. To the extent that we can be aware of our thinking, we can learn about it, improve it, and then control it. If students learn how to become more aware of their thinking during the process of problem development, they can control their thinking so that they can be good students. A good student, as Miles and Rauton informed us, is usually a consciously-thinking student. "Thinking is those conscious and unconscious mental skills we use when reacting to a choice", they said. Therefore, thinking, reading, and writing are necessary and important skills that must be used effectively at this stage of the learning process. Pitfalls to clear thinking include (a) emotions, (b) habits, (c) functional fixedness, (d) self-confidence, (e) laziness, (f) lack of knowing where to start, (g) time, (h) information flaws, (i) apparent lack of mental tools, and (j) others' opinions (Miles & Rauton). Listening skills are also important. We must listen to directions, our thoughts and those of others. A learner who practices good listening skills will enhance his or her reading and writing skills.

Critical Literature Review

There is a general consensus that the goals of a literature review are (a) to assist in conceptualizing a problem, refining it, and, if necessary, reducing it to a feasible size and scope; (b) to determine the major variables of importance in the phenomenon or phenomena; (c) to understand relationships among these variables; (d) to find the frontier of research on the problem (how far previous researchers could solidly reach); (e) to get suggestions about how to do the study, what previous mistakes to avoid, and what new methods might be effective; (f) to substitute shorter, less expensive time doing the literature search for lengthier, more expensive research time rediscovering what is already known; and (g) to put the conceptualized problem in the context of previous research, showing how the problem relates to it yet goes beyond it. The literacy skills discussed above must be utilized by every learner at the second stage of this model if a critical literature review is to be completed successfully. Once these goals are identified, the researcher then undertakes a critical review of the literature which consists of several steps or activities.

A critical review of the literature consists of a comprehensive search in which the researcher selects articles and critically discusses predominant findings in light of methodological limitations (Werthamer, 1999). As the narrative is developed, the author discusses the purpose of the studies being reviewed. The purpose of his or her study is compared and contrasted with that of other studies. A presentation of the research questions or problem statement is made, and these are related to the study. Important questions such as these are answered: What makes your questions the basis for an original research? Is your research going beyond other researchers' problems? A presentation of the statement of hypotheses (if any) is made and the theoretical frameworks (models) that are presented in the studies are critically reviewed. The author relates them to his or her proposed study and then determines the differences. In addition to Werthamer's (1999) suggestions regarding methods, Barham (1997) indicated that the following questions should be answered: What are the methods that were used? What are the research design(s), data collection methods (including sample selection and instrumentation), and data analytic techniques used to validate the hypotheses? Were they appropriate, valid, and reliable? Are the methods to be used in the study more valid and reliable than other studies reviewed? How or why?

The results of the studies should be reported and critiqued. Are they plausible? Are they questionable in light of possible invalidities? Do these results provide possible answers to the questions raised or investigated? Do we have a better understanding of the problem, a better explanation? If not, how will the proposed study possibly provide more plausible explanations or findings? Are conclusions drawn from these results sound in relationship to data and methods of validation?

The review continues with a discussion of the limitations of the studies reviewed. This discussion should indicate whether the study will eliminate those limitations thereby leading to more valid results. The author then shares with the reader insights that are not apparent. Understanding what we write involves the logical organization of the narrative. We must, therefore, organize a critical literature review by (a) using categories of variables or specific variable names that are the same as those used in the title as subheadings, (b) discussing similar theories under a broad subheading, and (c) discussing different theories under appropriate subheadings. In short, variable names in the model or theoretical framework should serve as subheadings.

Borg and Gall (1989) reported that every reviewer should avoid carrying out a hurried review of the literature in order to get started on the research project. This usually results in overlooking previous studies containing ideas that would have improved the researcher's (student's) project. It also represents an incomplete application of all the literacy skills necessary at this stage. Other common errors they warned about include (a) relying too heavily upon secondary data sources; (b) concentrating on research findings when reading research articles, thus overlooking valuable information on methods, measures, etc.; (c) overlooking sources other than education journals, such as newspapers and popular magazines that often contain articles on educational topics; and (d) failing to define satisfactorily the topic limits of the review of literature. Searching too broad an area often leads to the student's becoming discouraged or doing a slipshod job. Searching too narrow an area causes him or her to overlook many articles that are peripheral to the research topic but that contain information that would result in designing a better study. Borg and Gall mentioned two other common errors: (a) copying bibliographic data incorrectly and then being unable to locate the needed reference and (b) copying far too much material onto note cards. The latter often indicates that the student does not have clear understanding of his or her project and thus cannot separate important from unimportant information.

Designs or Methods

Phase 3 of this model is the designs or methods phase in which the writer develops the narrative using subareas such as subjects, situations, treatment (if any), observations or measures, basis for sensing attributes or changes, and procedures (Krathwohl, 1998). In the section involving subjects, the researcher should indicate in considerable detail how he or she will obtain subjects--the sample--to be used in the study. A random sample should be used whenever possible.

The situations or environments in which the research is carried out should be discussed. The researcher should also describe the treatment or design (experimental, quasi-experimental or any one of a number of other quantitative or qualitative designs). Observations or measures are presented along with the type of instrument(s) used to collect data. A discussion of validity and reliability of the instruments is expected. The basis for sensing attributes or changes is established through the theoretical framework on which a study is built and the use of various appropriate statistical techniques. The procedures that were established in the study are also discussed. Literary devices should be used effectively. The researcher should (a) use a narrative stance–he or she is the expert who did the research; (b) make a general point and support it with statistics, examples, quotations, etc.; and (c) write with immediacy, as if everything were here and now (Ogunyemi, 1997). Other suggestions for writing this and other sections effectively (Barham; Ogunyemi) are: (a) be concise: simple, brief, and clear; (b) engage a clear writing style: short, simple sentences and active verbs; (c) use concrete and easy language; (d) use short paragraphs and headings (such as the subareas above); and (e) use personal pronouns such as "I" and "you." In being concise, the writer should (a) eliminate redundancy such as "true and accurate," "full and complete," "my own personal," "few in number," "disappear from sight," "circle around," "adequate enough," and "still yet," and (b) avoid wordiness such as "In spite of the fact that," "Due to the fact that," and "came into the possession of." As the researcher develops each section of the proposed model, he or she will use various literary devices in the social sciences (including education) such as synecdoche and metaphor. Synecdoche is a rhetorical technique through which a part stands for a whole (e.g., individuals for a class; roof--house; gavel--law). We use a sample (a part) in scientific research to understand various parameters of a population (the whole).

Metaphor is the understanding and experiencing of one kind of thing in terms of another. For example, "a systematic approach" is a metaphor for "a social system."

Findings

Data collection and analysis are the subareas of section 4. This is usually presented under the broad area of findings. A discussion of data collection approaches would include ways in which subjects were identified for participation. Did they voluntarily agree to participate by signing a consent form? The instruments that were used must also be described and the process by which validity and reliability were established should also be described.

The data analysis subsection includes the results of the statistical techniques that were used to test the negation of the research hypotheses (the null hypotheses). This determines, to some extent, the basis for sensing attributes or changes.

Conclusions and Recommendations

Finally, section 5 of this model highlights all that one can possibly conclude from the study and presents any reasonable recommendation(s). A link to future studies is usually a concluding section. Here, as in all the major sections of this model, the narrative is used. It is the primary way through which humans organize their experiences into temporally meaningful episodes (Polkinghorne, 1988). The narrative is both a mode of reasoning and representation. Narrative structures frame both narrative and logico-scientific writings and as such should be taught as part of any research methods course within the preservice teacher preparation curriculum and the general undergraduate and graduate curricula. It is also important to note that the narrative provides access to time in the following ways: everyday, auto-biographical, cultural, and collective story.

Summary

In this chapter, I have attempted to describe a model of literacy skills that can assist students of diverse cultural backgrounds in conducting and understanding educational research. One could identify this also as a model of educational research which emphasizes the integration of literacy skills for better understanding. In an article entitled "Research in the Undergraduate Curriculum," Bierhanzl (1999) wrote:"In recent years, writing as a part of the undergraduate curriculum has increasingly been the subject of research" (p. 4). He said that many of the benefits of adding writing to the curriculum are "ultimately expressed as improvements in the clarity and structure of students' arguments, thinking and expression" (p. 4). I am arguing further that these literacy skills be integrated in any educational research course for all students. Bertoffs (as reported by Bierhanzl) described the process of writing which is beneficial to students this way: "The work of the active mind is seeing relationships, finding forms, making meanings" (p. 4). I agree with Bierhanzl that this is a description of the process of research as well. By presenting this model, I hope it will move us one step further in embracing Bierhanzl's ideas when he wrote:

Many benefits that flow from a structured program of writing could (and should) also be created by a program that introduces a structured method of research. Additional educational value can, in many areas, be created by occasionally shifting the focus from writing to research. Rather than seeing writing always as the primary end to be achieved, and research merely as a means to obtain fodder for writing, we can view the research process as a means of learning in and of itself. Writing is not thereby dismissed; it becomes a tool for communicating the results of research (p. 4).

This model, as Bierhanzl lamented, views the research process as a means of learning in and of itself. We would not teach these literacy skills in isolation but incorporate them in the structure of an educational research course. By doing this, it is likely that students will become better researchers themselves.

Afterword

Cultural diversity is a critical social issue that must be addressed in the new millennium. Although it is not new to higher education, some progress has been made as administrators and faculty have worked to solve problems and to make decisions about the challenges, opportunities, and promises of cultural diversity in American higher education. However, recent changes in admissions and financial aid policies and practices have resulted in a decline of and passive support for the modest progress made over the past decades.

The new faces on our college and university campuses demonstrate that students from culturally diverse groups are more visible than any other period in America's history; true diversity, nevertheless, remains a dream, rather than a reality in higher education.

Finally, in *Meeting the Challenge of Cultural Diversity in Higher Education in the New Millennium,* the authors present some of the research being done by faculty and administrators to respond to the needs of culturally diverse college students. Consequently, this book should prove useful for educators who need to become more knowledgeable about America's diversity in higher education.

Ada Harrington Belton and Herbert C. Chambers

Notes About Lead Author

Vernon L. Farmer is acting assistant vice president for Academic Affairs and dean of the School of Graduate Studies and Research at Grambling State University. He is a professor in the Department of Educational Leadership and former department head and director of doctoral studies in the College of Education. He earned the B. A. in sociology from the University of Michigan at Flint, the M. A. in counselor education and the Ph.D. in higher education from the University of Michigan at Ann Arbor.

Notes About Other Contributing Authors

Eleanor Agnew is an associate professor in the Department of Writing and Linguistics in the College of Liberal Arts and Social Sciences at Georgia Southern University. She earned the B. A. in history from the University of Vermont, the M. A. in composition and rhetoric from the University of Maine in Orono, and the Ph.D. in composition and rhetoric from Louisiana State University at Baton Rouge.

Wilton A. Barham is head of the Department of Educational Leadership and director of doctoral studies in the College of Education at Grambling State University. He is also a professor in the Department of Educational Leadership. He earned the B.S. in secondary mathematics from State University of New York at Oneonta, the M.P.H. in biostatistics, and the Ph.D. in educational research methods from the University of Michigan at Ann Arbor.

Ada Harrington Belton is an assistant professor in the Department of Curriculum and Instruction in the College of Education and Psychology at the University of Southern Mississippi. She earned her Ph.D. in curriculum and instruction from Fordham University.

Laura D. Browne is director of Developmental Education for Iowa Valley and the Student Success Center at the Iowa Valley Community College District in Marshalltown. She earned the B. A. in social work and the M. A. in education from the University of Northern Iowa in Cedar Falls, and the

Ph.D. in educational leadership and policy studies from Iowa State University.

Herbert C. Chambers is an associate dean of the Pre College at Rowan-Cabarrus Community College, in Salisbury. He earned the B. S. in political science from Livingstone College, the M.S. in reading education from the University of Southern Mississippi at Hattisburg, and a specialist in developmental education from Appalachian State University.

Frances Swayzer Conley is an assistant principal for administration at Woodlawn High School Magnet and Career Academies in Shreveport, LA. She earned the B. S. in English and speech from Grambling State University, the M.A. in English education from Louisiana Tech University, and the Ed.D. in developmental education from Grambling State University.

Martin O. Edu is director of the Graduate Program in the Department of Mass Communication in the College of Liberal Arts at Grambling State University. He is also an associate professor in the Department of Mass Communication. He earned the B. A. in broadcasting and public relations from Eastern Kentucky University, the M.A. in communication studies from The University of Iowa, the Ed.D. in developmental education from Grambling State University, and the Ph.D. in mass communication from The University of Southern Mississippi at Hattiesburg.

Betty J. Farmer is an associate professor in the School of Nursing at Grambling State University. She earned a B. S. in nursing at the University of Louisiana in Monroe, the M. S. in nursing at Northwestern University at Natchitoches, and the Ed.D. in higher education from the University of Arkansas at Little Rock.

Lee Jones is an associate dean in the College of Education at Florida State University. He is an associate professor in the Department of Educational Leadership. He earned the B. A. in drama and speech com-munications from Delaware State University, the M. A. in business and administration and the Ph.D. in organizational development from The Ohio State University.

Heather A. Katz is an instructional systems specialist with the United States Navy Naval School of Health Sciences at the National Naval Medical Center in Bethesda, MD. She earned the B.S. in environmental science and the M.Ed. in special education from Howard University, and the Ph.D. in curriculum and instructional technology from the University of Texas at Austin.

Gordon Kitto is transportation director for the Santee Sioux Tribe at Niobara, NE. He is also former dean of students at Nebraska Indian Community College in Niobara. He earned his B. S. in education from Fairfield University, and the M. S. degree in guidance counseling from Eastern Washington University.

Margaret A. McLaughlin is an associate professor in the Department of Writing and Linguistics in the College of Liberal Arts and Social Sciences at Georgia Southern University. She earned the B. A. in English from DePauw University, the M. A. in English and reading from Western Illinois University, and the D.A. in English studies from Illinois State University.

Evelyn Shepherd-Wynn is an assistant professor in the Department of English in the College of Liberal Arts at Grambling State University. She earned the B. S. in English from Grambling State University, the M. A. in English education from Louisiana Tech University, and the Ed.D. in developmental education from Grambling State University.

Gwen Spencer is director of Educational Planning and Advising at Highline Community College. She earned the B.A. in psychology and sociology from the University of Wisconsin at Eau Claire, the M. A. in counselor education from the University of Wisconsin at Oshkosh, and the Ed.D. in educational leadership at Seattle University.

Neari F. Warner is acting president and provost at Grambling State University. She is also a professor in the College of Education. She earned the B. A. in English from Grambling State University, the M. A. in English education from Louisiana Tech University, and the Ph.D. in curriculum and instruction from Louisiana State University at Baton Rouge.

APPENDIX 1

#	93 F	94 W	94 Sp	94 Su	94 F	95 W	95 Sp	95 Su	95 F	96 W	96 Sp	96 Su	96 F	97 W	97 Sp	97 Su	97 F	98 W	98 Sp	98 Su	Number of times in BW	Exit	VSAT
1		P	P	X	S																1	Y	260
2		D																			2	N	229
3	P	S	P	X				X			OK										1	Y	330
4		P	OK	X				X				X				X			G		1	Y	350
5		P	OK	X				X				X							G		1	Y	300
6		P	OK	X															G		1	Y	350
7				X	P	P															1	Y	300
8				X														G			1	Y	280
9		P	P				P														4	N	330
10	P	P	S				P	E							E						1	Y	320
11			X			P	OK	X	P												3	Y	230
12		P	X	S																	2	Y	340
13		P	P																		1	Y	330
14			X			P	S						E		P						3	Y	320
15			X			P	S	X	OK			X	P		E	OK				OK	1	Y	330
16			X	D																	3	Y	260
17		P	P	S	OK			X				X	P	E		P	E				1	Y	340
18		P	P	X	P	OK	P	X	S	E			E								2	Y	270
19		P	P	X	S		E														2	Y	360
20			OK																		1	Y	310
21		P	P	X	OK			X			P	X	S	E		E					1	Y	360
22	OK																				1	Y	410
23		P	P	X	P	S	OK	X												OK	2	Y	270
24	P	P	OK	X	P	S		P													2	Y	290
25		P	X	D																	1	Y	280
26			X														G				1	Y	360
27			X				X												OK		1	Y	320
28			X	P	P	OK								X		G					2	Y	310
29		P	OK	X	P	P	S	X	P	E		P	E	P	P	E	E				2	Y	310
30		P	S	X	E		P	X	P												1	Y	240
31			X															G			2	Y	330
32		P	X	S	OK		X	P	P	OK			P	OK				OK			2	Y	330
33			X				X						OK								1	Y	350
34			X	OK																	1	Y	290
35	P	P	P	X	S	E		P	OK								G				3	Y	290
36		P	OK	X		P	P	X	OK												1	Y	270
37										X							G				2	Y	310
38	OK			OK	D																3	N	320
39			X								X					G					1	Y	400
40		P	X	S	P																2	Y	290
41	D																				1	N	360
42		P	X	S	E	E	X	P		E	P										1	Y	350
43			X			P	OK							OK							2	Y	240
44			X			X		P	OK			G									1	Y	340
45	P	OK	X			X			X			X					G				1	Y	310
46		D																			1	Y	350
47				X													G				2	Y	340
48			X			X			X			X				G					2	Y	300
49	P	P																			3	Y	300
50			X										X			OK					1	Y	360
51	OK																G				1	Y	290
52		P	S	X	OK			X								G					1	Y	280
53		P	S	X	E	OK		X								G					1	Y	310
54			X					X				OK									1	Y	330
55		P																			1	Y	220
56		P	X	S	P	E															2	Y	290
57		P																			1	Y	330
58			X				X				X				G						1	Y	320
59			X											X	G						1	Y	310
60			X		P	P															1	Y	280
61	P	S																			1	Y	330

BASIC WRITERS FIVE YEARS LATER: PROFILES OF THEIR ACADEMIC PROGRESS

The horizontal lines show each student's progress, from Fall, 1993 through Summer, 1998.

| P = Probation | S = Suspension/Restricted Enrollment | E = Exclusion |
| D = Dismissal | G = Graduation | OK = Good Standing |

X = Did not attend summer school but still enrolled

McLaughlin and Agnew 17

APPENDIX 2

#	93 F	94 W	94 Sp	94 Su	94 F	95 W	95 Sp	95 Su	95 F	96 W	96 Sp	96 Su	96 F	97 W	97 Sp	97 Su	97 F	98 W	98 Sp	98 Su	Number of times in BW	Exit BW	VSAT
1		P	P	X	S																1	Y	260
2		D																			2	N	229
3	P	S	P	X				X			OK										1	Y	330
4		P	OK	X				X				X				X			G		1	Y	350
6																							
7				X	P	P															1	Y	300
8																							
9		P	P					P													4	N	330
10	P	P	S						P	E					E						1	Y	320
11			X		P	OK	X	P													3	Y	230
12		P	X	S																	2	Y	340
14		X			P	S					E		P								3	Y	320
15		X			P	S	X	OK			X	P		E	OK				OK		1	Y	330
16		X	D																		3	Y	260
17	P	P	S	OK			X			X	P	E		P	E						1	Y	340
18	P	P	X	P	OK	P	X	S	E		E										2	Y	270
20		OK																			1	Y	310
21	P	P	X	OK			X		P	X	S			E	E						1	Y	360
23	P	P	X	F	P	S	OK	X											OK		2	Y	270
24	P	P	OK	X	P	S	P														2	Y	290
25		P	X	D																	1	Y	280
27		X			X				X						OK						1	Y	320
28		X	P	P	OK		X						X	G							2	Y	310
29	P	OK	X	P	P	S	X	P	E	P	E	P	P	E	E						2	Y	310
30	P	S	X	E		P	X	P													1	Y	240
35	P	P	P	X	S	E	P	OK										G			3	Y	290
36	P	OK	X	P	P	X	OK														1	Y	270
38	OK			OK	D																3	N	320
39								X					G								1	Y	400
40	P	X	S	P																	2	Y	290
42	P	X	S	E	E	X	P		E	P											1	Y	350
44		X			X	P	OK			G											1	Y	340
45	P	OK	X			X			X			X	OK								1	Y	310
46		D																			1	Y	350
48		X			X			X			X	G									2	Y	300
49	P	P																			3	Y	300
54		X					X	OK													1	Y	330
55	P																				1	Y	220
56	P	X	S	P	E																2	Y	290
60	X		P	P																	1	Y	280
61	P	S																			1	Y	330

African-American Students Progress

The horizontal lines show each student's progress, from Fall, 1993 through Summer, 1998.

P = Probation   S = Suspension/Restricted Enrollment   E = Exclusion

D = Dismissal   G = Graduation   OK = Good Standing

X = Did not attend summer school but still enrolled

APPENDIX 3

	93 F	94 W	94 Sp	94 Su	94 F	95 W	95 Sp	95 Su	96 F	96 W	96 Sp	96 Su	97 F	97 W	97 Sp	97 Su	98 F	98 W	98 Sp	98 Su	Number of times in BW	Exit BW	VSAT
1																							
2																							
3																							
4																							
5		P	OK	X				X			X								G		1	Y	300
6		P	OK	X															G		1	Y	350
7																							
8			X																G		1	Y	280
9																							
10																							
11																							
12																							
13		P	P																		1	Y	330
14																							
15																							
16																							
17																							
18																							
19		P	P	X	S		E														2	Y	360
20																							
21																							
22	OK																				1	Y	410
23																							
24																							
25																							
26			X																		1	Y	360
27																							
28																							
29																							
30																							
31							X												G		2	Y	330
32		P	X	S	OK		X	P	P	OK			P	OK					OK		2	Y	330
33			X				X				X			OK							1	Y	350
34			X		OK																1	Y	290
35																							
36																							
37											X					G					2	Y	310
38																							
39																							
40																							
41	D																				1	N	360
42																							
43			X						P	OK							OK				2	Y	240
44																							
45																							
46																							
47							X												G		2	Y	340
48																							
49																							
50			X											X					OK		1	Y	360
51	OK																			G	1	Y	290
52		P	S	X	OK						X								G		1	Y	280
53		P	S	X	E	OK					X								G		1	Y	310
54																							
55																							
56																							
57		P																			1	Y	330
58			X				X				X					G					1	Y	320
59			X												X	G					1	Y	310

White Students' Progress

The horizontal lines show each student's progress, from Fall, 1993 through Summer, 1998.

P = Probation	S = Suspension/Restricted Enrollment	E = Exclusion
D = Dismissal	G = Graduation	OK = Good Standing
X = Did not attend summer school but still enrolled		

References

Chapter 1

Aguirre, A. (2000). *Women and minority faculty in the academic workplace: Recruitment, retention, and academic culture.* (ERIC Document Reproduction Service No. ED 446 723)

Anderson, J. A. (1991). *Diversity, excellence and achievement. 2* (2) 1-4. Indiana, PA: Department of Psychology.

Barham, W. A. (2001). A supplemental learning assistance model for developmental learners. In Farmer, V. L. & Barham, W. A. (eds.). *Selected Models of Developmental Education Pro-grams in Higher Education.* Lanham: University Press of America.

Carnevale, A. P. & Fry, R. A. (2000). *Crossing the great divide: Can we achieve equity when generation y goes to college?* Prepared for the *Educational Testing service Leadership 2000 Series.* New Jersey: Princeton.

Commission on National Challenges in Higher Education. (1988). *Memorandum to the 41st President of the United States.* Washington, DC: American Council on Education.

DuBois, N. (2001). A developmental information processing model: Metacognition and self-regulated learning. In Farmer, V. L. & Barham, W. A. (eds.). *Selected Models of Developmental Education Pro-grams in Higher Education.* Lanham: University Press of America. pp. 25-61.

Dunn, R., Dunn, K., & Perrin, J. (1994). *Teaching young children through their instructional learning styles: Practical approaches for grades K-2.* Boston, MA: Allyn & Bacon.

Farmer, V. L. & Barham, W. A. (2001). An integrated developmental education model: A comprehensive approach. In Farmer, V. L. & Barham, W. A. (eds.). *Selected Models of Developmental Education Programs in Higher Education.* Lanham: University Press of America. pp.427-447.

Gilbert II, S., & Gay, G. (1985). Improving the success of poor Black children. *Phi Delta Kappan, 67,* 133-137.

Granger, M. (1993). A review of the literature on the status of women and minorities in the professoriate in higher education. *Journal of School Leadership, 3*, 121-135.

Hocker, C. (1991). In search of black faculty. *Black Enterprise, 21*(10), 70-76.

LaBare, M. J. (1993). *Faculty development for inclusive curriculum: Principles and processes.* Paper presented at the College Teaching and Learning Exchange National Conference, San Jose, CA (ERIC Document Reproduction Service, No. ED 370 480)

Locke, D. C. (1992). *Increasing multicultural understanding.* Newbury Park, CA: Sage Publications, Inc.

Morganthau , T. (1997, January 27). Demographics: The face of the future. *Newsweek,* 58-60.

National Center for Education Statistics. (1997). Office of Educational Research & Improvement. Washington, DC: U. S. Department of Education.

Pine, G., & Hilliard, A. (1990). Rx for racism: Imperatives for America's schools. *Phi Delta Kappan, 71*(8), 593-600.

Roach, R. (June 2001). Is higher education ready for minority America? *Black Issues in Higher Education, 18*(8), 29-31.

Rodriguez, A. M. (1991). *Multicultural education: Some considerations for a university setting.* California State University, Hayward, CA   (ERIC Reproduction Document Service No. ED 337 094)

Shepherd-Wynn, E., Cadet, L. P., & Pendleton, E. P. (2001). A collaborative writing model for college students with emphasis on cultural diversity. In Farmer, V. L. & Barham, W. A. (eds.). *Selected Models of Developmental Education Programs in Higher Education.* Lanham: University Press of America.

Sleeter, C., & Grant, C. (1986). Success for all students. Phi Delta Kappan, 68, 297-299.

Tomlinson, L. M. (1989). *Postsecondary developmental programs: A traditional agenda with new perspectives* (Report No. 3). Washington, DC: School of Education and Human Development, The George Washington University.

Turner, C. & Sotello, V. (2000). New faces, new knowledge. *Academe,* *86*(5), 34-37.

Wadsworth, E. C. (1992). Inclusive teaching: A workshop on cultural diversity. *To Improve the Academy, 11,* 233-239.

Webster, S. (1974). *The education of Black Americans.* New York: The John Day Company.

Chapter 2

Abraham, A. A. Jr. (1991). They came to college: A remedial profile of first-time freshmen in SREB states. *Issues in Higher Education, 25,* 1-12.

Abraham, A. A. Jr. (1987). *Readiness for college: Should there be statewide placement standards?* Southern Regional Education Board. Atlanta, GA: SREB.

Astin, A. (1984). A look at pluralism in the contemporary student population. *NASPA Journal, 21*(3), 2-11.

Ausubel, D. P. (1968). *Educational psychology: A cognitive view.* New York: Holt, Reinhart, and Winston, Incorporated.

Beckett, G. (1985). *Developmental education.* (ERIC Document Reproduction Service No. ED 258 635)

Botan, C. H., & Hazleton, V. Jr. (Eds.). (1989). *Public relations theory.* Hillsdale, N. J.: Lawrence Erlbaum Associates, Publishers.

Brown, C. H. (1991). *The relationship between the attitudes of directors and instructors and student ratings in remedial and developmental students in Tennessee's community colleges.* (ERIC Document Reproduction Service No. ED 339 444)

Chen, G. & Starosta, W. J. (1998). *Foundations of intercultural communication.* Boston: Allyn and Bacon.

Chickering, A. W., & Associates (1989). *The modern American college.* San Francisco: Jossey-Bass Publishers.

Cohen, A. M., & Brawer, F. B. (1989). *The American community college* (2nd ed.). San Francisco: Jossey-Bass.

Cooley, W. W & Lohnes, P. R. (1971). *Multivariate data analysis.* New York: Wiley.

Combs, L. M., & Boylan, H. R. (1985). Federal viewpoint: A recent discussion. *Journal of Developmental Education.* *9*(1), 16-18.

Cutlip, S. M., Center, A. H., & Broom, G. M. (1985). *Effective public relations, 6th ed.* New Jersey: Prentice-Hall, Inc.

Davis, C. L. (Winter, 1979). Developmental education in Georgia. *Journal of Developmental and Remedial Education, 2*(2), 2-4, 26.

Desmond, J. (1989, Sept.-Oct.). Managing your media relations. *Physician Executive*, p. 24.

DiDomenico, M. (1992, May). Getting a restaurant to stand out in the crowd. *Nation's Restaurant News, 26*(20), 44.

Dodd, H. D. (1995). *Dynamics of intercultural communication*, 4th ed. Dubuque, IA: WCB Brown & Benchmark Publishers.

Dunn, S. W. (1986). *Public relations, a contemporary approach.* Homewood, IL: Irwin.

Egginton, E., Wells, R. L., Gaus, D., & Esselman, M. E. (1990). *Underlying factors associated with dropping out and factors impacting at-risk students' attitudes toward school: A comparison study of low income, white females.* (ERIC Document Reproduction Service No. ED 317 932)

The G. I. Bill of Rights. In Goodchild, L. F. & Wechsler, H. S. (Eds.) (1989). *ASHE reader on the history of higher education.* MA: Ginn Press, 627-629.

Hacker, A, (1997). *Money: Who has how much and why.* New York: Scribner.

Hardin, C. J. (1988). Access to higher education: Who belongs? *Journal of Developmental Education, 12(*1), 2-4, 19.

Harris, P. R. & Moran, R. T. (1996). *Managing cultural differences: Leadership strategies for a new world of business*, 4th ed. Houston: Gulf Publishing Company.

Hedden, B. (April, 1992). Image is everything. *Fueloil & Oil Heat Air Conditioning, 51*(4), 23.

Higbee, J. L., Dwinell, P. L., McAdams, C. R., Goldeberg-Belle, E., & Tardola, M. E. (1991). Serving underprepared students in institutions of higher education. *Journal of Humanistic Education and development, 30*(2), 73-80.

Higher Education Act of 1963; 1965. In Goodchild, L. F., & Wechsler, H. S. (Eds.)

Holstrom, E. I. (October, 1973). Older freshmen: Do they differ from typical undergraduates? *ACE Research Reports, 7 & 8.*

Jones, R. W., & Hattie, J. A. (1991). Academic stress among adolescents: An examination by ethnicity, grade, and sex. (ERIC Document Reproduction Service No. ED 336 668)

Kalat, J. W. (1990). *Introduction to psychology,* 2nd. ed. Belmont, CA: Wadsworth Publishing Company.

Lamons, B. (1992, June 8). If you don't care about your company image, no one will. *Marketing News, 26*(12), 13.

Landward, S., & Hepworth, D. (1984). Support systems for high risk students: Findings and issues. *College and University, 59,* 119 -128.

Lederman, M. J., Ribaudo, M., & Ryzewic, S. R. (1985). Basic skills of entering college freshmen: A national survey of policies and perceptions. *Journal of Developmental Education. 9*(1), 10-13.

Lowman, J. (1990). *Mastering the techniques of teaching.* San Francisco: Jossey-Bass Inc., Publishers.

Lustig, M. W. & Koester, J. (1998). *Intercultural competence: Interpersonal communication across cultures.* New York: Longman.

Martin, J. N., & Nakayama, T. K (2000). *Intercultural communication in contexts,* 2nd. ed. Mountain View, CA: Mayfield Publishing Company.

Maxwell, M. (1979). *Improving student learning skills.* San Francisco: Jossey-Bass Inc, Publishers.

Mead, G. H. (1934). *Mind, self, and other.* Chicago: University of Chicago Press.

Mickler, L. M., & Chapel, A. C.(1989). Basic skills in college: Academic dilution or solution? *Journal of Developmental Education, 13*(1), 2-4, 16.

Morvis, G. M. (1991, September). Public relations: New priority for banks today. *Bank Marketing, 23*(9), 44.

National Center for Education Statistics (1985). *The condition of education: A statistical report.* (ERIC Document Reproduction Service No. ED 258 365).

National Society for the Study of Education, Part 1. Chicago: University of Chicago Press. 336-337.

Nist, S. L. (1985). Developmental versus remedial: Does a confusion exist in higher education? *Journal of Developmental Education, 8*(3), 8-10.

Nolfi, G. F., Jr. & Nelson, V. I. (1973). Strengthening the alternative postsecondary education system: Continuing and part-time study in Massachusetts. Vol. 1: *Summary report and recommendation.* Cambridge, Mass: University Consultants.

Pilland, W. E. (1983). Remedial education in the states. (ERIC Document Reproduction Service No. ED 251 160)

Plisko, V. W., & Stern, J. (1985). *The condition of education: A statistical report, 1985 edition.* Washington D. C.: National education statistics. (ERIC Document Reproduction Service No. ED 258 365)

Platt, G. M. (1986). Should colleges teach below college-level courses? *Community College Review, 14*(2), 19-25.

Reynolds, M. C. (1985). Institutional implications of diagnostic reading tests. (ERIC Document Reproduction Service No. ED 262 102)

Roelfs, P. J. (1975). Teaching and counseling of older college students. *Findings, 2*(1).

Rudolph, F. (1990). *The American college and university: A history.* Athens: The University of Georgia Press.

Samovar, L. A. & Porter, R. E. (1997). *Intercultural communication: A reader,* 8th ed. Belmont, CA: Wadsworth Publishing Company.

Sandage, C. H., Fryburger, V., & Rotzoll, K. (1990). *Advertising: Theory and practice,* 12th. ed. NY: Longman, Inc.

Shimp, T. A. (1993). *Promotion management and marketing communications,* 3rd. ed. NY: The Dryden Press.

Sietel, F. P. (1993). *The practice of public relations.* New York: MacMillan Publishing Company.

Solmon, L. C., Gordon, J. J., & Ochsner, N. L. (1979). *The characteristics and needs of adults in postsecondary education.* Los Angeles: Higher Education Research Institute.

Southern Regional Education Board (1985). Access to quality undergraduate education: A report to The Southern Regional Education Board by its Commission for Educational Quality. Southern Regional Education

Board (1986). College-level study: What is it? *Issues in Higher Education, 22.*

Stuart, C. (1990, October, 1). Kiam buys advertising space to reiterate apology. *USA Today*, 2c.

Sullivan, E. (1992). Ewing sounds alarm on higher education. The *Ruston Daily Leader, 98*(280), 1.

Sullivan, H. S. (1947). *Conceptions of modern psychiatry.* Washington, DC: William A. White Foundation.

Sullivan, H. S. (1953). *The interpersonal theory of psychiatry.* New York: Norton.

Sumrall, L. (1993). *The name of God.* Springdale, PA: Whitaker House.

Turnball, W. W. (1986). *Can "value added" add value to education?* (ERIC Document Reproduction Service No. ED 281 869)

The President's Commission Higher Education for Democracy. In Goodchild, L. F., & Wechsler, H. S. (Eds.) (1989). *ASHE reader on the history of higher education.* MA: Ginn Press, 630-648.

Vaughan, G. B. (1982). *The Community College in America: A Pocket History.* Washington DC.: American Association of Community and Junior Colleges.

Wambach, C., & Brothen, T. (1990). An alternative to the prediction-placement model. *Journal of Developmental Education, 13*(3), 14-15, 24-26.

Wartick, S. L. (1992). The relationship between intense media exposure and change in corporate reputation. *Business and Society, 31*(1), 33-49.

Weathersby, R. (1977). A developmental perspective on adults' uses of formal education. In Chickering, A. W. & Associates. *The modern American college, Chapter 2.* San Francisco: Jossey-Bass Inc. Publishers, 51-75.

Wells, W., Burnett, J. & Moriarty, S. (1998). *Advertising principles & practice.* Stallies, 4th ed. Upper Saddle River, NJ: Prentice-Hall.

Wilcox, D. L., Ault, P. H., & Agee, W. K. (1998). *Public relations strategies a tactics.* 5th ed. United States: Addison Wesley Longman, Inc.

Wilson, J. G. (1997). Sexism, racism and other -isms. In S. Biagi & M. Kern-Foxworth. *Facing difference: Race, gender and mass media.* Thousand Oaks, CA: Pine Forge Press.

Yager, R. E., & Penick, J. E. (1989, January). An exemplary program payoff: What student perceptions reveal about science programs. *The Science Teacher, 56*(1), 54.

Zanden, J. W. V. (1981). *Social psychology.* New York: Random House.

Chapter 3

Balester, V. (1993). *Cultural divide: A study of African-American college level writers.* Portsmouth, N.H.: Boynton/Cook.

Ball, A. & T. Lardner (1997). Teacher constructs of knowledge and the Ann Arbor Black English case. *College Composition and Communication 48,* 469-485.

Dean, T. (1989). Multicultural classrooms, monocultural teachers. *College Composition and Communication 40,* 23-27.

Fidler, P. & M.A. Godwin. Retaining African-American students through the freshman seminar." *Journal of Developmental Education 17,* 34-40.

Gray, S. (1997, March 13). Study: blacks still lag behind whites in college education. *Savannah News Press,* p. A3; A5..

Harrold, V. (1995). *An investigation of faculty attitudes and oral communication programs for African American speakers of Black English at selected two-year private and public institutions of higher education in Michigan.* Unpublished dissertation. Wayne State University.

Kamusikiri, Sandra. (1996). African American English and writing assessment: An afrocentric approach. In E.M. White, W.D. Lutz, & S. Kamusikiri (Eds.). *Assessment of Writing.* New York: MLA.

Lipscomb, D. (1985). Introduction: writing. In C. K. Brooks (Ed.), *Tapping potential: English and Language Arts for the black learner* (pp. 149-53). Urbana: NCTE.

Pate, M. (1993). African American discourse: clarifying the conflict. *Journal of commonwealth and postcolonial studies, 4* (1), 78-87.

Ramsey, P. (1985). Teaching the teachers to teach black-dialect writers. In C. K. Brooks (Ed.), *Tapping potential: English and Language Arts for the black learner* (pp. 176-81). Urbana: NCTE.

Shuy, R. W. (1971). Social dialects: Teaching vs learning. *Florida FL reporter.* 28-33; 55.

Smitherman, G. (1977). *Talkin' and testifyin'.* Boston: Houghton Mifflin.

Smitherman, G. (1990). The "mis-education of the Negro"--and you too. In H. A. Daniel (Ed.), *Not only English: affirming America's multilingual heritage.* (pp.109-120). Urbana: NCTE.

Soliday, M. (1996). "From the Margins to the Mainstream: Reconceiving remediation." *College Composition and Communication 47*:(1), 85-101.

Taylor, H. (1991). *Standard English, Black English, and bidialectalism: a controversy.* New York: Peter Lang.

Wolcott, W. (1994). A longitudinal study of six developmental students' performance in reading and writing." *Journal of Basic Writing 13* (1), 14-39.

Ziegler, M.B. (1996). Postcolonial contexts of African American vernacular English. *Journal of commonwealth and postcolonial studies, 4* (1), 1-13.

Chapter 4

Agee, J. M. (1977). The realities of college composition courses. *English Journal, 66*(8), 58-60.

Anderson, T. (1995). Approaches to improving retention being investigated by the SUCCEED coalition. <http://mrsec.www.ecn. purdue. edu/v1/asee/fie95/4a2/4a23/4a23.htm>

Applebee, A. N. et al. (1989). *Crossroads in American education: A summary of findings. The nation's report card. Report no. 17-0V-01.* Princeton, NJ: National Assessment of Educational Progress. Educational Testing Service.

Applebee, A. N., Langer, J. A., & Mullis, I. V. S. (1986). *The writing report card: Writing achievement in American schools.* Princeton, J: Educational Testing Service.

Aronson, et.al. (1978). *The jigsaw classroom.* Beverly Hills, CA: Sage.

Bereiter, C. (1985). Toward a solution of the learning paradox. *Review of Educational Research, 55*(2), 201-226.

Bloom, L. Z. (1980, Mar.). *The composing process of anxious and non-*

anxious writers: A naturalistic study. Paper presented at the Annual Meeting of the Conference on College Composition and Communication, Washington, D. C. (ERIC Document Reproduction Service No. ED 185 559)

Bloom, L. Z., (1981, Mar.). *Why graduate students can't write: Implications of research on writing anxiety for graduate education.* Paper presented at the Annual Meeting of the Conference on College Composition and Communication, Dallas, TX. (ERIC Document Reproduction Service No. 199 170)

Boyer, E. L. (1987, Mar.). American higher education: The tide and the undertow. *International Journal of Institutional Management in Higher Education, 11*(1) 5-11.

Brandt, R. S. (1987). Is cooperation un-American? *Educational Leadership, 45*(3), 3.

Bruffee, K. A. (1972). *Collaborative learning: The relevance of social group work to innovation in college teaching.* A report written at Columbia University and circulated within the City University, 6, mimeographed.

Bruffee, K. A. (1980). *A short course in writing.* Cambridge, MA: Winthrop Publishers, Inc.

Bruffee, K. A. (1984). Collaborative learning and the conversation of mankind. *College English, 46*(7), 635-652.

Bruffee, K. A. (1985). *A short course in writing.* New York: Little, Brown and Company.

Bushman, J. H. (1984). *The teaching of writing.* Illinois: Charles C. Thomas Publisher.

Butler, N. M. (1981). *Project equality.* College Entrance Examination Board, New York, NY (ERIC Document Reproduction Service No. ED 212 194)

Cameron, R. G. & Guralnick, E. (1977). Score decline. *Journal of the National Association of College Admissions Counselors, 21*(4), 7-12.

Clifford, J. P. (1977). *An experimental inquiry into the effectiveness of collaborative learning as a method for improving the experiential writing performance of college freshmen in a remedial writing class.* (Doctoral dissertation, New York University, 1978). Dissertation Abstracts International, 38-12A, AAI7808455.

Connors, R. & Lunsford, A. (1993, May). Teachers' rhetorical comments on students papers. *College Composition and Communication, 44* (2), 200-223.

Dale, H. (1994). Collaborative writing interactions in one ninth-grade classroom. *Journal of Educational Research, 87*(6), 334-344.

Daly, J. A. & Hexamer, A. (1983). Statistical Power in Research in English Education. *Research in the Teaching of English, 17*(2), 157-61.

Daly, J. A. & Miller, M. D. (1975a). The empirical development of an instrument to measure writing apprehension. *Research in the Teaching English, 9*(3), 242-249.

Daly, J. A., & Miller, M. D. (1975b). Apprehension of writing as a predictor of message intensity. *Journal of Psychology, 89,* 175-177.

Daly, J. A. & Miller, M. D. (1975c). Further studies in writing apprehension: SAT scores, success expectations, willingness to take advanced courses, and sex differences. *Research in the Teaching of English, 9(3), 250-258.*

Daly, J. A. & Shamo, W. (1978). Academic decisions as a function of writing apprehension. *Research in the Teaching of English, 12*(2), 119-126.

Daly, J. A. & Shamo, W. (1976). Writing apprehension and occupational choice. *Journal of Occupational Psychology, 49,* 55-58.

Daly, J. A. & Wilson, D. (1983). Writing apprehension, self-esteem, and personality. *Research in the Teaching of English, 17*(4), 327-41.

Danis, M. F. (1980). Peer-response groups in a college writing workshop: Students' suggestions for revising compositions. (Doctoral dissertation, Michigan Sate University, 1980). *Dissertation Abstracts international, 41,* 5008A-5009A.

Daiute, C. & Dalton, D. (1988). Let's brighten it up a bit: Communication and cognition in writing. In B. A. Rafoth & D. L. Rubin (Eds.), *The Social Construction of Written Language* (pp. 249-269). Norwood, NJ: Ablex.

Deutsch, M. (1949). *An experimental study of the effects of cooperation and competition upon group process.*

DeVries, D. L., & Slavin, R. E. (1978). Teams-games-tournament (TGT): Review of ten classroom experiments. *Journal of Research and Development in Education, 12,* 28-38.

Dietrerich, D. J. (1977). The decline in students writing skills: An ERIC/RCS interview. *College English, 38*(5), 466-472.

Dudley, D. A. (1976). A plea for English. *Journal of National Association of College Admissions Counselors,* 21(1), 3-6.

Elbow, P. (1973). *Writing without teachers.* New York: Oxford University Press.

Ellman, N. (April 1978). Science in the English classroom. *English Journal,* 63-65.

Emerson, A., Phillips, J., Hunt, C., & Alexander, A. B. (1994, Fall). Case studies. *New Directions for Teaching and Learning, 59,* 83-91.

Emig, J. (1971). *Components of the composing process among twelfth graders.* (Doctoral dissertation, Harvard University, 1971). *Dissertation Abstracts International,* 31-01A, AAI7012418.

Emig, J. & King, B. (1979). *Emig-King attitude scale for students.* Test-Questionnaires. (ERIC Document Reproduction Service No. Ed 236 630)

Erickson, G. (1983). Student frameworks and classroom instruction. In H. Helm and J. Novak (Eds.), *Proceedings of the International Seminar on Misconceptions in Science and mathematics.* Ithaca, NY: Cornell University.

Faigley, L., Daly, J. A. & Witte, S. P. (1981). The role of writing apprehension in writing performance and competence. *Journal of Educational Research.,* 75(1), 16-21.

Felder, R. M. (1995). *A longitudinal study of engineering student performance and retention. IV.* Instructional methods and student responses to them.<http:\\turmac13.chem.columbia.edu/ LearnTeach/collab.html>

Felder, R. M. & Brent, R. (1994). *Cooperative learning in technical courses: Procedures, pitfalls, and payoffs.* <<http:// turmac13.chem columbia.edu/LearnTeach/collab.html>

Fleming, M. B. (1988). Getting out of the writing vacuum. NCTE Committee on Classroom Practices in Teaching English, *Focus on Collaborative Learning: Classroom Practices in Teaching English.* Urbana: NCTE, 77-104.

Flynn, E. A., McCulley, Gratz, (1982, Nov.). *Effects of peer critiquing and model analysis on the quality of biology student laboratory reports.* Paper presented at the Annual Meeting of the National Council of Teachers of English.

Washington, D. C. (ERIC Document Reproduction Service No. ED 234 403)

Ford, B. W. (1973). The effects of peer editing/grading on the grammar-usage and theme-composition ability of college freshmen. (Doctoral dissertation, The University of Oklahoma, 1973). *Dissertation Abstracts International, 33-12A,* AI173 15321.

Franklin, G., Griffin, R., & Perry, N. (1994-95). Effects of cooperative tutoring on academic performance. *Journal of Educational Technology Systems, 23*(1), 13-25.

Gabbert, B., Johnson, D. W., & Johnson, R. (1986). Cooperative learning, group-to-individual transfer, process gain, and the acquisition of cognitive reasoning strategies. *Journal of Psychology, 120*(3), 265-278.

Gebhardt, R. (1979). *Teamwork and feedback: Broadening the base of collaborative writing.* Paper presented at the 30th Annual Conference on college composition and communication, Minneapolis, Minnesota. (ERIC Document Reproduction Service No. ED 174 994)

Goldstein, G. S. (1993). Using a group workshop to encourage collaborative learning in an undergraduate counseling course. *Teaching of Psychology, 20,* 109-110.

Gossage, R. (1976). SAT scores and writing skills: A two-headed beasts. *Journal of the National Association of College Admissions Coun-selors, 21*(2), 17-19.

Groccia, J. E. & Miller, J. E. (1996, Winter). Collegiality in the classroom: The use of peer learning assistants in cooperative learning in introductory biology. *Innovative Higher Education, 2*(2), 87-100.

Grossack, M. (1954). Some effects of cooperation and competition upon small group behavior. *Journal of Abnormal and Social Psychology, 49,* 341-348.

Gunderson, B. & Johnson .(1980). Building positive attitudes by using cooperative learning groups. *Foreign Language Annals, 13*(1), 39-43.

Haaga, D. A. f. (1993, February). Peer review of term papers in graduate psychology courses. *Teaching of Psychology, 20*(1), 28-32.

Haines, D. B. & McKeachie, W. J. (1967). Cooperative versus competitive discussion methods in teaching introductory psychology. *Journal* of Educational Psychology, *58*(6), 386-390.

Hairston, M. (1982, Feb.). The winds of change: Thomas Kuhun and the revolution in teaching writing. *College Composition and Communication, 33*(1), 76-88.

Harmin, M. (1994). *Inspiring active learning: A handbook for teachers.* Association for Supervision and Curriculum Development, Alexandria, VA (ERIC Reproduction Document Services No. ED 368 709)

Hart, R. L. (1993). An investigation of the effects of collaborative learning on the writing skills of Composition II students at Gloucester County College: Applied educational research and evaluation. *Dissertation Abstracts International,* (University Microfilms No. ED 341 058).

Higgins, L., Flower, L., & Petraglia, J. (1992). Planning text together: The role of critical reflection in student collaboration. *Written Communication,* 9, 48-84.

Hillocks, G. (1984, Nov.). What works in teaching composition: A meta-analysis of experimental treatment studies. *American Journal of Education,* 133-170.

Horgan, D. D. & Barnett, L. (1991, Apr.). *Peer review: It works.* Paper presented at the Annual Meeting of the American Educational Research Association, Chicago, IL. (ERIC Reproduction Document Services No. ED 334 203)

Jacobs, L. C. (1983). *Basic academic skills expected of entering freshmen at Indiana Studies* in higher education. Number fifty (ERIC Reproduction Document Services No. ED 208 768)

Johnson, D. W., & Johnson, R. T. (1991). *Learning together and alone: Cooperative, competitive, and individualistic learning.* Englewood Cliffs, NJ: Prentice-Hall.

Johnson, D. W., & Johnson, R. T. (1975). *Learning together and alone.* Englewood Cliffs, NJ: Prentice-Hall.

Johnson, D W., Johnson, R. T., & Holubec, E. (1990). *Circles of learning: Cooperation in the classroom* (2nd ed.). Edina. MN: Interaction Books.

Jonassen, D. H. (1994). *Computers in schools: Mindtools for critical thinking.* Pennsylvania State University Press.

Koch, C. & Brazil, J. M. (1978). *Strategies for teaching the composition process.* National Council of Teachers of English, Urbana, IL. (ERIC Reproduction Document Services No. ED 147 880)

Light, R. (1990). *The Harvard assessment seminars.* Cambridge, MA: Harvard University Press.

Locke, D. C. (1992). *Increasing multicultural understanding.* Newbury Park, CA: Sage Publications, Inc.

Lupack, B. T. (1983, Oct.). *Writing across the curriculum: Designing on effective model.* Paper presented at the Annual Meeting of the Midwest Writing Center, Iowa City, IA (ERIC Reproduction Document Services No. ED 238 025)

MacGregor, J. T. (1992). Collaborative learning: Reframing the classroom. In A. S. Goodsell, M. R. Maher, V. Tinto B. L. Smith & J. MacGregor (Eds.), *Collaborative learning: A sourcebook for higher education* (37-40). University Park, PA: National Center on Postsecondary Teaching, Learning, and Assessment (NCTLA).

Madden, D. & Laurence, D. (1994). *An examination of college writing skills: Have they deteriorated?* Reports-Research/Technical. (ERIC Reproduction Document Services No. ED 364 909)

Maddox, R. M. (1981). The one-to-one student writing conference: An evaluation study of its effectiveness in improving writing skills. (Doctoral dissertation, Brigham Young University, 1981). *Dissertation Abstracts International, 42-08A,* AAI8126321.

Maller, J. B. (1929). *Cooperation and competition.* New York, NY: J. J. Little and Ives.

Manx, M. S. (1991). *Writing abilities, writing attitude, and the teaching of writing.* A Paper presented at the 42nd Annual Meeting of the Conference on College Composition and Communication, Boston, MA. (ERIC Document Reproduction Service No. ED 332 215)

Markman, M. C. (1983). Teacher-student dialogue writing in a college composition course: Effects upon writing performance and attitude. (Doctoral dissertation, University of Maryland College Park, 1983). *Dissertation Abstracts International, 45-06A,* AAI8419524.

Martin, O. L. (1985, Nov.). *A five-year analysis of basic skill competencies of two-year college freshmen.* Paper presented at the Annual Meeting of the Mid-South Educational Research Association, Biloxi, MS. (ERIC Reproduction Document Services No. ED 267 850)

Maxwell, M. (1988). *Improving student learning skills.* San Francisco, CA: Jossey-Bass Publishers.

McAndrew, D. A. (1983). *The effect of an unassigned rhetorical context of the holistic quality and syntax of the writing of high and low ability writers.* Unpublished manuscript. Indiana: Indiana University of Pennsylvania.

McBride, C. A. (1986). Peer and traditional instruction: A comparison of the effectiveness of peer tutoring/editing and traditional instruction on the writing abilities of freshman composition students. (Doctoral dissertation, University of Kansas, 1986). *Dissertation Abstracts International, 48-02A,* AAI8711191.

McColly, W. (1970, Dec.). What does educational research say about the judging of writing ability? *The Journal of Educational Research, 64*(4), 147-156.

McInerney, V., McInerney, D. M., Lawson, R. Roche, L. (1994, July). *Cooperative group computer competency instruction: Efficacy and effect on anxiety.* Paper presented at the International Congress of Applied Psychology, Madrid, Spain. (ERIC Reproduction Document Services No. ED 386 160)

Mead, D. G. (1994). *Celebrating dissensus in collaboration: A professional writing perspective.* Conference on College Composition and Communication. Nashville, TN. (ERIC Document Reproduction Service No. ED 375 427)

Meiklejohn, A. (1932). *The experimental college.* New York: Harper and Row.

Mellon, J. C. (1975). *National assessment and the teaching of English: Results of the first national assessment of educational progress in writing, reading, and literature-- implications for teaching and measurement in the English language arts.* National Council of Teachers of English, Urbana, IL (ERIC Reproduction Document Services No. ED 112 427)

Milligan, J. (1980). *Using the composing process and positive reinforcement to teach college basic students to write.* State University of New York College at Brockport. (ERIC Reproduction Document Services No. ED 198 524)

Morgan, M., Allen, N. Moore, T. Atkinson, D., & Snow, C. (1987). Collaborative writing in the classroom. *The Bulletin of the Association for Business Communication, 50*(3), 20-26.

Morganthau, T. (1997, January 27). Demographics: The face of the future. *Newsweek*, 58-60.

Myrick, R. D. (1993). *Developmental guidance and counseling: A practical approach.* Minneapolis, MN: Media Corporation.

Newkirk, T. R., Cameron, T. D., & Selfe, C. L. (1977, Nov.). Why Johnny can't write: A university view of freshman writing ability. *English Journal*, 65-69.

Nielson, D. C. (1994). Cooperative learning in graduate and undergraduate reading courses. *Journal of Reading.*

Ornstein, A. C. (1992, Sept.). The national reform of education: Overview and outlook. *NAASP: A Special Bulletin*, 89-101.

Piaget, J. (1972). Intellectual evolution from adolescence to adulthood. Human Development, 15(1), 1-12, 72.

Pfeifer, J. D. (1981). The effects of peer evaluation and personality on writing anxiety and writing performance in college freshmen. (Texas Tech University, Doctoral dissertation, 1981). *Dissertation Abstracts International, 42-04A.* (University Microfilms No. AAI8121895)

Pomplum, M. et al. (1991). *An exploration of the stability of freshman GPA, 1978-1985.* Educational Testing Service, Princeton, N. J.

Renninger, K., Hidi, S., & Krapp, A. (Eds.). (1992). *The role of interest in learning and development.* Hillsdale, NJ: Erlbaum.

Richardson, R. C. et al. (1983). *Literacy in the open-access college.* (ERIC Reproduction Document Services No. ED 320 650)

Rogoff, B. (1986). Adult assistance of children's learning. In T. E. Raphael (Ed.), *Contexts of school based literacy* (pp 27-40). NY: Randon House.

Sailor, S. H. (1996). *The effect of peer response groups on writing apprehension, writing achievement, and revision decisions of adult community college composition students.* (Doctoral dissertation, University of Florida, 1996). Dissertation Abstracts International, 57-09A, AAI9703607.

Scott, M. D., & Wheeless, L. R. (1977). Communication

apprehension, student attitudes and levels of satisfaction. *Western Journal of Speech Communication, 41*, 188-197.

Selfe, C. L. (1981). *The composing processes of high and low writing apprehensives: A modified case study.* Research prepared at the University of Texas. (ERIC Document Reproduction Service ED 216 354)

Sharan, S., & Sharan, Y. (1976). *Small-group teaching.* Englewood Cliffs, N.J.: Educational Technology Publications.

Shaughnessy, M. (1977). *Errors and expectations: A guide for the teacher of basic writing.* New York: Oxford University Press.

Shea, C. (1993, Feb. 3). What's happened to writing skills? *The Chronicle of Higher Education* A33-A35.

Shepherd-Wynn, E. (1999). The effects of collaborative learning on English composition students' writing anxiety, apprehension, attitude and writing quality. (Doctoral dissertation, Grambling State University, 1999). *Dissertation Abstracts International, 68*, 134.

Shrewsbury, M. B. (1995). The effects of collaborative learning on writing quality, writing apprehension, and writing attitude of college students in a developmental English program. (Doctoral dissertation, West Virginia University, 1995). *Dissertation Abstracts International,* 56-08A, AAI9543878.

Slavin, R. E. (1977). *Decomposing a student team technique: Team reward and team task.* Paper presented at the Annual Convention of the American Psychological Association. San Francisco, CA (ERIC Document Reproduction Services No. ED 160 575)

Slavin, R. E., (1986). *Using student team learning.* 3rd ed. Baltimore: Center for Research on Elementary and Middle Schools, Johns Hopkins University.

Slavin, R. E. (1987). Cooperative learning: Where behavioral and humanistic approaches to classroom motivation meet. *Elementary School Journal, 88*(1), 29-37.

Strang, S. (1984). Product and process: The author-led workshop. *College Composition and Communication, 35*(3) 327.

Swift, P. W. (1986). The effects of peer review with self-evaluation on freshman writing performance, retention, and attitude at Broward

Community College (Florida) (Doctoral dissertation, Florida Atlantic University, 1986). *Dissertation Abstracts International, 47-10A,* AAI8702377.

Thompson, M. O. (1981, Oct.). *The returning students: Writing anxiety and general anxiety.* Paper presented at the Northeast Regional Conference on English in the Two Year College, Baltimore, MD. (ERIC Reproduction Document Services No. ED 214 558)

Thompson, R. F. (1981, October). Peer grading: Some promising advantages for composition research and the classroom. *Research in the Teaching of English,* 172-74.

Triesman, U. (1985). Studying students studying calculus: A look at the lives of minority mathematics students in college. *The College Mathematics Journal, 23*(5), 362-372.

Vygotsky, L. S. (1986). *Thought and language.* Cambridge, MA: MIT PRess.

Walker, L. (1976). Writing skills and the demise of grammar. *English Quarterly, 9*(3), 31-41.

Wheeler, R., & Ryan, R, K. (1973). Effects of cooperating and competitive classroom environments on the attitudes and achievement of elementary school students engaged in social studies inquiry activities. *Journal of Educational Psychology, 65*(3), 402-07.

Wulff, D. H., Nyquist, J. D., & Abbott, R. D. (1987). Students' perception of large classes. In M. E. Weimer (Ed.) *Teaching Large Classes Well.* San Francisco, CA: Jossey-Bass.

Wynn, E. S. (2000).

Wynn, E. S., & Cadet, L. P. (1997). Developing a perspective for a culturally responsive collaborative writing model. *Research in Developmental Education, 14*(3), 1-4.

Chapter 5

Apple, J. (1979). *Ideology and curriculum.* Boston: Routledge & Kegan Paul.

Adler, J. (1900, September). Creating problems. *Newsweek,* pp. 16-22.

Alter, J. & Denworth, L. (1900, September). A (vague) sense of history. *Newsweek*, pp. 31-33.

Beckum, L., Zimmy, A., & Fox, A. (1989). The urban landscape: Educating for the twenty-first century. *The Journal of Negro Education, 58*, 430-441.

Birch, H. & Gussow, J. (1970). *Disadvantaged children: Health, nutrition and school failure.* New York: Harcourt Brace, Jovanovich.

Birren, J. (1987, May). The best of all stories. *Psychology Today*, pp. 91-92.

Blase, J. (1985). The socialization of teachers: An ethnographic study of factors contributing to the rationalization of the teacher's instructional perspectives. *Urban Education, 20*, 235-256.

Bowles, S. & Gintis, H. (1976). *Schooling in capitalist America.* New York: Basic Books.

Burling, R. (1973). *English in Black and White.* New York: Holt, Rinehart and Winston.

Clark, R. (1983). *Family life and school achievement: Why poor black children succeed or fail.* Chicago: The University of Chicago Press.

Cummings, S. (1977). *Black children in northern schools: The pedagogy of politics and failure.* San Francisco: Reed & Eterovich.

Dabney, N. & Davis, A. (1982). *An ethnographic description of a successful inner-city school and its community.* Philadelphia: Pennsylvania University, Graduate School of education. (ERIC Document Reproduction Service No. ED 220 546)

Devin, B. & Greenberg, B. (1972). *The Communication Environment of the Urban Poor.* East Lansing: Michigan State University.

Dixon, T. (1902). *The leopard's spot.* New York: Doubleday, Page & Co.

Doll, W. (1988). Curriculum beyond stability: Schon, Prigogine, Piaget. In W. Pinar (Ed.), *Contemporary curriculum discourse* (pp. 114-133). Scottsdale, AZ: Gorsuch Scarisbrick.

Doty, B. (1965). Why do mature women return to college? *Journal of National Association for Women Deans and Counselors, 29*, 171-174.

DuBois, W. E. B. (1903). *The Souls of black folks.* Greenwich, CN: Fawcett Publications.

Ediger, M. (1989). *The urban school of the future.* Kirksville, MO: Northeast Missouri State University. (ERIC Document Reproduction Service No. ED 304 503)

Eisner, E. (1985). The educational imagination. New York: Macmillan.

Filling, C. (1980). Prospects for an ethnographic approach to urban education. *Urban Education, 15,* 259-277.

Fischer, S. (1983). Sociology and life history: Methodological incongruence? *International Journal of Oral History, 5,* 29-40.

Fordham, S. (1985). *Black student's school success: Coping with the "burden of 'acting white'."* Presented at the annual meeting of the American Anthropological Association, Washington, D.C., (ERIC Documentation Reproduction Service No. ED 281 948)

Fordham, S. (1987). *Black student success: An ethnographic study in a large urban public school system.* Washington D. C.: The University of the District of Columbia, Department of Educational and Psychological Foundations. (ERIC Document Reproduction Service No. Ed 281 949)

Foster, W. (1954). *The Negro people in American history.* New York: International Publishers.

Franklin, B. (1986). *Building the American community.* Philadelphia: The Falmer Press.

Freire, P. (1986). *Pedagogy of the Oppressed.* New York: Continuum.

Fulghum, E. (1990, September). A bag of possible and other matters of the mind. *Newsweek,* pp. 88-92.

Geertz, C. (1973). Thick description: Toward an interpretive theory of culture. In. C. Geertz (Ed.), *The interpretation of cultures: Selected essays by Clifford Geertz* (pp. 3-32). New York: Basic Books.

Giroux, H. (1989). Education Reform in the age of George Bush. *Phi Delta Kappan, 70,* 728-30.

Glasgow, D. (1981). *The black underclass.* New York: Vintage Books.

Glenn, C. (1989). Just schools for minority children. *Phi Delta Kappan, 70,* 777-779.

Goodson, I. (1981). Life histories and the study of schooling. *Interchange, 11*, 62-76.

Grant, C. (1989). Urban teachers: Their new colleagues and curriculum. *Phi Delta Kappan, 70*, 764-770.

Grant, M. (1921). *The passing of the great race.* New York: Charles Scribners and Sons.

Greene, M. (1978). *Landscapes of Learning.* New York: Columbia University Press.

Hale-Benson, J. (1986). *Black children: Their roots, culture, and learning styles.* Baltimore: The Johns Hopkin's University Press.

Hammersley, M. & Atkinson, P. (1983). *Ethnography: Principles in practice.* New York: Tavistock.

Haskins, J. & Butler, H. (1973). *The psychology of black language.* New York: Barnes & Noble Books.

Henry, M. (1985). Black reentry females: Their concerns and needs. *Journal of the National Association for Women Deans and Counselors, 48*, 5-10.

Hess, F. (1988). *A comprehensive analysis of the dropout phenomenon in an urban school system.* Chicago: Panel on Public School Policy and Finance (ERIC Documentation Reproduction Service No. ED 287 202)

Hicks, E. (1981). Cultural Marxism: non-synchrony and feminist practice. In L. Sargeant (Ed.), *Women and revolution* (pp.219-2380. Boston: South End Press.

Horner, V. (1966). *Misconceptions concerning language in the disadvantaged.* IRCD Bulletin, 1966, 2, 1-2.

Jensen, A. (1969). How much can we boost I. Q. and scholastic achievement? *Harvard Educational Review*, Reprint Series No. 2, 1-123.

King, C. (1892). *The picturesque geographical readers.* Boston: Lew and Shepard Publishers.

Kliebard, H. (1986). *The struggle for the American curriculum.* Boston: Rouledge & Regan Paul.

Langness, L. & Frank, E. (1981). *Lives.* Novato, CA: Chandler & Sharp.

Leichter, H. (1973). The concept of educative style. *Teacher's College*

Record, 75, 239-250.

MacDonald, J. (1988). Curriculum, consciousness, and social change. In W. Pinar (Ed.), *Contemporary curriculum discourses* (pp. 156-174). Scottsdale, AZ: Gorsuch Scarisbrick.

McCarthy, C. (1988a).   Marxist theories of education and the challenge of a cultural politics of non-synchrony. In L. Roman & L. Christian Smith (Eds.), *Becoming feminine: The politics of popular culture* (pp. 185-203). London: Falmer Press.

McCarthy, C. (1988b). Rethinking liberal and radical perspectives on racial inequality in schooling. Making the case for non-synchrony. *Harvard Educational Review, 58,* 265-279.

McCord, W. (1969). *Lifestyles in the black ghetto.* New York: Norton.

McCormick, J. (1990, September). Where are the parents? *Newsweek,* pp. 54-58.

Miller, L. (1974). *The testing of black students.* Englewood Cliffs: Prentice-Hall.

Morganthau, T. (1990, September). The future is now. *Newsweek,* pp. 72-76.

Ogbu, J. (1978). *Minority education and caste.* New York: Academic Press.

Ogbu, J. & Matuke-Bianchi, M. (1986). Understanding, sociocultural factors: Knowledge, identity and school adjustments. In *Beyond Language: social and cultural factors in schooling language minority student.* (pp. 73-141). Los Angeles: California State University Press.

Perry, I. (1988). A Black student's reflection on public schools. *Harvard Education Review, 58,* 332-336.

Pierre, R. (1991, April 5). Teaching expert: U.S. education hasn't kept pace. *The Times Picayune,* p. B-2.

Pierre, R. (1991, April 6).   Schools should try scout philosophy, consultant says. *The Times Picayune,* p. B-4.

Prager, K. (1983). Educational aspirations and self-esteem in returning and traditional community college students. *Journal of College Student Personnel, 24,* 144-147.

Rashid, H. (1981). Early childhood education as a cultural transition for African American children. *Educational Research Quarterly, 6,* 55-63.

Rist, R. (1970). Student social class and teacher expectations: The self-fulfilling prophecy in ghetto education. *Harvard Educational Review, 40,* 411-451.

Robinson, I. (1973). The black classroom. In J. Haskins (Ed.), *Black manifesto for education* (pp. 12-18). New York: Morrow.

Roman, L. (1988). *Punk femininity: The formation of young women's gender identities and class relations in the extramural curriculum contemporary subculture.* Unpublished doctoral dissertation, University of Wisconsin-Madison.

Sarris, J. (1978). Vicissitudes of intensive life history research. *Personnel and Guidance Journal, 56,* 269-272.

Saslow, R. (1980). A new student for the eighties: The mature woman. *Educational Horizons, 60,* 41-46.

Scanzon, J. (1971). *The black family in modern society.* Boston: Allyn & Bacon.

Scheinfield, D. & Messerschmidt, D. (1979). *Teachers' classroom ideologies and notions of the person-world of relationship.* SSRC Conference St. Hildas.

Schubert, W. (1986). *Curriculum.* New York: Macmillan.

Sedlacek, W. & Brooks, G. (1976). *Racism in American education: A model for change.* Chicago: Nelson-Hall.

Semons, M. (1989, March). *Ethnographic description of a multiethnic school: A comparison to desegregated settings.* Paper presented at the annual meeting of the American educational Research Association, San Francisco. (ERIC Documentation Reproduction Service No. ED 309-214.

Shockley, W. (1969). "Negro I. Q. and heredity," *School and Society, 96,* 127-128.

Sickle cell anemia: New hope in fighting incurable blood disease. (1991, winter). *Health Scene,* p. 5.

Sleeter, C. & Grant, C. (1985). Race, class, and gender in an urban school. *Urban Education, 20,* 37-60.

Solomon, P. (1986). Black cultural forms in schools: A cross national comparison. In L. Weis (Ed.), *Class, race and gender in American education* (pp. 249-265). Albany: State University of New York.

Southern University at New Orleans Catalogue. (1989). New Orleans: Southern University.

Taylor, D. & Dorsey-Gaines, C. (1988). *Growing up literate.* Portsmouth, N.H.: Heinemann.

Thomas, J. (1983). Toward a critical ethnography. *Urban Life, 11*, 477-490.

Warren, C. (1982). The written life history as a prime research tool in adult education. *Adult Education, 32*, 215-218.

Weinberg, M. (1977). *Minority students: A research appraisal.* Washington D. C. : National Institute of Education.

Weis, L. (1985). *Between two worlds.* Boston: Routledge & Kegan Paul.

Wells, J. & Morrison, G. (1985). Putting the 'urban' in education. *Phi Delta Kappan, 67*, 142-143.

Willie, C. (1990). *Five black scholars: An analysis of family life, education and career.* New York: Abt Books.

Willis, P. (1977). *Learning to labour.* New York: Columbia University Press.

Woods, K. (1989, April 15). Nation must snap cycle of poverty, businessmen say. *The Times Picayune*, p. B-1.

Wyman, I. (1990, September). How to raise good readers. *Newsweek*, pp. 54-58.

Chapter 6

Arbona C., & Novy, D. (1990). Non-cognitive dimensions as predictors of college success among Black, Mexican-American, and white students. *Journal of College and Student Development, 31*(5). 415-422.

Arkin, R., & Maruyama, G. (1979). Attribution, affect, college performance. *Journal of Educational Psychology, 71*(1), 85-93.

Blaine, B., & Crocker, J. (1995). Religiousness, race, and psychological well-being: Exploring social psychological mediators. *Personal and Social Psychology Journal, 21*(10), 1031-1041

Crocker, J., Voelkl, K., Testa, M., & Major, B. (1991). Social stigma:

The affective consequences of attributional ambiguity. *Journal of Personality and Social Psychology* 60(2), 218-228.

Dalah, A. (1988). *Attribution theory and research.* New Delhi, India: Wiley Eastern Limited.

Evans-Hughes, G. (1992). The influence of racial identity and locus-of-control on the adjustment and academic achievement of African American college students. Dissertation Abstracts International, 54 (04-A). (*Dissertation Abstracts Online* No. AAD93-20784).

Fordham, S., & Ogbu, J. (1990). Black students' school success coping with the "burden" of 'acting white.'" *The Urban Review*, 18(3), 176-206.

Gerarldi, S. (1990). Academic self-concept as a predictor of academic success among minority and low-socioeconomic status students. *Journal of College Student Development, 31*(5), 402-407.

Gordon, K. (1995). Self-concept and motivational patterns of resilient African American high school students. *Journal of Black Psychology*, 21(3), 239-255.

Graham, S. (1994). Motivation in African Americans. *Review of Educational Research*, 64(1), 55-117.

Graham, S., & Long, A. (1986). Race, class and the attributional process. *Journal of Educational Psychology.* 78(1), 4-13.

Jenkins, A. (1995). *Turning corners.* Boston: Allyn and Bacon.

Johnson, I., & Ottens, A. (Eds.). The challenge for higher education: Retaining students of color. *New Directions for Student Services*, 74, 3-14.

Justiz, M., Wilson, R., & Bjork, L. (1994). *Minorities in higher education.* Phoenix, AZ: The Oryx Press.

Olivas, M. (Ed.), (1986). *Latino college students.* New York: Teacher College Press, Columbia University.

Pascarella, E., Smart, J., & Nettles, M. (1987). The influence of college on self-concept: A consideration of race and gender differences. *American Educational Research Journal*, 2191), 49-77.

Pintrich, P., & Schunk, D. (1996). *Motivation and education.* Englewood Cliffs: NJ: Prentice-Hall.

Platt, C. (1988). Effects of causal attribution on success on first-term college performance: A co-variance structure model. *Journal of Educational Psychology*, 80(4), 569-578.

Powers, S., & Rossman, M. (1984). Attribution for success and failure among Anglo, Black, Hispanic, and Native American community college students. *The Journal of Psychology*, 117(1), 27-31.

Rendon, L., & Associates. (1996). *Educating a new majority.* San Francisco: Jossey-Bass.

Smith, J., & Price, R. (1996). Attribution theory and developmental students as passive learners. *Journal of Developmental Education*, 19(3), 228-233.

Spencer, G. (1998). The relationship of causal attribution and academic success for ethnic minority college students. Dissertation Abstracts International. (Number not assigned)

Steele, C. (1992). Race and the schooling of Black Americans. *The Atlantic Monthly*, April, 1992.

Stevens-Arroyo, A. M. (1996). The Latino religious resurgence, 1967-1983. PARAL Occasional Paper No. 1.

Stevens-Arroyo, A., & Diaz-Stevens, A. (Eds.). (1994). *An enduring flame: Studies on Latino popular religiosity.* New York: Bildner Center of Hemisphere Studies.

Taylor, E., & Olswang, S. G. (1997). Crossing the color line: African Americans and predominantly white universities. *College Student Journal*, 31(March), 11-18.

Valencia, R. (Ed.). (1991). *Chicano school failure and success: Research and policy agendas for the 1990's.* New York: The Falmer Press.

Weiner, B. (1985). An attributional theory of achievement motivation and emotion. *Psychological Review*, 92(4), 548-573.

Weiner, B. (1986). *An attributional theory of motivation and emotion.* New York: Springer Verlag.

Weiner, B., & Kukla, A. (1970). An attributional analysis of achievement and motivation. *Journal of Personality and Social Psychology*, 15(1), 1-20.

Wilhite, S. (1990). Self-efficacy, locus of control, self-assessment of memory ability and study activities and predictors of college course achievement. *Journal of Educational Psychology.* 82(4), 696-700.

Wlodkowski, R. (1985). *What motivates adults to learn.* San Francisco: Jossey-Bass.

Chapter 7

Appleson, W. B. (1994). *We are all related. A model for successful collaboration in American Indian education* (Report No. JC 940 442). (ERIC Document Reproduction Service No. ED 373 808)

Arnold, J. F. (1994). A sample of Montana's Native American tribal college students' perceptions of the mental health field: Utilization and career interests. *Dissertation Abstracts International, 54* (09), 4905B. (University Microfilms No. AAC94-05134)

Badwound, E. D. (1991). Leadership and American Indian values: The tribal college dilemma. *Dissertation Abstracts International, 51* (09), 2991A. (University microfilms No. AAC91-04847)

Beaty, J., & Chiste, K. B. (1986). University preparation for Native American students: Theory and application. *Journal of American Indian Education, 26* (1), 6-13.

Beaulieu, D. (1991). The state of the art: Indian education in Minnesota. *Change, 23* (2), 31-35.

Ben, L. W. et al. (1992). *Wellness circles: The Alkali Lake model in community recovery processes* (Report No. SP 034 208). (ERIC Document Reproduction Service No. ED 352 347)

Benjamin, D. P., Chambers, S., & Reiterman, G. (1993). A focus on American Indian college persistence. *Journal of American Indian Education, 32* (2), 25-39.

Benshoff, J. M., & Lewis, H. A. (1992). *Nontraditional college students.* Ann Arbor, MI: ERIC Clearinghouse on Counseling and Personnel Services. (ERIC Document Reproduction Service No. ED 347 483)

Bold Warrior, S. (1992). *For the administrators: Realities for the Native American and education* (Report No. 018 841). (ERIC Document Reproduction Service No. ED 351 164)

Boyer, P. (1989-90). The tribal college: Teaching self-determination. *Community, Technical, and Junior College Journal, 60* (3), 24-29.

Browne, D. B., & Evans, W. H. (1987). *Native Americans in higher education* (Report No. RC 016 752). (ERIC Document Reproduction Service No. ED 299 082)

Buteyn, R. J. (1989). *Gender and academic achievement in education* (Report NO. PS 018 258). Washington, DC: U. D. Department of Education (ERIC Document Reproduction Service No. ED 313 303)

Carbone, G. J. (1987). *Academic support services for developmental and high-risk students in community colleges.* IN K. M. Ahrendt (Ed.), Teaching the developmental education student (pp. 23-47). San Francisco: Jossey-Bass, Inc., Publishers.

The Carnegie Foundation for the Advancement of Teaching. (1989). *Tribal colleges: Shaping the future of Native America.* Princeton, NJ: The Carnegie Foundation for the Advancement of Teaching.

Carstens, S. P. (1994). Use of noncognitive variables to predict the academic persistence and graduation of high-risk students who are admitted using special admissions standards. *Dissertation Abstracts International, 55* (03), 478A. (University Microfilms No. DA94-20133)

Chaney, B., & Farris, E. (1991). *Survey on retention at higher education institutions* (Report No. HE 025 308). Washington, DC: Department of Education. (ERIC Document Reproduction Service No. ED 342 334)

Charleston, G. M. (1994). Toward true Native American education: A treaty of 1992 final report of the Indian Nations at Risk Task Force. *Journal of American Indian Education, 33* (2), 10-56.

Cohen, D. (1989). Tribal enterprise. *The Atlantic Monthly, 264* (4), 32-34; 36; 38; 42-43.

Coladarci, T. (1983). High school drop out among Native Americans. *Journal of American Indian Education, 23* (1), 1522.

Conley, F. S. (1998). The relationship of achievement and academic and support services for developmental students at tribal American colleges. In V. L. Farmer & W. A. Barham (Eds.), A Preview of Student and Faculty research in Developmental Education at Grambling State University: Part II.

Research in Developmental Education, 14(5), 1.

Counseling to enhance self-esteem.   Ann Arbor, MI: ERIC Clearhinghouse on Counseling and Personnel services.   (ERIC Document Reproduction Service No. ED 328 827)

Dehyle, D. (1992).   Constructing failure and maintaining cultural identity: Navajo and UTE school leavers. *Journal of American Indian Education, 31* (2), 24-47.

Dick, R. W., Manson, S. M., & Beals, J. (1993).   Alcohol use among male and female Native American adolescents; Patterns and correlates of student drinking in a boarding school. *Journal of Studies on Alcohol, 54* (2), 172-176.

Eberhard, D. R. (1989).   American Indian education: A study of dropouts, 1980-87. *Journal of American Indian Education, 29* (1), 32-41.

Embree, B. G., & Whitehead, P. C. (1993).   Validity and reliability of self-reported drinking behavior: Dealing with the problem of response bias. *Journal of Studies on Alcohol, 54* (3), 334-343.

Falk, D. R., & Aitken, L. P. (1984).   Promoting retention among American Indian college students. *Journal of American Indian Education, 23* (2), 24-31.

Farabaugh-Dorkins, C. (1991). *Beginning to understand why older students drop out of college: A path analytic test of the Bean/Metzner model of nontraditional student attrition* (Report No. HE 024 559).   (ERIC Document Reproduction Service No. ED 332 598)

Flannery, K. (1992).   Smokeless tobacco among Native American Indians enrolled in tribally controlled colleges (Doctoral dissertation, The Pennsylvania State University, 1991).   *Dissertation Abstracts International, 52,* A2827.

French, L. A. (1992). *Cultural disintegration perpetuated through substance abuse among American Indians* (Report NO. CG 024 408).   (ERIC Document Reproduction Service No. ED 438 590)

Gold, J., Burrell, S., Haynes, C., & Nardecchia, D. (1990). *Black undergraduate adaptation to college as a predictor of academic success* (Report No. UD 028 303).

Goodchild, L. & Wechsler, H. (Eds.) (1997). *The history of higher education*, 2nd ed. Needham Heights, Mass: Simon and Schuster.

Griffin, D. J. (1990). The effectiveness of a mandatory developmental education program on academic success, retention, and graduation rates at a 2-year technical college. *Dissertation Abstracts International, 52* (02), 404A. (University Microfilms No. AAC92-18760)

Guyeth, S., & Heth, C. (1983). *American Indian higher education: Needs and projections* (Report No. JC 014 221). Montreal, Quebec, Canada: American Educational Research Association. (ERIC Document Reproduction Service No. ED 232 810)

Haeuser, P. N. (1993). *Public accountability and developmental (remedial) education* (Report No. JC 930 186). Arnold, MD: Anne Arundel Community College Office of Planning and Research. (ERIC Document Reproduction Service No. ED 356 003)

High-risk students and higher education: Future trends. Washington, DC: ERIC Clearinghouse on higher education. (ERIC Document Reproduction Service No. ED 325 033)

Hill, N. (1991). AISES: A college intervention program that works. *Change, 23* (2), 24-26.

Hodgkinson, H. (1992). *The current condition of Native Americans* (Report No. RC 018 910). Washington, DC: Office of Educational Research and Improvement. (ERIC Document Reproduction Service No. ED 348 202)

Hoover, J. J., & Jacobs, C. C. (1992). A survey of American Indian college students: Perceptions toward their study skills/college life. *Journal of American Indian Education, 32* (1), 21-29.

Hornett, D. (1989). The role of faculty in cultural awareness and retention of American Indian college students. *Journal of American Indian Education, 29* (1), 12-17.

Houser, S. (1991). *Underfunded miracles: Tribal colleges* (Report No. RC 061 6731). (ERIC Document Reproduction Service No. 343 772)

Houston, D. M. (1993). An exploration and analysis of the relationship among learning styles, teaching styles, gender, and performance in a college computer science course. *Dissertation Abstracts International, 54*(8),

2867B. (University Microfilms No. DA94-02706)

Huffman, T. E., Sill, M. E., & Brokenleg, M. (1986). College achievement among Sioux and White South Dakato students. *Journal of American Indian Education, 25* (2), 32-38.

Hurlburt, G., Gade, E., & McLaughlin, J. (1990). Teaching attitudes and study attitudes of Indian education students. *Journal of American Indian Education, 29* (3), 12-17.

Idaho Committee on Indian Education. (!993). *Goals & recommendations for improving American Indian education* (Report No. RC 019 219). (ERIC Document Reproduction Service No. ED 359 016)

Indian Nations at Risk: An educational strategy for action (report No. RC 018 443). Washington, DC: Department of Education (ERIC Document Reproduction Service No. ED 339 587)

Isaac, S., & Michael, W. B. (1990). Handbook in research and evaluation (2nd ed.). San Diego, CA: Edits Publishers.

Jensen, S. (1993). Native Americans energized, skeptical about new policies: Interns get close-up look at government's inner workings. *Black Issues in Higher Education, 10* (15), 34-35.

Jones, C. E. (1992). Academic achievement of college students as a function of involvement, gender, race, satisfaction, and participation status. *Dissertation Abstracts International, 53* (10), 3454A. (University Microfilms No. DA93-04004)

Kasworm, C. E., & Marienau, C. (1993). Assessment strategies for adult undergraduate students. In T. W. Banta & Associates (Eds.), *Making a difference: Outcomes of a decade of assessment in higher education* (pp. 121-134). San Francisco: Jossey-Bass Publishers.

Kleinfeld, J., Cooper, J., & Kyle, N. (1987). Postsecondary counselors: A model for increasing Native Americans' college success. *Journal of American Indian Education, 27* (1), 9-15.

Lamarine, R. J. (1993). A pilot study of sources of information and substance abuse patterns among selected American Indian high school seniors. *Journal of American Indian Education, 32* (3), 30-39.

Latham, G. I. (1985). The educational status of federally recognized

Indian students. *Journal of American Indian Education, 25* (1), 25-33.

Leung, P. K., Kinzie, J. D., Boehnlein, J. K., & Shore, J. H. (1993). A prospective study of the natural course of alcoholism in a Native American village. *Journal of Studies on Alcohol, 54* (6), 733-737.

Lin, R. L., LaCounte, D., & Eder, J. (1988). A study of native American students in a predominantly White college. *Journal of American Indian Education, 27* (3), 8-15.

Manzo, K. K. (1994). Breaking point for tribal colleges. *Black Issues in Higher Education, 11* (16), 34-37.

Martin, J. V. (1994). Factors influencing Native American persistence and graduation at a two-year institution of higher learning (Doctoral dissertation, Kansas State University, 1993). *Dissertation Abstracts International, 54,* A2447.

Mooney, C. J. (1988, April 6). In a barren land, a tribal college flourishes. *The Chronicle of Higher Education,* pp. A1, 16-17.

Noar, G. (1981). *Sensitizing teachers to ethnic groups.* New York: Allyn and Bacon, Inc.

Nolte, W. H. (1994). *Student outcomes and performance standards: Issues and challenges for community and technical colleges* (Report No. JC 940 503). (ERIC Document Reproduction Service No. ED 373 849)

O'Brien, E. M. (1990). The demise of Native American education. *Black Issues in Higher Education, 7* (1), 15-22.

Oppelt, N. T. (1990). *The tribally controlled colleges: The beginnings of self determination in American Indian education.* Tsaile, AZ: Navajo Community College Press.

Osborne, V. C., & Cranney, A. G. (1985). *Elements of success in a university program for Indian students* (Reports No. RC 015 296). (ERIC Document Reproduction Service No. ED 257 611)

Patty, K. J. (1989). An investigation of the relationship of selected variables as potential predictors of academic persistence among developmental students at a state university. *Dissertation Abstracts International, 50* (07), 1923A. (University Microfilms No. AAC 89-23256)

Pavel, D. M. (1992). *American Indians and Alaska natives in higher education: Research on participation and graduation* (Report No. RC 018 905). Washington, DC: Office of Educational Research and Improvement. (ERIC Document Reproduction Service No. ED 348 197)

Pego, D. (1993). Native American leaders to prioritize youth education. *Black Issues in Higher Education, 10* (18), 18-19.

Pego, D. (1994). American Indian education in Montana: U. S. Civil Rights Commission asked to study conditions. *Black Issues in Higher Education, 11* (4), 12-13.

Peterson's Guide to Two-Year Colleges. (1992). Princeton, NJ: Peterson's Guides.

Pottinger, R. (1989). Disjunction to higher education: American Indian students in the Southwest. *Anthropology & Education Quarterly, 20*, 326-345.

Purvis, D., & Watkings, P. C. (1987). Performance and retention of developmental students: A five-year follow-up study. *Research in Developmental Education, 4* (1), 1-4.

Raymond, J. H., III. (1986). *American Indian education and the reservation community college* (Report No. JC 870 016). University of South Florida. (ERIC Document Reproduction Service No. ED 276 489)

Red Horse, J. H. (1986). Editorial comment: Education reform. *Journal of American Indian Education, 25* (3), 40-44.

Reeves, M. E. (1993). Mathematics and gender: A general history of recent research and common perceptions. *Dissertation Abstracts International, 55* (03), 500A. (University Microfilms No. DA94-19919)

Reyhner, J. (1991). *Plans for dropout prevention and special school support services for American Indian and Alaska Native students* (Report No. RC 019 621). Washington, DC: Department of Education (ERIC Document Reproduction Service No. 343 762)

Roueche, J. E. (1984). Between a rock and a hard place. *Community and Junior College Journal, 54* (7), 21-24.

Rowland, F. C. (1994). Tribal education: A case study of Northern Cheyenne elders. *Dissertation Abstracts International, 55* (08), 2252A. (University Microfilms NO. AAC95-02319)

St. Pierre, N., & Rowland, F. C. (1990). Educational issues in Montana's tribal colleges. *Adult Literacy and Basic Education, 14* (3), 212-219.

Sanderson, J. (1980). *State services for California Indians* (Report No. RC 013 531). Sacramento, CA: California State Department of Housing and Community Development (ERIC Document Reproduction Service No. ED 220 230)

Scalley, E. (1993). Gender differences in the attrition process of nontraditional college students; A case study of a private four-year university in Puerto Rico. *Dissertation Abstracts International, 54* (04), 1313A. (University Microfilms No. DA93-24627)

Schlossberg, N. K., Lynch, A. Q., & Chickering, A. W. (1989). *Improving higher education environments for adults.* San Francisco: Jossey-Bass Publishers.

Schuckit, M. A., Klein, J. L., Twitchell, G. R., & Springer, L. M. (1994). Increases in alcohol-related problems for men on a college campus between 1980 and 1992. *Journal of Studies on Alcohol, 55* (6), 739-742.

Spann, N. (1990). Student retention: An interview with Vincent Tinto. *Journal of Developmental Education, 14* (1), 1823.

Special Report, (1995, July 17). *Community College Week,* pp. 6-13.

Steward, R. J. (1993). Two faces of academic success: Case studies of American Indians on a predominantly Anglo university campus. *Journal of College Student Development, 34* (3), 191-195.

Stone, L. E. (1992). Effectiveness of developmental education as an intervention strategy in promoting student success (Doctoral dissertation, The University of Iowa, 1991). *Dissertation Abstracts Inter-national, 52* (12), A4199.

Swisher, K., & Hoisch, M. (1992). Dropping out among American Indian and Alaska Natives: A review of studies. *Journal of American Indian Education, 31* (2), 3-23.

Tierney, W. G. (1991). Native voices in academe: Strategies for empowerment. *Change, 23* (2), 36-39.

Tierney, W. G. & Kidwell, C. S. (1991). The quiet crisis. *Change, 23* (2), 4-5.

Tippeconnic, J. W., III. (1998). A survey: Attitudes toward the education of American Indians. *Journal of American Indian Education, 28* (1), 34-36.

United States Department of Education. (1996-97). *Student financial assistance programs: The student guide [Brochure].* Washington, DC: Author.

Washington, T. (1993). NASULGC endorses tribal college land-grant status. *Black Issues in Higher Education, 10* (17), 20-21.

Weibel-Orlando, J., Weisner, T., & Long, J. (1984). Urban and rural Indian drinking patterns: Implications for intervention policy development. *Substance and Alcohol Actions/Misuses, 5,* 45-57.

Wetsit, D. (1994-95). American Indian higher education curriculum: A counseling case study. *Tribal College, 6* (3), 33-37.

White, W. G., Jr., & Schnuth, M. L. (1990). College learning assistance centers: Places for learning. In R. M. Hashway (Ed.), *Handbook of developmental education* (pp. 155-177). New York: Praeger.

Wicks, D. H., & Price, F. H. (1981). *The American Indian controlled community college movement* (Report No. JC 820 166). (ERIC Document Reproduction Service No. 214 611)

Wildy, E., III. (1989). Native American educational plight described as national disgrace. *Black Issues in Higher Education, 6* (3), 8-9.

Williford, A. M., & Moden, G. O. (1993). Using assessment to enhance quality. In T. W. Banta & Associates (Eds.), *Making a difference: Outcomes of a decade of assessment in higher education* (pp. 40-53). San Francisco: Jossey-Bass Publishers.

Wilson, M. G., & Lamarine, R. J. (1990). A health promotion marketing analysis of adolescent information sources. *Wellness Perspectives: Research, Theory, and Practice, 6* (4), 67-74.

Wright, B. (1985). Programming success: Special student services and the American Indian college student. *Journal of American Indian Education, 24* (1), 1-7.

Wright, B., & Tierney, W. G. (1991). American Indians in higher education: A history of cultural conflict. *Change, 23* (2), 11-18.

Wright, B., & Weasel Head, P. (1990). Tribally controlled community colleges: A student outcomes assessment of Associate Degree recipients.

Community College Review, 18 (3), 28-33.

Chapter 8

Ambler, M. (1997). Revisioning American Indian education. *Tribal College: Journal of American Indian Higher Education, 9*(2), 8-10.

Banks, J. A. (1975). *Teaching strategies for ethnic studies.* Boston, MA: Allyn and Bacon, Inc., p. 139-178.

Belgarde, L. (1994). Seize the day: Tribal colleges must focus on the future. *Tribal College: American Indian Journal of Higher Education, 5*(4), 7-10.

Bigart, R. (1997). Tribal college land-grant future: promise and peril. *Tribal College: American Indian Journal of Higher Education, 8*(4), 36-37.

Boyer, E. (Ed.). (1989). *Tribal college: Shaping the future of Native America.* Princeton, NJ: University Press.

Boyer, P. (1989). Higher education and Native American society. *Tribal College: American Indian Journal of Higher Education, 1*(1), 10-18.

----(1990). Building a tribal college: Six criteria for a college of quality. *Tribal College: American Indian Journal of Higher Education, 2*(1), 13-17.

----(1997). *Native American colleges: Progress and prospects.* Princeton, NJ: Carnegie Foundation for the Advancement of Teaching.

Boylan, H. R., Bonham, B. S. & Bliss, L. (1994). Who are developmental students? *Research in Developmental Education, 11*(2).

Boylan, H. R., Bliss, L. B. & Bonham, B. S. (1993). The performance of minority students in developmental education. *Research in Developmental Education, 10*(2).

Chavers, D. (1996, October 28-November 4). Correcting untruths, half-truths and the exaggeration of college statistics. *Indian County Today*, Rapid City, SD: Native American Publishing, Inc., p. A12.

Conley, F. C. (1998). The relationship of achievement and academic and support services for developmental students at tribal American colleges. In Barham, W. A., & Farmer, V. L. (Eds.). A preview of student and faculty research in developmental education at Grambling State University: Part II. *Research in Developmental Education, 14*(5).

Crum, S. (1989). The idea of an Indian college or university in twentieth century American before the formation of Navajo Community College in 1968. *Tribal College: American Indian Journal of Higher Education, 1*(1), 20-23.

Irving, V. (1971). *I have spoken: American history through the voices of the Indians.* Ohio: Swallow Press.

Kidwell, C. S. (1994). Higher education issues in Native American communities. In Justiz, M. J., Wilson, R. & L. G. Bjork (Eds.). (1994). *Minorities in Higher Education,* 239-257. Phoenix, AZ: The Onyx Press.

Miller, C. A. (1990). Minority Student Achievement: A comprehensive perspective. *Journal of Developmental Education, 13*(3), 6-11.

National Congress of American Indians. [On-line]. http:// www:ncai.org.

O'Brien, E. (1992). American Indians in higher education: Research brief. Washington, D.C.: American Council on Education.

Olivas, M. A. ((1997). Indian, Chicano, and Puerto Rican Colleges: Status and issues. In Goodchild, L. F. & H. S. Weschler (Eds.). *The History of Higher Education,* New York, New York: Simon and Schuster Custom Publishing, 677-697.

Oppelt, N. T. (1984). The tribally controlled colleges in the 1980s: Higher education's best-kept secret. *American Indian Culture and Research Journal, 8*(4), 27-45.

----(1990). *The Tribally Controlled Indian College: The beginning of Self-determination in American Indian Education.* Tsaile, AZ: Navajo Community College Press.

Reyhner, J. (1992). *American Indian/Alaska Native Education.* Bloomington, IN: Phi Delta Kappa Educational Foundation.

Stein, W. (1992). *Tribally controlled colleges: Making good medicine.* New York: Peter Lang Publishing, Inc.

Utter, J. (1993). American Indians: Answers to today's questions. Lake Ann, MI: National Woodlands Publishing Co.

Wenzlaff, T. L. & A. Biewer. (1996). Native American students define factors for success. *Tribal College: American Indian Journal of Higher*

Education, 7(4), 40-44.

Chapter 9

Agresti, A. (1990). *Categorical data analysis.* New York: John Wiley & Sons.

American Nurses' Association. (1984). *Standards for professional nursing education.* Kansas City, MO: Author.

Aspinall, M. J. (1979). Use of a decision tree to improve accuracy of diagnosis. *Nursing Research, 28,* 182-185.

Bandman, E. L., & Bandman, B. (1988). *Critical thinking in nursing.* Norwalk, CT: Appleton & Lange, Publisher.

Bauwens, E. E., & Gerhard, G. G. (1987). The use of the Watson Glaser Critical Thinking Appraisal to predict success in a baccalaureate nursing program. *Journal of Nursing Education, 26(7),* 278-281.

Beare, P. G. (1991). Davis' *NCLEXRN review.* Philadelphia: F. A. Davis Company.

Bechtel, G. A., Smith, J. A., Printy, V. & Gronseth, D. Critical thinking and clinical judgment of professional nurses in a career mobility program. *Journal of Nursing Staff Development, 9(5),* 218-222.

Becker, H. A., & MacCabe, N. (1994). Indicators of critical thinking, communication, and therapeutic intervention among first line nursing supervisors. *Nurse Educator, 19(2),* 15-19.

Berger, M. C. (1984). Clinical thinking ability and nursing students. *Journal of Nursing Education, 23,* 306-308.

Boyle, K. K. (1986). Clinical thinking ability and nursing students. *Journal of Nursing Education, 23.* 306-308.

Bower, F. (1976). Relation of the learning environment to ethnic minority achievement. *Communicating Nursing Research, 7,* 205-224.

Brooks, K. L., & Shepherd, J. M. (1990). The relationship between clinical decision making skills in nursing and general critical thinking abilities of senior nursing students in four types of nursing programs. *Journal of Nursing Education, 29(9),* 391-399.

354   *Meeting the Challenge of Cultural Diversity in Higher Education*

Claerbaut, D. (1978). Expansionist trends in health care and the role of minority students: a challenge for nursing education. *Journal of Nursing Education, 17(4)*, 42-47.

Creighton, H. (1984). Nursing judgment. *Nursing Management, 15(5)*, 60, 62-63.

Dagenais, D. L. (1984). The use of probit model for the validation of selection procedures. *Educational and Psychological Measurement, 44*, 629-645.

de Tornyay, R., & Russell, M. (1978). Helping the high risk student achieve. *Nursing Outlook, 26(9)*, 576-580.

Deardoff, M., Denner, P., & Miller, C. (1976). Selected national league for nursing achievement test scores. *Nursing Research, 25*, 35-38.

Dell, M. A. & Halpin, G. (1984). Predictors of success in nursing school and on the state board examinations in a predominantly black baccalaureate nursing program. *Journal of Nursing Education, 23(4)*, 147-150.

Dell, M. A., & Valine, W. J. (1990). Explaining differences in NCLEXRN scores with certain cognitive and non cognitive factors for new baccalaureate nurse graduates. *Journal of Nursing Education, 29(4)*, 158-162.

Ennis, R. H. (1985). Critical thinking and the curriculum. *National Forum, 65(11)*, 28-31.

Felts, J. (1986). Performance predictors for nursing courses and NCLEXRN. *Journal of Nursing Education, 25(9)*, 372-377.

Frierson, H. T., Malone, B., & Shelton, P. (1993). Enhancing NCLEXRN performance: assessing a three pronged intervention approach. *Journal of Nursing Education, 32(5)*, 222-224.

Glaser, E. M. (1985). Critical thinking: educating for responsive citizenship in a democracy. *National Forum, 65(1)*, 24-27.

Grier, M. R. (1976). Decision making about patient care. *Nursing Research, 25*, 105-110.

Grobe, S. J., Drew, J. A., & Fonteyn, M. E. (1991). A descriptive analysis of experienced nurses' clinical reasoning during a planning task. *Research in Nursing and Health, 14*, 305-314.

Gross, Y. T., Takazawa, E. S., & Rose, C. L. (1987). Critical thinking and nursing education. *Journal of Nursing Education, 26(8)*, 317-323.

Halpern, D. F. (1984). *Thought and knowledge: An introduction to critical thinking.* New Jersey: Lawrence Erlbaum Associates.

Hartley, D., & Aukamp, V. (1994). Critical thinking ability of nurse educators and nursing students. *Journal of Nursing Education, 33(1),* 34-35.

Holl, R. M. (1994). Characteristics of the registered nurse and professional beliefs and decision making. *Critical Care Nursing Quarterly, 17(3),* 60-66.

Homs, P. N., O'Sullivan, P., & Goodman, R. (1991). The use of progressive indicators as predictors of NCLEX-RN success and performance of BSN graduates. *Journal of Nursing Education, 3,* 9-14.

Horns, R. M. (1994). The use of progressive indicators as predictors of NCLEXRN success and performance of BSN graduates. *Journal of Nursing Education, 30(1),* 9-14.

Hughes, K. K., & Young, W. B. (1992). Decision making stability of clinical decisions. *Nurse Education, 17(3),* 12-16.

Jenkins, H. M. (1985). Improving clinical decision making in nursing. *Journal of Nursing Education, 24,* 242-243.

Johnson, J. (1988). Differences in the performance of baccalaureate, associate degree and diploma nurses: A metaanalysis. *Research in Nursing and Health, 11(3),* 183-197.

Jones, S. A., & Brown, L. N. (1991). Critical thinking: Impact on nursing education. *Journal of Advanced Nursing, 16,* 529-533.

Justus, M. A., & Montgomery, J. A. (1986). Current status of nursing process in programs. *Journal of Nursing Education, 25(3),* 118-120.

Katzell, M. (1970). Upward mobility in nursing. *Nursing Outlook, 18,* 36-39.

Ketefian, S. (1981). Critical thinking, educational preparation, and development of moral judgment among selected groups of practicing nurses. *Nursing Research, 30(2),* 98-103.

Kissinger, J. F., & Munjas, B. A. (1982). Predictors of student success. *Nursing Outlook,* Jan, 53-54.

Klein, L. W. (1985). Passing NCLEX. *Issues, 6(21),* 1-5.

Kurfiss, J. (1988). Critical thinking: Theory, research, practice and possibilities. *ASHE-ERIC Higher Education Report No. 2*, Washington, DC: Association for the Study of Higher Education.

Levenstein, A. (1981). Nursing judgement. *Nursing Management, 12(9)*, 67-68.

Levenstein, A. (1983). Professional judgment. *Nursing Management, 14(8)*, 32-33.

Levenstein, A. (1984). Logic vs. feeling. *Nursing Management, 15(4)*, 64-66.

Louisiana State Board of Nursing. (1994). *The Examiner, 2(2)*, 1-8.

McKinney, J., Small, S., O'Dell, N., & Coonrod, B. (1988). Identification of predictors of success for the NCLEXRN and students at risk for NCLEXRN failure in a baccalaureate nursing program. *Journal of Professional Nursing, 4(1)*, 55-59.

McMillian, J. (1987). Enhancing college students' critical thinking: A review of studies. *Research in Higher Education, 26*, 3-29.

McPeck, J. E. (1981). *Critical thinking and education.* New York: St. Martin's Press.

McPeck, J. E. (1990). *Teaching critical thinking.* New York: Routledge.

Miller, M. (1987). Impact of a baccalaureate registered nurse program in the critical thinking skills of students, *Dissertation Abstracts International* (University Microfilms No. 88 08292).

Miller, M. A. (1992). Outcome evaluation: Measuring critical thinking. *Journal of Advanced Nursing, 17*, 1401-1407.

Miller, M. A., & Malcolm, N. S. (1990). Critical thinking in the nursing curriculum. *Nursing & Health Care, 11(2)*, 67-73.

National League for Nursing. Council of baccalaureate and higher degree programs. (1991). *Criteria for the evaluation of baccalaureate and higher degree programs in nursing.* NLN Publication No. 15 2474. New York: Author.

Outtz, J. H. (1979). Predicting the success on state board examinations for Blacks. *Journals of Nursing Education, 18(9)*, 35-40.

Pardue, S. F. (1987). Decision making skills and critical thinking ability among associate degree, diploma, baccalaureate, and master's prepared nurses. *Journal of Nursing Education, 26(9)*, 354-361.

Paul, R. (1993). *Critical thinking: What every person needs to survive in a rapidly changing world.* Santa Rosa, CA: Foundations for Critical Thinking.

Perry, W. (1981). Cognitive and ethical growth: The making of meaning, in Chickering, A. & Associates, *The Modern American College.* San Francisco: Jossey-Bass.

Philpot, W., & Bernstein, S. (1978). *Minorities and women in the health fields: Applicants, students and workers.* Health Manpower References. Health Resources Administration (DHEW/PHS). Bethesda, MD: Bureau of Health Manpower.

Rachel, M. M. (1989). The relationship between critical thinking abilities and performance on NCLEXRN, with special reference to age at graduation and previous educational experience, *Dissertation Abstracts International* (University Microfilms No. 90 05397).

Rami, J. S. (1992). Predicting nursing students success on NCLEXRN. *The Association of Black Nursing Faculty Journal, Summer,* 67-71.

Rausch, T., & Rund, D. (1981). Nurses' Clinical Judgements. *Nursing Management, 12(12),* 24-26.

Richards, M. A. (1977). One integrated curriculum: An empirical evaluation. *Nursing Research, 26,* 90-95.

Rubenfeld, M. G., & Scheffer, B. K. (1995). *Critical thinking in nursing: An interactive approach.* Philadelphia: J. B. Lippincott Co.

Saarman, L., Freitas, L., Rapps, J., & Riegel, B. (1992). The relationship of education to critical thinking ability and values among nurses: Socialization into professional nursing. *Journal of Professional Nursing, 8(1),* 26-34.

SAS Institute Inc. (1997). Release 6.12 (Orlando II), [Computer Software]. Cary, NC: Statistical Software.

SAS/STAT User's Guide, Version 6. (1989). Fourth Edition, Volume 2. Cary, NC: SAS Institute Inc.

Sharp, T. (1984). An analysis of the relationship of seven selected variables to state board test pool examination performance of the University of Tennessee, Knoxville, College of Nursing, *Journal of Nursing Education, 23(2),* 57-63.

Siegel, H. (1980). Critical thinking as an educational ideal. *The Educational Forum, 45*, 7-23.

Siegel, H. (1988). *Educating, reasoning: rationality, critical thinking, and education.* New York: Routledge Chapman, & Hall, Inc.

Snead, L. (1983). Teaching and evaluating minorities. *Nurse Education, 8(4)*, 15-16.

Stokes, M., Davis, C., & Koch, G. (1995). *Categorical data analysis using the SAS system.* Cary, NC: SAS Institute Inc.

Sullivan, E. J. (1987). Critical thinking, creativity, clinical performance, and achievement in RN students. *Nurse Educator, 12(2)*, 12-16.

Tschikota, S. (1993). The clinical decision making processes of student nurses. *Journal of Nursing Education, 32*(9), 389-398.

Watson, G., & Glaser, E. M. (1980). *Watson-Glaser critical thinking appraisal manual: Forms A and B.* New York: Harcourt Brace Jovanovich, Inc.

Whitley, M. P., & Chadwick, P. L. (1986). Baccalaureate education and NCLEX: The causes of success. *Journal of Nursing Education, 25*(3), 94-101.

Wold, J. E., & Worth, C. (1990). Baccalaureate student nurse success prediction: A replication. *Journal of Nursing Education, 29*(2), 84.

Yinger, R. (1980). Can we really teach them to think? *New Directions for Teaching and Learning, 3*, 11-29.

Yocom, C. J., & Scherubel, J. C. (1985). Selected preadmission and academic correlates of success on state board examinations. *Journal of Nursing Education, 24(6)*, 244-249.

Yura, H., & Walsh, M. B. (1983). *The nursing process: assessing, planning, implementing, evaluating.* (4th ed.). Norwolk, Conn.: Appleton-Century-Crofts.

Chapter 10

(1994 - 1998). *HIV and AIDS Knowledge*, [Web Page]. The Measurement Group and the HRSA SPNS Program Adolescent CARE Projects. Available: http://www.tmg-web.com/ Documents/ adolspns/ mods/bnhi.pdf [2000, October 28].

Altun, A. (1999). Patterns in cognitive processes and strategies in hypertext reading: A case study of two experienced computer users. *Journal of Educational Multimedia and Hypermedia, 8*(4), 423-443.

Ambrose, D. W. (1991). The effects of hypermedia on learning: A literature review. *Educational Technology, 31*(12), 51-55.

Ames, C. (1992). Classrooms: Goals, structures, and student motivation. *Journal of Educational Psychology*, 84, 261-271.

Ames, C., & Archer, J. (1988). Achievement goals in the classroom: Student's learning strategies and motivation processes. *Journal of Educational Psychology*, 80, 260-267.

Anderman, E. M., & Young, A. J. (1994). Motivation and strategy use in science: Individual differences and classroom effects. *Journal of Research in Science Teaching, 31*, 811-831.

Borsook, T. K., & Higginbotham-Wheat, N. (1992). *A psychology of hypermedia: A conceptual framework for R & D.* Paper presented at the Annual Meeting of the Association for Educational Communications and Technology, Washington, D.C.

Burton, J. K., Moore, M. M., & Holmes, G. A. (1995). Hypermedia concepts and research: An overview. *Computers in Human Behavior, 11*(3-4), 345-369.

Crosby, M. E., & Stelovsky, J. (1995). From multimedia instruction to multimedia evaluation. *Journal of Educational Multimedia and Hypermedia, 4*(2/3), 147-162.

Cunningham, D. J., Duffy, T. M., & Knuth, R. A. (1993). The textbook of the future. In A. D. C. McKnight, J. Richardson (Ed.), *Hypertext: A Psychological Perspective* . Chichester, West Sussex: Ellis Horwood Limited.

Deci, E., & Ryan, R. (1985). *Intrinsic motivation and self-determination in human behavior.* New York: Plenum.

Dewey, J. (1963). *Experience and education.* New York: Collier Macmillan Publishers.

Dweck, C. S., & Leggett, E. L. (1988). A social-cognitive approach to motivation and personality. *Psychological Review, 95*, 256-273.

Elliot, A. J., & Harackiewicz, J. M. (1996). Approach and avoidance achievement goals and intrinsic motivation: A mediational analysis. *Journal of Personality and Social Psychology, 70*(3), 461-475.

Grabe, M., Petros, T., & Sawler, B. (1989). An evaluation of computer based instruction. *Journal of Computer Based Instruction, 16*, 110-116.

Graham, S. (1994). Motivation in African Americans. *Review of Educational Research, 64*, 55-117.

Hagen, A. S., & Weinstein, C. E. (1995). Achievement goals, self-regulated learning, and the role of classroom context. In P. R. Pintrich (Ed.), *Understanding Self-regulated Learning* (Vol. 63,). San Francisco, CA: Jossey-Bass.

Hammomd, N. V., & Allinson, L. (1989). Extending hypertext for learning: An investigation of access and guidance tools. In A. Sutcliffe & L. Macaulay (Eds.), *People and Computers*. Cambridge, MA: Cambridge University Press.

Hardiman, B., & Williams, R. (1990). Teaching developmental mathematics: The interactive video approach. *T.H.E. Journal, 17*, 154-159.

Health, A. A. f. W. (1998, December 1, 1998). *World AIDS Day Resource Book: How Much Do You Know About HIV/AIDS?*, Washington, DC.

Higgins, K., & Boone, R. (1992). Hypermedia computer study guides: Adapting a Canadian history text. *Social Education, 56*(3), 154-159.

Jacobson, M. J., & Spiro, R. J. (1995). Hypertext learning environments, cognitive flexibility, and the transfer of complex knowledge: An empirical investigation. *Journal of Educational Computing Research, 12*(4), 301-333.

Janda, K. (1992). Multimedia in political science: Sobering lessons from a teaching experiment. *Journal of Educational Multimedia and Hypermedia, 1*(341-354).

Kaplan, A., & Midgley, C. (1997). The effect of achievement goals: Does level of perceived academic competence make a difference? *Contemporary Educational Psychology, 22*, 415-435.

Katz, H. A. (2001). *The Relationship Between Learners' Goal Orientation and their Cognitive Tool Use and Achievement in an Interactive Hypermedia Environment.* Unpublished Doctoral Dissertation, University of Texas at Austin, Austin.

Katz, H. A. (2002). Focus on Solutions: Multimedia HIV/AIDS Prevention Education for Undergraduate African and Latina American Women. In D. J. Gilbert & N. Wright (Eds.), *African American Women and HIV/AIDS* : Prager Press, NY.

Kim, H., & Hirtle, S. C. (1995). Spatial metaphors and disorientation in hypertext browsing. *Behaviour and Information Techno-logy, 14*, 239-250.

Kommers, P. A. M., Grabinger, S., & Dunlap, J. C. (1996). *Hyper-media learning environments: Instructional design and integration.* Mahwah, NJ: Lawrence Erlbaum Associates.

Lajoie, S. P. (1993). Computer environments as cognitive tools for enhancing learning. In S. P. Lajoie & S. J. Derry (Eds.), *Computers as Cognitive Tools* (pp. 261-288). Hillsdale, NJ: Lawrence Erlbaum.

Leader, L. F., & Klein, J. D. (1996). The effects of search tool type and cognitive style on performance during hypermedia database searches. *Educational Technology, Research and Development, 44*(2), 5-15.

McDonald, S., & Stevenson, R. J. (1999). Spatial versus conceptual maps as learning tools in hypertext. *Journal of Educational Multimedia and Hypermedia, 8*(1), 43-64.

Meece, J., Blumenfeld, P., & Hoyle, R. (1988). Students' goal orientations and cognitive engagement in classroom activities. *Journal of Educational Psychology, 80*, 514-523.

Mickelson, R. A. (1990). The attitude-achievement paradox among Black adolescents. *Sociology of Education, 63*, 44-61.

Middleton, M., & Midgley, C. (1997). Avoiding the demon-stration of lack of ability: An under-explored aspect of goal theory. *Journal of Educational Psychology, 89*, 710-718.

Midgley, C., Maehr, M., Hicks, L., Roeser, R., Urdan, T., Anderman, E., Kaplan, A., Arunkumar, R., & Middleton, M. (1997). *Patterns of Adaptive Learning Survey* (PALS). Ann Arbor, MI: University of Michigan.

Moore, D. M., Burton, J. K., & Myers, R. J. (in press). Multi-media/Multiple Channel research.

In D. H. Jonassen (Ed.), *Handbook of Research on Educational Communications and Technology*. Washington, D.C.: Association for Educational

Communications and Technology.

National Center for HIV, S., and TB Prevention. (2001). *HIV/AIDS Among US Women: Minority and Young Women at Continuing Risk.* Atlanta: Centers for Disease Control & Prevention.

Nelson, W. A., & Palumbo, D. B. (1992). Learning, instruction, and hypermedia. *Journal of Educational Multimedia and Hypermedia, 1*(4), 445-464.

Nicholls, J. G. (1984). Conceptions of ability and achievement motivation. In R. Ames & C. Ames (Eds.), *Research on motivation in education: Student Motivation* (Vol. 1, pp. 39-73). New York: Academic Press.

Nolen, S. B. (1988). Reasons for studying: Motivational orientations and study strategies. *Cognition and Instruction, 5*, 269-287.

Park, I., & Hannafin, M. J. (1993). Empirically-based guidelines for the design of interactive multimedia. *Educational Technology, Research, and Development, 41*(3), 63-85.

Park, O. (1991). Hypermedia: functional features and research issues. *Educational Technology, 31*(8), 24-31.

Park, S. (1995). Implications of learning strategy research for designing computer-assisted instruction. *Journal of Research on Computing in Education, 27*(4), 435-456.

Patton, M. Q. (1987). *How to use qualitative methods in evaluation* (2 ed.). Los Angles, CA: Sage Publications, Inc.

Peterson, L. R., & Peterson, M. J. (1959). Short-term retention of individual verbal items. *Journal of Experimental Psychology*, 58, 193-198.

Pintrich, P., & Garcia, T. (1994). Self-regulated learning in college students: Knowledge,
strategies, and motivation. In P. R. Pintrich, D. Brown, & C. E. Weinstein (Eds.), *Perspectives on student motivation, cognition, and learning: Essays in honor of Wilbert J. McKeachie* (pp. 113-133). Hillsdale, NJ: Erlbaum.

Pintrich, P. R., & Garcia, T. (1991). Student goal orientation and self-regulation in the college classroom. In M. L. Maehr & P. R. Pintrich (Eds.), *Advances in motivation and achievement: Goals and self-regulatory processes* (Vol. 7, pp. 371-402). Greenwich, CT: JAI Press.

Pintrich, P. R., & Schrauben, B. (1992). Students motivational beliefs and their cognitive engagement in classroom tasks. In D. H. Schunk & J. Meece (Eds.), *Student perceptions in the classroom: Causes and consequences* (pp. 149-183). Hillside, NJ: Lawrence Erlbaum Associates.

Pintrich, P. R., & Schunk, D. H. (1996). *Motivation in education: Theory, research, and applications.* Englewood Cliffs, NJ: Merrill Prentice-Hall.

Pittman, K., Wilson, P. M., Adams-Taylor, S., & Randolph, S. (1992). Making sexuality education and prevention programs relevant for African American youth. *Journal of School Health, 62*(339-344).

Reinking, D., & Rickman, S. S. (1990). The effects of computer-mediated texts on the vocabulary learning and comprehension of intermediate-grade readers. *Journal of Reading Behavior, 22*, 395-411.

Schroeder, E. E., & Kenny, R. F. (1995). Learning strategies for interactive multimedia instruction: Applying linear and spatial notetaking. *Canadian Journal of Educational Communication, 24*(1), 27-47.

Spiro, R. J., & Jehng, J. C. (1990). Cognitive flexibility and hypertext: Theory and technology for the nonlinear and multidimensional traversal of complex subject matter. In D. Nix & R. Spiro (Eds.), *Cognition, Education, and Multimedia* (pp. 163-205). Hillsdale, N.J.: Lawrence Earlbaum.

Stephens, T., Braithwaite, R. L., & Taylor, S. E. (1998). Model for using hip-hop music for small group HIV/AIDS prevention counseling with African American adolescents and young adults. *Patient Education and Counseling, 35*, 127-137.

Stevenson, H. C., & Davis, G. (1994). Impact of Culturally Sensitive AIDS Video Education on the AIDS risk knowledge of African American adolescents. *AIDS Education Prevention, 6*, 40-52.

Stevenson, H. C., McKee Gay, K., & Josar, L. (1995). Culturally Sensitive AIDS Education and Perceived AIDS Risk Knowledge: Reaching the "Know-it-all" Teenager. *AIDS Prevention and Education, 7*(2), 134-144.

Stuber, M. L. (1991). Children, Adolescent and AIDS. *Psychiatric Medicine, 9*, 441-454.

Tierney, R. J., & Shanahan, T. (1991). Research on the reading-writing relationship interactions, transaction, and outcomes. In P. D. Pearson (Ed.), *Handbook of Reading Research.* New York, NY: Longman.

Vanderbilt, C. a. T. G. a. (1992). The Jasper Series as an example of anchored instruction: Theory, program description, and assessment data. *Educational Psychologist, 27*(3), 291-315.

Weinstein, C. E. (1996). Self-regulation: A commentary on directions for future research. *Learning and Individual Differences, 8,* 269-274.

Weinstein, C. E., & Mayer, R. E. (1986). The teaching of learning strategies. In M. Wittrock, C. (Ed.), *Handbook of research on teaching* (pp. 3rd ed., 315-327). New York: Macmillan.

Wingood, G. M., & DiCelemente, R. J. (1992). Cultural, gender and psycho-social influences on HIV-related behavior of African American female adolescents: Implications for the development of tailored prevention programs. *Ethnicity and Disease, 2*(4), 381-388.

Winne, P. H., & Hadwin, A. F. (1997). Studying as self-regulated learning. In D. J. Hacker, A. C. Graesser, & J. Dunlosky (Eds.), *Metacognition in educational theory and practice* (pp. 279-306). Hillsdale, NJ: Erlbaum.

Winne, P. H., & Stockley, D. B. (1998). Computing technologies as sites for developing self-regulated learning. In D. H. Schunk & B. J. Zimmerman (Eds.), *Self-regulated Learning: from Teaching to Self-Reflective Practice* (pp. 106-136). New York, NY: The Guildford Press.

Wolters, C. A., Yu, S. L., & Pintrich, P. R. (1996). The relation between goal orientation and students' motivational beliefs and self-regulated learning. *Learning and Individual Differences, 8*(3), 211-238.

Yang, C.-S., & Moore, D. M. (1995-6). Designing hypermedia systems for instruction. *Journal of Educational Technology Systems, 24*(1), 3-30.

Zimmerman, B. J. (1989). A social cognitive view of self-regulated academic learning. *Journal of Educational Psychology, 81*(3), 329-339.

Chapter 11

Adams, M., (ed). (1992, Win.). Promoting diversity in college classrooms: Innovative responses for the curriculum, faculty, and institutions. *New Directions for Teaching and Learning,* 52.

Barr, R. B. & Tagg, J. (1995). From teaching to learning: A new paradigm for undergraduate education. *Change*. November-December. p. 13-25.

Bryan, W. A. (1996). What is quality management? *New Directions for Student Services*, No. 76, p. 3-15.

Carreathers, K. R., Beekmann, L., Coatie, R. M. & Nelson, W.L. (1996). Three exemplary retention programs. *New Directions for Student Services*, No. 74, p.35-52.

Crosson, P. (1988). Four-year college and university environments for minority degree achievement. *Review of Higher Education, 11*(4), p. 365-382.

Gray, P. J. (1997). Viewing assessment as an innovation: Leadership and the change process. *New Directions for Higher Education*, No. 100, p. 5-15.

Howard, N. L. (1996). Pros and cons of TQM for student affairs. *New Directions for Student Services*, No. 76, p. 17-31.Kinnick, M. K. & Ricks, M. F. (1993). Student retention: Moving from numbers to action. *Research in Higher Education, 34*(1), p. 55-69.

Kobrak, P. (1992). Black student retention in predominantly white regional universities: The politics of faculty involvement. *Journal of Negro Education, 61*(4), p. 509-530.

Lozier, G. G. & Teeter, D. J. (1993). Six foundations of total quality management. *New Directions for Institutional Research; 78*, 5-11 Sum 1993.

Love, B. J. (1993). Issues and problems in the retention of Black students in predominantly White institutions of higher education. *Equity and Excellence in Education, 26*(1), p. 27-36.

Madison, E. (1993). Managing diversity: Strategies for change. *CUPA Journal, 44*(4), p.23-27.

Mallinckrodt, V. & Sedlacek, W. (1987). Student retention and the use of campus facilities by race. *NASPA Journal, 24*(3), p. 28-32.

McDaniel, T. R. (1994). College classrooms of the future: Megatrends to paradigm shifts. *College Teaching, 42*(1), p. 27-31.

McNairy, F.G. (1996). The challenge for higher education: Retaining students of color. *New Directions for Student Services*, No.74, 3-14.

Melan, E. H. (1993). Quality improvement in higher education: TQM in administrative functions. *CUPA Journal, 44*, p. 7-8, 10, 12, 14-18.

Obiakor, F. E. & Harris-Obiakor, P. (1997). *Retention models for minority college students* (Report No. HE 030 081) Emporia, KS: Research and Creativity Forum. (Eric Document Reproduction Service No. ED 406 907).

Pang, V. O. (1995). *Asian Pacific American students: A diverse and complex population.* (ERIC Document Reproduction Service No. ED 382 718)

Parker, C.E. (1997, February 20). Making retention work. *Black Issues in Higher Education, 13*(26), 120.

Rowser, J.F. (1997). Do African American students' perceptions of their needs have implications for retention? *Journal of Black Studies, 27*(5), 718-726.

Sailes, G.A. (1993). An investigation of Black student attrition at a large, predominately White, Midwestern university. *The Western Journal of Black Studies, 17*(4), 179-182.

Takaki, R. (1989). *Strangers from a different shore. A history of Asian Americans.* (ERIC Document Reproduction Service No. ED 319 839)

Tinto, V. (1987). *Leaving college: rethinking the causes and cures of student attrition.* Chicago: The University of Chicago Press.

Sotello Viernes Turner, C. (1994). Guests in someone else's house: Students of color. *Review of Higher Education, 17*(4), 355-70.

Chapter 12

Banks, J. A. & Banks, C. A. M. (1997).(Eds.). *Multicultural education: Issues and perspectives (Third Ed.).* Boston, MA: Allyn and Bacon.

Barham, W. A. (1997). *Professional writing seminar.* Conducted at The University of Arkansas at Fayetteville, September 27.

Berhanzl, E. J. (1999). Research in the undergraduate curriculum. *University Faculty Voice/Vol. 3*, No. 10/June 1999, pp. 4-5.   Borg, W. R., & Gall, M. D. (1989). *Educational research: An introduction.* New York: Longman. Brown, A., & Dowling, P. (1998). *Doing research/reading research: A mode of interrogation for*

education. Washington, D.C.: Falmer Press.

Craft, M. (1996). *Teacher education in plural societies: An international review.* Washington, D.C.: Falmer Press.

Crowl, T. K. (1996). *Fundamentals of educational research (Second Ed.).* Madison, WI: Brown & Benchmark Publishers.

Grant, C. A. (1995). (Ed.). *Educating for diversity: An anthology of multicultural voices.* Boston, MA: Allyn & Bacon.

Grant, C.A. (1999) (Ed.). *Multicultural research: A reflective engagement with race, class, gender and sexual orientation.* Philadelphia, PA: Falmer Press.

Krathwohl, D. R. (1998).*Methods of educational and social science research: An integrated approach (Second Edition).* New York: Longman Publishing Group.

Krathwohl, D.R. (1993). *Methods of educational and social science research: integrated approach.* New York: Longman Publishing.

Lingua Links (1997). *Http//:www.sil.org/lingualinks/library.*

Maxwell, J. A. (1996). *Qualitative research design: An interactive approach.* Thousand Oaks, CA: Sage Publications.

Miles, C., & Rauton, J. (1985). *Thinking tools: Academic, personal, and career applications.*

Clearwater, Florida: H & H Publishing Company, Inc.

Mitchell, J. P. (1989). *Writing with a computer.* Boston, MA: Houghton Mifflin Company.

Ogunyemi, O. (1997). *Professional writing and reporting practicum course: Lecture notes.* College of Education, Grambling State University.

Polkinghorne, D. E. (1988). *Narrative knowing and the human sciences.* Albany, New York: State University of New York Press.

Richardson, L. (1990). *Writing strategies: Reaching diverse audiences.* Qualitative Research Methods Series 21: A Sage University Paper. Newbury Park, CA: Sage Publications.

Timm, J. T. (1996). *Four Perspectives in Multicultural Education.* New York: Wadsworth Publishing Company.

Tuckman, B. (1994). *Conducting educational research (4th ed.).* New York: Harcourt Brace Jovanovich, Publishers.

Tuckman, B. (1988). *Conducting educational research (3rd Ed.).* New York: Harcourt Brace Jovanovich, Publishers.

Wassman, R., & Rinsky, L. A. (1997). *Effective reading in a changing world (2nd Ed.).* Upper Saddle River, New Jersey: Prentice-Hall, Inc.

Werthamer, L. (1999). *Elements of a well-written proposal.* Presented at the National Technical Assistance Proposal Development Workshop sponsored by the National Institute on Drug Abuse (NIDA), July 8-9, Bethesda, Maryland.

Wolpert, E. M. (1991). *Understanding Research in Education: A consumer guide to critical reading (Third Ed.).* Dubuque, IA: Kendall/ Hunt Publishing Company.

education institutions
and, 4; student
involvement and, 28;
student/teacher and, 24
Clifford, J. P. 48, 50-51, 58, 65-
66, 75
Coatie, A. M. 281
Cognitive Tools 232, 235-237,
243
Cohen, D. 146, 148-149, 171
Cohen, A. M. 17
Coladarci, T. 145-147, 170
Collaborative Learning 54
selected research on, 57;
study on Black
students and,
Collaborative Writing 45,
54,76
Constructivist Theory 51
Combs, L. M. 14
Commission on National
Challenges in Higher
Education 1
Connors, R. 55
Cooley, C. H. 28
Coonrod, B. 211, 214
Cooper, J. 146
Craft, M. 296, 299
Cranney, A. G. 148, 155,
157-158, 166, 172, 178,
181
Creighton, H. 201
Critical Thinking 196
and academic
performance, 201-210;
definition of, 198-
201; and nursing
process, 196-198
Crocker, J. 138, 141

Crosby, M. E. 234
Crosson, P. 276
Crowl, T. K. 296
Crum, S. 188-190, 193
Cultip, S. M. 21
Cultural Perceptions 20
from public relations, 20;
peer pressure, 29;
public relation, 20;
student/teacher
relations, 24; student
involvement, 28
Cummings, S. 91, 94, 101
Cunningham, D. J. 234

D

Dabney, N. 103
Daily, J. A. 77
Daiute, C. 57
Dalah, A. 139-140
Dale, H. 52-53, 55
Daly, J. A. 48, 51, 77
Danis, M. F. 58,75
Davidson, A. L. 24
Davis, A. 100, 103
Davis, A. 242, 261
Davis, C. L. 17
Dean, T. 43
Deci, E. 255
Dehyle, D. 147
Dell, M. A. 212-216,
219-220
Demographic Trends 266
and college enrollment,
266-268; and college
graduation rates, 268;

academic services for,
143-156; achievement
and academic support
services for, ;
factors affecting
achievement of, 144-146;
persistence and success
of, 148-149;
unmet needs of, 145;
wellness/substance
abuse of, 156-160
Nelson, V. I. 19
Nelson, W. A. 235
Nelson, W. L. 281
Newkirk, T. R. 46
Nicholls, J. G. 237
Nielson, D. C. 53
Nist, S. L. 23
Noar, G. 146, 149
Nolen, S. B. 237
Nolfi, G. F., Jr. 19
Nolte, W. H. 168

O

Obiakor, F. E. 277
O'Brien, E. M. 166
Ochsner, N. L. 18
O'Dell, N. 211, 214
Ogbu, J. 95-98, 100
Ogunyemi, O. 305
Olivas, M. A. 137, 187
Olswang, S. G. 138
Oppelt, N. T. 143-144, 148-149,
153, 187-190, 192-194
Ornstein, A. C. 46
Osborne, V. C. 148 155, 157-
158, 166, 172, 178, 181
O'Sullivan, P. 213-214

Outtz, J. H. 215, 216

P

Palumbo, D. B. 235
Pang, V. O. 270
Pardue, S. F. 354, 361
Parker, C. E. 188, 281-282
Park, I. 235
Pate, M. 42
Patton, M. Q. 250
Patty, K. J. 174
Paul, R. 199
Pavel, D. M. 145, 147, 171, 177
Pedhazur, E. J.
Pego, D. 145, 147, 149, 159,
170-171
Pendleton, E. 9
Penick, J. E. 25
Perrin, J. 9
Perry, N. 56
Perry, W. 198
Perry, I. 121
Peterson, L. R. 260
Peterson, M. J. 260
Petraglia, J. 55
Petros, T. 234
Pfeifer, J. D. 48, 58, 75
Pheland P. 24
Philpot, W. 221
Piaget, J. 52
Pierre, R. 123
Pilland, W. E. 16
Pine, G. 5
Pintrich, P. 132-133, 137, 139,
236-237
Pittman, K. 242
Platt, C. 132, 135
Platt, G. M. 15

Plisko, V. W. 16
Polkinghorne, D. E. 307
Pomplum, M. 46
Porter, R. E. 11, 20
Pottinger, R. 145-146, 170
Powers, S. 140
Prager, K. 106, 108
Price, F. H. 132
Price, R. 148, 152
Purvis, D. 174

R

Rachel, M. M. 211-212
Rami, J. S. 219
Ramsey, P. 42
Randolph, S. 242
Rapps, J. 206-207
Rashid, H. 93, 101
Rauton, J. 301-302
Raymond, J. H., III. 144-147, 149, 171
Red Horse, J. H. 146, 149
Reeves, M. E. 173
Reiterman, G. 145, 170
Retention
    with learning paradigm, 283-285; with Total Quality Management, 283-285
Retention Model
    characteristics of, 279-283; retention plan for, 285-292
Reyhner, J. 145-147, 170-171, 187, 191
Reynolds, M. C. 25
Ribaudo, M. 16
Richards, M. A. 201

Richardson, R. C. 47
Richardson, L. 297
Ricks, M. F. 293
Riegel, B. 206
Rinsky, L. A. 300
Rist, R. 103
Roach, R. 2-3, 7
Robinson, I. 91, 93, 101
Roderguiz, A. M. 1
Roe, B.D. 6
Roelfs, P. J. 18-19
Rogoff, B. 52-53
Roman, L. 103
Rose, C. L. 140, 201-204, 207, 227
Ross, E. P. 6
Rossman, M. 140
Rotzoll, K. 22
Roueche, J. E. 155, 171
Rowland, F. C. 145, 148, 157-158, 171-172, 175, 177
Rowser, J. F. 276
Rubenfeld, M. G. 201
Rudolph, F. 18
Russell, M. 221
Ryan, R. K. 255
Ryzewic, S. R. 16

S

Saarman, L. 206-207
Sailes, G. A. 278
Sailor, S. H. 46, 50-51, 58, 75
Samovar, L. A. 11, 20
Sandage, C. H. 23
Sanderson, J. 146
Sarris, J. 108
Saslow, R. 115

Y